COM IDL
& Interface Design

Dr. Al Major

Wrox Press Ltd. ®

COM IDL and Interface Design

wrox

Published by Wrox Press Ltd.
Arden House, 1102 Warwick Road, Acocks Green, Birmingham, B27 6BH, UK
Printed in USA
ISBN 1-861002-25-4

Trademark Acknowledgements

Wrox has endeavored to provide trademark information about all the companies and products mentioned in this book by the appropriate use of capitals. However, Wrox cannot guarantee the accuracy of this information.

Credits

Author
Dr. Al Major

Development Editor
John Franklin

Editors
Jon Hill
Karli Watson

Technical Reviewers
Richard Anderson
Peter French
Richard Grimes
Kevlin Henney
Mary Kirtland
Sing Li
Jonathan Miller
Christian Nagel
Krishna Pant
Arthur Wang
Jason Whittington

Cover
Andrew Guillaume
Concept by Third Wave

Design/Layout
Tony Berry

Index
Seth Maislin

About the Author

Dr. Al Major is a Denver-based software developer, trainer and entrepreneur.

Al has been writing code for fun and profit for over 17 years and has hacked hundreds of thousands of lines of code in that time. He has been researching COM-based object models for several years.

Along the way, Al has picked up a Computer Science PhD from Yale University, co-founded one of the first e-commerce startups, "BrainPlay.Com", been a Wall Street Rocket Scientist, and consulted for Microsoft.

His comprehensive knowledge of software development and ability to communicate it in a simple, direct and relevant fashion make Dr. Major a sought after speaker by corporations large and small.

When he's not relaxing writing code, Al relaxes by watching Rockies games, doing Yoga or whipping up a gourmet Indian meal.

Dr. Major can be reached at AlMajor@boxspoon.com

Acknowlegements

I'd like to thank the various excellent reviewers whose advice (even when it was ignored) has immeasurably improved the book. First, I'd like to thank Bill Andreas for suggesting the language independent approach to the first 3 chapters. It was a *lot* harder, and took a lot longer, to write without C++ code samples, but the concepts came through much more clearly.

Many thanks are due to the main technical reviewers. Mary Kirtland for taking the time out of her real job to review the book and coordinate the Microsoft feedback. Dr. Richard Grimes for giving this book the benefit of his peerless knowledge of COM and ATL. Christian Nagel for the benefit of his substantial COM experience.

I cannot thank the Wrox team enough. Jon Hill and Karli Watson kept me honest, pointed out my various errors and omissions, amd worked completely insane hours to meet the publication schedule. Chris Hindley 'marshal'ed this final push to publication, and gently chivvied me when I needed it. And, of course, John Franklin who had the vision to push me into writing a much better and more relevant book than I'd initially conceived.

Finally, I'd like to thank Kavi Singh at Microsoft for introducing me to Mary and facilitating the early MS review process.

Table of Contents

Table of Contents

Table of Contents

Table of Contents

Table of Contents

1

Introduction

It took me a long time to see the COM forest from the trees. I climbed the usual COM learning curve, finding out about vtables and how to use C++ to implement them, the details of Automation interfaces, type libraries and ODL, marshaling and IDL, and so on.

But it just wouldn't fall into place! What I really wanted to do was build reusable object models in COM, not spend time learning about various esoteric details of the plumbing (undeniably fascinating though that can be). What I needed were answers to questions that ranged from the extremely broad:

> *"How do I apply standard OO methodologies to COM interfaces?"*
>
> *"What makes one interface design better than another?"*

to the extremely detailed:

> *"When should I use Alternate Identities, and how do I implement them in ATL?"*
>
> *"When should I use a smart proxy?"*

What I needed was a compilation of common design techniques and idioms, so that I wasn't constantly reinventing the wheel, or wasting time creating sub-optimal designs.

Language Bindings

A second problem area was this: I do most of my serious programming in C++. It's not that I think *everything* should be written in C++, but it is still the best option for the core of any large application, which is what I spend my time building. Despite this fact, I was acutely conscious of the practical importance of other languages, especially scripting ones, and their position in the programming food chain. I knew that I had to design my object models so that they could be called from any of the COM-capable languages.

Here I found confusion! It seemed as though every language had its own abstraction of COM, with no particular common design. Each one constrained the COM model in various ways and had its own little quirks. Given Microsoft's well-known emphasis on a market-driven, multi-pronged, multi-team approach to developing products, this is not particularly surprising, but it does make life a little difficult for those of us trying to build portable, re-usable object models. To make headway, I needed to know how the syntax of each language bound to the underlying COM architecture.

IDL and Type Information

A third source of frustration was the poor quality of information surrounding IDL and type libraries. Despite the official rhetoric about COM being a binary standard, it was quite obvious that the IDL file (and its compiled equivalent, the type library) was the source of the true interface descriptions used to *support* binary inter-operability. As such, it is used by all kinds of COM support tools, perhaps the most important being the MIDL compiler, generator of standard marshaling code.

It became clear to me that the true *lingua franca* of COM was embodied by these and related type information systems. In order to talk meaningfully about COM interfaces and objects in a language-independent fashion, one has to resort to a separate language that describes these details. Currently, the best candidate for this is COM IDL (Interface Definition Language). In fact, to the extent that humans need a textual notation to work with COM, it is the only viable candidate at present.

A Synthesis

IDL is a language that can be used to describe the basics of COM interfaces. To this end, all the bindings of different languages with COM can be explained in relation to it. In addition, IDL is also the obvious notation for interface and object design.

It turns out that there is no authoritative source of information on topics like these. The COM documentation and many of the best existing books focus on the details of the COM infrastructure, or look at COM primarily from a C++ programmer's perspective. Books on other languages tend to describe everything purely within the framework of the language itself, rather than in universal COM terms.

It's not that the knowledge doesn't exist. There are numerous pieces available, with sources ranging from Crispin Goswell's excellent *COM Programmer's Cookbook* to discussions on the various Usenet newsgroups and the DCOM mailing list. The problem is that no one has synthesized all this knowledge into an authoritative guidebook – everyone has been forced to learn this important information in a fragmented and piecemeal manner.

This book is my attempt to provide such a synthesis.

Synopsis

Over the next couple of pages, I want to give you an idea of the ground we'll be covering over the course of the book. By doing so, I hope to provide a frame of reference such that when you read each chapter, you'll have a better idea of where the subject 'fits' with respect to the rest of the material.

Chapter 2: COM and IDL Basics

I'll begin the next chapter by presenting some background material on the scope and application of type information, and then placing IDL within this context.

There are a number of basic facts about COM that you need to know before you can successfully embark on interface and object model design, and there are entire books devoted to explaining them. I will not make any attempt to reiterate that; instead, I will provide a super-fast summary of the features of COM that are most important to the design of interfaces and object models. This summary covers COM basics such as box-spoon diagrams, classes, the various interface types, errors and the COM rich error protocol, outgoing interfaces, events, and the connectable object protocol.

The rest of the chapter then focuses on the basics of IDL. I'll start by explaining the compilation process for IDL files, and by describing the IDL file structure (along with the complexities of IDL file inclusion). The chapter continues with explanations of the basic IDL syntax for base types, user-defined types, functions and constants, and then progresses to deal with the IDL syntax for COM-specific constructs, such as the various kinds of interfaces and COM classes.

The chapter ends with a summary that provides a list of design guidelines based on the contents of the earlier sections.

Chapter 3: Remote Method Calls

Remote method calls are at the heart of what COM has to deal with, and marshaling is one of the crucial functions provided by the COM infrastructure. Chapter 3 explains this process in some detail. I begin by summarizing the problems that need to be dealt with by any marshaling architecture, and then outline COM's approach to solving them.

I then go into the specifics of the IDL code required to configure the marshaling process, fleshing out the details of the COM remoting architecture as I do so. This includes the simple IDL code needed for scalar data types, as well as that for arrays, pointers and interfaces.

The chapter also contains a section on the heap memory ownership rules of COM, and how they are determined by the IDL used to specify pointer parameters. Once again, I conclude with a section on design guidelines.

Chapter 4: Automation and Tool Support

There are many aspects of COM IDL that originated from the support for Automation in Visual Basic, including keywords for the description of Automation and the implementation of dual interfaces. Along with these, I also describe in this chapter the IDL for the various Automation types that are encapsulated by the Visual Basic `Variant` type.

One of the benefits of Automation-style interfaces is the support they provide for various flavors of dynamically typed behavior, including late binding, optional parameters, dynamic parameter types and variable numbers of parameters. In the second part of the chapter, I explain these features of Automation, and the IDL that is required to support them.

There are a number of IDL (originally ODL) keywords that are not strictly necessary for interface *or* object model description; many of them grew out of various requirements of the Visual Basic design time environment. Support exists for outgoing interfaces and property notifications, visibility, optimization and documentation, and the keywords involved are also covered in this chapter.

Chapter 5: Application Design

Chapter 5 centers on the high level design of a fully-fledged COM application. I begin it by providing a large collection of standard COM techniques/protocols/idioms – a suite of 'best-design' practices that should flatten the learning curve for application design. Some of the techniques are useful only in the implementation/optimization stage of an object model, but it is a good idea to be aware of them even during the design phase. Taken as a whole, they should provide a context for evaluating the various options that are available to you at any point in the design.

The second part of the chapter is my attempt to provide, by example, a methodology for COM application design. Like others in the OO community, I split object model design into a specification stage and an implementation stage; this section focuses on the specification model. Beginning with the functional specification of the application, I provide a case study of creating a model of it. The use cases for the system are analyzed, and from this most of the interfaces are obtained. The model is then rounded out with additional structural and utility interfaces.

Chapter 6: Client Language Bindings

Chapter 6 contains the details of client language bindings, beginning with an examination of the RAD support for COM built into various Microsoft development environments. For each one, I describe the support available for building a forms-based application, and how various COM components, both visual and otherwise, are included.

I then move on to a detailed examination of the various COM/Automation data types and how they are mapped into the various client languages, before finally examining the bindings for creating and using classes and interfaces in each client language. This includes details of memory allocation, error and event handling, and the quirks of individual languages.

The chapter ends with an example of building a forms-based UI to the specification model that was developed in Chapter 5. To show how a real COM object model is used from the different languages, I build functionally identical user interfaces using each of the client languages.

Chapter 7: Server Bindings and Implementation

The final chapter of the book shows how to build object models in C++ with ATL. In it, I begin with a description of the C/C++ bindings for base and user-defined IDL data types, as well as bindings for IDL interfaces. Next, I look at the implementation of a COM class using ATL. This illustrates all aspects of the ATL server bindings, including those for errors and events. It also discusses all the details that must be addressed by production code, including preparing parameters, return values on error, and HRESULT transformations.

The remaining part of the chapter focuses on the design and implementation of the COM server, starting with a fully specified implementation model that is derived from the specification model. This implementation, which uses some of the more sophisticated techniques discussed in Chapter 5, is illustrated with IDL and box-spoon diagrams.

The rest of the section focuses on the actual implementation of this object model using very sophisticated ATL techniques – including some ATL extensions of my own invention. If you are programming serious COM implementations in ATL, this material should merit some very close study.

Finally, the chapter describes the use of user-defined types with embedded pointers, indicating the potential performance benefits of such types and illustrating the methods required for their correct use, paying close attention to heap allocation. The last section of all focuses on the implementation of a DHTML control that was used in Chapter 6.

What You Need to Use this Book

In order to run the code examples presented in this book, you need a computer running Windows 95, Windows 98 or Windows NT 4.0 (with Service Pack 4.0). However, much of the material – particularly in the early chapters – doesn't actually require you to be at a computer while you read. The information on the COM infrastructure, IDL attributes and application design can usefully be read by anyone with a working knowledge of COM and C/C++ programming.

The majority of the code was developed and tested using Visual C++ 6.0 and ATL 3.0, although the nature of the book is such that a number of other languages are also used for the development of client code. Visual Basic, Visual J++ and Visual InterDev are all utilized in Chapter 6, but while being able to test and develop the code is a valuable addition to the learning process, having access to these languages is not a prerequisite for reading the book.

Conventions Used

We use a number of different styles of text and layout in the book to help differentiate between different kinds of information. Here are some examples of the styles we use and an explanation of what they mean:

> **These boxes hold important, not-to-be forgotten, mission critical details that are directly relevant to the surrounding text.**

Background information, asides and references to information located elsewhere appear in text like this.

❑ **Important Words** are in a bold font
❑ Words that appear on the screen, such as menu options, are in a similar font to the one used on the screen – the File menu, for example
❑ Keys that you press on the keyboard, like *Ctrl* and *Delete*, are in italics
❑ All filenames are in this style: Pidl.cpp
❑ Function names look like this: SHBrowseForFolder()

Code that's new, important or relevant to the current discussion will be presented like this:

```
[
    uuid(93C255B0-2AC9-11D2-A5B6-000000000002)
]
dispinterface DMyInterface
{
properties:
    [id(3)] long lMyProp;
methods:
    [id(4)] long MyMethod([in] long, [in] long);
};
```

However, code that you've seen before, or which has little to do with the matter at hand, looks like this:

```
[
    uuid(93C255B0-2AC9-11D2-A5B6-000000000002)
]
dispinterface DMyInterface
{
properties:
    [id(3)] long lMyProp;
methods:
    [id(4)] long MyMethod([in] long, [in] long);
};
```

Tell Us What You Think

We've tried to make this book as accurate and enjoyable as possible, but what really matters is what the book actually does for you. Please let us know your views, either by returning the reply card in the back of the book, or by contacting us via e-mail at feedback@wrox.com

Source Code

All the source code from the examples in this book is available for download from the Wrox Press web site:

http://www.wrox.com
ftp://ftp.wrox.com/professional
ftp://ftp.wrox.co.uk/professional

Support

We've made every effort to make sure there are no errors in the text or the code. However, to err is human and as such we recognize the need to keep you, the reader, informed of any mistakes as they're spotted and corrected. The web site acts as a focus for providing the following information and support:

- ❑ Errata sheets
- ❑ Information about current and forthcoming titles
- ❑ Sample chapters
- ❑ Source code downloads
- ❑ An e-mail newsletter
- ❑ Developer's Journal subscription
- ❑ Articles and opinion on related topics

Errata sheets are available for all our books – please download them, or take part in the continuous improvement of our products and upload a 'fix' or a pointer to the solution.

2

COM and IDL Basics

This chapter introduces the basics of COM IDL. As you'll see, IDL is a language for defining interfaces and capturing type information for distributed systems. By using IDL effectively, you can improve the efficiency of your COM marshaling code and make life easier for the users of your COM components. In these first few sections, I want to give you an idea of how both these goals can be achieved.

I'm going to begin by placing IDL within the larger context of, "ways of describing type information." After that, we'll take a super-fast tour through the basic COM concepts that are modeled in IDL, incorporating the notion of classes, the different kinds of interfaces, error notifications and events. I'll follow this with a look at the IDL compilation process and the output of the MIDL compiler, including the type library, proxy-stub DLL and RPC headers. We'll then examine the structure of an IDL file, and see how the contents of IDL files can be re-used.

Next, I will get into the basics of IDL syntax and semantics: the concepts of decorations, IDL base types, user-defined types, and function and constant definitions. This will be followed by the parts of IDL that are COM specific, the declaration of various kinds of interfaces, and the rules that govern such interfaces. Finally, I'll close the chapter with a list of interface design guidelines that are based on the things we've looked at up to that point.

What is IDL?

IDL stands for **Interface Definition Language**. It is an ASCII or human-readable representation of interface definitions and type information that together describe the important features of a COM distributed object model, in a manner that doesn't depend on any other language. The IDL that this book deals with is the one that's used in the definition of COM-style interfaces. It is a subset of the language that is recognized by the **Microsoft IDL** (**MIDL**) **compiler**.

The MIDL compiler was originally designed to generate **marshaling code** for RPC interfaces (an interface paradigm that is not object-oriented). Since COM interfaces also required marshaling, MIDL was extended to generate marshaling code for the COM RPC (also known as ORPC) architecture, and we'll be covering this use of IDL in Chapter 3. Although ORPC is built on top of Microsoft RPC, that's only an implementation detail and I will not be looking at RPC IDL in this book.

The function of generating **type libraries** used to be served by a language called **ODL** that was compiled by a tool named **MkTypLib**. However, the similarities between 'old' IDL and ODL were so striking (they both described a different aspect of program metadata) that all the functionality was merged into a single language (modern IDL) and a single tool (the MIDL compiler).

In this book, I shall adopt the term "type information" as shorthand to mean all kinds of program metadata. The most important aspects of IDL are those that deal with defining interfaces, but as we shall see in Chapters 4 and 6, it also serves various other uses.

Type Information: The Big Picture

IDL itself has only quasi-official status in the COM universe. Officially, COM is a binary standard in which descriptions of interfaces in source code are simply a notational convenience. The actual infrastructure is described in terms of binary memory layouts and API calls, and it's these binary representations that are supposedly the 'real' description of an object model. At the moment, however, IDL is the only widespread ASCII representation of the type information associated with COM object models, and that's why this book has the acronym IDL in the title.

This official position regarding binary layout is getting increasingly hard to justify, since COM is no longer tied exclusively to Wintel platforms. In the broader context of multiple architectures and OS platforms, a purely binary standard for interoperability doesn't make much sense. (Are the vtable entries in a 64-bit architecture going to remain 32-bit pointers?) Clearly, some kind of language/architecture/OS-neutral interface description is required, and this function is currently served by the combination of the type library, IDL and the NDR wire-level data representation format.

For the purposes of the book, I will treat a type library as being the compiled form of an IDL file, which means that I'll describe the contents of a type library in terms of the equivalent IDL code. In fact, Microsoft is often at pains to separate the two descriptions. This book is described in terms of IDL syntax, but I've tried very hard to stay focused on the essential concepts underlying type information. These will remain relevant whatever type information syntax is used in the future.

At present, it is not strictly true that a type library is the compiled form of a source IDL file because the translation from the latter to the former loses information. Furthermore, there is no guarantee that the type information API will remain completely compatible with IDL. At the moment, though, there is enough overlap to make this statement approximately correct.

The Scope of Type Information

The scope of type information can be appreciated by looking at the various uses to which it can be put. Type information is used by a number of tools that require information about the object model in order to fulfill their function. Some of the most visible uses of type information are:

❑ Its use by the Visual Basic design-time environment to generate the call that corresponds to a COM/Automation interface invocation.

❑ Its use in the generation of COM client side bindings for J++ (creating COM wrappers) and C++ (the `#import` directive).

❑ The Visual C++ ClassWizard uses it to insert an ActiveX control into a project and make it available in the dialog editor toolbar.

❑ IntelliSense technology (which is now available in all Microsoft language environments) uses it to provide auto-completion and context-sensitive help for interface members.

❑ Various containers (Visual Basic, the ActiveX Test Container) use type information to implement the event interfaces that are supported by an object.

❑ The type library marshaler reads the description of an interface to do interpretive standard marshaling on the interface.

❑ The Automation side of a dual interface is 'automagically' implemented by means of the **Dispatch API**. This API uses the description of an interface to convert Automation calls into the equivalent vtable calls.

In addition, the metadata contained in the type information can be used by various flavors of CASE tools. These applications are limited only by the imagination of the tool developer.

A Super-fast Introduction to COM

In order to understand how IDL works, you need to understand the various aspects of COM that are represented in IDL. The most important of these concepts are interfaces and, to a lesser extent, classes. In addition, any production-standard object model needs to specify errors and be able to perform callbacks. I will review these important COM ideas in this section.

If you're an experienced COM programmer, you may just want to skim this section very quickly to get a handle on my notation, and for the occasional design recommendation.

Box-Spoon Diagrams

I intend to introduce these COM concepts in the context of a graphical notation that has become familiar to COM programmers. Some people call them **lollipop diagrams**; I use the term **box-spoon diagram** and have extended the notation to simplify the depiction of errors, events and interface types.

Broadly speaking, the box-spoon system is used to represent COM classes and interfaces. The figure below shows just such a diagram:

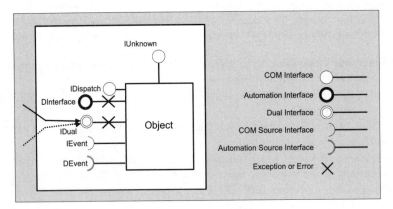

Classes

The box (the inner rectangle) represents a COM class (or an object – that is, an instance of a class). However, because of the interface-based design philosophy used in COM, classes are not particularly relevant – they are only required at object creation time. The overwhelming majority of COM code just deals with interfaces, although classes *are* a useful construct when you're viewing the object model as a whole, or if you have tools that need to be aware of objects. You'll see examples of this in Chapters 4 and 6.

Interfaces

The spoons protruding from the box represent the interfaces exposed (or exported, or implemented) by a class (or object). Conceptually, an interface is a group of related methods (or properties exposed as pairs of 'get' and 'set' methods) implemented by a COM class.

An arrow pointing at the interface represents a reference to it – in other words, it means a client has a pointer to the interface. A dotted arrow represents a weak reference – that is, a pointer to the interface that hasn't been reference counted.

A cross on the handle of a spoon indicates that the interface generates an error object, almost certainly using the COM error protocol. The cup shape indicates an outgoing interface – generally one that uses the connectable object protocol for sink registration. These two concepts are explained in greater detail below.

The Different Interface Types

There are two distinct physical mechanisms for exposing a logical interface:

❑ A COM-style or vtable mechanism. An interface like this is characterized by a very specific binary memory layout, and is physically invoked by a mechanism very similar to that used to call an API level compiled function. It is identical to the vtable mechanism used by the Visual C++ compiler to call virtual functions, hence the use of the term **vtable interface**.

❑ An Automation mechanism. This is based on a COM-style interface called `IDispatch`. Unlike vtable invocation, the physical invocation mechanism looks like a lot like the one used by a language interpreter to invoke interpreted functions.

This is hardly an accident, since the mechanism grew out of the Visual Basic interpreter.

❑ The Automation mechanism has recently been extended to support highly dynamic interface semantics. The new mechanism is based upon an extension to the `IDispatch` interface, named `IDispatchEx`, and this too is covered in greater detail in Chapter 4.

There is also a hybrid interface type that can be invoked using *either* mechanism. Such a hybrid interface is called a **dual interface**.

Why Have Different Interface Types?

Why have two different mechanisms for invoking interfaces? Why not just standardize on one? The simple answer is that historically, Visual Basic was designed with Automation interfaces and there are just too many legacy interfaces to get rid of the mechanism. The complex answer has to do with the difference between compiled and interpreted languages.

Immutability

Vtable interfaces are designed for the use of clients written in compiled languages. They are inherently strongly typed, because the client has to set up the call stack with the exact number and types of values that the method invocation expects. This works very well for clients written in strongly typed, compiled languages, since the compiler can ensure that the call matches the method prototype.

This is also the reason why vtable interfaces are **immutable**. If the type signature or semantics of an interface were changed, all clients that were compiled on the basis of the old type signature would break – in fact they would crash and burn in truly spectacular fashion.

Late Binding

In contrast, Automation interfaces are designed for the use of interpreted clients. The method call is set up at runtime, and there is no strong type checking. This means that the following situations can and will occur at runtime:

❑ A function may be called with the wrong number of parameters
❑ A function name may be misspelled

Because of its strongly typed nature, the vtable invocation mechanism cannot deal with situations like these. If the first case were to occur with a vtable interface (and if the compiler allowed it to compile at all), the program could not recover gracefully, and would be almost certain to crash immediately. The second example makes no sense at all within the vtable framework, since the misspelled method simply would not compile. With Automation interfaces, both scenarios are possible because of the way Automation interfaces are invoked. This feature of Automation interfaces that allows method calls to remain unresolved until runtime is known as **late binding**.

In principle, all interpreted languages can be modified to allow compilation, as has happened with Visual Basic. There is no longer a technological reason for maintaining dynamically (or loosely) typed, interpreted language semantics. The existence of interpreted languages is attributable to market needs: interpreted languages are easier to learn (this is why there are so many Visual Basic and script programmers). Novice programmers can start producing working code without having to understand the intricacies of a type system and compiler-enforced strong typing (isn't that why it takes so long to become a C++ expert?). Late binding is a necessary component of a loosely typed language.

Automatic Automation

A final point worth making is this: given an IDL description, it isn't hard to generate an Automation interface that proxies a vtable interface automatically. As a matter of fact, there is an API that is designed to serve this very purpose. As we shall see later, this is the easiest way of implementing a dual interface.

It is possible to take this a step further and automatically wrap a non-dual vtable interface in an Automation-style proxy *at runtime*. The figure below displays the structure of such a proxy:

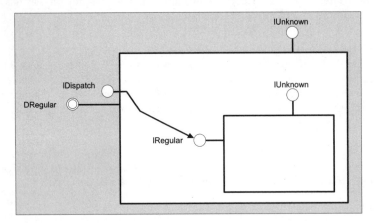

Representing the Different Interfaces

Take another look at the above figure. Although it's not standard practice, I distinguish between the different kinds of interfaces by drawing Automation interfaces using a pair of concentric circles on the spoon, and dual interfaces using a circle with a thick border. The `IDispatch` interface will sometimes be shown as a little stub next to the Automation interface, indicating its special involvement in the implementation of that interface.

Errors

COM requires that all the methods on a remotable interface return an HRESULT. The rationale for this is straightforward: any method on a remotable interface can fail as a result of transport failure, even if the underlying implementation semantics never allow failure. For this reason, the type signature of such a method must allow for the *possibility* of failure, and so it must return a 32-bit HRESULT status code.

The most significant bit is a severity code that can be used to indicate success (0) or failure (1), while the next two bits are reserved for future use, and must be set to 0. The following 13 bits represent a **facility code** that's used to identify the group of status codes that this value belongs to. Examples of such groups (or facilities) are: FACILITY_STORAGE, used to describe status codes related to persistent storage; and FACILITY_RPC, used to describe errors generated from the underlying RPC implementation. Because they must be globally unique, only a central coordinating authority (this is assumed to be Microsoft) can assign new facility codes.

The table lists the facility codes that are currently in use, and their descriptions from the Platform SDK:

Name	Value	Description
FACILITY_NULL	0	For broadly applicable common status codes such as S_OK.
FACILITY_RPC	1	For status codes returned from remote procedure calls.
FACILITY_DISPATCH	2	For late-binding IDispatch interface errors.
FACILITY_STORAGE	3	For status codes returned from IStorage or IStream method calls relating to structured storage. Status codes whose code (lower 16 bits) value is in the range of DOS error codes (that is, less than 256) have the same meaning as the corresponding DOS error.
FACILITY_ITF	4	For most status codes returned from interface methods. The value is defined by the interface, which means that two SCODEs or HRESULTs with exactly the same 32-bit values returned from two different interfaces might have different meanings.
FACILITY_WIN32	7	Used to provide a means of handling error codes from functions in the Win32 API as an HRESULT. Error codes in 16-bit OLE that duplicated Win32 error codes have also been changed to FACILITY_WIN32.
FACILITY_WINDOWS	8	Used for additional error codes from Microsoft-defined interfaces.
FACILITY_CONTROL	10	Used for OLE Controls-related error values.

The 16 least significant bits of the HRESULT are used to return a code that indicates the actual status value. Only the central coordinating authority can define status values for facilities other than FACILITY_ITF.

More Complex Status Information

What if you want to return a more complex status type, or find the HRESULT type too restrictive? Using a parameter, you can always have your methods return any user-defined status type that you'd like.

Exception Style Error Mechanism

Most modern programming languages offer some form of exception handling mechanism. At the method level, an exception is a way for an invocation to signal an unusual or abnormal return condition to the calling method. Typically, the calling method then has the option either to continue its control flow, or to propagate the exception further.

Standard exception handling mechanisms are language specific and ill suited to cross-process invocation. Therefore, COM takes the route of using a COM-based protocol for exception handling. For the protocol to work correctly, both server (the entity that signals the error) and client (the entity that catches the error) have to agree on the details.

Before taking a look at the 'standard' error protocol, it is worth making the point that theoretically not only is this protocol optional (your server need not support it), but also it can be replaced by a completely different protocol if you really need it to be. As long as you are in control of both client and server, the error protocol that you use is completely up to you. However, there are two that make the protocol I shall describe here the *de facto* standard:

❑ All Microsoft-created clients, servers and tools work with it.
❑ The DCOM implementation of the protocol has a body extension that conveys the error information as part of an ORPC response or fault packet. This means that the information is made available to the caller without the need for an extra network round trip.

If you're willing to incur the cost of the extra round trip (or to write a body extension to the DCOM protocol), you are perfectly free to implement any error protocol of your choosing. Put like that, it doesn't sound like much of an option, does it?

The COM Error Protocol

Let us now take a look at the COM error protocol. As a comparison, you may be aware that a method in a pure Automation interface can raise an error with rich information simply by returning that information in one of the parameters of IDispatch::Invoke(). However, there is no obvious opportunity of this kind for vtable-based interfaces, so how can we specify a rich error in this case?

Could we use the C++ exception handling mechanism? Not really, because not only is that mechanism C++ specific, but also it has strong thread affinity. As I mentioned earlier, a generalized COM error mechanism must work across a process boundary. The protocol that we wind up using, then, is a COM-based protocol. Individual language implementations are expected to layer their language-specific mechanism on top of this protocol.

Logical Threads and Error Objects

The COM runtime has a notion of **logical threads** that keep track of method invocations as they cross apartment (or process, or machine) boundaries. Each such thread can have an **error object** associated with it that may be accessed using the COM error API.

When a thread first begins using COM, no error object exists. When a COM method wishes to signal an error, it creates a new error object on its logical thread, sets the rich error information on that object, and returns a failure HRESULT. On detecting this, the ORPC mechanism checks for the existence of an error object and (if it finds one) transfers it across apartment boundaries. This is done by the body extension to the DCOM protocol that I mentioned earlier.

The details of this protocol are mapped out in the following sections.

Classes and Interfaces

The figure below shows the classes and interfaces required for the protocol to work. In addition to the primary object class, there is an error object class that exports the ICreateErrorInfo and IErrorInfo interfaces. Note that this object is actually implemented by the COM runtime, and you do not need to implement it yourself. Your object class, however, must export the ISupportErrorInfo interface, which you *are* required to implement.

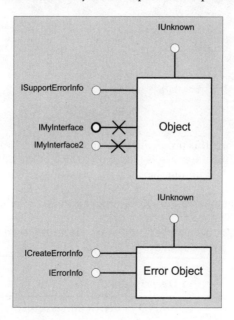

Sequence Diagram

The next diagram shows the sequence of operations that take place during a conversation under the COM error protocol. The important steps are described in the following section.

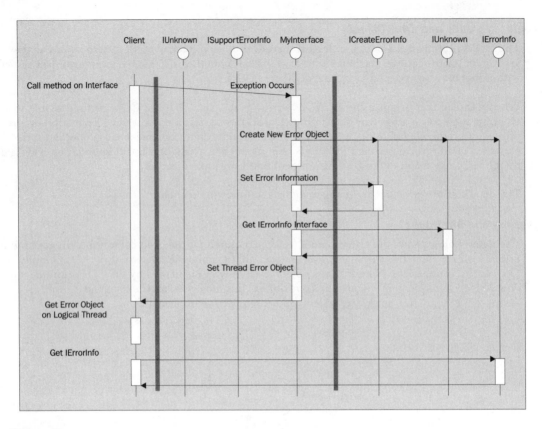

Signaling an Error

A COM server class that supports this protocol *must* implement the ISupportErrorInfo interface. However, the only function of this interface is to identify which of the other interfaces on the object raise errors using the protocol. Not all interfaces on the object have to use the protocol.

When a method on an error-supporting interface hits an exception condition, it creates a generic COM error object using the COM API call CreateErrorInfo(). The state of this object is then set using the methods of the ICreateErrorInfo interface that is returned by the API call. The pieces of information captured in the error object are

Item	Description
Source	ProgID of the COM class that raised the error
IID	Interface ID of the interface that raised the error
Description	A textual description of the error
Help File	A path to a help file that describes the error
Help Context	Help Context Identifier

The API call `SetErrorInfo()` is then used to associate the `IErrorInfo` interface on the error object with the current 'logical thread', releasing a previous instance of `IErrorInfo` if there is one.

Catching an Error

Prior to using the interface, the client checks to see if it supports error objects. If it does, the client resets the error object for the current logical thread to `NULL` before invoking the interface method. Upon getting a failure `HRESULT` back from the method invocation, the client uses the COM API call `GetErrorInfo()` to get the `IErrorInfo` interface on the error object associated with the current 'logical thread'. This interface gives access to the error state that was stored in the error object by the `ICreateErrorInfo` interface in the method implementation.

Events

Another form of communication between object and client is the **event**. An event is a mechanism that allows the *server* to notify a *client* (the opposite of what usually happens) in an asynchronous manner when something 'interesting' happens.

When you're dealing with ordinary, non-COM programming, a **callback** is typically a simple, client-implemented function with an agreed-upon signature. The address of this function is passed to the server using some registration protocol. The server then calls the client back (hence the name), using this function with the appropriate parameters when the 'interesting' situation arises.

Outgoing Interfaces

The problem, of course, is that the COM callback mechanism must work across process boundaries, but the solution isn't hard to deduce. Rather than making a callback on a function entry point, we do it on a COM interface method instead, since the COM remoting mechanism *guarantees* that this will work across process boundaries. A COM interface that is used in this fashion is called an **outgoing** or **source interface** because the server *invokes* its methods, rather than *implementing* them. It is also sometimes called an **event set**. The client is required to implement the interface and inform the server object of its existence; on the client side, it is known as an **incoming** or **sink interface**.

The trickiest part of this process is the registration of the sink interface with the server object, but happily a 'standard' way of performing this task does exist. In the next section, I will describe the **connectable object** (or **connection point**) **protocol**, which was first defined for use with ActiveX controls. Again, it is worth making the point that there is absolutely no requirement that you use this protocol to register outgoing interfaces in your own object models – it has been criticized in the past as being too generic for many specific situations. Although less 'wired' into the COM infrastructure than the COM error protocol, this protocol is also a *de facto* standard because all the Microsoft clients, servers and tools support it.

The Connectable Object Protocol

The diagram below shows the classes and interfaces associated with the connection point protocol. A class that supports events is required to export the `IConnectionPointContainer` interface. It must also contain one instance of a connection point object for each source interface, and each connection point object is required to export the `IConnectionPoint` interface.

In addition, there are a couple of classes that may be instantiated to provide enumerators. The first of these iterates over all `IConnectionPoint` interfaces contained in the main object, and exports the `IEnumConnectionPoints` interface for this purpose. The second iterates over all sink interfaces currently registered with a given connection point, and exports the `IEnumConnections` interface.

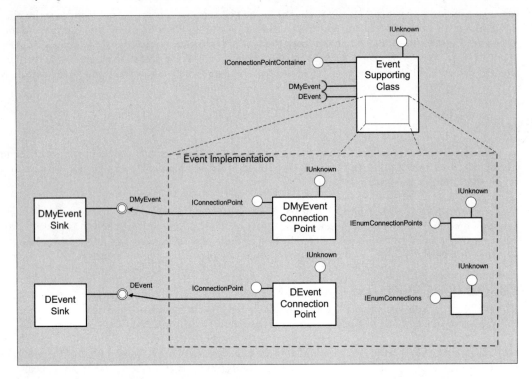

The client needs to implement objects that implement the various sink interfaces that it wishes to be notified upon.

Sequence Diagram

The next figure shows the order in which operations occur in a sample two-way conversation using the connection point protocol. This sequence is not the most general – for instance, it does not use the enumerator interfaces at all.

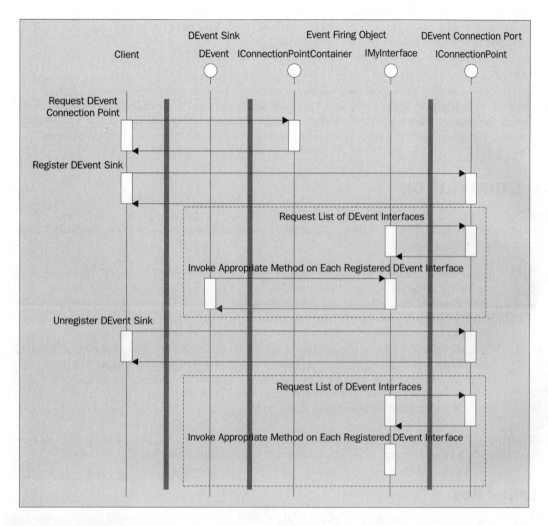

Client Registration

If it wants to be advised of events, the client registers in two steps. First, it uses methods of `IConnectionPointContainer` to retrieve the `IConnectionPoint` associated with its sink interface.

A variation on the protocol requires the client to enumerate over all connection points supported by the container. This might be done, for instance, by a client that creates custom sinks to match the events available on a server object.

Next, the client uses this `IConnectionPoint` to request that it be advised when the event occurs, and you should be aware there is a potentially serious flaw in the signature of the `IConnectionPoint::Advise()` method that is used for this purpose. The first parameter to the method is a pointer to the `IUnknown` interface on the sink object, which means that an additional `QI()` (and network round-trip) is necessary to retrieve the actual sink interface itself.

Eventually, when the client no longer wishes to receive events, the client uses `IConnectionPoint` again to request that event notifications be terminated. The client does not receive any events that occur prior to registration, or after de-registration.

Event Firing

When the event occurs, the server uses the connection point object to enumerate over all the registered sink interfaces (it may or may not choose to use the enumerator interface if it has direct access to the connection point's state). It then calls the method on sink interface that is appropriate to the event. The process of invoking the method on all registered interfaces is called **event firing**.

IDL Compilation

Having reviewed the basic COM concepts that are described in IDL, I'm going to move on to examine the process of IDL compilation. The MIDL compiler is the primary consumer of IDL source code, and it serves two major functions:

❑   It generates the standard marshaling code for the interfaces described in the IDL file. Standard marshaling, described in greater detail in Chapter 3, is the process by which COM creates interface proxies and stubs, and marshals method parameters and return values across apartment, process or machine boundaries. This marshaling code, which is implemented in a so-called **proxy-stub DLL**, is then distributed with any object that exposes the relevant interfaces.

❑   It compiles the IDL file into a type library, and it's this type library that is used by the majority of tools that depend on type information. (More precisely, it is the type-querying API we'll be covering later in the book that's used by these tools.) As currently implemented, the MIDL compiler does not carry all the source-level IDL information into the type library. Some marshaling-specific information is lost in the process.

If MIDL could include marshaling information in the type library, it wouldn't need to generate the marshaling code as well. A separate tool that worked with type libraries could do it instead.

Output Files

As a result of a successful compilation with MIDL, a number of files are generated from a single IDL file. By default, all the new files have names prefixed with the name of the IDL file (in the example below, the prefix is `foobar`), but this can be overridden by supplying replacements using the appropriate command line flags to MIDL. (See Appendix A.)

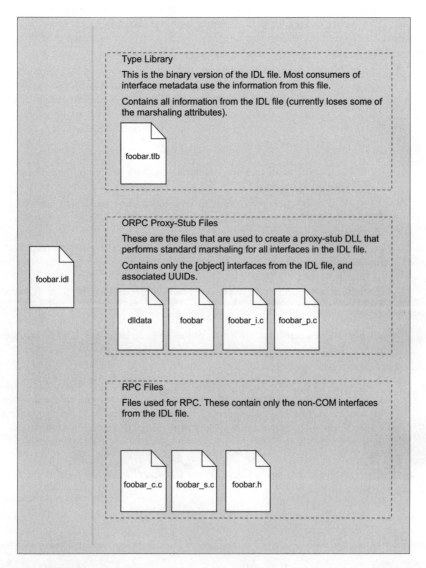

The above figure shows the files that are output by the MIDL compiler in the process of compiling an IDL file. Not counting the ones that deal with RPC interfaces, there are three kinds of files being generated:

- ❑ Files for creating the proxy-stub DLL that's used to marshal COM interfaces.
    - ❑ `foobar_p.c` is a C file that contains the code used to create the client proxy, server stub, and the marshaling and unmarshaling code required to remote the interfaces defined in `foobar.idl`.
    - ❑ `dlldata.c` is a C file that contains the DLL entry points required by a COM object server. In reality, the proxy-stub DLL is implemented by means of COM objects that implement the interface marshalers. Therefore, the DLL must expose the same entry points as any other COM object server.

❏ Files used to describe interfaces. The proxy-stub DLL is the primary consumer of these files, but they are also commonly used for C/C++ server bindings (described in Chapter 7). They also used to be used for client bindings, but that function is increasingly being taken over by the header files generated by the new `#import` directive, which we'll look at shortly.

  ❏ `foobar.h` is a header file that contains C++ and C declarations for each of the interfaces defined in the IDL file. The C++ interfaces are simply C++ abstract base classes that have a one-to-one correspondence with the corresponding IDL interface. The C interfaces are a little more complicated because the vptr and vtable have to be 'hand-built'. This header file is used within the server when the interface is referenced or realized using C/C++ code.

  `foobar.h` also contains forward declarations that are used in the interface marshaling code in the proxy-stub DLL.

  ❏ `foobar_i.c` is a C file that contains definitions of variables that hold the various UUIDs (IIDs, CLSIDs and LIBIDs) introduced in the IDL file. By convention, these variables have names like `IID_<interfacename>`, `CLSID_<classname>` and `LIBID_<libraryname>`, where the words in angled brackets correspond to the human-readable 'names' assigned to the corresponding entities in the IDL file.

  These names are no longer strictly necessary when using a compiler that support the UUID extensions defined by Microsoft. These extensions consist of the compiler directives `__declspec(uuid())` and the `__uuidof()` operator, and make it possible to associate a UUID with a object and retrieve the UUID of an object respectively.

❏ A file that contains the type library.

  ❏ `foobar.tlb` contains a binary, tokenized version of the IDL file. At the time of writing, the textual and tokenized versions of the IDL are not identical (some information is lost when going from `.idl` to `.tlb`, primarily the marshaling attributes), but this difference may disappear over time and with evolution of the tools.

The figure also shows the files that are generated for the RPC interfaces, but we won't be examining them any further in this book. These files are not actually generated unless you have defined RPC interfaces in your IDL file.

IDL File Structure

We've seen how IDL files get compiled, so let's look now at the structure of an IDL source file. Broadly speaking, an IDL file is split into two sections: one that generates the proxy-stub code for standard marshaling, and another that generates the type library. The type library is generated from the body of a `library` statement, while everything outside this statement is used to generate marshaling code.

The following listing shows a sample IDL file based on the examples that are coming up later in this chapter. Obviously, it won't all be clear to you until you've read through to the end of the chapter, but even at this stage you should be able to appreciate some of the structure – in many ways it's a lot like C/C++ code:

```
#include "stdio.h"
import "wtypes.idl"

cpp_quote("// Url History Interfaces.")

enum OLECMDF
{
   OLECMDF_SUPPORTED = 0x00000001,
   OLECMDF_ENABLED   = 0x00000002,
   OLECMDF_LATCHED   = 0x00000004,
   OLECMDF_NINCHED   = 0x00000008,
};

typedef struct tagMSG
{
   HWND    hwnd;
   UINT    message;
   WPARAM wParam;
   LPARAM lParam;
   DWORD  time;
   POINT  pt;
} MSG, *PMSG, *NPMSG, *LPMSG;

[
   object,
   uuid(93C255B0-2AC9-11D2-A5B6-000000000001)
]
interface IMyInterface : IUnknown
{
   HRESULT MyMethod([in] long, [in] long, [out, retval] long*);
   HRESULT MyGet([out] long*);
   HRESULT MySet([in] long);
};

[
   uuid(93C255B1-2AC9-11D2-A5B6-000000000002)
]
library Foo
{
   importlib("stdole32.tlb");

   typedef [public] GUID GUID;

   interface IMyInterface;

   [
      dllname("somemod1.dll")
   ]
   module SomeModule
   {
      const ULONG MAGIC_NUMBER = 356;
      [entry("profound"), usesgetlasterror] long profound([in] double x);
   };
};
```

This rather strange structure reflects the dual heritage of the current IDL language, and the same reason explains why there are three different ways of re-using IDL descriptions from other files, as we shall see shortly.

MIDL and the C Preprocessor

Prior to running the IDL compiler itself, MIDL runs the C preprocessor on the input file it's passed. This means that familiar C preprocessor directives such as #include, #define and #if are available in IDL.

As you would expect, any macros created using #define in the IDL file are expanded prior to compilation and do not make it into the C/C++ code that is the output of the MIDL compiler. In situations where it is *desirable* for some pieces of code to make it through the preprocessor and into the final C/C++ files intact, a cpp_quote() statement should be used. This technique is generally used to insert #define directives, #if directives and comments into the generated files. For example, this statement introduces the declaration into the generated C header file:

```
cpp_quote("EXTERN_C const CLSID CLSID_StdComponentCategoriesMgr;")
```

While this statement saves the comment from the preprocessor:

```
cpp_quote("// Url History Interfaces.")
```

Since a cpp_quote() statement can always be avoided by having an auxiliary header file, it should be used only when it is absolutely essential. One such use is to provide conditional definitions for legacy types whose C/C++ declarations provide insufficient information for marshaling, and that therefore require separate IDL definitions that are only seen by the marshaling code. We'll discuss this subject again in Chapter 3, but it shouldn't be an issue if you're only using 'new' types.

cpp_quote() does not have any effect on the type library generated from the source file; it only inserts text into the marshaling code.

Including the Contents of Other Files

As I mentioned above, there are three mechanisms in IDL for including the contents of other files, and the differences between them can be confusing at first sight. The options are #include, import, and importlib.

#include

#include works as you would expect it to: the contents of an included file are placed into the including file verbatim, just as if they had been typed in.

```
#include "stdio.h"
```

If the above statement appeared in the file example.idl, all of stdio.h would be included within example.idl. All legitimate declarations, including function prototypes, would make their way into the generated example.h file.

import

The import directive is the standard method for bringing in definitions from other IDL, ODL or C/C++ header files into the main IDL file. All type and constant definitions (including those for interfaces) in the imported file can be referenced in your file. Unlike the #include directive, import ignores other kinds of declarations, such as function prototypes.

The `import` directive has a slightly different effect in the type library than it does in the generated C/C++ header files. If a type from the imported file is referenced in the `library` section, then the declaration of that type is inserted into the type library. On the other hand, the C/C++ header files never have any code inserted from the imported file. Instead, the file simply `#includes` the header file corresponding to the imported IDL file.

If that's not quite clear, consider that the `GUID` data structure used throughout COM is defined in the `wtypes.idl` file. If we have code like this:

```
import "wtypes.idl"

...

library Foo
{
    typedef [public] GUID aGUID;
};
```

Then the generated header file will contain this:

```
#include "wtypes.h"
```

However, it will have no actual declaration for `GUID` (it is assumed that `wtypes.h` will provide one). This is in contrast to the `#include` directive, which would have inserted the contents of `wtypes.idl` into the generated file.

On the other hand, the generated type library file will have a declaration for `GUID` inserted into the library — that is, the de-compiled library has the following form:

```
library Foo
{
    typedef struct tag_GUID
    {
        unsigned long Data1;
        unsigned short Data2;
        unsigned short Data3;
        unsigned char Data4[8];
    } _GUID;

    typedef [public] _GUID aGUID;
};
```

The C preprocessor is invoked separately for an imported file **prior** to it being imported, so any preprocessor definitions in the imported file are not visible in the importing file.

importlib

What if we wanted to avoid including the definition of `GUID` in every type library (unnecessary duplication of declarations generally resulting in harder-to-maintain code)? This is where the `importlib` directive comes in. The `importlib` directive can only occur within the body of a `library` statement, and must precede any other definitions. Type definitions in the imported library are **not** duplicated in the importing library. Therefore, any referenced type libraries have to be distributed along with the importing library, so that the referenced types are available at runtime.

```
library Foo
{
    importlib("stdole32.tlb");

    typedef [public] GUID aGUID;
};
```

The above code, for example, results in a situation where the declaration of GUID is *not* inserted into the type library. This results from the fact that GUID is declared in the stdole32.tlb file. stdole32.tlb must be available on any machine on which the Foo type library is installed. The best way to make it available is by properly registering the type library on the target machine.

Usage Patterns

Unless you need to support legacy types, it is best not to use #include. Use import to get at IDL declarations, and importlib to reduce redundancies caused by declarations that seep into the type library.

Entities Described by an IDL File

The ultimate purpose of an IDL file is to describe various features of a COM object model – most importantly, the declarations of COM interfaces. In addition, it is also used to describe COM classes and DLL modules. The entities involved in this task are:

Entity	Description
interface	An interface represents a vtable interface, and describes the order, names and signatures of the methods (and pseudo-properties) that make up that interface.
dispinterface	A dispinterface represents an Automation interface, and describes the order, names, and signatures of the methods and properties that make up that interface.
	In modern practice, it is common to define dual interfaces, rather than pure dispinterfaces.
coclass	A coclass describes a COM class in terms of the interfaces and dispinterfaces that it exposes, and the outgoing (source) interfaces that it supports.
	The coclass statement is also used for type information, as we'll see in Chapters 4 and 6.
library	Only the portion of the IDL file that falls within the library statement is actually inserted into the type library that is generated by MIDL.
	However, this can include declarations from outside the block that are referenced from within it, as with the interface statements in the earlier listing.
module	A module describes a DLL module in much the same way that a DEF file does – it lists the names and ordinals of exported functions and global variables.

The complete specification of interfaces, functions and variables also requires the ability to declare user-defined types. IDL supports this with the help of the `typedef` statement, and the `struct`, `union` and `enum` keywords.

Basic IDL Syntax

Because of its historical roots in RPC IDL, COM IDL is based on C syntax. This means that if you're a C/C++ programmer, IDL declarations should look very familiar to you. As a matter of fact, IDL can be viewed as an extension to C that is specialized to give very precise definitions of data types and interfaces. At present, IDL has no support for specifying computations.

The Structure of an IDL Declaration: Decorations

An IDL declaration looks identical to a C declaration, with the addition of so-called **decorations**. A decoration precedes the C declaration, and is delimited by brackets. The decoration consists of a (comma-separated) list of **attributes** that qualify the C construct by specifying extra type information that can't be expressed in ordinary C. Thus, the parameters in an ordinary C function declaration like this:

```
void f(int, long*);
```

Would be decorated in IDL with the direction of parameter transfer – that is, whether data is traveling into or out of the function:

```
void f([in] int, [in, out] long*);
```

The decorations are the expressions in brackets that precede the parameter declarations. The individual keywords, `in` and `out` in this example, specify the attributes.

Base Types

Like any other programming language, IDL has a set of primitive or base data types. These are: `boolean`, `byte`, `char`, `double`, `float`, `hyper`, `int`, `long`, `short`, `small`, `void`, and `wchar_t`. IDL also allows `signed` and `unsigned` versions of all the integer types, and pointers to all data types. Pointers in IDL are very similar to C pointers.

The base types in IDL all have a fixed size and sign (and therefore a predetermined range of values). This contrasts with the base types in C/C++, where the range of values associated with a type can be compiler- and platform-dependent. Since IDL is used to generate code that is architecture neutral this is a critical property of the IDL base types.

Character Types in IDL

You may have heard that COM uses Unicode strings, and this is true inasmuch as the parts of the COM API that use strings expect Unicode-encoded, wide character strings. The native `BSTR` and the `OLESTR` that is used by other methods are both Unicode types.

The COM specification demands Unicode because it is the only way to ensure that strings can be interpreted as the same sequence of characters regardless of the underlying architecture. There is nothing stopping you from declaring char* strings and using them in your own methods, but this is probably not a particularly smart idea. The problem associated with using char* strings is that the default IDL char type and the default C/C++ char type differ in their signed-ness, giving you plenty of potential for confusion in their interpretation. My advice is that you stick to wchar_t and use Unicode encoding for characters.

User Defined Types

Beyond the base types, IDL provides constructs to create user-defined types. These are the data composition primitives enum, struct and union.

enum

An enum works exactly like the equivalent construct in C. It is used to generate an enumerated data type – that is, a range of identifiers (or names) that are mapped onto integer values. Just like the C enum (and *unlike* the C++ enum), an IDL enum injects all its identifiers into the top-level namespace, rather than into the scope in which it is defined. For this reason, enum identifiers are frequently prefixed with a scope name:

```
enum OLECMDF
{
    OLECMDF_SUPPORTED  = 0x00000001,
    OLECMDF_ENABLED    = 0x00000002,
    OLECMDF_LATCHED    = 0x00000004,
    OLECMDF_NINCHED    = 0x00000008,
};
```

The above code, for example, declares an enum called OLECMDF with four named values that represent bit flags. An enum can be decorated with additional attributes that we'll be looking at later on.

struct

An IDL struct is identical to a C struct, with the added feature that each field in a struct can be decorated with additional attributes. In addition, bit fields and function declarations are not permitted in structs that participate in marshaling.

```
typedef struct tagMSG {
    HWND    hwnd;
    UINT    message;
    WPARAM  wParam;
    LPARAM  lParam;
    DWORD   time;
    POINT   pt;
} MSG, *PMSG, *NPMSG, *LPMSG;
```

This sample declares a C-style structure called `tagMSG` and several aliases. Win32 API programmers will recognize this as the window message type.

union

IDL allows two kinds of unions: an **encapsulated union** and a **non-encapsulated union**. In either case (and unlike C/C++ `union` types), it is a *discriminated* union – there is a tag value that identifies which sub-type of the union is currently valid. As we will see later, the point of defining unions in this fashion is to provide enough information to marshal a value.

Encapsulated Unions

In an encapsulated union, the discriminating tag is declared *as part of the union*, and the IDL compiler automatically compiles the union into a `struct` that contains the discriminator as well as the union type.

```
typedef union _userHMETAFILE switch(long fContext)
{
    case WDT_INPROC_CALL:    long        hInproc;
    case WDT_REMOTE_CALL:    BYTE_BLOB*  hRemote;
    default:                 long        hGlobal;
} userHMETAFILE;
```

Here, the union `_userHMETAFILE` is either a `long`, a `BYTE_BLOB*` or a `long`, depending on the value of the discriminating field `fContext`. Notice the use of the `switch`, `case` and `default` keywords, mirroring the syntax of the C `switch` statement.

Non-Encapsulated Unions

The non-encapsulated union is very similar, except that it permits one to separate the declaration of the union from the declaration of the discriminating type:

```
typedef [switch_type(VARTYPE)] union tagTYPEUNION
{
    [case(VT_PTR, VT_SAFEARRAY)]  struct tagTYPEDESC*  lptdesc;
    [case(VT_CARRAY)]             struct tagARRAYDESC* lpadesc;
    [case(VT_USERDEFINED)]        HREFTYPE            hreftype;
    [default];
} TYPEUNION;

typedef struct tagTYPEDESC
{
    [switch_is(vt)] TYPEUNION tu;
                    VARTYPE   vt;
} TYPEDESC;
```

The discriminating `case` syntax is now present in the form of decorations to the individual fields. The use of two separate attributes – `switch_type()` and `switch_is()` – in place of the single `switch` keyword permits the separation of the union from its tag.

Having this separation makes it possible to have a union embedded in a `struct` such that the tag is contained in the `struct`, away from the union. The syntax is also useful in declaring parameter lists in which the union and the tag are separate parameters into a method call. This affords an extra degree of flexibility that's not available to encapsulated unions. IDL semantics require that the discriminating variable be declared at the same level (that is, in the same structure or parameter list) as the union itself.

typedef

As you can see from the examples above, IDL permits the use of the `typedef` statement to allow named, user-defined types. As with the identifiers declared by `enum`, the new names are injected into the top-level namespace, and may therefore need to be prefixed with a scope identifier.

There is a slight twist to the use of a `typedef` in IDL. By default, an IDL `typedef` is only introduced into the marshaling headers, *not* into the type library. In the type library, every occurrence of an aliased name is fully expanded to the underlying type expression. In order to introduce a `typedef`'d alias into the type library, it must be decorated with the `public` attribute, like this:

```
library Foo
{
    typedef [public] long* FooBar;

...

};
```

This is the only use of the `public` keyword, and it's useful when you want the end user to be able to declare variables of the type decorated as such.

Function and Constant Definitions

IDL is also used to declare entities associated with ordinary procedural programming, specifically function entry points and constants. This is accomplished by means of the IDL `module` statement, which you also saw in the earlier listing.

The purpose of the `module` statement is to serve as a language-independent header for a DLL function, in the same way that `interface` declarations (coming up soon) serve as a language-independent header for object interfaces. A `module` statement can only occur inside a `library` declaration, and it looks something like this:

```
[
    dllname("somemodl.dll")
]
module SomeModule
{
    const ULONG MAGIC_NUMBER = 356;
    [entry("profound"), usesgetlasterror] long profound([in] double x);
};
```

Here, we're defining entry points and global constants in the `somemodl.dll` file, as specified by the value of the `dllname()` attribute in the `module` decoration. Note that the type library in which the module is declared doesn't need to be included as part of the DLL named in the module. Any number of DLLs can be documented in a single type library, and the `module` statement can selectively include or exclude specific exported functions or constants.

This module declaration is exposing a `ULONG` constant called `MAGIC_NUMBER`, and a function entry point named `profound`. A complete type signature is specified for both the constant and the function.

The precise name of the DLL entry point for the function is provided by means of the `entry()` attribute, and it can be supplied either as a string representing the entry point, or the ordinal for it. The declared name is the one that is visible in the type library, while the `entry()` name or ordinal is the 'true' function being called.

Finally in the above code, the `usesgetlasterror` attribute indicates that the module uses the Win32 `SetLastError()` call to pass information when an error occurs. The caller can then use `GetLastError()` to retrieve this information about the error.

Object Models and Function Entry Points: A Warning

There is a danger related to using DLL entry points in conjunction with a COM object model. Imagine, for instance, that the `somemodl.dll` file had actually been a COM object server. It might seem quite reasonable to use the global functions to extract global data from the server, while at the same time using the COM API to create objects using the DLL.

Beware! There is no guarantee that the global data will be associated with the same instance of the DLL as the one being used to serve up COM objects. In general, when trying to associate global or class-wide data with an object model, it is best to use COM techniques like application or class objects (we'll be discussing these in Chapter 5). DLL globals should only be used to document non-COM functionality.

Although we will have occasion to resort to modules in this book, they are not particularly relevant to COM programming, and I will not discuss their syntax any further.

COM-specific Syntax

Having looked at some of the broader features of IDL, we'll turn our attention to address the parts of the syntax that were designed specifically to support COM.

interface: COM-style Interfaces

The interface is a kind of IDL construct we haven't looked at so far – one that doesn't have its roots in C. It was originally used in RPC IDL to package together a group of entry points into an RPC server. However, this syntax was overloaded in COM IDL to represent something fundamentally different: a group of related methods and properties that are exposed by an object – a COM interface. In this respect, it is somewhat similar to the C++ `class` statement.

A C++ class with only pure virtual members is almost identical to a COM interface. (In fact, the implementation under Visual C++ is identical to a COM interface). A class like this is sometimes even called an interface in modern C++ usage.

The `interface` statement is used to declare a COM-style interface. Let's begin with an example of an interface declaration:

```
[
    object,
    uuid(93C255B0-2AC9-11D2-A5B6-000000000001,
    pointer_default(unique)
]
interface IMyInterface : IUnknown
{
    HRESULT MyMethod([in] long, [in] long, [out, retval] long*);
    HRESULT MyGet([out] long*);
    HRESULT MySet([in] long);
};
```

object

One of the attributes decorating this interface declaration is the `object` keyword. This identifies the interface as being a COM-style, object-oriented interface. If the attribute is left out, the interface is assumed to be a procedural RPC interface. Since the subject of this book is COM IDL, all the interfaces that we discuss will have the `object` attribute.

uuid()

The `interface` keyword is also decorated with a `uuid()` attribute that associates a string containing 32 hexadecimal characters with the interface. This string represents a 128-bit integer.

As you know, COM uses 128-bit numbers as the 'real' names of various entities, instead of relying on character string identifiers as names. The `uuid()` keyword is used in IDL whenever an entity needs to have a 128-bit name associated with it. When you're dealing with an interface, the UUID is usually referred to as an IID (Interface Identifier).

Of course, the interface also has the 'name' `IMyInterface`, but ultimately this is only used to provide notational convenience for us poor hex-challenged humans!

pointer_default()

The `pointer_default()` attribute is used to set the pointer type of any unattributed pointers that are reachable from the interface declaration. We will examine this notion in greater detail in Chapter 3.

Interface Methods

The body of the interface definition consists of declarations of the three methods `MyMethod()`, `MyGet()` and `MySet()`. Each declaration completely specifies the signature of the method – that is, the order and types of the parameters to the method, and the type of the result. Each parameter may in turn be decorated with additional attributes that will be examined in subsequent chapters.

Since COM interfaces are based on a binary standard, the actual names used to declare the methods are not important, and nor are the names used for the parameters. The two things that *are* significant are:

❑ The position of the method in the declaration order – whether it is the first, second or third method

❑ The signature of the method: the order and types of parameters, and the return type

It's important to recognize that, as in C++, there is also an implicit parameter to each interface method: a pointer to the interface itself. This pointer can be used by the method implementations to gain access to the private state of the object.

Directional Attributes

Notice that the parameters have been decorated with the directional attributes in and out, which we've already seen in passing. These attributes specify the semantics of data transfer during the method invocation. An in attribute specifies a read-only parameter of the call, an out parameter specifies a write-only parameter of the call, while an in, out parameter can be both read and written.

IDL method signatures have C-style call-by-value semantics, and so all parameters with an out attribute have to be *pointers* to the type actually being returned. In addition, you should note the retval parameter, which is used to tag a parameter as the 'return value' of the method. As we'll see later on, this information is used in the creation of Automation interfaces.

Interface Definition and Status Codes

There are several non-obvious facts about HRESULTs that you need to be aware of when you're writing interfaces. For a start, values that have the severity bit set to 0 are called **success codes**. The success codes that may be returned by interface methods are part of the interface definition, and cannot be changed after the interface has been published. Conversely, HRESULT values that have the severity bit set to 1 are called **failure codes**, and these are *not* a binding part of the interface contract. Implementers are allowed to return undocumented failure codes, including newly created ones.

The restrictions on creating new facilities mean that the average user can only create new status codes within FACILITY_ITF. This pretty much guarantees that different programmers are going to use the same values to mean different things. To minimize the problems that might arise from such duplication, status codes are defined only in the context of the interface that returned the code – that is, the same value is allowed to have different meanings when being returned from different interfaces. The interface designer is responsible for defining the status codes returned by the interface.

These rules are sufficient for success codes, because those are fixed at the time the interface is published. Failure codes are a little more complicated, since an interface implementer is allowed to add failure codes over time. An interface *client*, on the other hand, must continue to respond gracefully in the presence of all failures, even the ones it doesn't know about. How can it do this in general? It turns out there are some constraints:

❑ Any COM-defined interface or function can legally return any COM-defined failure code (including ones that may be defined by COM in the future).

In order to rule out the possibility of a COM-defined interface returning a user-defined failure code, we need to ensure that a user-defined failure code never has the same value as a COM-defined failure code. This is easy to do, since all the COM-defined failure codes in FACILITY_ITF are guaranteed to have status codes in the range 0x0000 to 0x01FF.

An exception to this rule is IAccessControl.

❑ *Any* interface (COM- or user-defined) may return *any* failure code (present or future) of facilities other than FACILITY_ITF. This covers the situation where an interface call fails due to a failure of plumbing, such as an RPC transport failure or a hard disk failure.

The above rules establish what the client can expect in terms of receiving 'well-known' failure codes, and it is assumed that the client will take actions that are appropriate to the type of failure. But what about user-defined failure codes? How is a client supposed to react to an undocumented, user-defined code? A couple of rules cover this scenario:

❑ The failure code E_UNEXPECTED is legal for *any* method on *any* interface (COM-defined or otherwise). Clients are expected to provide some form of generic handling for E_UNEXPECTED.

❑ The client should handle any undocumented FACILITY_ITF failure code as if it were E_UNEXPECTED. An interface implementation that returns such a failure code must ensure that the generic client handling of E_UNEXPECTED will work in its new situation.

Interface Pointer Data Types

When you have methods that deal with interfaces, IDL only allows values of type 'pointer to interface' to be passed to them. A value of type 'interface' is not permitted because all interface methods must be invoked with a hidden first parameter that contains the pointer to the interface. De-referencing an interface pointer into a plain interface value would cause this information to be lost, rendering the methods of the interface unusable. Since this belies the basic point of having an interface, it has been disallowed, but *pointers* to any interface type are valid types in IDL.

The following, then, would be a typical example of IDL code for a method to which an interface is passed:

```
interface IShowUnknown
{
    HRESULT SetObject([in] IUnknown* pUnk);
};
```

As you know, the IUnknown interface serves as the identity of an object. In this sense, a parameter of type IUnknown* can always serve as an object reference. In addition, any other interface on the object can be obtained from the IUnknown interface. A final use of the IUnknown type is to stand in for a dynamically typed interface pointer; this scenario is explained in greater detail in Chapter 3.

In legacy COM code, you will sometimes see void* *being used instead of an* <interface>*
type. While this is still valid, it is less type-safe than using (say) IUnknown*, *and should
therefore be considered deprecated. I recommend not using it in new code.*

IDL Inheritance

The syntax of an interface declaration is reminiscent of C++ inheritance syntax. In this case, the syntax of the interface with which I started this discussion indicates that `IMyInterface` is derived from `IUnknown`.

The COM specification requires that every COM interface be derived from some other COM interface (and ultimately from `IUnknown`) – in fact, `IUnknown` is the only case of an interface that has no base interface. The declaration of `IUnknown` looks something like this (I've dropped some more advanced IDL for now):

```
interface IUnknown
{
    HRESULT QueryInterface([in] REFIID riid, [out] void** ppvObject);
    ULONG AddRef();
    ULONG Release();
};
```

Although syntactically similar to C++ inheritance, IDL interface inheritance has very limited semantics by comparison. It simply serves as shorthand to indicate that the derived interface has, as its first members, the methods of the base interface in the order they were declared. Thus, `IMyInterface` has the methods of `IUnknown` as its first three members. The full definition of `IMyInterface` therefore includes six methods, in the order `QueryInterface()`, `AddRef()`, `Release()`, `MyMethod()`, `MyGet()`, `MySet()`.

A secondary purpose of IDL inheritance is to document the evolution of an interface. Unlike C++ inheritance, IDL inheritance does not serve as the basis for polymorphism. Note also that since IDL has no notion of implementation, IDL inheritance is interface inheritance, not implementation inheritance.

Polymorphism, Aggregation and Multiple Inheritance

If IDL inheritance is simply a notational convenience, how *does* polymorphism work in COM? Recall that polymorphism is the ability of different objects to respond differently to the same message/method invocation. In COM, polymorphism is accomplished by having different classes provide different implementations of the same interface. This interface-based polymorphism does not require inheritance in order to make it work.

Another concept that crops up often in COM is its aggregation mechanism, which is frequently likened to implementation inheritance. However, whatever the merits of aggregation, there is currently very limited IDL support for the concept.

Why doesn't IDL support multiple inheritance as well as single inheritance? Let's examine the options. IDL has no notion of implementation inheritance, so the only form of multiple inheritance that's feasible in IDL is interface inheritance. However, the COM approach to multiple interfaces is to expose them individually, rather than exposing a 'joint' interface that derives multiply from all the individual interfaces.

Many experts consider multiple inheritance to be a very poor way of using existing interfaces to define new interfaces, since you are mixing together potentially unrelated interfaces to create new ones, breaking the rules of interface programming. For this reason, the lack of multiple inheritance in IDL is not a serious omission from the language.

Binary Layout of the IDL Interface

Finally, let us look at the correspondence between an IDL interface declaration and its COM binary equivalent.

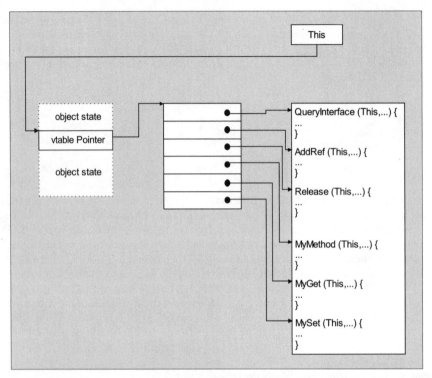

As you can see, the interface corresponds to a binary memory layout that looks almost exactly like the vtable structure that is generated for polymorphic types by some C++ compilers (notably Visual C++). Note especially that the IDL inheritance structure is lost in the translation: the binary layout consists of a flat array of pointers to functions. Each of the functions that implement the interface methods takes a pointer as its first parameter; this is the implicit or hidden interface pointer that doesn't show up in the signature. The purpose of this parameter is to allow the object method implementation (*not* the client, which cannot see this state) to get access to the object.

Notice also that this binary structure, which (apart from the object's state) is what the client actually sees, loses the name information for the functions and parameters. A method is invoked only by its position in the vtable and by setting up the stack to contain the data types that are implied by its signature; that's why it's safe to omit parameter names as I have done in a couple of the earlier examples.

dispinterface: Automation-style Interfaces

IDL has a different syntactic mechanism for defining Automation-style interfaces. As I mentioned earlier, an Automation interface is a logical interface that has an alternative, non-vtable mechanism for invoking methods. If I were to rewrite the interface we've been using in our discussions so far as its Automation-style equivalent, I would wind up with the following IDL code:

```
[
    uuid(93C255B0-2AC9-11D2-A5B6-000000000002)
]
dispinterface DMyInterface
{
properties:
    [id(3)] long lMyProp;
methods:
    [id(4)] long MyMethod([in] long l1, [in] long l2);
};
```

We'll spend the whole of Chapter 4 looking at the IDL attributes associated with Automation-style interfaces, but for now we can just focus on the essentials.

An Automation-style interface is declared with the `dispinterface` (short for dispatch interface) statement, which automatically implies that the actual implementation will be an implementation of the `IDispatch` interface. However, the syntax for this is not entirely consistent with that for the `interface` statement.

uuid()

Dispinterfaces have UUIDs just as regular interfaces do, although they are sometimes referred to as DIIDs (Dispatch Interface Identifiers). As before, the UUID is the 'real' name of the interface, but it's not used as commonly as an IID because an Automation client can typically use the one and only Automation interface exposed by an Automation object.

Properties and Methods

The most obvious difference between `dispinterface` and `interface` statements is the presence of individual sections for `properties` and `methods`. These sections both have to be present (even if one is empty), and they must appear in the order I've shown you here. Automation interfaces appear to expose a property as a data value, rather than as a pair of functions.

Despite all these rules, though, there are *two* ways to declare properties in a dispinterface. The first is to list a type and a name in the `properties` section, as you can see in the above example, which declares a property that may be read and written. If you wish to restrict a property to be read-only using this syntax, the `readonly` attribute must be used:

```
[id(3), readonly] long lMyProp;
```

However, in an omission that testifies to the ad-hoc nature of some of the IDL that descends from ODL, there is no corresponding `writeonly` attribute. Instead, there is the alternative way to declare properties, which is to use the method syntax:

```
dispinterface DMyInterface
{
properties:
methods:
    [id(3), propget] long lMyProp();
    [id(3), propput] void lMyProp([in] long l);
    [id(4)] long MyMethod([in] long l1, [in] long l2);
};
```

The propget and propput Attributes

A `propget` method returns a value of the same type as the property, while a `propput` method takes a parameter of the same type as the property. This syntax gives finer control over the declaration and is closer to the actual property implementation, making it the preferred way to declare properties. There is no compelling reason ever to declare a property in the `properties` section, unless you *really* hate typing in those extra lines.

Member Ordering

The next thing to notice is the `id()` attribute decorating each member of the interface. We will look at this attribute in greater detail later on, but for now be aware of the fact that each member (method or property) is identified not by its order in the declaration list, but by the value of the `id()` attribute. This value, called the DISPID (short for dispatch identifier), is used to identify the member during interface invocation. There is no requirement that the DISPIDs start at 1, or that they be contiguous. The guidelines for DISPID numbering are presented in Chapter 4.

Return Type

You will probably have spotted this change too: `MyMethod()` has a return type of `long`, rather than having an `out` parameter. This is in contrast to the method in the COM interface that returned an `HRESULT` status code. What's going on here? How are the methods supposed to return error status? For that matter, what if a property get (or set) fails?

The answer to all these questions is that the invocation of an Automation interface member returns error information in a separate structure. The COM error objects actually grew out of the exception raising mechanism built into Automation invocation, which is implemented by the `IDispatch::Invoke()` COM method. This method *does* return an `HRESULT`, but typically an Automation programmer sees neither the method nor its return value.

Missing Elements

As well as all these new things, you should have noticed that some elements of the COM interface declaration are missing. For a start, there's no `object` attribute − it's not necessary because there was no legacy `dispinterface` keyword in RPC. Furthermore, there is no inheritance mechanism.

Type Restrictions and Variants

My final point about Automation interfaces (for now) is that the data types to be used in an Automation property or method cannot be arbitrary, user-defined types. There is a limited set of data types that can occur in an Automation interface, consisting of those types that can be encapsulated in the `Variant` type first introduced in Visual Basic. We'll take a closer look at this set of types in Chapters 4 and 6.

IDispatch: Implementing Automation

An Automation interface must be implemented on a COM object, since it requires the presence of the COM interface `IDispatch`. When you do so, the object becomes an **Automation object**. A client of the Automation interface gets access to the interface implementation by querying for `IDispatch` on the Automation object. Once the client has a valid pointer to `IDispatch`, it can access members of the Automation interface by calling the `Invoke()` method of `IDispatch`.

A COM object can only expose one IDispatch interface – it doesn't make semantic sense to have QueryInterface() able to return two completely different implementations of the same interface. The implication is that an Automation object can only expose one interface to users of 'ordinary' Automation (such as the current generation of scripting languages), and this is an annoying limitation of the Automation mechanism.

As will be explained in Chapter 4, though, an Automation interface is extensible – the IDispatch implementation can add methods and properties at runtime. However, there is no IDL support for representing this behavior.

The IDispatch Interface

The IDispatch interface has (approximately – once again, I'm leaving some material for later) the following IDL definition:

```
[
    object,
    uuid(00020400-0000-0000-C000-000000000046)
]
interface IDispatch : IUnknown
{
    HRESULT GetTypeInfoCount([out] UINT* pctinfo);

    HRESULT GetTypeInfo([in] UINT iTInfo,
                        [in] LCID lcid,
                        [out] ITypeInfo** ppTInfo);

    HRESULT GetIDsOfNames([in] REFIID riid,
                          [in] LPOLESTR* rgszNames,
                          [in] UINT cNames,
                          [in] LCID lcid,
                          [out] DISPID* rgDispId);

    HRESULT Invoke([in] DISPID dispIdMember,
                   [in] REFIID riid,
                   [in] LCID lcid,
                   [in] WORD wFlags,
                   [in, out] DISPPARAMS* pDispParams,
                   [out] VARIANT* pVarResult,
                   [out] EXCEPINFO* pExcepInfo,
                   [out] UINT* puArgErr);
};
```

As you can see, it looks pretty much like any other COM interface. It has four methods (plus the IUnknown methods), of which the most important one is Invoke().

Invoke()

As its name suggests, the problem that Invoke() solves is the invocation of methods on the Automation interface. Invoke() also evaluates/assigns properties by calling the appropriate get/set method. It takes a large number of parameters, the most important of which are shown in the table overleaf:

Parameter	Description
dispIdMember	Contains the DISPID of the member being invoked. This can be considered to be the 'real name' of the Automation member, since the string identifier for the name can be changed (for localization purposes).
pDispParams	A structure containing an array of parameters that will be passed into the method invocation. The structure is flexible enough to describe a combination of positional and named parameters, as well as a variable number and type of parameters.
pVarResult	Contains the 'result' of the invocation – that is, the return value of the Automation method.
pExcepInfo	Contains a structure with rich error information. This is how the invocation of an Automation method or property would return error information. The client of an Automation interface is expected to check this value if DISP_E_EXCEPTION is returned by Invoke(). A client such as the Visual Basic runtime wraps this check and converts it into a Visual Basic exception.

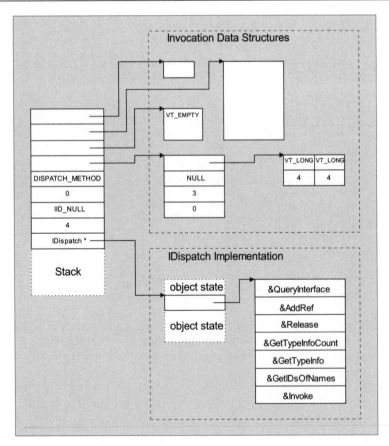

The above figure shows the stack frame and data structures involved in the invocation of the Automation method `MyMethod()` (from our earlier example). It also serves to illustrate the invocation of a method in a vtable interface, `IDispatch`. As it would be for the invocation of any vtable method, the first parameter into `Invoke()` is the `IDispatch` pointer itself. Recall that the whole purpose of this pointer is to allow the method to gain access to the state of the COM (in this case, Automation) object.

An Automation *property* is invoked in almost exactly the same way, reflecting its implementation as a pair of get and set methods.

Late Binding and the Significance of Names

What is it that makes late binding possible? How can a method name remain unresolved until runtime? Doesn't the DISPID for the method need to be known at compile time?

The answer to these questions lies with the `GetIDsOfNames()` method of `IDispatch`, which is used to discover the DISPID associated with a string that represents a method name. Optionally, it can be used to discover the IDs of named parameters to the method as well.

`GetIDsOfNames()` is called at runtime, and the resulting IDs are then used in a corresponding call to `Invoke()`. This is the technique that allows names to remain unresolved until runtime.

Since Automation interfaces allow late binding, names are significant in Automation interfaces. A name string can be used to invoke a method, and even to identify parameters. This is in contrast to vtable interfaces, where only position and type is significant.

Type Information and Early Binding

The `GetTypeInfoCount()` and `GetTypeInfo()` methods on the `IDispatch` interface provide support for various tools to query the Automation interface for type information. `GetTypeInfoCount()` returns either 0 or 1, indicating the absence or presence of type information for the Automation object. This implies that each object can only support one set of type information: that associated with `IDispatch`. Passing 0 as the first parameter to `GetTypeInfo()` retrieves this set.

In particular, a compiler can look up the DISPID corresponding to a method name, and the names and types of the parameters to that method. This allows the compiler to do strong type checking on method calls and generate optimized code. For example, it permits the compiler to eliminate the run-time call to `GetIDsOfNames()`, instead calling `Invoke()` directly with the appropriate arguments. The latter usage is sometimes called **early binding**, since names are resolved at compile time rather than runtime.

For the most part, these functions are now redundant because the majority of tools have direct access to the type information for the entire type library, and not just for this one interface.

Locales

Since name strings are significant in Automation, it would be nice to allow script programmers to create names that make sense in their native language, instead of being forced to write in English.

This is made possible in Automation by using the LCID parameter that occurs in three of the four IDispatch methods. An LCID (Locale Identifier) has a value that specifies the locale for national language support. This means that the various members of the interface can have a different name in each locale, tailored to the appropriate language. In practice, this generally involves having a physically distinct type library for each language, such that the Automation interfaces they contain will have names that have been localized to that language.

The LCID can also be used by the method implementation to perform other kinds of localization, such as output character strings, date formats, etc.

The Implicit Object

Just as in the case of a COM interface, there is always an implicit parameter into an Automation call that identifies the state of the object being accessed by the interface (recall that this state is only visible from the object implementation, not from the client). In the case of Automation, it is the implicit first parameter in the call to IDispatch::Invoke() that identifies the object state.

Dual Interfaces

You've seen that Automation interfaces have the desirable property of supporting late binding and allowing method invocations to be dynamically typed. However, there is a cost to be paid for this flexibility: the performance of an in-apartment Automation interface is up to two orders of magnitude slower than that of the equivalent vtable interface.

IDL Inheritance from IDispatch

The **dual interface** was devised as a way of gaining the benefits of dynamic typing without sacrificing the speed of vtable interfaces. Here's how it works.

A dual interface is a COM interface that derives from IDispatch instead of being derived from IUnknown. For instance, the dual interface corresponding to the Automation interface described earlier would be declared as follows; as you can see, it's very similar to using only the method section of a dispinterface:

```
[
    object,
    dual,
    uuid(93C255B0-2AC9-11D2-A5B6-000000000001)
]
interface DIMyInterface : IDispatch
{
    [id(4)] HRESULT MyMethod([in] long l1, [in] long l2, [out, retval] long* pl);
    [id(3), propget] HRESULT MyGet([out] long* pl);
    [id(3), propput] HRESULT MySet([in] long l);
};
```

This is a COM interface just like any other, but what's special about it is that the methods of IDispatch make the vtable methods available as an Automation interface. This means that scripting clients can use it *as if it were an Automation interface* – they would be completely unaware of the fact that there are valid vtable entries below the IDispatch entry. A vtable-aware client, on the other hand, could use the vtable side of the interface.

A client such as Visual Basic can use this interface *either* from its Automation *or* from its vtable side. The use of the vtable side of a dual interface by Visual Basic is sometimes called **very early binding** or **vtable binding**.

Salient Features

Let us examine some of the features of this interface. A few things are noteworthy:

❑ The dual attribute is used to decorate the interface and mark it as being a dual interface. Doing so also subsumes the oleautomation attribute discussed below in the section on *Automation-compatible Interfaces*.

❑ Like all COM interfaces, it also has the object attribute.

❑ The methods of the dual interface must all return HRESULT, like the methods on every other COM interface. However, the methods must *also* be associated with a DISPID so that they can be called appropriately from IDispatch.

❑ The property is specified by a pair of read and write methods that are decorated with the attributes propget and propput respectively, just as you saw being used for dispinterfaces.

❑ The methods of a dual interface *must* return HRESULTs, so the retval attribute is used to decorate the last parameter of the method. The return value of the Automation interface method corresponds to the out, retval final parameter of the equivalent method in the dual interface.

The retval keyword is used to mark the one and only parameter that is to be considered the 'return value' of the method. This parameter also has to be the last parameter in the list. An Automation interface method with a void return value is replaced in a dual interface by an HRESULT-returning method with no addition to the parameter list.

Dual vs. Pure Vtable Interfaces

The primary advantage that a dual interface has over a plain vtable interface is that the former can be called in a late-bound fashion. The primary disadvantage is that a dual interface absolutely has to be Automation-compatible, and we'll discuss the limitations that this brings in a moment.

Dual vs. Pure Dispatch Interfaces

Dual interfaces are the preferred way of building Automation-capable interfaces, and there are a couple of significant advantages to implementing dual interfaces instead of implementing an Automation interface. First, a client can query for a dual interface by its IID instead of always having to query for IDispatch. This makes it possible for an Automation object to expose more than one Automation interface. At present, however, most Automation clients cannot take advantage of this added flexibility.

Second, it is complicated to implement Invoke() for an Automation interface, but the direct correspondence between a dual interface and the Automation interface it supports makes it possible to create a boilerplate implementation of the IDispatch methods in a dual interface. This implementation checks the incoming parameters against the known type signature for the method, and if everything is kosher, delegates the call to the vtable method implementation.

This delegation, which involves setting up the correct stack frame before calling the function entry point, can be done mechanically as long as a description of the method signature is available. Such a description is present in the type library, which is what the boilerplate implementation uses. The standard boilerplate implementation is called the **Dispatch API**, and once the call is complete it takes the return values and packages them up for consumption by the Automation client. Thus, it is only necessary to implement the vtable side of a dual interface – you get the Automation side for free.

The biggest potential disadvantage of implementing dual interfaces is that they are immutable, while pure Automation interfaces can be modified in most circumstances. I shall discuss this in greater detail in Chapter 4.

Automation-compatible Interfaces

A regular COM interface is considered **Automation-compatible** if all the parameters of all its methods belong to the restricted set of Automation types that I referred to earlier. By definition, all dual interfaces are Automation-compatible.

The oleautomation Attribute

An Automation-compatible interface should be decorated with the `oleautomation` attribute, which is applicable only to `interface` statements. The `dual` keyword implies the `oleautomation` keyword, so it is not necessary to apply `oleautomation` to a dual interface explicitly. Similarly, all Automation-only interfaces (dispinterfaces) are assumed to imply `oleautomation`.

The question must then be asked, "Why would you ever bother marking ordinary COM interfaces as being Automation-compatible? You can't use them directly from an Automation client (as you can a dual interface), so what's the point?"

The basic reason is that interfaces decorated with the `oleautomation` attribute do not require a proxy-stub DLL in order to be marshaled. As long as their corresponding type libraries are registered with the system, they can be marshaled using the **type library marshaler**. As you will discover in the next chapter, this pays off in a smaller working set at runtime, and potentially higher performance.

coclass: COM Class Descriptions

You've now seen that COM IDL has a great deal of support for declaring interfaces. When you consider that the acronym stands for Interface Definition Language, and that COM is an interface-centric object system, this is hardly likely to have come as a surprise. Over time, however, the need for metadata for other COM constructs has become apparent, if only for use by the various tools that a modern programming environment seems to require.

Chief among these constructs is the COM class, which is declared by means of the `coclass` statement. This code, for example, declares a creatable COM class with the human-readable alias `WebBrowser_V1`:

```
[
    uuid(EAB22AC3-30C1-11CF-A7EB-0000C05BAE0B),
    control
]
coclass WebBrowser_V1
{
                        interface        IWebBrowser2;
    [default]           interface        IWebBrowser;
    [source]            dispinterface DWebBrowserEvents2;
    [default, source]   dispinterface DWebBrowserEvents;
}
```

uuid

Like other COM entities, the true name of the coclass is supplied by the `uuid()` attribute that decorates the statement. This time, the UUID is called a CLSID (class identifier).

control

The `control` attribute is used to mark a COM class as being a full (OCX style) ActiveX control. This is done for the benefit of containers that distinguish controls (objects with user interfaces) from non-visual objects.

Class Members

The declaration of this coclass indicates that it exposes the two interfaces `IWebBrowser` and `IWebBrowser2`. Of these, `IWebBrowser` is marked as the default interface, and we will see the significance of this declaration in Chapters 4 and 6.

The declaration also indicates two outgoing dispatch interfaces (`DWebBrowserEvents` and `DWebBrowserEvents2`), of which the first is the default. These are event interfaces of the coclass, exposed via the connectable object protocol.

Missing Members

Clearly, there are a number of interfaces that have not been declared here – specifically, all the interfaces that a COM object must export in order to be an ActiveX control. Historically, the `coclass` declaration has been used largely to declare ActiveX controls and other Automation objects, and since Automation ignores the non-`IDispatch` interfaces on a COM object, these interfaces have traditionally been left out.

Prior to Visual C++ 6, there were problems importing a type library that had well-known, Microsoft-defined interfaces listed in a `coclass` declaration. In my new IDL code, I tend to list *all* the interfaces that are exported by a coclass. Not everyone considers this to be good form, but I prefer to err on the side of a more complete specification.

Missing Types and Features

IDL seems to have many of the C/C++ data structuring and typing features, but what's missing?

Here's my wish list of syntactic features that IDL should have:

❑ It would be nice if C++-style scoping was available in IDL, thus avoiding pollution of the global namespace. In the same vein, some form of modern namespace mechanism is desirable.

❑ C++-style reference types. IDL has pointer types that can be decorated to behave quite like references, but explicit dereferencing is still required.

❑ C++-style templates would be handy for pattern-centric programming styles.

❑ C++-style `const`, `mutable` and `volatile` modifiers or similar attributes would be helpful for optimizing Wizard-generated code.

Summary

In this chapter, I've tried to cover the basics of IDL, beginning with a very rapid introduction to those features of COM that you need to know in order to begin to understand interface-based programming. Subsequently, we looked at the MIDL compiler, its basic functions, and the files that are outputs of the compilation process.

The next section went into the basic structure of an IDL file including:

❑ The two basic pieces that came out of the old IDL and ODL languages

❑ The interaction of MIDL with the C preprocessor

❑ The different ways of re-using IDL from other files

❑ A brief description of the basic IDL entities

❑ The fundamentals of IDL: syntax, base types, user-defined types and `typedef`s, functions and constants

After that, I told you about COM-specific IDL syntax, including the syntax and semantics of the different interface types. For COM interfaces, you saw:

❑ The basic interface attributes: `object`, `uuid()` and `pointer_default()`

❑ The basics of declaring interface methods

❑ The directional attributes: `in` and `out`

❑ Rules regarding the valid range of values for `HRESULT` status codes

❑ The declaration and use of interface variables in IDL

❑ How inheritance works in IDL (and especially what it *cannot* specify)

❑ The correspondence between the interface definition and the vtable layout

Then you saw the very basics of Automation interfaces, including:

❑ The syntactic differences between declaring COM and Automation interfaces

❑ The implementation of Automation using `IDispatch`

❑ The binary layout of an Automation call

❑ The benefits of Automation – that is, late binding

❑ A quick introduction to locales

Finally, we took a quick look at the concepts of dual interfaces and coclasses.

Design Implications

At the end of each chapter, I want to provide you with a list of the implications that the things we've discussed have for your COM application designs. Here are the thoughts that you should be taking away from this chapter.

Class Design

- ❑ Keep event sets (outgoing interfaces) in mind when you are designing your class
- ❑ If you will be working with Microsoft clients, you will need to support the connectable object protocol
- ❑ For custom clients, you can choose to implement other event registration protocols

Interface Design

You almost certainly want to implement some systematic error reporting mechanism in production object systems.

- ❑ If you're working with Microsoft clients, particularly Visual Basic, it makes a lot of sense to support the COM error protocol.
- ❑ If you're working with custom clients, you can choose a custom error protocol. Bear in mind, though, that the COM error protocol will require one fewer network round trip because the DCOM protocol already has a body extension that supports it.

Always use the UUID algorithm to generate UUIDs. The easiest way to use the algorithm is by employing one of the two programs Uuidgen or Guidgen. Don't make up your own UUIDs from scratch, because that defeats the purpose of having them in the first place! If you need a systematic way to name all your related COM entities then generate a large block of UUIDs and use ranges from within that block.

When do you decide that an interface has been published and cannot be changed? Use one of two approaches:

- ❑ If you have complete control over all clients and implementations, use a cost metric. When it costs more than $X to fix existing clients, you should deem the interface published. You decide what $X is, and how to measure it.
- ❑ If you do not have such control, and you no longer know who has implemented the interface or what clients might be using it, you should deem it published.

Try to re-use existing HRESULT codes to the greatest possible extent. Remember that success codes are part of the interface definition: you cannot change them after the interface has been published. If you have to define your own result codes, remember to use FACILITY_ITF and failure codes in the range 0x0200 to 0xFFFF.

You can always have complete control over status codes by having a separate output parameter for error status, rather than using HRESULT codes. As you'll see in Chapter 6, there is at least one good reason for avoiding HRESULTs: they are not accessible from many languages. Similarly, you can have a user-defined error type as an output parameter instead of a custom exception protocol. This technique will not work with Automation-compliant interfaces.

Use IUnknown* instead of void* to represent interface pointers or object references. This adds an extra degree of type safety to the interface without having any real downside.

Miscellaneous

Don't use DLL entry points to gain access to the global state of a COM object server.

What's Next

The next two chapters examine further details of IDL syntax. Chapter 3 examines the details of marshaling method invocations and examines the IDL that is required to describe this. Chapter 4 examines Automation-related IDL, as well as the IDL that is used for tool support.

3

Remote Method Calls

In Chapter 2, I covered the fundamentals of IDL, the file structure and syntax, and the basics of how COM objects, interfaces, errors and events are specified in IDL. This chapter introduces some more advanced IDL syntax: that related to the mechanics of **remote method calls** (**RMC**), the COM feature that is responsible for location transparency.

The chapter is organized into two major segments. The first of these outlines the general problems that have to be solved by *any* mechanism for remote method calls. The approach taken by COM to solve these problems is also outlined, including summaries of standard, custom and handler marshaling. The second segment goes into the details of RMC and parameter marshaling, and explains the various IDL attributes that have been defined to provide fine-grained control over marshaling semantics. In addition to these topics, this chapter contains shorter sections on heap memory allocation and ownership, an important RMC topic. Finally, there is a short discussion of interpretive, inline and type library marshaling.

The Problem

So far, we have looked at the correspondence between IDL interfaces and COM interfaces, but in the process we glossed over an important issue. As you know, the code in COM clients remains unchanged regardless of whether the server is executing in process, out-of-process, or even on a different machine altogether.

Invoking an interface method in the in-process (in-apartment) case can be assumed to follow normal procedure call semantics. The caller and callee share the same address space, use a single stack on which arguments are passed, and execute on a single thread. In the out-of-process case, there is a lot more going on than meets the eye. The caller and callee (potentially) live in different address spaces, execute on different threads, and use different stacks.

Local Method Calls

The difficulty can be most easily demonstrated by examining the client's address space before and after a method invocation when the caller and object both execute on the same stack. Consider a method called `Bar()`, with the following IDL signature:

```
typedef struct tagB
{
    long        m_l;
    struct tagB* m_pB;
} B;

typedef struct tagA
{
    long        m_l;
    B*          m_pB1;
    B*          m_pB2;
} A;

interface IMyInterface
{
    HRESULT Bar(long, long**, A**);
};
```

The figure below shows the stack and address space before this method is called:

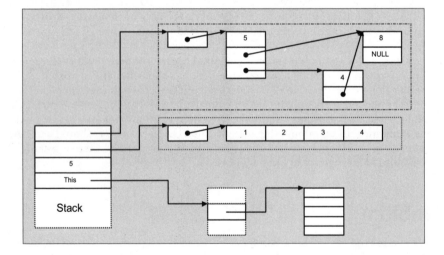

The stack contains the following three arguments:

- ❏ The value 5
- ❏ A pointer to a pointer to an array that currently has 4 elements with values 1, 2, 3, 4
- ❏ A pointer to a pointer to a linked data structure with complex internal linkage

There is also the hidden 'first' argument that is a pointer to the interface itself. The next figure shows the stack and address space after the call has been completed:

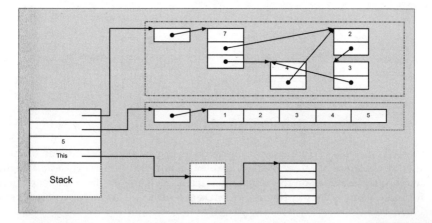

Notice the following:

- ❑ As expected, the first parameter is unchanged (it is being passed by value, so there is no point in modifying it).
- ❑ The second parameter has been changed by the method: the array has been extended with an additional element whose value is 5.
- ❑ The third parameter has also been changed. An additional node has been added to the linked structure, and some of the existing links and values have changed. Note the presence of a cycle in the linked structure.

This is easy enough to grasp in the case of a single address space, but how do things change when the client and server are in different address spaces? There lies the rub: things *cannot* change. The client *must* see the same state after the method invocation, regardless of whether the call is being made on its stack, or in a different process altogether.

Remote Method Calls

This is where remote method calls come in. The purpose of the RMC mechanism is to forward a method invocation to a remote object in such a way that the semantics appear indistinguishable from those of a local invocation.

In order to make the process transparent to the client, the first requirement is the presence of a **proxy object** in the client's address space. To the client, this object looks indistinguishable from the actual server object – it exposes identical interfaces. The proxy object can communicate with **stub code** in the server's address space. The stub code has access to the 'real' object implementation in the server, and can therefore get hold of any required information and communicate it to the proxy. The proxy then makes the appropriate modifications in the client's address space before returning to the original caller. This is illustrated below:

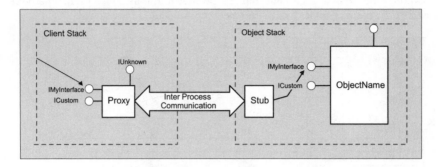

The proxy interface in the client's address space must be an in-process representation of the actual interface. In other words, there has to be a proxy vtable that contains (the addresses of) methods with the same signatures as the methods on the actual interface. Depending on the implementation of the proxy object, it can be a simple **forwarding** or '**by reference' proxy**, or it can incorporate various degrees of 'intelligence'.

Forwarding or Marshal-by-Reference Proxies

The most straightforward kind of proxy object is the one that simply forwards every method invocation on to the real object. The real object calls the method and passes the results of the invocation back to the proxy, which modifies the client address space and returns to the caller. A marshal-by-reference proxy must solve the following problems:

❑   The mechanism requires that the stack frame for the invocation be replicated exactly from the client thread to the server thread. As we saw in the example above, this process is not straightforward – the linked data structure needs to be copied to the remote address space recursively (any pointer being meaningless outside the context of its original address space). Once the entire stack frame has been replicated in this fashion, the actual interface method must be invoked in the remote address space. When the invocation is complete, the output arguments and return value need to be sent back to the address space that originated the invocation.

❑   There are situations where the call semantics require memory to be allocated by the callee and released by the caller (or vice versa). In our example, the new node that is introduced into the linked structure must be allocated on the server, and released in the client. In order to prevent a memory leak in this kind of situation, heap operations in the client and server address spaces have to be coordinated by the proxy mechanism.

We'll deal with the last of these problems first. The next two diagrams illustrate how in-process heap allocation translates to a cross-process heap coordination mechanism involving the proxy and the stub. The first of these illustrates a situation in which the caller allocates memory that the callee must release. Since both caller and callee are in the same address space, this is simple: the two have only to agree upon which heap API to use.

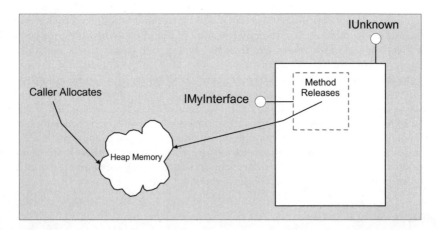

The next figure shows how this works in the cross-process case. The caller and callee must continue to work as before (after all, that's the whole point of a transparent RMC mechanism), and so the *proxy and stub* need to provide the extra functionality that makes transparency possible. The stub needs to allocate the memory in the callee's address space prior to invoking the method, while the proxy must release the memory in the caller's address space after the RMC is complete. A similar procedure is followed if the callee allocates memory that the caller must free.

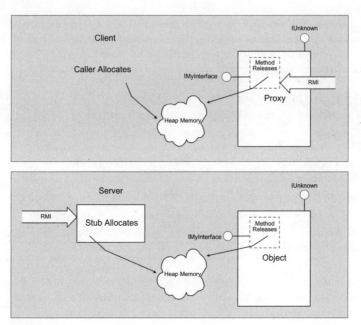

Smart Proxies

Marshaling by reference (forwarding) is a completely general mechanism for proxying method calls. It can be applied to any method invocation on any kind of server. However, it has no 'intelligence' of any kind, so it cannot be easily optimized for special circumstances.

To see what I mean, consider a situation where the state of the callee object is constant, so the results of the method call depend only on the parameters passed into the method. An efficient way to proxy such an object would be to replicate it – to copy the state of the object when the proxy and stub are being set up. A local version of the object can then be created with exactly the same state, and all method invocations on the proxy can call the *local* version of the object, instead of having to communicate with the 'real' one. This kind of marshaling is sometimes called **marshal-by-value**.

Clearly, marshaling by value is not applicable in the general RMC case, since it depends on the semantics of the object implementation. However, in the cases where it *is* appropriate, it can result in enormous performance improvements. It may be, for instance, that you're faced with a hybrid situation, where some method invocations can be performed locally and others need to communicate with the remote object. All situations of this kind can be addressed by using smart proxies, which can use various custom protocols to communicate between client and server.

Apartments

In COM, the situation regarding marshaling is made even more complex by its roots in Win16, and certain limitations of the Windows UI architecture. Because the original mechanism used to implement cross-process COM calls had thread affinity (it used the Windows message pump), legacy COM objects are not thread-safe. More modern COM objects used by elements of the user interface are afflicted by the same problem, since the UI elements that call them will themselves have thread affinity.

In order to provide a measure of thread safety for such objects, the COM runtime had to introduce the notion of **apartments**. In COM programming, it is not sufficient to be concerned about inter-process communication – we also need to be concerned about *intra*-process communication. Here are the rules that govern apartments, at least until the introduction of Windows 2000:

❑ Each COM process is made up of a number of apartments
❑ Each COM thread and object can belong to exactly one apartment
❑ There are two kinds of threads. An STA thread uses window messages to enforce synchronized access to objects in an apartment. An MTA thread provides no synchronization.
❑ There are two kinds of apartments: a **single-threaded apartment** (**STA**) can contain only one STA thread, while a **multithreaded apartment** (**MTA**) can have many MTA threads.
❑ A COM process can have one or more STAs, or an MTA and zero or more STAs

*It is intended that Windows 2000 will introduce a new apartment type called **Neutral**. An object in a neutral apartment is always invoked on the thread of the caller.*

The figure below shows the apartment structure of a COM process with three STAs and an MTA. The box-spoon notation is used for objects, and a stack depicts a thread in the apartment. The dotted rectangles enclose proxy-stub pairs.

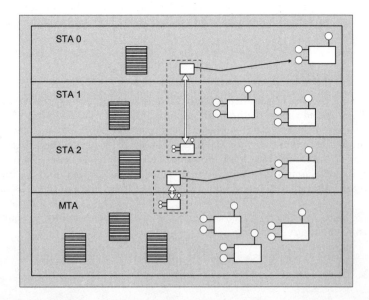

A COM STA is a scheduling context (think of it as a mini-process) inside a process. All method invocations on objects in an STA are transparently serialized by COM. As illustrated in the figure, however, any method invocation that crosses an apartment boundary has to be proxied so that this serialization can occur. The intent of this particular proxy is to facilitate synchronization (rather than to transfer data between address spaces), but the calling method and the called method execute on different threads, and therefore use different stacks. This makes it possible to re-use the RMC architecture to proxy inter-apartment method invocations within a single address space.

The COM RMC architecture is thus used whenever a method invocation crosses an *apartment* boundary, not just a process boundary (although the underlying plumbing used in this case is an optimized "local RPC" protocol). This is generally a source of surprise to experienced programmers doing their first COM programming.

The COM RMC Architecture

So far, we've discussed the general problems that have to be solved by an RMC mechanism. In this section, I'm going to give you an overview of how the COM RMC architecture goes about doing just that.

It turns out that COM supports both types of proxies that I mentioned in the previous section, but by far the more common is the marshal-by-reference type. In COM, proxies like these use the **standard marshaling** architecture.

The other kind – the smart proxies – can be implemented by using **custom** or **handler marshaling**. However, the mechanism for implementing such proxies is not easily portable, so it is best to approach them with caution.

Standard Marshaling

Marshaling refers to the process of serializing *all* the data (input arguments and – where necessary – what they point at) associated with a method call into a flat data buffer. This data buffer is then transferred to the apartment in which the server method executes. At this point, the flat data buffer needs to be transformed back into the equivalent stack frame; predictably, the process of recreating the stack frame is called **unmarshaling**. After the server stack frame has been created, the server method is invoked, the output arguments and return values are marshaled, and the buffer is transferred back to the client apartment and unmarshaled onto the original client stack.

The correspondence between the marshaled and unmarshaled representations for our sample method invocation is shown in the figure below:

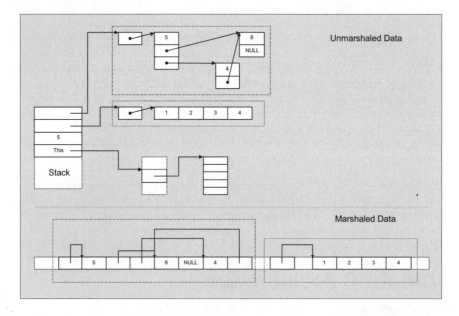

This illustrates how the arbitrarily linked memory structures that are required for the call are transformed into a series of bytes that exactly represent this data. You can see why the process is also called **serialization**. Note that this picture only shows a *sample* serialization schema; it does not represent the actual schema used by COM.

Network Data Representation

What is the format of the flat data buffer? Do we just perform a binary dump of the contents of the stack and the memory that it points at? We could do so, but this would be dependent on the following:

❑ *Language*: interpretation of data types is different in different programming languages – a C++ int, for example, is not the same as a Visual Basic Integer

❑ *Platform*: a C++ int under Win32 is a different size from a C++ int under Win16

❑ *Architecture*: Intel processors have different endian-ness and alignment constraints from RISC processors

Instead, a well-specified intermediate data format called **network data representation** (NDR) is used. NDR is a format specified by DCE RPC (upon which COM RPC is based) that permits complete specification of the range of values, endian-ness, and format (for floating point numbers) of a wide variety of standard scalar types.

Indeed, these scalar types are the base types in IDL. As long as the marshaling and unmarshaling code understand NDR, a remote method call can be completely language, platform, and architecture independent.

NDR is also quite an *efficient* data representation, because it allows different binary formats to be used that can be native to specific architectures. It uses a 'reader makes right' policy, where the representation is actually identical to the binary format of the machine sending the data. It is up to the receiving machine to change this to its own native representation. In the (very common) scenario where the sending and the receiving machine have the same (Wintel) architecture, no conversion needs to be performed.

Proxies and Stubs

One of the interesting features of the standard COM RMC infrastructure is that it is based on remoting individual interfaces, rather than objects as a whole. This is an important tenet of interface programming. Each proxy knows how to marshal and unmarshal the individual methods of a *single interface*. The big benefit of doing things in this fashion is that the proxy code can be re-used whenever *any* class exports the interface. The following figure illustrates roughly how this works by means of a representative proxy object:

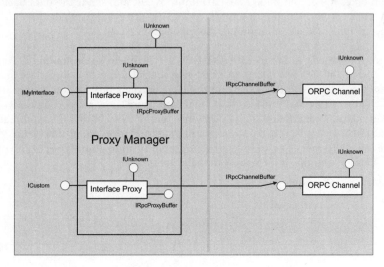

61

As you can see, the interface is exported by a separate, interface-specific proxy that's aggregated within an outer proxy manager object. The interface-specific proxy object belongs to the class that is implemented by the (usually MIDL-generated) proxy-stub DLL.

The proxy-stub DLL is loaded into the client's address space *and* the server's address space. On the client side, it is used to create the client proxy that I keep mentioning. On the server side, it creates the stub that (as we saw earlier) is used by the RMC mechanism to call the actual interface method on the real object. The following figure illustrates the structure of the server side stub code:

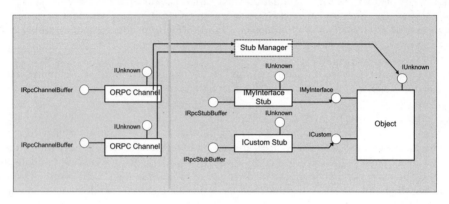

You can't have failed to notice the presence of the "ORPC Channel" in both pictures. This object is physically present in the client apartment, but it's the piece that actually communicates with the stub manager and therefore the interface stubs.

The interface-specific proxy implements the code that marshals the client stack into NDR, transfers the data buffer to the server, and (using the stub manager) eventually causes the interface stub to be invoked via the IRPCStubBuffer interface. The stub receives the data buffer, converts from NDR, unmarshals the buffer onto its stack, and then calls the actual interface method. When the method returns, the stub takes the output data, marshals it into NDR, and sends the data back via the ORPC Channel to the client proxy. Finally, the interface-specific proxy unmarshals this NDR in the transfer buffer back onto the client stack, completing the invocation.

A special case of this process is the so-called **system** or **type library marshaling**. For an interface that is Automation compliant, it is not necessary to have a specialized proxy-stub class that understands the signatures of the methods. It turns out that the IDL interface description, stored in the type library, is sufficient to allow the interface to be marshaled and unmarshaled by the **type library** (also **universal** or **Automation**) **marshaler**. This is a by-product of the fact that the Automation data types are all self-descriptive – that is, they contain complete information about their own type and size. The only things the marshaler needs to know are the order and Automation types of the parameters to a method, and it can look up this information in the type library.

User Defined Types

So far, so good: I've explained how scalar parameters can be marshaled across processes, and I've also described how pointer parameters are marshaled by copying the actual data that is being pointed at, rather than just the meaningless binary value of the pointer.

How do user-defined types like enumerations, structures and (discriminated) unions fit into this picture? Well, enumerations are simple enough: they can be translated to some integer type. Structures and unions are also easy, provided that they are composed only from base NDR types. The marshaling code just needs to be able to deconstruct the structure or (discriminated) union into its component types, and to create an NDR representation of the structured type from the NDR representations of the base types. The union *must* be discriminated; if it isn't, the marshaling code cannot know how to perform the translation.

An added complexity, though, is that structures and unions can contain embedded pointers. In such cases, the marshaling/unmarshaling code must recursively copy/reconstruct the actual data being pointed to by the embedded pointers.

All of this, of course, is contingent on the marshaling/unmarshaling code 'understanding' the specifications of the various user-defined types, and we'll be dealing with that topic later in the chapter.

Marshaling Interfaces

I've described to you how the proxy-stub mechanism works, and how method parameters of simple and user-defined types get marshaled and unmarshaled. However, I haven't yet talked about how to approach marshaling parameters that are themselves COM objects.

What does it mean to marshal an object? Well, since we're talking about COM, we actually marshal *interfaces*, rather than objects as a whole. Let's try that again.

What does it mean to marshal an interface? Clearly, the intent of marshaling an interface is to make it available for use from the 'other side' of the RMC invocation. How does RMC use an interface? That's an easy one: it invokes the methods on the interface. What is the mechanism for invoking methods on a remote interface? The proxy-stub mechanism, of course! The process of marshaling an interface, then, involves creating a proxy-stub pair that can be used to perform RMC on that interface.

The next question must be to ask where the proxy is created – in other words, which thread is going to call the interface? Logically, this must be the recipient of the interface: the unmarshaling code. Conversely, the stub is created by the originating, or marshaling, code. In a situation where an interface is an *input* parameter into a method, the stub is created in the client apartment and the proxy is created in the server apartment. On the other hand, when an interface is an *output* parameter of a method, the stub is created in the server apartment and the proxy is created in the client apartment. Thus, a proxy-stub pair is created by the marshaling code whenever an interface is passed as a method parameter. This is illustrated in the figure overleaf:

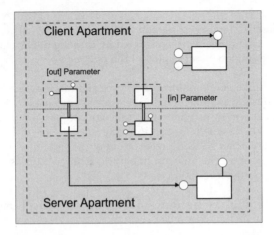

You might be wondering about the NDR corresponding to a marshaled interface. Since it isn't object-oriented, DCE RPC NDR does not have any support for marshaling interfaces. However, COM RPC extends the DCE RPC NDR with a new type (an IPID) to represent a marshaled interface pointer. This is the only Microsoft extension to DCE RPC NDR.

Incidentally, calls to COM API functions such as `CoCreateInstance()` that return new interface pointers work very similarly to method invocations with interfaces as output parameters. A stub is created in the server apartment, and a proxy is created in the client apartment. The similarity is due to the fact that these functions are actually implemented by calls to appropriate COM interface methods.

Weak References

There is a known issue with **weak references** (ones whose reference counts have not been incremented) and interface marshaling. Typically, weak references are used to prevent **reference cycles** – chains of references that loop back on themselves, such as when two interfaces maintain references to each other.

Reference cycles are explained in greater detail in Chapter 5.

Generally speaking, weak references are not dangerous in the in-apartment case because they are only maintained on an interface whose lifetime is *guaranteed* to be longer than the lifetime of the interface holding the link. Thus, IB holds a weak reference to IA only when the semantics of the situation guarantee that IA has a longer lifetime than IB.

As soon as marshaling enters the picture, however, there is a new consideration: the interface proxy-stub pair. In our example, if IA and IB are in different apartments, and IB holds a weak reference to IA, there is no guarantee that the *stub* for IA will have a lifetime that is longer than the lifetime of IB, even if IA itself is long-lived. As soon as the last out-of-apartment strong reference to IA is released, the stub disappears, even if IA itself is still alive. This means that an out-of-apartment weak reference is not guaranteed to work, and hence should not be used at all.

> In particular, the COM aggregation mechanism uses a weak reference to the outer object, and therefore won't work across apartment boundaries.

This problem does have a solution – there *is* a COM mechanism that can be used for controlling the lifetime of a stub for an object with weak references. Our savior is the `IExternalConnection` interface and its protocol, of which details are provided in Chapter 5. However, it should only be used as a last resort: do not get into the habit of holding weak references on objects unless you absolutely need to do so.

Tear-Off Interfaces

Another issue that comes up as a consequence of the marshaling process has to do with **tear-off interfaces**. These are interfaces whose vtables are only created when they're actually queried for (normally, an object will create the vtables of its interfaces when it is constructed). The advantage of a tear-off is that you have delayed initialization, which is good if the interface is rarely used and uses a resource that is expensive (in time or memory) to create.

> *Chapter 5 examines tear-off interfaces in greater detail.*

For the in-apartment case, tear-offs can also be used to *release* resources early, when the *interface* is released rather than when the *object* is released. This works because tear-off interfaces implement 'per interface' reference counts. However, this stops working as soon as a proxy-stub pair enters the picture. A proxy holds extra references to each interface to avoid network round trips caused by `AddRef()` and `Release()`. This means, however, that the semantics of per-interface reference counting don't work as you might expect. In this situation, the entire proxy has to disappear before the stub releases the interface, finally causing the tear-off to be released.

Memory Allocation

As soon as we start considering pointer (or array) parameters, memory allocation rears its ugly head. For the semantics of heap-allocated memory to make sense in a world of seamless remoting, the calling code and the method code must follow some conventions or protocol regarding ownership of memory – that is, where in the code heap memory is to be allocated and freed. Simply stated, these are the rules:

- ❑ Memory for `in`-only parameters is always allocated and freed by the caller
- ❑ Memory for `out`-only parameters is always allocated by the method, and always freed by the caller
- ❑ Memory for `in`, `out` parameters can be allocated at either end, and freed at either end

The protocol is thus completely specified by the signature of a method. This is necessary because the 'other end' of a memory allocation operation must be dealt with by automatically generated RMC marshaling code. Such code *cannot* contain information on the semantics of the interface; it can only depend on the signatures of the methods.

We will examine the details of the memory allocation rules after looking at the IDL syntax for arrays and pointers later in the chapter.

Custom and Handler Marshaling

The COM specification also explicitly allows for **smart proxies** that are understood by the marshaling infrastructure. In order to override the use of a standard marshaler, an object must implement either or both of the interfaces IMarshal and IStdMarshalInfo.

In each of these cases, there are conceptually two programmer-supplied COM classes: the object class itself, and a handler class. The handler class serves the same function as the client proxy manager did in standard marshaling – it becomes the in-process proxy for the object. Sometimes, you will find both classes implemented on the same COM class, which makes some sense for intra-process, inter-apartment marshaling, but would be strange for inter-process marshaling.

'Simple' custom marshaling is used if an object implements only IMarshal. When the remoting infrastructure on the server detects that the object implements IMarshal, it executes the following sequence of steps instead of setting up standard marshaling:

- ❑ It queries for CLSID of the handler class.
- ❑ It asks the server object to serialize an initialization state for a client-side proxy into a stream (via an IStream interface), after querying for the maximum size of that stream.
- ❑ The stream is returned to the client-side infrastructure, along with the handler CLSID.
- ❑ The CLSID of the handler class is used to create the client proxy, instead of using the standard marshaling proxy manager.
- ❑ An object of the handler class is created, and its IMarshal interface (which it must also implement) is used to load the server-created stream information. This initializes the handler.

From this point on, the relationship between the handler and the object looks like this:

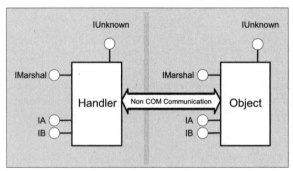

The handler must implement all of the interfaces that are implemented by the object. These interfaces are expected to use the state of the handler to mimic the behavior of the object. If necessary, the handler can communicate back to the object, but there's no support for this in the COM infrastructure, so you're completely on your own.

This mechanism can be used to implement a number of alternatives to marshaling by reference, of which marshaling by value is only one. Other possibilities are using shared memory for intra-process method invocation, and even the free-threaded marshaler provided by the COM runtime. However, there are some obvious difficulties with it:

- ❑ It is not possible to override remoting for some interfaces while retaining the use of marshaling by reference for others. It is an all-or-nothing proposition.
- ❑ The use of the `IStream` interface for persistence is inherently architecture specific. This is not a portable mechanism.
- ❑ Being forced to write custom code to communicate back to the object is very painful. One of the whole points of COM remoting was to save the programmer the drudgery of writing code that does this sort of plumbing work.

For all of these reasons, it is best to avoid custom marshaling if at all possible, but there is (or will be) an alternative that provides a much more flexible architecture. Although **handler marshaling** has been in the specification for a while, implementation is not expected until Windows 2000, but here is a brief description of how it is supposed to work.

The objective of handler marshaling is to make it possible to use custom marshaling for only selected interfaces, while using standard marshaling for all the rest. The `IStdMarshalInfo` interface is used to implement handler marshaling; it can be used in conjunction with `IMarshal` to pass some client state from the server to the handler, or it can be used in a stateless manner without `IMarshal`. This is achieved by having the handler class aggregate the standard marshaling proxy manager. Any interface that is not directly implemented by the handler class is delegated to the standard marshaler. This is illustrated in the following figure:

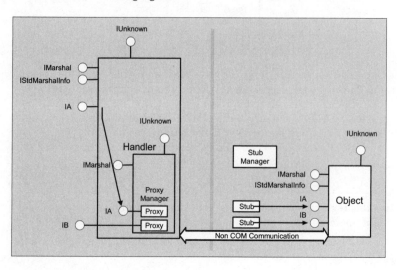

I will not examine custom marshaling or handler marshaling any further in this book.

The Proxy-Stub DLL

Before getting into the IDL that is required for marshaling, let me quickly describe the structure of a standard, MIDL-generated proxy-stub DLL, and how it is used by the COM remoting infrastructure.

The proxy-stub DLL is generated by compiling dlldata.c, foo_p.c and foo_i.c. As we saw in Chapter 2, these three files are generated by MIDL as the result of compiling a file called foo.idl. The resulting DLL is actually a self-registering, in process COM server.

The classes registered by this DLL are ordinary COM classes. Each class implements the proxy *and* the stub for a single interface. In addition, each class also has a class object that implements IPSFactoryBuffer, the interface used to create new instances of proxies and stubs. The proxy must expose the interface it is responsible for remoting *and* IRPCProxyBuffer, while the stub must expose the IRPCStubBuffer interface. We've already seen how these interfaces are used by the standard marshaling infrastructure; the structure of each class in a proxy-stub DLL is shown in the following figure:

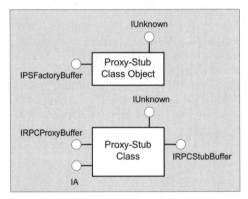

Just like any other COM classes, the proxy-stub classes must be registered in the system registry. In addition, however, there needs to be a new sub-key under the Interface key in HKEY_CLASSES_ROOT. For example, if the interface ID is {3B90C6D0-B632-11D2-A71D-000086056448} and the CLSID of the proxy-stub class for this interface is {475ABA20-B632-11D2-A71D-000086056448}, then the registry entry would be:

```
[HKCR\Interface\{3B90C6D0-B632-11D2-A71D-000086056448}\ProxyStubClsid32]@=
                            {475ABA20-B632-11D2-A71D-000086056448}
```

The nice thing is that this registration code can be built into the ordinary self-registering process for a COM server, making it operationally simple to register the proxy-stub DLL.

IDL and RMC

If you've been following along closely, you've probably noticed that I haven't mentioned any IDL specifics yet, but those of us who build COM servers using the ATL support built into Visual C++ 5.0 and above have become accustomed to defining all interfaces in terms of IDL. As I've said, there is nothing sacrosanct about either IDL or type libraries: people can build COM object servers without the benefit of IDL or the MIDL compiler. There is nothing about the COM remoting architecture that *requires* an IDL specification of the interfaces involved. However, trying to do without IDL would be incredibly tedious and error-prone.

So, exactly what information is required in the IDL to support automatic generation of interface marshaling code? Essentially, the IDL has to be able to specify the following:

❑ The direction of data transfer for each method parameter – input, output, or both

❑ The type (and therefore the size) of data that is pointed to by each pointer reachable from a parameter

❑ The type and bounds of each array reachable from a parameter, as well as the number of elements to be transmitted

❑ A specification of memory allocation policy for each pointer reachable from a parameter – that is, where allocation and de-allocation take place

❑ Information to allow the dynamic creation of proxies and stubs in the appropriate places for interface parameters

We will look at the specifics of the IDL required for all these purposes over the next few sections.

Direction of Data Transfer

The most obvious IDL attributes are the directional ones, in and out. The in attribute is used to decorate an input parameter of interface method, while the out attribute similarly signifies an output parameter. A parameter that serves for both input and output is decorated with both attributes. For example, the following Skip() method takes a single input parameter of type long:

```
[helpstring("Skip over the next N elements")]
HRESULT Skip([in] long a_vulCount);
```

Similarly, the following Count 'property' has a single output parameter called a_pl of type long. This parameter also happens to be the 'return value' of the method:

```
[propget, helpstring("Count")]
HRESULT Count([out, retval] long* a_pl);
```

Notice that the type of the parameter is actually a *pointer* to a long, and this is because IDL methods follow C-style call-by-value semantics. The only way to have an output parameter is by passing a pointer to the type, and using that pointer to assign the actual value. All output parameters must be pointers.

Of course, an input parameter may also be a pointer. For instance, if we were to have a method called SetItem() that set the value of an item of a (user-defined) type called stBid, we could pass in a parameter of type stBid:

```
HRESULT SetItem([in] stBid a_vitm)
```

Or we could pass in a pointer to a stBid:

```
HRESULT SetItem([in] stBid* a_pitm)
```

The latter usage is the C idiom (it's also slightly more efficient in the in-apartment case, since we don't need to copy the entire structure onto the stack), and the preferred way to pass input parameters that are not simple 32-bit scalar values. It would be nice if IDL were extended to have C++-style reference types and the const modifier, so that we could use the 'const reference' idiom to pass input parameters, but for now we have to make do with what we've got.

The directional attributes are also used to optimize data transfer. Only in and in, out parameters are transferred from the proxy to the stub upon method invocation, and only out and in, out parameters are transferred from the stub to the proxy on method completion. This has the potential to reduce network traffic by up to a factor of two.

The final use for directional attributes is in conjunction with **pointer attributes** (which we'll be looking at shortly) to specify how and where memory should be allocated.

Marshaling Data

Next, we need to examine the IDL syntax that governs the marshaling of scalar and user-defined data types.

Base Types

Nothing special needs to be done to specify the marshaling of scalar data types such as long or double; the only point to be aware of is that the IDL specification of a type such as long is platform and architecture *invariant*. The base types in IDL are defined in terms of the range of values that they can hold, rather than being tied to the local C/C++ compiler's definition of the base types. This is done to make the IDL specification language, platform and architecture independent, and makes the mapping to NDR straightforward. Thus, an IDL base type could be mapped to different compiler. types, depending on the platform and compiler.

> *One peculiar exception to this rule is the* int *type, which has a well-defined NDR representation, but not a well-defined C/C++ translation. For legacy reasons, it is always translated to a C/C++* int, *which has different value ranges on Win16 and Win32 For this reason it is best to avoid the use of* int *types in IDL.*

All this makes using IDL #define'd equivalents of the base types (like LONG instead of long) particularly handy. Since the C++ declarations of these #define'd types can expand to different base types on different compilers, it keeps the C++ source code portable and in visual harmony with the IDL. This reduces the potential for confusion when comparing the IDL interface with C++ implementations.

It's possible to change the defaults for some of the base integral types from signed to unsigned by using command line switches to the MIDL compiler (see Appendix A), but doing so is a bad idea because it renders your IDL non-portable (defeating the purpose of having an IDL specification). In fact, you might even want to go the extra mile for portability and explicitly qualify the signs of all integral types in your IDL code.

Enum Types

Essentially, enums are 16-bit integer types. By default, they are mapped to a 16-bit `unsigned short` for network transmission. enum values outside the range 0 to 32,767 can cause a run-time error to be generated by the MIDL-generated proxy-stub code, depending on the value of the `/error` flag passed to MIDL (see Appendix A).

To speed up the marshaling code on 32-bit architectures, it is desirable to cause enum values to be transmitted as 32-bit values. This can be accomplished by using the `v1_enum` attribute to decorate the enum declaration. Here's an example of this in code:

```
[
    helpstring("Exceptional Bid Prices"),
    v1_enum
]
enum auctAIBidStatus
{
    [helpstring("No Bid Available")] auctAIBSNoBid = -1
};
```

Structures

IDL structures are identical to C structures, except for a few modifications to allow 'remotability'. Specifically, structures that will be transmitted as part of an ORPC call cannot have bit fields or function pointers in them; all other C-style members are allowed. In addition, structure members may themselves have decorations specifying one or more attributes. For instance, the following `tagBid` structure has a member pointer that is decorated with a `ref` attribute:

```
struct tagBid
{
    [ref]  stBidder*  m_pbdrMember;
           LONG       m_vlPrice;
           LONG       m_vlTime;
           SHORT      m_vsNumber;
};
```

Here's another example of an individual member being given an attribute:

```
struct tagBSTRBLOB
{
                       ULONG cbSize;
    [size_is(cbSize)] BYTE* pData;
};
```

We will see what the `size_is()` and `ref` attributes actually signify shortly.

Unions

As we saw in Chapter 2, unions in IDL must be discriminated by a tag. Here, for example, is the definition of a simple union structure:

```
struct _var
{
    USHORT vt;
    USHORT Reserved1;

    [switch_type(ULONG), switch_is(vt)] union
    {
        [case(0L)] LONG lVal;
        [case(1L)] SHORT sVal;
    };
};
```

You probably recall the use of the switch_type() and switch_is() attributes from Chapter 2. In the context of remoting, it is clear why these attributes are required: it's a way of letting the marshaler know how to convert the union into the equivalent NDR buffer.

Care must be taken when using unions as in, out parameters, and the reasons for this are explained in the section called *Storage for Marshaled in, out Parameters*.

Arrays

In IDL, arrays of elements are represented using either array syntax, or the so-called **sized pointer syntax**. IDL array support can be a little confusing at first, but it's actually fairly straightforward.

Arrays vs. Pointers

It is in its usage of pointers and arrays that IDL can get confusing to the longtime C programmer, but the problem actually stems from a shortcoming that was designed into the C type system. C programmers are accustomed to thinking of pointers and arrays as being interchangeable, with a declaration like this one referring to either a pointer to a single long, or the beginning of an array of longs:

```
long* plLong;
```

Similarly, the next declaration could be a pointer to a pointer to a single long, a pointer to an array of longs, an array of pointers to longs, or an array of arrays of longs.

```
long** pplLong;
```

However, this ambiguity, which is central to many of the most excruciatingly delightful C idioms, cannot be left unresolved in IDL. An IDL description has to be specific enough to let an automatically generated proxy-stub class marshal the parameters to a method call. In the case of a pointer, its dimensionality and bounds have to be made explicit.

In IDL, an unqualified pointer is *always* a pointer to a single item, rather than the beginning of an array. Thus, the plLong declared above is a pointer to a single long. An array of longs might be declared like this:

```
long alLong[MAX_SIZE]
```

The important distinction is that the size of an array is specified so that the marshaler knows how much data to transmit at runtime.

Sized Pointers

A pointer in IDL may also be qualified with a size; a **sized pointer** is functionally equivalent to an array. Thus, the array above could be declared as the equivalent sized pointer:

```
[size_is(MAX_SIZE)] long* alLong;
```

In general, my advice is that you should use the sized pointer syntax instead of the array syntax. First, it is closer in spirit to the C/C++ notion of an array, and second, at the time of writing the MIDL compiler has several bugs (or 'features') associated with the pure array syntax.

IDL Array Types

From the perspective of marshaling code, arrays can be classified as **fixed**, **conformant**, **varying** or **open**.

Fixed Arrays

A **fixed array** is one that has its dimensions and size completely specified in IDL. In particular, this means that the size expressions in the IDL must either be constant, or able to be evaluated at IDL compile time. The generated marshaling code then has these sizes hard-wired. Here is an example of an array of longs:

```
long alLong[MAX_SIZE];
```

The #define'd expression MAX_SIZE must evaluate to a constant at compile time.

Conformant Arrays

A **conformant** array is one whose size is determined at runtime. The size of the array is specified in IDL by means of the size_is() attribute. Here is the IDL for a function that sends an array of longs into a method call:

```
HRESULT SendData([in] ULONG uSz, [in, out, size_is(uSz)] long* plB);
```

Note that the size_is() attribute takes an argument that can be a non-constant expression – in this case, the value of the first parameter. This expression is evaluated in the marshaling code at runtime, just before data transfer occurs.

The size_is() parameter has very similar semantics when applied as a field attribute in a structure. Consider the example that we saw earlier:

```
struct tagBSTRBLOB
{
                        ULONG cbSize;
    [size_is(cbSize)] BYTE* pData;
};
```

The second member of the structure is really the beginning of an array whose size is specified by the first member. This structure is called a **conformant structure**; it can have at most one conformant array member, and this must be the last member in the structure. A conformant structure must also be the last member of any structure that contains it.

Be careful not to use a dereferenced, unique pointer in a size_is() expression, since these pointers are allowed to be null.

The semantics of a size_is() expression can also be achieved by means of a max_is() expression. The latter specifies an array size by means of the largest index in an array, rather than as a count of the number of elements. Thus, a one-dimensional array of size N has a largest index of N - 1. In our first example above, we could have the equivalent expression:

```
HRESULT SendData([in] ULONG uSz, [in, out, max_is(uSz - 1)] long* plB);
```

Varying Arrays

What about the situation where the number of elements to be transmitted is sometimes less than the total size of the array? Or where more elements need to be transferred in one direction than in the other? These are important optimizations, since the performance of ORPC can be expected to be quite sensitive to the actual amount of data that needs to be transferred during an RMC.

IDL has this situation covered with the use of **varying arrays**. The length_is(), first_is() and last_is() attributes together specify the number of elements to be transferred. For example:

```
HRESULT SendPart(
    [in, out] long* lFirst,
    [in, out] long* lLast,
    [in, out, first_is(lFirst), last_is(lLast), size_is(100)] long* al);
```

The method specifies a method invocation where only the elements of the array al[100] between lFirst and lLast inclusive get sent in each direction. The server is allowed to change the values of lFirst and lLast (since they are also in, out), and the marshaling code will automatically change the range of values to be transmitted back to the client.

The same example may be written by using length_is() instead of last_is() as follows:

```
HRESULT SendPart(
    [in, out] long* lF,
    [in, out] long* lL,
    [in, out, first_is(lF), length_is(lL - lF + 1), size_is(100)] long* al);
```

This code also illustrates the relationship between the three values: length = last - first + 1. You need to exercise particular caution when using in, out length_is() or size_is() parameters, and the reasons for this are made clear below.

Open Arrays

A conformant, varying array is called an **open array**. The array parameter in the SendPart() method described above would have been an open array, had the argument to the size_is() attribute been a variable.

Performance Considerations in Array Marshaling

The array attributes serve to specify the number of array elements to be transferred during the marshaling and unmarshaling of a remote invocation. The distinction between the different kinds of arrays is important only because the marshaling algorithm is slightly different for fixed and varying arrays.

Non-varying arrays (whether fixed or conformant) are transmitted in their entirety. Also, once the data has been received, it can be manipulated by the server code in-place – that is, in the data buffer that was used during message reception. Varying arrays, on the other hand, have an extra memory buffer with space for the entire array (the value of the size_is() expression) allocated for them by the server stub. The array elements from the incoming data buffer have to be copied into the allocated memory buffer.

This means that varying arrays incur the overhead of an extra buffer copy in each direction. The rationale for this extra buffer copy is not entirely clear, because the semantics of remoting slices of arrays are not completely straightforward. When deciding which type of array to use, the cost of the extra allocation and copying must be offset against the cost of transmitting all the data over the network.

Multidimensional Arrays

As mentioned earlier, IDL permits the specification of multidimensional arrays in a way that resolves the ambiguity surrounding nested pointers in C. The size_is() and length_is() (and the associated max_is(), first_is() and last_is()) attributes each have a multidimensional syntax variant. A doubly nested C pointer comes in several IDL flavors. For example:

```
HRESULT SendData1([in] long** ppl);
```

The above line of code means that the variable ppl refers to a pointer to a pointer to a single long.

```
HRESULT SendData2([in] ULONG uSz, [in, size_is(,uSz)] long** pal);
```

This line, however, uses the multidimensional syntax variant of size_is() to decorate the variable pal. This syntax permits a comma-separated list of parameters to the attribute, where each parameter is an expression that is evaluated at runtime. Each position in the list specifies the extent of the corresponding dimension of the array. In this example, reading the parameters of the size_is() attribute from left to right, we see that the leftmost parameter, corresponding to the outermost pointer level, is empty. The right-hand parameter has the value uSz. This declaration is specifying that the variable pal is a pointer to an array of uSz longs.

```
HRESULT SendData3([in] ULONG uSz, [in, size_is(uSz,)] long** apl);
```

In the same fashion, the apl parameter to SendData3() is an array of uSz pointers to longs.

```
HRESULT SendData4([in] ULONG uSz1,
                  [in] ULONG uSz2,
                  [in, size_is(uSz1, uSz2)] long** aal);
```

Finally the single parameter to this function, aal, is an array of uSz1 arrays of uSz2 longs.

Strings

Strings are a special case of arrays: they are one-dimensional arrays of type char, wchar_t or byte. Unlike the COM IDL convention we have seen so far, however, C string APIs typically do not pass the length of the string as a separate parameter, or as a byte count member of a string structure. In order to make it convenient to inter-operate with legacy C string APIs, then, IDL has a string attribute.

The string attribute is used instead of a length_is() attribute to describe the actual size of a null-terminated character array. At runtime, the marshaler will use a function such as strlen() or wcslen() to determine the actual number of characters to transmit. The string attribute can be used in conjunction with a size_is() attribute to specify the *maximum* string length; if this is not done, the size of the input string is assumed also to be the maximum size. This is obviously not possible for out-only parameters, since there is no input string to serve as the maximum size.

Pointers

A typed pointer is a memory address that points at memory holding a specific type of data. From the standpoint of RMC, pointers need two kinds of attributes: one kind to specify what sort of **aliasing** may take place in the data passed into a method invocation, and a second kind to specify marshaling and memory allocation policy.

As it turns out, only one set of attributes is actually defined, but in conjunction with the directional attributes, it serves both purposes.

Pointer Attributes

There are attributes for defining three different kinds of pointers in IDL:

❑ A ref pointer corresponds to a C++ reference parameter. It must be initialized with a valid (non-null) address at method invocation. This value cannot change during method execution.

❑ A unique pointer is a curious beast, designed for superior marshaling performance without the restrictions of a ref pointer. The value of a unique pointer may be null, and may also change during method execution.

❑ A ptr pointer is the most general kind of pointer, closest in spirit to a 'normal' C pointer.

Aliasing Properties

Two pointers are said to be **aliased** when they both point to the same object (memory address). To ensure correctness, it is important to know when the arguments in the parameter list of a remote method call may contain (or be used to obtain) aliased pointers. To see what this means, consider this method:

```
HRESULT SetTo10And12([in, out] long* pl1, [in, out] long* pl2);
```

Its purpose is to assign 10 to its first parameter and 12 to its second parameter (yes, it's a silly function). What happens if the same variable, say lVar, is passed into both parameters (in other words, the parameters are aliased)?

For the in-process case, the answer is clear: whichever assignment the server code performs later is the value that will stick. If 12 is the later value to be assigned, the new value of lVar is 12.

The answer for the remote case, however, is not clear. If the marshaler worked on the assumption that pointers are never aliased, it would marshal the pointers back to the client as two independent variables with values 10 and 12. The value assigned to lVar would then depend on which assignment happened later *during unmarshaling*, not on which assignment happened later in the server.

Consider a second example – a ring buffer implemented as a singly linked list using this structure:

```
typedef struct tagRB
{
   long    lVar;
   tagRB* pRB;
} RB;
```

In this instance, the final element of the ring buffer is linked back to the first element. I can pass a pointer to the first element as a parameter into a method that manipulates the buffer, and this will work fine for an in-apartment method. However, if I try to do the same thing on a remote invocation, a simple marshaling algorithm that assumes no aliasing would get caught in an infinite loop as it chased the pointers round the ring buffer.

We might resolve simply to use a marshaler that recognizes aliasing in all cases, but the algorithm it uses is much more expensive than the non-aliasing algorithm. Since aliasing is relatively rare in practice, it seems unreasonable to force the extra performance hit on all remote method invocations with pointers in them. The IDL solution is to use pointer attributes to specify aliasing properties:

❑ A ref pointer cannot be aliased – no other pointer in the method invocation can point to storage pointed at by a reference pointer.
❑ A unique pointer cannot be aliased, either.
❑ A ptr pointer *can* be aliased – in fact, this is the only difference between a ptr pointer and a unique pointer. ptr pointers should be used sparingly, if at all.

In our examples above, if we wanted to allow aliasing in the method calls, we would change the declarations to be:

```
HRESULT SetTo10And12([in, out, ptr] long* pl1, [in, out, ptr] long* pl2);
```

```
typedef struct tagRB
{
        long    lVar;
   [ptr] tagRB* pRB;
} RB;
```

The marshaler would then use the aliasing algorithm while remoting. The programmer does not need to do anything else for this to work correctly.

Aliasing is not a very common problem if you're dealing with relatively simple parameter types. In more complex cases, where you may have large and nebulous networks of nodes that may be aliased, it is almost certainly not a smart idea to pass the entire network as a parameter to a method invocation. There are more efficient ways of distributing such data. The need for ptr-style semantics really is quite rare, and can probably be eliminated completely when designing new interfaces from scratch.

Rules for Assigning Pointer Types to Variables

IDL assumes certain defaults for pointer types, but in practice it's a good idea to specify explicit pointer attributes wherever these are known, rather than depending on implicit IDL typing. This makes the precise semantics clear without forcing the reader to think about what the default behavior is.

Top-Level vs. Embedded Pointers

The pointer closest to the variable name (the outermost pointer) in a function parameter is referred to as a **top-level pointer**.

```
HRESULT foobar([in] long* pL1, [out] long* pL2, [in, out] long** ppL3);
```

In the above method, pL1 and pL2 are both top-level pointers, ppL3 is a top-level pointer, but *ppL3 is not.

On the other hand, any *non-sized* pointer that is reachable from a top-level pointer, including those inside arrays, structures and unions reachable from a top-level pointer, is referred to as an **embedded pointer**. In the example above, *ppL3 would be an embedded pointer. A *sized* pointer in IDL is an array, and therefore not really a pointer at all.

This is further illustrated in the figure below:

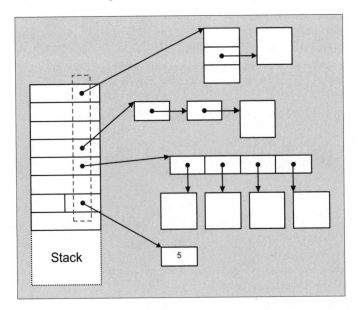

The diagram depicts the stack frame and memory values before a typical method invocation; the arrows all represent pointer values. It is easy to see the difference between the types of pointers; those on the stack (enclosed in the dotted rectangle) are top-level, while the rest are embedded.

Top-Level Pointers

- ❑ A top-level pointer that is not otherwise attributed is always assumed to be a `ref` pointer
- ❑ A top-level pointer that is an `out`-only parameter *must be* a `ref` pointer – it cannot be a `ptr` or a `unique` pointer. This is because IDL follows the call-by-value semantics of C – in order for a parameter to be an output parameter, it must be a pointer (reference) to a variable.

Explicit Pointer Attribution

When a pointer is explicitly decorated by an attribute, the attribute always qualifies the *outermost* level of indirection of the pointer type. Thus, in this declaration:

```
HRESULT foo([in, out, ptr] long** ppL);
```

The `ptr` attribute qualifies `ppL`, not `*ppL`. Similarly, in this structure:

```
typedef struct tagFoo
{
            long    lVar;
    [unique] long** ppL;
} Foo;
```

`ppL` is qualified as being `unique`, but `*ppL` is not. An inner nested pointer cannot be explicitly given an attribute in this fashion.

The pointer_default() Attribute

Clearly, we need some way of specifying a type for embedded pointers that cannot be, or have not been, explicitly qualified by being decorated. This is done by using a `pointer_default()` attribute in the interface header, as you saw in the last chapter.

The `pointer_default()` attribute qualifies all undecorated pointers that are reachable from the interface declaration, including those within structures and in multiply-nested pointer data types. Notice the implication here that a pointer in a structure declaration can be attributed differently *depending on the interface that it appears in.* Since this can lead to subtly different semantics in different method invocations, it is a good idea to decorate all pointers embedded in structures explicitly whenever the attribution is known.

Default Pointer Attribution

If an interface has no `pointer_default()` attribute, all undecorated, embedded pointers reachable from it are assumed to be `unique`.

Memory Management

So far, we've examined the rules that govern pointer variables. We now switch focus to the rules that govern memory ownership policy for pointer variables. There are a couple of issues of interest here: one related to variables that can vary in size, and the other to the general subject of heap allocation.

Storage for Marshaled in, out Parameters

A variable that's marshaled as an in, out parameter has certain aspects of its size fixed at the time when marshaling occurs in the client proxy, prior to method invocation (marshaling in the in direction). This information is particularly significant in the context of variables for which the values of certain fields can affect the size of the whole – in other words, conformant variables and unions.

Conformant Variables

The difference between sized pointers and non-sized (that is, normal) pointers can lead to subtle misunderstandings of an IDL specification, especially on the part of those of us who are experienced C/C++ programmers.

The fact is that the size_is() attribute of a sized pointer is fixed when the parameter that points to it is first marshaled. Thus, when the following method is called, the size of the array al is fixed at the value of *pl that the caller passed into the invocation:

```
HRESULT Fixed1([in, out] LONG* pl, [in, out, size_is(*pl)] LONG* al);
```

The server code can subsequently change the value of *pl, but it *cannot* change the size that the stub unmarshaler allocated for al. The size_is() attribute is therefore only applied in the in direction.

This only seems weird to us as C programmers because we are not accustomed to thinking of arrays as a first class type. Once a variable has been allocated for any *first class* type, you can't change its size, but you *can* change its contents. In IDL, sized pointers just happen to be more like first class types than pointers are in C.

How then can we change the size of an array within the function? It turns out that we can't, and in the face of such blatant provocation, our only recourse is to cheat (well, sort of...)! Instead of changing the size of an allocated variable, we simply create a new variable of a different size and return that instead. The IDL for specifying this is:

```
HRESULT Fixed2([in, out] LONG* pl, [in, out, size_is(,*pl)] LONG** pal);
```

In this instance, the variable *pal, which is a sized pointer of size *pl, can be replaced in the out direction by a newly allocated variable *pal of a different size. The parameter *pl would, of course, be updated to reflect the new size. We are not actually changing the size of the top-level pointer variable pal; we're just assigning a new variable of a different size to it.

Exactly the same situation arises for other conformant types – a conformant structure with an embedded, sized pointer, for example, is subject to the same issues of resizing.

Union Variables

Although unions are not conformant types, an analogous problem exists. The size of a union is fixed when it is first marshaled, and is dependent on the switch type. Any attempt to assign a new value to a union variable that changes the switch is potentially hazardous, since the actual memory allocation of the variable doesn't change. If the new switch value implies a larger allocation than the old, the assignment will overwrite memory that doesn't belong to the union.

The solution to this problem is the same as in the case for conformant type. Instead of passing a union variable, pass a *pointer* to a union variable in its place.

Heap Allocation Conventions

It's about time that I filled in the details of the memory allocation conventions I outlined earlier. Remember that the basic problem here is *ownership* of heap memory – whose job it is to allocate and release it. There are four distinct places where this is an issue: the client application, the client proxy, the server stub, and the server application.

Heap Operations that Cross Address Spaces

The principal source of trouble with memory allocation arises from the situation where memory has to be allocated on one side of a method invocation, and freed on the other. The problem is easiest to see in the case where caller and callee are in different address spaces – there is no way they can share the same heap, as heaps are local to an individual address space.

As I suggested earlier, what happens to resolve the problem is that the marshaling code acts as the 'other side' of each memory allocation operation that crosses between client and server code.

Consider a situation where the client allocates memory, and the method implementation is required to free it. In the in-apartment case, this is simple: the client and the method implementation have access to the same heap, and can perform the operation trivially. What happens in the remote case? Since COM is location transparent, the client and server cannot do anything different – the client still allocates the memory, and the server still frees it. In order to make this work and prevent memory leaks in both the client and the server, the marshaling infrastructure must take up the slack. The client proxy acts as the server would, and de-allocates the memory in the client's heap after the method has been remotely invoked. Similarly, the server stub acts as the client would, and allocates memory in the server's heap prior to calling the actual method.

The COM Task Memory Allocator

For the above process to work in a language-independent and location-transparent manner, the calling function, the server interface method and the proxy-stub code all have to agree to use the same heap API, and the one used is the **COM task memory allocator**, implemented by the `IMalloc` interface. This interface can be accessed with the `CoGetMalloc()` function, but the new and improved way of getting at the heap is via the `CoTaskMemAlloc()`, `CoTaskMemRealloc()` and `CoTaskMemFree()` API calls. These functions wrap calls to `CoGetMalloc()` and the subsequent invocation of the corresponding methods on the `IMalloc` interface.

Whenever a pointer comes in across a remotable interface (that is, one that can participate in COM marshaling), any allocation or freeing of memory pointed to by the pointer *must* be performed with the COM task memory allocator. Pointers that never have to cross a remotable interface can be allocated and released with any old heap API. As we'll discuss later in the chapter, the only *non-remotable* interfaces are those marked with the `local` attribute.

Pointer Types and Memory Allocation

Since the marshaling code is generated automatically from the IDL definition of a method, the memory allocation operations performed by the code are also affected by the values of IDL attributes.

A `ref` pointer cannot have newly allocated memory assigned to it. This is just a consequence of the fact that a `ref` pointer should not have *anything* assigned to it after its value has been initialized. For similar reasons, you shouldn't de-allocate memory pointed to by a `ref` pointer, either. Basically, a `ref` pointer should not participate in heap operations at all.

As with all good rules, though, there is one exception: an embedded, out-only ref pointer. Such a pointer might occur, for instance, as an aggregated member of an out-only structure. For memory allocation purposes, this kind of pointer behaves as if it were a unique pointer. The reason for this is that an embedded, out-only pointer *has* to be initialized on the server, and therefore eventually freed by the client.

> **Pointers with the unique and ptr attributes can always participate in heap operations.**

Marshaling and Heap Allocation

Now let's examine each of the scenarios in which heap operations can occur in rather more detail.

in-only Parameters

in-only pointer parameters constitute the simplest case. By definition, an in-only parameter, whether top-level or embedded, cannot be changed in any way by the server code. This includes any changes that involve the allocation or de-allocation of memory.

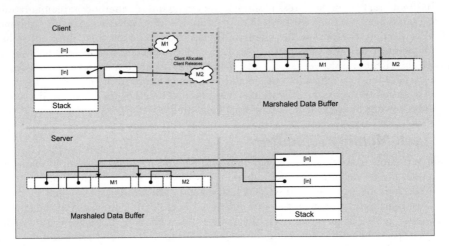

On the client side, the marshaler chases all pointers and marshals the actual data into the serialized data buffer. It then invokes the remote stub. Upon return from the stub, the proxy simply frees the data buffer (if necessary) and returns to the caller. No heap operations need to be performed on the in-only parameters.

On the server side, the stub leaves the data sitting in the serialized data buffer (except in the case of a varying array, where a separate buffer is created) and unmarshals only the top-level pointers onto the stack. It then calls the actual server method. Upon return from the method invocation, it releases the data buffer if necessary, and returns to the client proxy. Again, no heap operations are performed.

Top-level out Pointers

Top-level pointer parameters are also a relatively simple case. The in-only case is subsumed by the above discussion, so let us now look at out parameters.

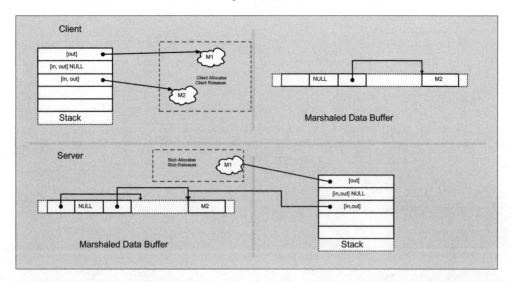

If the pointer is an out-only parameter, it must be a ref pointer and hence allocated on the client. If the pointer is in, out, then its value can be null on input (and that cannot be changed by the server) *or* a valid address on the client. In either case, any memory allocation must occur only in the client code.

The client proxy allocates no memory for an out-only top-level pointer. The server stub unmarshals the top-level pointers onto its stack and provides a static allocation for the out variable. No heap operations are performed in either proxy or stub.

Embedded out-only Pointers

An out parameter with an embedded (and possibly sized) pointer exhibits a greater level of complexity: who is responsible for allocation of the space that is pointed to by the embedded pointer? The only reasonable answer is that the method being called must be responsible. In general, the caller cannot know the size of the array or the depth of pointer recursion for an out-only variable. The sensible choice here is for the server code to allocate the storage, and to return the pointer. The client code must release the storage when the call is complete.

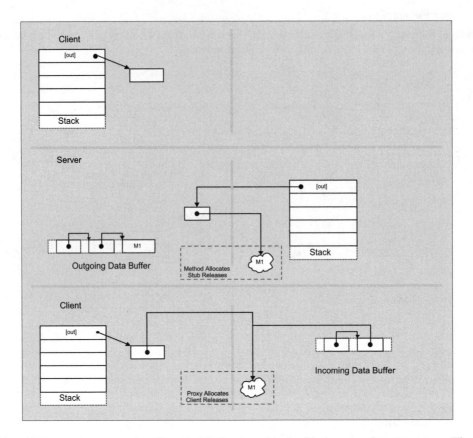

The above diagram represents the allocation behavior of embedded out-only parameters. The first panel shows the client state prior to invocation, while the last panel shows the state of the client afterwards. The state of the server post-invocation, and outgoing data buffer, is displayed in the middle panel.

As you can see, memory is allocated on the server by the method. Upon completion of the method, the stub marshals the output parameters, chases all embedded pointers and marshals their data, and transmits the data buffer to the proxy. It then needs to traverse all the output parameters, chase the embedded pointers, and release the storage that was allocated by the server code.

The client proxy simply unmarshals the embedded out-only parameters, allocating heap storage in which to store the values copied out of the received data buffer. This heap storage must eventually be released by the client code.

Embedded in, out Pointers

Embedded in, out pointers represent the most complex case of all. Here, both client and server can allocate *and* free memory. The marshaling code has to contend with all possible combinations of heap operations.

As if that weren't bad enough, the situation is further complicated by a couple of other factors that we have already discussed:

- ❑ All `in, out` variables (including conformant, sized pointers) have their sizes fixed at the time the client proxy marshals the variable. The server code cannot change the size of conformant variables, although it can change the values within.

- ❑ Embedded `in, out, ref` pointers cannot be allocated, released or modified.

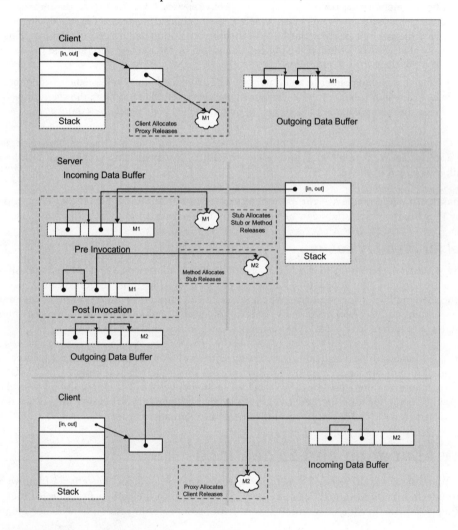

For non-sized pointers, the server can:

- ❑ Change a null pointer to a new value allocated on the heap. In this case, the server stub must release the allocated memory, and the client proxy must allocate it on the client. Finally, the client code must release the memory.

❑   Change a non-null pointer to a new value allocated on the heap. In this situation, the server code must first release the old non-null value and then allocate the new non-null value. The server stub must release the allocated memory; the client proxy must release the old pointer and allocate memory for the new value; and finally the client itself must release the new memory.

This is the most general case of memory allocation, and the previous diagram represents this scenario. Initially, the embedded pointer is pointing to a client-allocated piece of memory, M1. After this memory has been marshaled, the proxy releases it. On the server, the stub allocates M1, which gets released and reallocated as M2 by the method invocation. After marshaling the return values, the stub releases M2 (or M1 if the method invocation had left M1 untouched). Finally, the proxy allocates M2 (or M1, if it had been untouched by the method and returned by the stub), which the client then has to release.

❑   Change a non-null pointer to a null pointer. The server code must release the existing memory before setting the pointer to null. This time, the server stub does nothing; the client proxy must release the memory and set the pointer to null; the client code need do nothing at all.

Clearly, the marshaling code has to be sophisticated enough to detect various pointer changes and take the appropriate steps to allocate and release memory. Not surprisingly, this case has the highest marshaling overhead of the lot.

The semantics of embedded in, out parameters are complicated enough that they should be used sparingly. For the most part, they can be replaced by independent in and out parameters.

Potential for Memory Leaks

There are certain shortcomings in the MIDL-generated marshaling code that makes it possible for memory to be orphaned by apparently legitimate server code. The most important of these is shortening the length of a varying array whose elements contain embedded pointers. The marshaling code does not attempt to clean up memory that is potentially orphaned by such a length change. Do not change the length of a varying array (using length_is()) of this type.

The IDL documentation also indicates that changing the value of a unique or ptr pointer variable from non-null to null can cause memory orphaning, but this is strictly true only for RPC IDL. In COM IDL, the marshaling code *does* keep track of such changes for unique pointers (by releasing the old pointer and allocating the new one), but not for ptr pointers. However, this is not done for aliased pointers, for which the application is expected to manage memory.

Memory Allocation and Exceptions

Another situation in which we need a memory allocation protocol is for the return of failure codes. When an interface method returns a failure code, it isn't clear to the calling function (or the marshaling code) whether the out and in, out parameters contain results, or whether memory was allocated.

The protocol is designed to keep error handling simple, especially in the case where the caller immediately propagates the error back to its *own* caller. Obviously, the best convention is something that does not require the caller to do *any* clean up.

❑ For embedded out-only pointers, you are required to set them to null explicitly. This is best achieved by setting all embedded out pointers to null upon entry into the method invocation.

❑ For embedded in, out pointers, the values are best left at the caller-initialized state. If this is not achievable, the pointers should be freed and set to null. This has the downside that it changes the caller's state, requiring cleanup, but it does so in such a way that the normal cleanup routine (especially that used by the marshaler) continues working.

Why make this a requirement for out pointers? Simply put, the marshaling code expects to be able to marshal the contents of the pointer, regardless of whether the call succeeded or failed. If such a pointer is pointing at garbage, the marshaling code will have problems – it will crash and burn.

This rule has no effect on the ability of the proxy-stub code to clean up heap memory correctly. It is merely designed to simplify client-side error handling.

Interfaces

Finally, let us look at the IDL specification for interface marshaling. COM IDL has native support for marshaling interfaces (indeed, that's its whole *raison d'être*). To pass an interface IFoo into a method invocation, one simply declares an in parameter of type IFoo*:

```
HRESULT ExportFoo([in] IFoo* pIFoo);
```

The declaration above, for example, will marshal the interface into the method invocation. As we discussed earlier, this creates a stub for IFoo in the client apartment, and a proxy for IFoo in the server apartment of the original object. All COM's reference counting rules are automatically enforced by the marshaling code.

Similarly, this method will unmarshal the interface out of the method invocation:

```
HRESULT ImportFoo([out] IFoo** ppIFoo);
```

In this case, the stub will be created in the server apartment of the original object, and the proxy will be created in the client apartment. Once again, the MIDL-generated marshaling code will enforce all the rules of COM.

A Query Over QueryInterface()

You're almost certainly familiar with the IDL for IUnknown::QueryInterface(), and at this point in the discussion, you might well be thinking it's rather strange. As a reminder, it looks like this:

```
HRESULT QueryInterface([in] REFIID riid,
                       [out, iid_is(riid)] void** ppvObject);
```

What's odd about this is the use of void** as the type of the out parameter. In fact, this is the only permissible use of void pointers in COM IDL, and exists for legacy reasons.

Now think about what `QueryInterface()` is supposed to do. Among other things, it should perform the appropriate marshaling for the returned interface. However, the type of the returned interface is not known until runtime, when it is passed in as the first parameter to the method call. The `iid_is()` attribute lets the MIDL-generated marshaling code load the correct proxy-stub DLL for this interface at runtime, and the proxy-stub DLL, of course, knows how to marshal the interface.

The same idiom can be used in many situations where an interface has to be returned from a function call and the interface designer doesn't want to hard-wire a specific interface into the IDL of the method:

```
HRESULT ReceiveInterface([in] REFIID riid,
                         [out, iid_is(riid)] IUnknown** ppvObject);
```

Why would you want to use the `iid_is()` attribute instead of specifying an actual interface as the type, when if anything the former usage is not as type-safe as the latter. The biggest reason for using this idiom is that it allows you to avoid hard-wiring a specific interface into the method signature. This gives your interface implementation an extra degree of freedom, although it does make the interface semantics less strict.

Non-Remotable Interfaces

It is possible to designate an interface as being non-remotable by using the keyword `local` in its attribute list. No marshaling code is generated for such an interface. Because a `local` interface can't be used by COM clients in general, it could be argued that there is not much point to including non-remotable interfaces in your IDL code. However, if you view your IDL file as documentation of your object model, including interfaces that are only called internally, you may choose to list those too.

MIDL Generated Standard Marshalers

The MIDL compiler is capable of generating two different sorts of marshaling code. There are the older kind, known as **inline marshalers**, and the newer kind, which are called **interpretive marshalers**. (The latter are also sometimes called "`/Oicf` marshalers", after the flag that you pass to MIDL in order to specify them.) In this section, I want to outline the differences between the two types.

Inline and Interpretive Marshaling

An interpretive marshaler simply contains a description of the types that need to be marshaled, and the signatures of the methods in the remotable interface. A marshaling interpreter takes these descriptions and uses them to marshal an actual method invocation. By contrast, an inline marshaler consists of compiled C code that steps through the process of marshaling each method in pieces.

To illustrate the difference between these two kinds of marshalers, I'm actually going to show you the marshaling code that is generated by MIDL in each case for a very simple method invocation.

Consider the sample interface:

```
[...]
interface IShowMarshal : IUnknown
{
    HRESULT SMSimple([out] long*);
};
```

When this interface is compiled with MIDL using the inline compilation option (/Os), the following C code is generated for the client proxy:

```
HRESULT STDMETHODCALLTYPE IShowMarshal_SMSimple_Proxy(
        IShowMarshal __RPC_FAR* This, /* [out] */ long __RPC_FAR* __MIDL_0015)
{
    HRESULT _RetVal;
    RPC_MESSAGE _RpcMessage;
    MIDL_STUB_MESSAGE _StubMsg;

    RpcTryExcept
    {
        NdrProxyInitialize((void __RPC_FAR*)This,
                           (PRPC_MESSAGE)&_RpcMessage,
                           (PMIDL_STUB_MESSAGE)&_StubMsg,
                           (PMIDL_STUB_DESC)&Object_StubDesc,
                           3);
        if(!__MIDL_0015)
        {
            RpcRaiseException(RPC_X_NULL_REF_POINTER);
        }

        RpcTryFinally
        {
            _StubMsg.BufferLength = 0U;
            NdrProxyGetBuffer(This, &_StubMsg);
            NdrProxySendReceive(This, &_StubMsg);
            if((_RpcMessage.DataRepresentation & 0X0000FFFFUL)
                                            != NDR_LOCAL_DATA_REPRESENTATION)
                NdrConvert((PMIDL_STUB_MESSAGE)&_StubMsg,
                           (PFORMAT_STRING)&__MIDL_ProcFormatString.Format[0]);

            *__MIDL_0015 = *((long __RPC_FAR*)_StubMsg.Buffer)++;
            _RetVal = *((HRESULT __RPC_FAR*)_StubMsg.Buffer)++;
        }
        RpcFinally
        {
            NdrProxyFreeBuffer(This, &_StubMsg);
        }
        RpcEndFinally
    }
    RpcExcept(_StubMsg.dwStubPhase != PROXY_SENDRECEIVE)
    {
        NdrClearOutParameters((PMIDL_STUB_MESSAGE)&_StubMsg,
                              (PFORMAT_STRING)&__MIDL_TypeFormatString.Format[2],
                              (void __RPC_FAR*)__MIDL_0015);
        _RetVal = NdrProxyErrorHandler(RpcExceptionCode());
    }
    RpcEndExcept
    return _RetVal;
}
```

It's tricky (to say the least!), but you should be able to see a couple of things in this listing. First of all, because I didn't give a name to the SMSimple() function's single parameter in my IDL code, the MIDL compiler has created its own – it has called it __MIDL_0015. You can skip the names in any IDL interface, and MIDL will always generate them on your behalf.

Second, it's pretty clear that this code is calling various functions in the RPC runtime. These functions initialize the transmission and then send, receive and convert the resulting buffer to and from NDR. Any heap memory is also freed as allocated, and out parameters are cleared upon error. All of this is done in a way that guards the code from exceptions.

The corresponding stub code in C is as follows:

```
void __RPC_STUB IShowMarshal_SMSimple_Stub(IRpcStubBuffer* This,
                                           IRpcChannelBuffer* _pRpcChannelBuffer,
                                           PRPC_MESSAGE _pRpcMessage,
                                           DWORD* _pdwStubPhase)
{
    long _M0;
    HRESULT _RetVal;
    MIDL_STUB_MESSAGE _StubMsg;
    long __RPC_FAR*__MIDL_0015;

    NdrStubInitialize(_pRpcMessage, &_StubMsg,
                                    &Object_StubDesc, _pRpcChannelBuffer);
    (long __RPC_FAR*)__MIDL_0015 = 0;
    RpcTryFinally
    {
        __MIDL_0015 = &_M0;
        *_pdwStubPhase = STUB_CALL_SERVER;

        _RetVal = ((((IShowMarshal*)((CStdStubBuffer*)This)->pvServerObject)->
        lpVtbl)->SMSimple((IShowMarshal*)((CStdStubBuffer*)This)->pvServerObject,
        __MIDL_0015);

        *_pdwStubPhase = STUB_MARSHAL;
        _StubMsg.BufferLength = 4U + 4U;
        NdrStubGetBuffer(This, _pRpcChannelBuffer, &_StubMsg);
        *((long __RPC_FAR*)_StubMsg.Buffer)++ = *__MIDL_0015;
        *((HRESULT __RPC_FAR*)_StubMsg.Buffer)++ = _RetVal;
    }
    RpcFinally
    {
    }
    RpcEndFinally

    _pRpcMessage->BufferLength =
            (unsigned int)((long)_StubMsg.Buffer - (long)_pRpcMessage->Buffer);
}
```

The stub code is similar in flavor to the proxy, but has no obvious connection to a vtable. This is because the stub code is not actually called through a vtable. Rather, it is called at the appropriate time by IRpcStubBuffer::Invoke().

In sharp contrast, the code generated for interpretive marshaling by the /Oicf flag to MIDL doesn't even have clear entry points for stubs (hence the misleading term "stubless proxy"). Provided instead is a detailed, tabular description of the various method signatures in the interface, as well as a table of various user-defined types that may be used by the interface. In our example, the table that describes the SMSimple() method invocation has the following structure:

```
{
/* Procedure SMSimple */
        0x33,                   /* FC_AUTO_HANDLE */
        0x6c,                   /* Old Flags:  object, Oi2 */
/*  2 */ NdrFcLong(0x0),        /* 0 */
/*  6 */ NdrFcShort(0x3),       /* 3 */
#ifndef _ALPHA_
/*  8 */ NdrFcShort(0xc),       /* x86, MIPS, PPC Stack size/offset = 12 */
#else
        NdrFcShort(0x18),       /* Alpha Stack size/offset = 24 */
#endif
/* 10 */ NdrFcShort(0x0),       /* 0 */
/* 12 */ NdrFcShort(0x10),      /* 16 */
/* 14 */ 0x4,                   /* Oi2 Flags:  has return, */
        0x2,                    /* 2 */

/* Parameter __MIDL_0015 */
/* 16 */ NdrFcShort(0x2150),    /* Flags:  out, base type, */
                                /* simple ref, srv alloc size=8 */
#ifndef _ALPHA_
/* 18 */ NdrFcShort(0x4),       /* x86, MIPS, PPC Stack size/offset = 4 */
#else
        NdrFcShort(0x8),        /* Alpha Stack size/offset = 8 */
#endif
/* 20 */ 0x8,                   /* FC_LONG */
        0x0,                    /* 0 */

/* Return value */
/* 22 */ NdrFcShort(0x70),      /* Flags:  out, return, base type, */
#ifndef _ALPHA_
/* 24 */ NdrFcShort(0x8),       /* x86, MIPS, PPC Stack size/offset = 8 */
#else
        NdrFcShort(0x10),       /* Alpha Stack size/offset = 16 */
#endif
/* 26 */ 0x8,                   /* FC_LONG */
        0x0,                    /* 0 */
        0x0
}
```

Although this is quite cryptic (the format being undocumented and subject to change), it seems reasonably clear that it is describing a method invocation including parameters, return values, and possibly the stack convention. There is no stub code as such, although there is a client method (for the proxy vtable) that simply calls into the marshaling interpreter. What does exist is the marshaling interpreter that understands the /Oicf structures and translates this data into run-time calls to functions very similar to those used by the compiled, inline marshaling code.

The primary benefit of /Oicf marshaling is that since they consist largely of tables describing types, the proxy-stub DLLs are significantly smaller (sometimes by an order of magnitude) than inline marshaling code. This size reduction eventually manifests itself in a smaller working set and a smaller overall application footprint. The systemic gains (less swapping) from the smaller footprint make up for the somewhat slower performance of the interpreted marshaler.

Interpretive marshaling has evolved over time to its current form, and MIDL can still generate earlier versions of the interpretive marshaling code. However, unless you really want to maintain a number of versions of the marshaling code, it is simpler to have just two: /Oicf and inline code.

Interpretive Marshaling and Type Library Marshaling

When you think about it, marshaling based on a description of the interface signature is very similar to what the type library marshaler does. In fact, the current implementation of the type library marshaler translates the signatures into /Oicf strings at runtime. These strings are then used dynamically to create run-time interpretive marshalers from the type library information. Various caching optimizations are performed to amortize the cost associated with creating the marshalers at runtime.

As the type library format gets more sophisticated and includes *all* the information present in source IDL, we can anticipate a time when the proxy-stub DLL might eventually become obsolete due to the type library containing all the marshaling information in a more abstract and portable form than the /Oicf strings.

> *To see a complete example of all the issues that come up while creating interfaces that have complex marshaling requirements, take a look at Chapter 7.*

Special Marshaling Requirements & Aliasing

Occasionally, situations arise where a legacy interface or data type cannot be handled by the standard marshaling code generated by MIDL. Equally, there are times when detailed knowledge of the problem domain allows a data structure to be transformed into a much more compact representation that is better suited to transmission across the wire.

Problem Areas

IDL has attributes and hooks that can be used to address both these situations. In this section, I'll show you the kind of problem areas that demand special treatment, as well as the IDL solution.

Inappropriate Method Semantics

The classic example of the problem posed by legacy interfaces is the declaration of the Next() method of the IEnumVARIANT interface (or indeed any of the IEnum*XXXX*::Next() methods). Here is its declaration:

```
HRESULT Next([in] ULONG celt,
             [out, size_is(celt), length_is(*pCeltFetched)] VARIANT* rgVar,
             [out] ULONG* pCeltFetched);
```

This looks like perfectly reasonable IDL code, but it turns out that the semantics of this method were defined before IDL was in widespread use, and they're inconsistent with those of IDL. Specifically, the third parameter (pCeltFetched) is allowed to be null if the first parameter has the value 1. However, as you've already seen in this chapter, all top-level out-only parameters are **required** to be ref pointers, and a ref pointer *can't* have a null value under any circumstances. If it does, there are likely to be problems in the marshaling code.

Legacy Data Types

Another of the problems caused by legacy types is demonstrated by the familiar BSTR data type. You'll recall that the BSTR declaration is not truly representative of the actual structure of a BSTR; the IDL declaration of a BSTR is:

```
typedef OLECHAR* BSTR;
```

While its true structure is actually something more like this:

```
typedef struct tagBSTR
{
                        unsigned long  fFlags;
                        unsigned long  clSize;
   [size_is(clSize)] unsigned short asData[];
} *wireBSTR;
```

The relationship between these two is that the OLECHAR* points to the beginning of the conformant data member asData[]. Can MIDL automatically generate the more complex structure when it sees a BSTR parameter into a method invocation? Of course it can, and I'll show you how in the next section.

There is a further complication with variables of the BSTR data type, which is that they are not allocated with the standard COM allocator. Instead, they use the "SysAlloc" API that is specific to BSTR values. How can the MIDL-generated marshaling code know that it needs to use a different heap when dealing with BSTR values?

Transmission Efficiency

There are still other situations where the programmer realizes that a specific complex data type could be 'intelligently' marshaled – that it could be transformed into a much more compact representation based on special domain knowledge. This transformation will doubtless require extra processing, and may not be worth doing in the in-process case, but it might be justified in a marshaled invocation.

In this case, the ideal solution is for MIDL to generate code that transforms the data into its compact representation, marshals the compact data type to the server, unmarshals it, performs the reverse transformation to generate the original data type, and then calls the server method with the original type. The only part of the code that is aware of the compact representation is then the marshaling code.

An example of such a situation might be a simple, doubly linked list. A doubly linked list whose node data field is one word long incurs an overhead of 2 extra words because of the two pointers per list node – put another way, two-thirds of its storage is pointer overhead. To marshal such a list naïvely would be quite expensive because two-thirds of the work is being wasted (in addition to requiring the marshaler to recognize the cyclic node dependencies). However, if we could convert this list into an array that contains only the data fields of interest, and then marshal the resulting array, that would be a big performance win. On the other side, we could unmarshal the array and convert it back into a doubly linked list.

IDL Solution: Aliasing

It turns out that IDL has an approach for solving all these problems. The technique has been termed **"aliasing"** in the literature, which is a little confusing because of the use of the same term for pointer semantics. Essentially, the solution boils down to creating a new method or data type that can be used as a proxy (or alias) for the original method or data type during the marshaling process.

local and call_as()

The first technique is applied when you have an interface method whose marshaling behavior needs to be overridden. To continue our example from above, let's look at how we'd fix the problem with the `IEnumVARIANT::Next()` method.

Recall the problem: the client needs to be able to call the method with the original semantics that were defined for it – that is, with a null value for a `ref` parameter. However, the marshaling code will complain if we try to pass in such a value as a `ref` parameter. The general solution to this problem is to interpose a layer between the method invocation as seen by the client and the actual marshaling code as generated by MIDL. This layer is responsible for cleaning up any inappropriate call semantics.

The first thing to do is to tag the original method as one that doesn't generate any marshaling code. As you know, this is done by applying the `local` attribute, as follows:

```
[local] HRESULT Next(
                [in] ULONG celt,
                [out, size_is(celt), length_is(*pCeltFetched)] VARIANT* rgVar,
                [out] ULONG* pCeltFetched
);
```

The next step is to provide an alternative signature for which marshaling code *will* be generated. This method is tagged with the `call_as()` attribute. In our case, this is:

```
[call_as(Next)] HRESULT RemoteNext(
                [in] ULONG celt,
                [out, size_is(celt), length_is(*pCeltFetched)] VARIANT* rgVar,
                [out] ULONG* pCeltFetched
);
```

In this case, the two methods have identical signatures, reflecting the fact that the problem lies in the semantics of the method, rather than its signature. In general, the two signatures can be completely unrelated. What's important is that MIDL uses the signatures to generate calls that convert from one form to the other.

Code is generated for two functions that marshal the remotable method call – in this case, `RemoteNext()`. The functions are called `IEnumVARIANT_RemoteNext_Proxy()` and `IEnumVARIANT_RemoteNext_Thunk()`..

The only thing left for the programmer to do is to provide implementations of the two functions that are needed to perform the layering described earlier. The first transforms the `local` version of the call to the `call_as()` version, and it's used on the client side of the RMC.

In our case, the function has the name `IEnumVARIANT_Next_Proxy()`, and might look something like this:

```
// Same signature as 'local' method .
HRESULT STDMETHODCALLTYPE IEnumVARIANT_Next_Proxy(IEnumVARIANT* This,
                                                  ULONG         celt,
                                                  VARIANT*      rgVar,
                                                  ULONG*        pCeltFetched)
{
    // Translate from local to call_as()

    ...

    // Call the call_as() proxy
    return IEnumVARIANT_RemoteNext_Proxy(This, celt, rgVar, pCeltFetched);
}
```

Note that this programmer-supplied function is simply converting a call from the `local` signature to the MIDL-generated proxy for the remotable signature.

The second function is used on the server side of the RMC and is used to translate the `call_as()` version of the method to the `local` version. In our case, this function has the name `IEnumVARIANT_Next_Stub()`, and might look like this:

```
// Same signature as call_as() method
HRESULT STDMETHODCALLTYPE IEnumVARIANT_Next_Stub(IEnumVARIANT* This,
                                                 ULONG         celt,
                                                 VARIANT*      rgVar,
                                                 ULONG*        pCeltFetched)
{
    // Call the local stub
    HRESULT hr = This->Next(celt, rgVar, pCeltFetched)

    // Translate from local to call_as()

    ...
    return hr;
}
```

As you can see, the two programmer-supplied routines are effectively translating from the `local` signature to the `call_as()` signature on the client side, and from the `call_as()` signature to the `local` signature on the server side. The precise semantics of the translation are completely defined by the programmer. Note also that it is up to the programmer to ensure that the appropriate method (`IEnumVARIANT_RemoteNext_Proxy()` on the client and `This->Next()` on the server) is actually called by the translation routine.

wire_marshal() and transmit_as()

Just as the `local` and `call_as()` keywords provide marshaling translations for method calls, the `wire_marshal()` and `transmit_as()` keywords provide marshaling translations for data types. Both keywords do roughly the same thing in that they convert from a local representation to a marshaling representation; `wire_marshal()` is the more efficient way of accomplishing this goal, but it only works on more recent versions of the COM runtime (Windows NT 4 and DCOM 95).

Either keyword may be used to implement marshaling translations. The general technique is to associate a **wire** (marshaling) **type** with the **user** (local) **type**, and then require the programmer to supply routines that convert between the two. The programmer also needs to supply routines to release the memory used to hold the converted data.

When the MIDL-generated marshaling code reaches a point where it has to marshal such a data type, it calls the appropriate entry points to perform the conversion and marshal the data into a transmission buffer. Since the marshaled data is represented as another type that is known to MIDL (the wire type), the NDR engine is quite capable of converting it to NDR once marshaling is complete.

A similar sequence of operations occurs when the MIDL-generated unmarshaling code reaches a point where it has to unmarshal the wire type. By this time, the NDR engine has already finished its work, and the data is sitting in the transmission buffer in the format of the wire-type. The MIDL-generated code simply calls the appropriate user-defined entry points to unmarshal the data and free the buffer as necessary.

The primary operational difference between the `transmit_as()` and `wire_marshal()` attributes is that the entry points for the former need to do one extra allocation and de-allocation, and one extra copy to get the data into the transmission buffer. The code that uses the `wire_marshal()`-style helpers works directly on the transmission buffer. This makes the latter the preferred approach to take when you have a choice.

I have focused on `wire_marshal()` in this section. The concepts for `transmit_as()` are very similar, but the precise semantics of the entry points are a little different. Let's continue our example and look at the entry points for the `BSTR` data type that I described earlier.

Using wire_marshal()

There is a restriction on the wire type that may be used in a `wire_marshal()` attribute. It must either be a flat data type (with no embedded pointers), or it must be a pointer to some other type. The second rule pretty much allows *any* type to be a wire type, provided that you create one extra level of indirection. This also explains why `wireBSTR` in the above code had to be a pointer to a structure, rather than a structure itself.

The only changes that need to be made to the IDL code are the declarations that associate the wire type with the local type. This is done in the `typedef` for the `BSTR`, as follows:

```
typedef [wire_marshal(wireBSTR)] OLECHAR* BSTR;
```

What remains to be done is to provide the entry points that are expected by the MIDL-generated code. This turns out to involve the following four functions:

In general, the `wire_marshal()` *-related entry points for a type named* `<type>` *have names prefixed with* `<type>_`.

```
unsigned long __RPC_USER BSTR_UserSize(unsigned long* pulFlags,
                                       unsigned long  ulStartingSize,
                                       BSTR*          pBSTR);
```

```
unsigned char* __RPC_USER BSTR_UserMarshal(unsigned long* pulFlags,
                                           unsigned char* pBuffer,
                                           BSTR*          pBSTR);

unsigned char* __RPC_USER BSTR_UserUnmarshal(unsigned long* pulFlags,
                                             unsigned char* pBuffer,
                                             BSTR*          pBSTR);

void __RPC_USER BSTR_UserFree(unsigned long* pulFlags,
                              BSTR*          pBSTR);
```

`BSTR_UserSize()` is used to return the size in bytes of the RMC buffer after the data has been converted. The initial size is passed into the function in the `ulStartingSize` parameter. The `BSTR` to be converted is passed in the third parameter.

`BSTR_UserMarshal()` is used to transfer the `BSTR` data in `pBSTR` into the transmission buffer `pBuffer` after converting it into the wire type `wireBSTR`.

`BSTR_UserUnmarshal()` is used to recreate `BSTR` data in `pBSTR` using the wire type `wireBSTR` that is present at the current offset `pBuffer` of the transmission buffer. This routine is also responsible for memory allocation of any data pointed at by the pointer. In this case, it is responsible for allocating a `BSTR` using the 'SysAlloc' API.

`BSTR_UserFree()` is used in the server stub to free any lingering `BSTR`s. In this case, it frees `*pBSTR` using the 'SysAlloc' API. `pBSTR` itself is freed by the marshaling code.

Problems With Aliasing

There are a couple of problems associated with the use of the aliasing keywords in IDL:

❑ The type library generated from the IDL file displays only the `call_as()` method and the wire type in the relevant signatures. This means the information in the type library is useless for actual use by a client. Hopefully, this will be fixed in a future release of the MIDL compiler.

This is an issue to the extent that you may be unaware of aliasing going on in an interface whose type library description is essential to the operation of your system.

❑ The way in which aliasing works requires the programmer to provide implementations of helper functions that can then be used by the marshaling code. However, this presupposes the existence of a proxy-stub DLL. If such DLLs should become obsolete in the future, completely replaced by type library marshaling, there might be a problem with supporting aliased types.

Note that this is not a huge issue when it comes to supporting legacy types, which you should be phasing out at this time anyway. It does make a difference, however, in the case where you want to have a separate wire type to optimize the transmission format. You may then be forced to do the conversion in the client and server implementations explicitly, rather than have MIDL perform it 'automatically'.

The nature of these problems should make you cautious about using IDL aliasing in your designs.

Summary

In this chapter, I've shown you the details of the COM remoting architecture and the ways in which the MIDL-generated standard marshaling code interacts with it. In particular you should understand the following concepts:

❑ The issues that must be addressed by a generic remote method call
❑ How the COM standard marshaling architecture handles these issues
❑ A general idea of how custom and handler marshaling may be used to create client proxies

You should also understand not just the marshaling related syntax of IDL, but how it relates to the COM standard marshaling architecture. In particular, you should be happy with:

❑ The way simple types and enums get remoted
❑ How more complex `struct`s and unions get remoted, including issues with types of variable size
❑ How arrays are represented in IDL, and the flexibility and performance tradeoffs associated with the different types of arrays
❑ Pointer semantics, including the effects of the various pointer attributes
❑ Details of the COM memory allocation policy, including use of the COM task allocator
❑ Memory allocation during error returns
❑ The way interfaces are marshaled, and the various issues that arise from interface marshaling

You should also have a good idea of the difference between inline and interpretive standard marshalers, and when to choose one over the other. You should also understand the close relationship between type library marshaling and interpretive marshaling.

Finally, you should understand the sorts of situations in which you might want to tweak the marshaling provided by MIDL, and how to use IDL aliasing for this purpose. You should also be aware of the potential problems this can entail.

Design Implications

Finally, here is a listing of some rules of thumb and design guidelines that you can take away from this chapter.

Parameter Passing

❑ Try to pass parameters of user-defined types by reference pointers rather than by value. Although this makes no difference to the efficiency of RMC calls, it is more efficient in the in-apartment case. It is also more compliant with the C/C++ idiom.

Interfaces

❑ You cannot have a weak reference that crosses an apartment boundary.
❑ In particular, you cannot use aggregation unless you can guarantee that both containing and aggregated objects are in the same apartment.
❑ Be careful with marshaled tear-off interfaces. They do not get released in the manner you might expect.

Base Types

- ❏ Do not change the signed-ness of IDL base types. If you have special sign requirements, use explicitly signed types.
- ❏ Do not use the `int` base type. Although it has a well-defined NDR type, it doesn't have a well-defined C/C++ translation.
- ❏ Consider using the `#define`'d IDL types from `wtypes.idl`. They map onto the corresponding `#define`s in C/C++. Unfortunately, this rule is not perfect – there are problems with the `CHAR`, `LPSTR` and `LPTSTR` types. If you stick only to wide characters and wide character strings, however, you will not encounter these issues.
- ❏ If you're concerned about performance, define all remotable `enum`s with the `vi_enum` attribute.

Arrays

- ❏ Use sized pointers in preference to arrays.
- ❏ The `length_is()` attribute saves on transmitted data while incurring extra buffer allocation and copying overhead in the server stub. In performance sensitive interfaces, the tradeoff should be considered before committing to it one way or the other.

Pointers

- ❏ When defining new interfaces from scratch, avoid aliased pointer semantics like the plague!
- ❏ Explicitly attribute all pointers with their type, whenever this is known. As with any typing mechanism, use the strongest (most constraining) type that you can.
- ❏ Always specify a `pointer_default()` attribute so that the type of nested pointers is made explicit.

Parameter Size

- ❏ Beware of the potential for memory corruption caused by changing the size of a variable. A simple way to avoid such leaks is to consider a `size_is()` parameter to a method invocation to be a constant. In practice, this is not a significant restriction.
- ❏ For the same reasons, you should treat the discriminating tag in a union as a constant.
- ❏ If you really need a variable `size_is()` or discriminating tag, use a doubly-nested pointer variable. This is semantically equivalent to creating a new variable instead of modifying an existing one.

Strings

- ❏ If you already have the string length computed, you can improve performance by using the `size_is()` attribute rather than the `string` attribute.
- ❏ By the same reasoning as given earlier for parameter size, `in`, `out` strings should always be doubly nested.

Memory Allocation

- ❏ Be careful when you have an `in`, `out`, `length_is()` parameter. It's easy to orphan memory.
- ❏ All interface semantics should be defined so that the caller has to do nothing on error return but return the `HRESULT` to its own caller.
- ❏ In particular, follow the on-error memory allocation convention religiously.

Chapter 3

IDL Aliasing

- ❏ IDL aliasing can be handy if you're trying to override the marshaling of legacy types and interfaces.
- ❏ It can also be useful if you need to optimize the marshaling behavior of an interface.
- ❏ However, it doesn't come without its problems. If you're trying to use IDL aliasing to optimize marshaling behavior, consider doing it explicitly instead.

Miscellaneous

- ❏ Consider having dynamically typed (`iid_is()`) interface parameters to a method. This buys you flexibility at the expense of semantic strictness.
- ❏ Using `structs` and unions instead of properties on a dual interface can greatly increase performance.

What's Next

In the next chapter, we'll focus on some details of Automation that we haven't looked at as yet, as well as various type attributes that were introduced largely for the benefit of the various tools that work with type libraries.

Automation & Tool Support

So far, we've looked at COM interfaces and marshaling. In this chapter, I want to examine Automation interfaces in greater detail than we've done to date. From a design standpoint, the most interesting feature of Automation interfaces is that they enforce much weaker typing than COM interfaces. I'm going to look at the various features of Automation that make this possible and explore the design consequences, introducing the relevant IDL keywords as I proceed.

After completing this look at Automation interfaces, I'll examine a miscellaneous collection of IDL that was introduced to facilitate usage by "visual" tools. These IDL features are relatively ad-hoc, having been introduced originally for use by Visual Basic at design time, which is the context in which I will illustrate them. In principle, however, they can be extended to any design time environment.

Before discussing Automation in depth, it is reasonable to review the reasons for its existence. Automation interfaces were originally created to allow interpreted languages to access user-defined OO functionality. The idea was that the client should not have to keep track of different vtable interfaces, or know how to set up the stack, or even be aware of any marshaling details – it only had to understand the single interface `IDispatch`. Over time, however, the technology for using COM interfaces has become fairly accessible (Visual Basic, the original Automation controller, now uses vtable interfaces directly), so why bother with Automation any more?

❑ An Automation-style interface allows dynamically typed invocations. This property, also known as **late binding**, has the following important characteristics:

  ❑ Names of methods and parameters can be bound at runtime

  ❑ The data type of a property does not have to be static

  ❑ The number and type of parameters to a method can vary

  ❑ Interface properties and methods can be added and deleted after the interface is 'published', even dynamically at runtime

Strictly speaking, only the first and last characteristics actually distinguish Automation interfaces from vtable interfaces. As we will see, varying the number and type of parameters in Automation is achieved by the use of a catchall VARIANT type, an option that is also available to ordinary vtable interfaces.

❑ VBScript and other scripting languages are still unable to use vtable interfaces. This means that if you want to script objects from Internet Explorer (for instance), you are restricted to using Automation interfaces. This is a strong practical incentive for caring about Automation. Although it would be technologically feasible to throw the full Visual Basic engine into VBScript, keeping scripting languages late-bound and 'type-less' increases their ease-of-use for novice programmers. Because of this, it is not desirable to make scripting languages strongly typed.

Automation and Dynamic Interfaces

This chapter begins by examining the use of dynamically defined interfaces. I shall then look at further details of Automation and dual interfaces, including details of the VARIANT type that makes much of the dynamic behavior of Automation interfaces possible.

In order to illustrate some of the effects of the IDL being introduced we will need some client-side code. Since the primary beneficiaries of Automation-style interfaces are Visual Basic and the scripting languages, the client samples are in Visual Basic and JScript.

If you're not familiar with the use of COM objects from these languages, jump ahead and quickly skim Chapter 6.

Dynamic or Weakly Typed Interfaces

From an interface designer's perspective, the most interesting feature of Automation is that it allows a certain degree of weak or dynamic typing. In situations where your interface functionality *must* be dynamic, Automation-style interfaces are the only viable option. When is this kind of dynamic functionality required?

❑ The ability to add members to an interface after it has been published can be quite handy. It allows an interface to be extended in various directions by various classes in ways that could not have been predicted when it was created. The clients of such extended interfaces can then use any extensions they know about in addition to the base interface. From the standpoint of inheritance, each interface so extended really 'derives' from the original.

❑ The ability to add members dynamically can be used to permit different objects of a class to be distinguished by the members that each has added to the base interface. This kind of conditional interface extension can be viewed as a form of 'dynamic' interface inheritance.

❑ The ability to call a method with different numbers and types of parameters is perhaps the most commonly used feature of Automation-style interfaces. It serves the same design function as method name overloading does in strongly typed languages, but while it's much more flexible, it's also much less type-safe.

The first two applications are both ways of deriving new interfaces from existing ones in a loosely typed fashion. There are few situations in which this kind of run-time or delayed inheritance is essential, but when it is, nothing else will do. The third application of dynamic typing allows the programmer to overload an interface member with different semantics depending on the actual call signature – it's a form of polymorphic method call.

Yet another form of dynamic typing is possible: an 'expando' interface is one that can be modified by the *client*, which can add or delete members. This kind of interface is required in order to allow script programmers to define new interfaces from scratch when working in a purely interpreted environment. The new interface is defined by adding members to an 'empty' or previously existing interface. Automation has been extended to allow this kind of functionality by the creation of the `IDispatchEx` interface, which we will look at in a later section.

Bear in mind that dynamic interfaces are intrinsically weakly typed, with all the problems that are associated with this. They should only be used to solve problems that cannot be solved by strongly typed COM interfaces.

The dispinterface: IDispatch

To refresh your memory, let's look again at the `IDispatch` interface definition from Chapter 2:

```
[
    object,
    uuid(00020400-0000-0000-C000-000000000046)
]
interface IDispatch : IUnknown
{
    HRESULT GetTypeInfoCount([out] UINT* pctinfo);

    HRESULT GetTypeInfo([in] UINT iTInfo,
                        [in] LCID lcid,
                        [out] ITypeInfo** ppTInfo);

    HRESULT GetIDsOfNames([in] REFIID riid,
                          [in] LPOLESTR* rgszNames,
                          [in] UINT cNames,
                          [in] LCID lcid,
                          [out] DISPID* rgDispId);

    [local] HRESULT Invoke([in] DISPID dispIdMember,
                           [in] REFIID riid,
                           [in] LCID lcid,
                           [in] WORD wFlags,
                           [in, out] DISPPARAMS* pDispParams,
                           [out] VARIANT* pVarResult,
                           [out] EXCEPINFO* pExcepInfo,
                           [out] UINT* puArgErr);
};
```

Many users of 'ordinary' Automation, such as the current generation of scripting languages, are only capable of using the primary Automation interface of a class – that is, the interface returned upon querying for `IDispatch`. Other users (like Visual Basic) that are capable of using type libraries can query for and use *any* Automation-capable interface made visible in this way. They can thus use *multiple* Automation interfaces on an object.

Also recall that Automation-only interfaces are defined in IDL using the `dispinterface` keyword. Declaring a dispinterface in IDL automatically implies that the actual implementation will be an implementation of the `IDispatch` interface. However, as mentioned in Chapter 2, the IDL for dispinterfaces has no notion of inheritance associated with it, unlike the IDL for COM interfaces. Let's now take a more detailed look at some of the attributes associated with dispinterfaces that we didn't see in Chapter 2.

The propputref Attribute

You may remember `DMyInterface` from Chapter 2; we used it to demonstrate some of the IDL attributes we were looking at there. Here it is again with a small addition that certainly needs some explanation:

```
dispinterface DMyInterface
{
properties:
methods:
    [id(3), propget] long lMyProp();
    [id(3), propput] void lMyProp([in] long l);
    [id(3), propputref] void lMyProp([in] IDispatch* pDisp);
    [id(4)] long MyMethod([in] long l1, [in] long l2);
};
```

The `propputref` attribute is an odd little thing that has its origins in the idiosyncrasies of Visual Basic syntax. Consider the following Visual Basic code:

```
Dim val as DMyOtherInterface
Dim var as DMyInterface

...

Set var.lMyProp = val
var.lMyProp = val
```

The two assignments are both permissible, but mean completely different things. The use of the `Set` keyword in the first assignment indicates that `lMyProp` is being assigned an interface – in this case, the `DMyOtherInterface` interface contained in the `val` variable. The second assignment is a simple one, where the *value* of the `val` object, which is the value of the default member of the `DMyOtherInterface` interface (the default member is the member tagged by the `DISPID_VALUE` ID, as will be explained shortly), is being assigned to the `lMyProp` property of the `DMyInterface` interface.

The first assignment is carried out using the `propputref` method associated with the `lMyProp` property, while the second assignment uses the `propput` method. In order for this to work, both the `propputref` *and* `propput` methods must be defined. If you're confused by this way of doing things, you're not alone. While Visual Basic has many good features that have fundamentally changed the nature of programming, the definition of the language was predominantly market-driven rather than being designed, and sometimes it shows.

Notice the signature of the `propputref` method: it takes a single `[in] IDispatch*` parameter. As we shall see in Chapter 6, this is how Visual Basic passes object references (hence the 'ref' in `propputref`).

The id() Attribute

As you know, the Automation invocation mechanism uses 32-bit DISPIDs to identify methods and properties. At runtime, the Automation client can use either the name (late binding) or the DISPID (early binding) to invoke Automation properties and methods. When a name is used, an extra step (calling `GetIDsOfNames()`) is required to look up the DISPID corresponding to that name.

Each interface member in an Automation or dual interface *must* be assigned a DISPID. Also, each DISPID in an Automation or dual interface must be assigned to *at most* one member (except in the case where a property is declared using multiple methods, each with its own separate declaration, but all referring to the same member property). Although MIDL will generate IDs for you if you don't specify them (using the DISPID rules coming up in the next section), it is best to specify DISPIDs in your IDL code explicitly, since they are the 'real' names of Automation members.

Dispatch ID Format

Ideally, the dispatch ID should conform to some rules that are designed to ensure there are no clashes between DISPIDs that are independently generated. If IDs are not specified for an interface, MIDL automatically generates DISPIDs that follow these rules:

Bits	Value
0–15	Offset. Any value is permissible.
16–21	The nesting level of this type information in the inheritance hierarchy. The nesting level goes as follows: `IUnknown` = 0; `IDispatch` (inherits from `IUnknown`) = 1; any dual interface (inherits from `IDispatch`) = 2. To be consistent with the numbering of an equivalent dual interface, Automation interfaces should be numbered 2 as well.
22–25	Reserved; must be zero.
26–28	DISPID value. Used to aggregate related DISPIDs. Typically 0 in user code.
29	TRUE if this is the ID for a method, otherwise FALSE. This will always be 1 if you want to be consistent with the numbering scheme for dual interfaces, which can only use the method syntax for properties.
30–31	Must be 01 (that is, positive).

For example:

```
[propget] long lMyProp();
```

If we follow the rules strictly, the DISPID for this property of the `DMyInterface` interface will be made up like this:

Bits	Value	Reason
0-15	0x1	Pick 1 because it's the first property in the list.
16-21	0x2	This is an Automation interface, so treat it as if it were a dual interface. This keeps things consistent with what the ID would be if we were defining a dual interface instead.
22-25	0x0	*See above table*
26-28	0x0	There is only one set of IDs for this interface, so pick 0.
29	0x1	*See above table*
30-31	0x1	*See above table*

Put all this together, and we have the hexadecimal number 0x60020001. The rules might seem a little peculiar, especially the one about inheritance depth for bits 16-21 (why would it ever be anything but 2?), but their origins betray the fact that the DISPID format grew out of a more generalized type information scheme that was not restricted to COM/IDL dispatch/dual interfaces. In the broader context, where IDs needed to be assigned to interfaces that were related by inheritance, there were possibilities of clashes. As an example of what could go wrong, consider the following two Automation-capable interfaces (these are dual interfaces, but they're needed for this discussion):

```
interface IFirstLevel : IDispatch
{
    [propget, id(1)] HRESULT Prop1Level1(long*);
};

interface ISecondLevel : IFirstLevel
{
    [propget, id(1)] HRESULT Prop1Level2(char*);
};
```

`IFirstLevel` doesn't pose any problems at all, but `ISecondLevel` does because we've reused the DISPID value 1 to refer to a different property. This violates the rule that a DISPID can only be associated with a single interface member. If we had used IDs that followed the DISPID numbering rules, the fact that `IFirstLevel` is at level 2 and `ISecondLevel` is at level 3 would have forced the DISPID values to be different. In practice, this is not how most dual interfaces are defined, so the problem is seldom made apparent.

Unfortunately, not all tools create IDs that conform to this format, although MIDL *will* generate conforming DISPIDs for those interface members that do not have them explicitly specified. The Visual C++ property and method Wizards are notable culprits for not adhering to these rules. As I've said, this does not tend to cause problems in practice, since most interfaces are defined in a manner that avoids the issue, and no tools seem to expect this format.

Special DISPID Values

I mentioned the 'default' member of an interface in an earlier example, but I haven't yet shown you how it is specified in IDL. How, for example, would we specify the default value of the DMyOtherInterface dispinterface above? The answer is that we use a special DISPID, DISPID_VALUE:

```
dispinterface DMyOtherInterface
{
properties:
methods:
   [id(DISPID_VALUE), propget] long Value();
};
```

The DISPID_VALUE macro is #define'd to the constant 0. Any member, property or method, that has an id() attribute of 0 is presumed by Visual Basic (and other Automation clients) to be the default member of the interface. Like all other dispatch IDs, the value should be assigned to *at most* one interface member, since the consequences of not doing so are undefined.

This is an example of a general technique for extending attribute specification without introducing new keywords into IDL. Many non-positive dispatch ID values have special meanings to specific users of interfaces. The most common of these DISPID values other than DISPID_VALUE are:

❑ DISPID_NEWENUM (-4) is used to tag a property in a collection interface that returns an IEnumVARIANT enumerator for the collection

❑ DISPID_EVALUATE (-5) is used to tag an evaluation function that is called by the Visual Basic interpreter whenever it encounters square braces in an expression

Consider the following IDL:

```
dispinterface IMyRecord : IDispatch
{
   [id(DISPID_EVALUATE)] VARIANT _MyEvaluate([in] VARIANT Name);
};
```

Thus, the Visual Basic expression

```
record[fieldname] = 10
```

(where record is an Automation interface of type IMyRecord) is translated to this expression:

```
record._MyEvaluate("fieldname") = 10
```

As you can see from the IDL code, _MyEvaluate() is the method on the interface that is identified by the ID DISPID_EVALUATE. Special or 'well known' IDs like these always have values that are negative (or 0 for DISPID_VALUE). Microsoft has reserved several ranges of negative numbers for specific tools and technologies, so in general it is safest not to use negative DISPIDs in your own interfaces (in fact it's impossible if you stick to the DISPID creation rules).

Another common set of predefined DISPIDs is the one defined for ActiveX control technology. Users of ActiveX controls – in other words, ActiveX control containers – recognize these IDs as having special meanings, and you'll find a list of them in the Olectl.h header that ships with Visual C++.

Extensible Interfaces

By default, all Automation interfaces are assumed to be extensible – the user of an interface should assume that methods and properties may be added to it at runtime. For a user such as Visual Basic, this restricts the amount of compile-time type checking that's possible. For instance, look at the following Visual Basic code:

```
Dim Foo as DMyInterface
Dim FooBar as DMyOtherInterface

...

Foo.lMyProp = FooBar
Foo.lMyProp10 = FooBar
```

We know that `lMyProp10` has not been declared a property of `DMyInterface`, but this 'error' won't be caught at compile time because the compiler cannot know if the interface will create the property at runtime. To force the compiler to register this as an error, the interface should be declared to be non-extensible, as follows:

```
[
    nonextensible,
    uuid(...)
]
dispinterface DMyInterface
{
    ...
};
```

IDispatch Interface Constraints

Extensible interfaces raise an interesting question about the binding of names to DISPIDs. Are there any constraints to this binding? It turns out that the rules for extensible Automation interfaces are:

❑ The DISPID of an existing method cannot be reused when extending the interface
❑ A dynamically created member cannot be deleted during the lifetime of the object
❑ The DISPID of a dynamically created member must remain constant for the lifetime of the object

Example

To summarize the use of dispinterfaces, consider an object model with two interfaces: an object interface called `DSimple` and a collection interface called `DSimples`. Here is the IDL for this interface:

```
dispinterface DSimple
{
properties:
methods:
    [id(DISPID_VALUE), propget] VARIANT ValueProp();
    [id(DISPID_VALUE), propput] void ValueProp([in] VARIANT vnt);
    [id(DISPID_VALUE), propputref] void ValueProp([in] IDispatch* pDsp);
    [id(0x60020000)] void DoSomething();
    [id(0x60020001), propget] IDispatch* SomeObject();
};
```

```
dispinterface DSimples
{
    [id(DISPID_VALUE), propget] VARIANT Item(VARIANT vnt);
    [id(DISPID_EVALUATE), propget] VARIANT Eval(VARIANT vnt);
    [id(DISPID_NEWENUM), propget] IUnknown* _NewEnum();
};
```

Let's see how this can be used in Visual Basic:

```
Dim smp as DSimple
Dim scoll as DSimples
Dim vnt as Variant

Set smp = scoll(10)          ' Return the 10th item in collection

vnt = smp.ValueProp          ' Get the value of property named ValueProp
vnt = smp                    ' Get the value of the default member,
                             ' which is also ValueProp

vnt = scoll(10)              ' Get the value of the 10th item, i.e. value of
                             ' default member of object that is 10th item.
                             ' Same as above

smp.ValueProp = "Hello"      ' Set the value of ValueProp to the string "Hello"

Set smp.ValueProp = smp.SomeObject   ' Set the object reference of ValueProp
                                     ' to the object returned by SomeObject

vnt = scoll[foo]             ' Call the Evaluate method Eval()
vnt = scoll.Eval("foo")

For Each smp In scoll Do     ' Iterate over collection using IEnumVARIANT
    vnt = smp
Next smp
```

Note the heavy use of the 'well-known' DISPIDs to abbreviate the code. Unfortunately, in my opinion this also obscures what is really going on. The equivalent lines of code that do not depend on the implicit use of DISPIDs look much clearer to me.

Truly Dynamic Interfaces: IDispatchEx

So far, the dynamic behavior that we have seen has been restricted to allowing the object implementation to *add* additional members to an Automation-capable interface at runtime. What about the situation where we want to *delete* members at runtime, or allow the *user* (rather than the object implementation) to add and delete members at runtime? Straight Automation does not permit either to happen.

Although the ability to delete interface members at runtime seems a fairly dubious practice, there is certainly a sensible application for programmatically *adding* members. Allowing a client to add interface members is a potentially useful feature for scripting languages that allow dynamic type creation.

Here is an example in JScript; at the time of writing, VBScript does not permit this extreme form of dynamically typed interface:

```
function AddBar()
{
   this.bar = "Hello World";
}

function Foo()
{
   this.func = AddBar;
}

function Run()
{
   obj = new Foo;
   obj.func();
}
```

The JScript function `AddBar()` simply assigns the value `"Hello World"` to the `bar` property of the `this` variable – that is, the object being used to invoke `AddBar()`. If the `bar` property doesn't already exist on the `this` object, it will be created.

The function `Foo()` is assigning the `AddBar()` method to the `func` member of the object pointed to by the `this` pointer. This is how a method is assigned to an interface. Note that the method could have been dynamically assigned to *any interface at all*, and would continue to work correctly. This is a big change from the static interface/object model that we have become accustomed to. As before, the `func` member will be created if it doesn't already exist.

The first line of the `Run()` function creates a new object called `obj`, using the function `Foo` as a constructor. This initializes the `func` member to `AddBar()`. The second line calls the member method `func` (that is, `AddBar()`). This has the effect of adding the member `bar` to `obj`. Thus, the interface is progressively changed by the addition of new members.

Regardless of whether you believe this behavior to be a feature or a bug of scripting languages, it is a fundamentally new kind of interface. In fact, the behavior is enabled by an extension of the `IDispatch` interface called `IDispatchEx`, which enables the following:

- ❑ Programmatic addition of members to an existing interface
- ❑ Programmatic deletion of members from an existing interface
- ❑ Passing a `this` parameter into a method invocation
- ❑ Navigation and informational querying of the members of an interface

`IDispatchEx` is derived from the `IDispatch` interface, and can be considered an extended version of it. Its declaration is as follows:

```
[
    object,
    uuid(A6EF9860-C720-11D0-9337-00A0C90DCAA9),
    pointer_default(unique)
]
```

```
interface IDispatchEx : IDispatch
{
    HRESULT GetDispID([in] BSTR bstrName,
                      [in] DWORD grfdex,
                      [out] DISPID* pid);

    [local] HRESULT InvokeEx([in] DISPID id,
                             [in] LCID lcid,
                             [in] WORD wFlags,
                             [in] DISPPARAMS* pdp,
                             [out] VARIANT* pvarRes,
                             [out] EXCEPINFO* pei,
                             [in, unique] IServiceProvider* pspCaller);

    HRESULT DeleteMemberByName([in] BSTR bstr,
                               [in] DWORD grfdex);

    HRESULT DeleteMemberByDispID([in] DISPID id);

    HRESULT GetMemberProperties([in] DISPID id,
                                [in] DWORD grfdexFetch,
                                [out] DWORD* pgrfdex);

    HRESULT GetMemberName([in] DISPID id,
                          [out] BSTR* pbstrName);

    HRESULT GetNextDispID([in] DWORD grfdex,
                          [in] DISPID id,
                          [out] DISPID* pid);

    HRESULT GetNameSpaceParent([out] IUnknown** ppunk);
};
```

InvokeEx()

The most important method of this new interface is `InvokeEx()`, which is an extension of the `IDispatch::Invoke()` method. You can see that its signature is very similar to that of `Invoke()`, although the `IID` parameter (which was unused) and the final `UINT` parameter (which was redundant) have both been dropped. More importantly, a new `IServiceProvider*` parameter has been introduced.

The new parameter is used to provide a generic way to pass caller context information into the method invocation. The `IServiceProvider` interface has one method – `QueryService()` – that can be used to query for arbitrary services in objects associated with the caller. A JScript object, for instance, might use this parameter to gain access to the scripting engine or some other service associated with the web browser.

The other extensions provided by InvokeEx() are:

❑ The ability to specify that a method invocation is actually the constructor for the object. This is achieved by passing a wFlags value of DISPATCH_CONSTRUCTOR, and is the secret of the code that lies behind a JScript constructor such as this line that we saw earlier:

```
obj = new Foo;
```

❑ The ability to pass the this parameter into a method. This is accomplished by passing in a 'named' parameter in the DISPPARAMS structure. The named parameter must have a DISPID of DISPID_THIS, and be the first parameter in the named parameter array. This is how the this parameter is transmitted in the translation of a JScript call into IDispatchEx::Invoke():

```
obj.func();
```

Interface Querying Functionality

For the most part, the other new methods in IDispatchEx provide functionality to manipulate interface metadata.

❑ New members can be added to an interface by using GetDispID()
❑ DeleteMemberByName() and DeleteMemberByDispID() allow removal of existing interface members
❑ GetMemberProperties() retrieves the properties associated with a given interface member
❑ GetNextDispID() allows enumeration over all members
❑ GetMemberName() allows a lookup of a member name given its DISPID
❑ For scripting clients that support namespaces, GetNameSpaceParent() gets the namespace to which the object belongs

IDispatchEx Interface Constraints

Naturally, there are restrictions on the behavior of IDispatchEx interfaces, and these are different from the restrictions on IDispatch interfaces, since the former allows members to be deleted.

❑ The mapping between a member name and a DISPID is constant, so the ID of a deleted member can only be used to add a member of the same name
❑ GetNextDispID() must continue to return the ID during enumeration
❑ All other methods that work with members must fail gracefully when an attempt is made to pass a deleted member as an argument

At the time of writing, there is no IDL support specific to interfaces implemented using IDispatchEx.

Automation Data Types

You'll recall that methods of Automation interfaces are restricted to parameters that fall within the set of Automation types, but what exactly *are* these types? In addition to the base IDL data types, Automation supports a number of typedef'd scalar types for specific purposes. It also supports a couple of complex types to represent character strings and arrays, and finally it has the catchall VARIANT type that is a union of all other supported types.

For now, we'll just examine the IDL associated with these data types. In the next chapter, we'll take a closer look at the various client language constructs that these types are bound to.

Scalar Types

The new `typedef`'d scalar types used by Automation are:

Type	Description
VARIANT_BOOL	This is a 16-bit value (`typedef`'d to a `short`) corresponding to a Visual Basic `Boolean`. Atypically, `VARIANT_TRUE` is defined to be −1, while `VARIANT_FALSE` is 0. By contrast `BOOL` is a more traditional 32-bit C/C++ Boolean value.
CURRENCY	This is a 64-bit value that's used to represent amounts of money.
DATE	A floating-point type (`typedef`'d to a `double`) that's used to represent instants in time.
DECIMAL	A 16-*byte* (96 bits plus scale and sign) fixed point number.

Strings

Automation uses the Visual Basic `String` type as its way of representing strings; it is given the type name `BSTR` in IDL. Here's the IDL declaration for `BSTR`:

```
typedef wchar_t WCHAR;
...
typedef WCHAR OLECHAR;
...
typedef [wire_marshal(wireBSTR)] OLECHAR* BSTR;
```

So, a `BSTR` is the same as a pointer to a wide character... or is it? It turns out that this is not the case. As a matter of fact, a `BSTR` is actually (a C-style pointer to the beginning of) an array of wide characters (usually encoded in Unicode) that is prefixed by a header containing its length (number of bytes not including the final null character, stored as a `long`). This prefix immediately precedes the first character in memory. The character following the last character in the string is null, although the array may also contain other null characters.

You saw the meaning of the `wire_marshal()` *attribute in the previous chapter.*

This situation is best illustrated by looking at the memory taken up by a sample `BSTR`, in this case the string 'Hello World!':

```
00143660   18 00 00 00 48 00 65 00   ....H.e.
00143668   6C 00 6C 00 6F 00 20 00   l.l.o. .
00143670   57 00 6F 00 72 00 6C 00   W.o.r.l.
00143678   64 00 21 00 00 00 AD BA   d.!...-°
```

The length of the string (12 characters taking up 24 bytes) is given by the hexadecimal value 18, which corresponds to decimal 24. An interesting feature of the length being stored separately is that it's possible to include null characters as part of the string – you don't have to rely on them as delimiters.

BSTR and OLESTR

Be *very* careful not to mix up BSTR values with WCHAR* variables and vice versa. BSTRs *have* to be allocated, released and manipulated using the BSTR API calls (see Chapter 6), whereas regular wide character strings *must not*. Unfortunately, the C++ type system allows the one to be substituted for the other, since they both look like pointers to wide characters, so you the programmer have to exercise extra caution.

Arrays

Just as the BSTR is based on Visual Basic strings, the Automation multidimensional array type is based on Visual Basic multidimensional arrays. The type is denoted by SAFEARRAY, whose IDL declaration looks like this:

```
typedef struct tagSAFEARRAYBOUND
{
    ULONG           cElements;        // Count of elements
    LONG            lLbound;          // Lower bound
} SAFEARRAYBOUND;

...

typedef struct tagSAFEARRAY
{
    USHORT          cDims;            // Number of dimensions
    USHORT          fFeatures;        // Flags
    ULONG           cbElements;       // Size of individual element
    ULONG           cLocks;           // Number of accessors
    PVOID           pvData;           // Pointer to beginning of array data
    SAFEARRAYBOUND  rgsabound[];      // Array of dimensional bound values
} SAFEARRAY;
```

The rgsabound member is an array of SAFEARRAYBOUND values, each describing the extents (lower bound and size) of a single dimension of the array. Two of the remaining members of the structure keep track of the number of dimensions and the size of an individual element in the array; the others are a pointer to the actual data, a variable for holding other properties, and an access count.

A SAFEARRAY is unusual in that the individual elements of the array can be of *any* Automation type (including the VARIANT type that we'll look at next). This enables Automation arrays to be parameterized by type, so the IDL for a SAFEARRAY parameter takes this form:

```
HRESULT Test([in] SAFEARRAY(DATE) a_psaDATE);
```

Here, the array declaration is parameterized by the type of its element. This IDL actually indicates a pointer to a SAFEARRAY structure.

Variants

Finally, we have the VARIANT type. This is equivalent to the Variant type used in Visual Basic to provide a catchall that is the *actual* type underlying an 'untyped' Visual Basic expression. A VARIANT is a discriminated union of all the Automation types – NULL (database NULL value), EMPTY (no value), signed and unsigned 1, 2, 4 and 8 byte integers, FLOAT, DOUBLE, VARIANT_BOOL, SCODE, CY, DATE, DECIMAL, BSTR, IUnknown*, IDispatch* and SAFEARRAY*. The latest versions of VARIANT also allow a user-defined type to be stored.

The (abbreviated) IDL for VARIANT is:

```
typedef struct tagVARIANT VARIANT;

struct tagVARIANT {
   union
   {
      struct __tagVARIANT {
         VARTYPE vt;
         WORD    wReserved1;
         WORD    wReserved2;
         WORD    wReserved3;
         union
         {
            LONG           lVal;        /* VT_I4           */
            // Remaining VARIANT types

         } __VARIANT_NAME_3;
      } __VARIANT_NAME_2;
      DECIMAL decVal;
   } __VARIANT_NAME_1;
};
```

The VARTYPE member holds the discriminating field that specifies what type is actually being held in the VARIANT at present.

The VARIANT type in IDL can be a little confusing because it is used not only to represent values that can be Visual Basic Variants, but also values that can be arguments to a Visual Basic method invocation. (This makes the IDL VARIANT a slightly more general type than the Visual Basic Variant.) 'Variant' types are also used in TYPEDESCs, OLE property sets and SAFEARRAYs; each of these applications grants a slightly different set of permissible sub-types.

VARIANT Variation

Not only is the VARIANT type used in various applications other than Automation, its use in Automation has changed over the years. There are more types usable in Automation today than there were a few years ago. However, the changes have been made in a backward-compatible fashion, so code compiled several years ago will still work correctly with today's VARIANTs – it will just be unaware of the new options that have been introduced into the discriminated union.

It is therefore not safe to assume that an old implementation of an Automation interface will correctly support the newer VARIANT options (such as VT_RECORD, for instance). An Automation controller must therefore make conservative assumptions about Automation types. This is not generally a problem, since controllers such as Visual Basic have not really expanded the set of native types in a while.

This is another reason to encourage the creation of system-supplied, type-library driven, run-time generated, automatic implementations of Automation interfaces that proxy programmer-supplied dual or vtable interfaces. Such a proxy can always be recompiled to reflect the newest version of the VARIANT type, but continue working with the subset of types implemented by the old interface.

In fact, this is why each new version of the type library marshaler continues working with all the old interfaces – the set of types it can marshal only grows with time.

Parameter Variation

The following techniques can be used to permit dynamic parameters in both Automation and vtable interfaces.

Dynamic Parameter Typing

What does it mean to have a parameter whose type is determined at runtime? How is one to declare such a parameter? If you declare the parameter to be of type VARIANT, the actual argument can be of any type that a VARIANT can encapsulate. At runtime, the server code must determine the actual type in the VARIANT argument, and perform the appropriate actions for that type.

In general, a parameter should be declared a VARIANT *only* if the method is prepared to take different actions for different actual parameter types – to behave in true polymorphic fashion. This is in keeping with the general principles of strong typing; a declaration should have the strongest possible type that is sufficient for its intended use. It is a misconception that you need to declare a VARIANT parameter just to help the client avoid a type conversion – in most cases, a system-supplied translation layer (such as the Dispatch API) that sits between the client and the server will automatically perform such conversions.

Consider, for instance, an Add() method declared like so:

```
HRESULT Add([in] VARIANT v1, [in] VARIANT v2, [out, retval] VARIANT* v);
```

This might perform integer addition on integer types, floating point addition on floating point numbers, string concatenation on BSTRs, and string creation and concatenation on wchar_ts. For mixed types, it might choose to widen the narrower type, but it should not be used to convert all parameters to integers in order to perform integer addition. That is better accomplished by the method with this signature, where the conversions are performed explicitly by the client or by a translation runtime sitting between client and server:

```
HRESULT Add([in] LONG v1, [in] LONG v2, [out, retval] LONG* v);
```

One common scenario in which a VARIANT is employed as suggested above is where it holds a value from a database field. Many databases require their fields to be typed, but allow the untyped NULL value to represent an empty field. The Microsoft client-side database APIs can return a VARIANT in such an instance that will have a value of either the field type or the VT_NULL type. The method implementation will typically take different actions in the two cases.

Optional Parameters

IDL allows the specification of optional parameters to a method with the optional attribute. Such parameters must have a base type that is one of the Automation types. If the parameter is omitted, a default value can be passed into the actual invocation.

If the parameter is of type VARIANT then, in the event of an absent parameter, the error value (tag VT_ERROR) DISP_E_PARAMNOTFOUND is supposed to be passed into the method. It is the responsibility of the client or the Automation controller (if a runtime is present) to make this substitution.

Here is the Add() function, modified to make the second parameter optional:

```
HRESULT Add([in] VARIANT v1,
            [in, optional] VARIANT v2,
            [out, retval] VARIANT* v);
```

This method could be called from Visual Basic as follows:

```
Dim v as Variant
v = Add(1)
v = Add("Hello ", "World")
```

In the first case, the Visual Basic runtime will automatically substitute an error Variant for the missing parameters of the call.

Here is another example of a function with optional parameters; this time, the parameter type is specified to be LONG rather than an unspecified VARIANT:

```
HRESULT AddLong([in] LONG l1,
                [in, optional] LONG l2,
                [out, retval] LONG* l);
```

Here is the Visual Basic calling code:

```
Dim v as Variant
v = AddLong(1)
v = AddLong(1, 2)
```

This time, the translation layer substitutes the value 0 for the missing parameters of the call. The VT_ERROR value can't be used directly because the type of the parameter is not VARIANT. For the same reason, a call such as this would fail in the translation layer:

```
Dim v as Variant
v = AddLong("Hello ", "World")
```

> In order to avoid ambiguity, all in parameters following the first optional parameter must also be optional.

Default Values

Of course, when a parameter is optional in the manner just described, you will want to specify what value should be plugged in as the default value when the parameter is missing. This is true even if there is no obvious default value to use, since if you don't select one, the translation layer will pick one for you.

IDL provides the `defaultvalue` attribute for just this eventuality. The `defaultvalue` attribute can only be applied to typed (non-`VARIANT`), optional parameters (it implies the `optional` attribute). The supplied default must be an expression that evaluates to a scalar constant of an Automation base type. Thus, we might have this method:

```
HRESULT Multiply([in, optional, defaultvalue(1)] LONG l1,
                 [in, optional, defaultvalue(1)] LONG l2,
                 [out, retval] LONG* pl);
```

For which any missing parameters default to 1 instead of zero, and this method:

```
HRESULT Concatenate([in, optional, defaultvalue("Hello")] BSTR s1,
                    [in, optional, defaultvalue("Hello")] BSTR s2,
                    [out, retval] BSTR* ps);
```

For which the missing parameters default to the string 'Hello'.

Variable Number of Parameters

You've seen that a method with optional parameters can be called from Visual Basic as if it were a method that takes a variable number of parameters. In reality, of course, the runtime has to plug in default values for all the parameters that the programmer omitted.

There is a separate mechanism for *actually* calling a method with a variable number of arguments, involving passing a `SAFEARRAY` of `VARIANT`s as the last parameter to the method. This array contains all the remaining parameters to the method, and can have any length and contain any mixture of Automation-typed values. The method implementation is responsible for unpacking and using this array.

A method that uses this mechanism must be decorated with the `vararg` keyword. In order to prevent ambiguity about a call, such a method cannot have any `optional` parameters.

For example, we can replace our earlier `Add()` function with an `AddN()` function that takes an arbitrary number of parameters, as follows:

```
[vararg] AddN([in] SAFEARRAY(VARIANT) a_av, [out, retval] VARIANT* a_pv);
```

Localization

If you remember, I said in Chapter 2 that the late-bound characteristic of Automation implies that method and parameter names can be localized to different languages, and there is IDL support for this feature too.

The lcid() Attribute

Localization may be considered another dynamically determined aspect of a method invocation. IDL allows one of the parameters of a method on a vtable interface to be labeled with a **locale ID** – a 32-bit `long` value specifying a locale.

Libraries

Consider this IDL code:

```
[
    ...
    lcid(0x0409)
]
library LocaleLib
{
    dispinterface DHello
    {
    properties:
    methods:
        [id(0x60020000), propget] long Foo();
        [id(0x60020001)]          long Bar(short as);
    };

    interface IHello : IDispatch
    {
        [id(0x60020000), propget] HRESULT Foo([in, lcid]    long  lcid,
                                              [out, retval] long* pl);

        [id(0x60020001)] HRESULT Bar([in]          short as,
                                     [in, lcid]    long  lcid,
                                     [out, retval] long* pl);
    };
};
```

As you can see, the `library` statement is decorated with an `lcid()` attribute that allows all the strings, names, etc. in the library section of the IDL file to be localized. When you're localizing a library section in this fashion, you will need multiple IDL files – one for each locale. This will then be translated into multiple type library files, again one for each locale.

This IDL code identifies the library as being created for locale ID `0x0409`, which corresponds to US English. There are two interfaces in the body of the library: one is the Automation interface `DHello`, while the other is the equivalent dual interface `IHello`.

Parameters

In Chapter 2, I mentioned that three of the `IDispatch` methods, including `Invoke()`, took an `LCID` parameter. In our example, notice that the methods on `DHello` have no parameters decorated with the `lcid` attribute, whereas the `IHello` methods each have an in, `lcid` parameter of type `long`. The boilerplate, vtable-delegating implementation of `IDispatch::Invoke()` will pass the value of its `LCID` parameter into the method parameter that has the `lcid` attribute. In turn, the method implementation must use the parameter value to perform the actual localization.

The locale ID parameter has to be an `in`-only `long` parameter decorated with the keyword `lcid`. As you can see, it is the parameter immediately preceding the one marked `retval`. For a `propput` or a `propputref`, it must precede the parameter representing the new value.

As the example shows, a dispinterface method does not contain a locale ID (it isn't necessary); only a method on a COM interface can have a locale ID.

Afrikaans

Here is the same IDL file, localized to Afrikaans (with apologies to my Dutch and Afrikaner readers). You can see that I have a pretty simplistic view of the language!

```
[
    ...
    lcid(0x0436)
]
library LocaaleLib
{
    dispinterface DHeello
    {
    properties:
    methods:
        [id(0x60020000), propget] long Foooo();
        [id(0x60020001)]          long Baar(short as);
    };

    interface IHeello : IDispatch
    {
        [id(0x60020000), propget] HRESULT Foooo([in, lcid]    long  lcid,
                                                [out, retval] long* pl);

        [id(0x60020001)] HRESULT Baar([in]          short as,
                                      [in, lcid]    long  lcid,
                                      [out, retval] long* pl);
    };
};
```

As you can see, all I did was change various strings in the library section of the file. In general, the strings will not be represented in Latin characters, but the transformation is equally trivial. The type library that is compiled from this file will be the one that is actually used by the Dispatch API implementation of the dual interface. The boilerplate IDispatch implementation based on the Dispatch API simply points at this library, instead of the English one. This is easily arranged by having the install program set the configuration to point at the appropriate file.

Parameter Ordering

To resolve any potential for ambiguity in a method call, there are rules about the ordering of different parameters in a method signature. The parameters must be in the following order:

- ❑ All non-optional parameters
- ❑ optional or vararg parameters:
    - ❑ All optional parameters with explicitly specified default values
    - ❑ All optional parameters without default values

  or:

    - ❑ A SAFEARRAY of VARIANTs representing a variable number of parameters
- ❑ An lcid parameter
- ❑ The retval parameter (the RHS value in a propput or propputref method)

Tool Support

IDL has a number of attributes that were created largely for use by various tools, beginning with the Visual Basic design-time environment. These attributes are related to Automation only inasmuch as both sets of attributes grew out of Visual Basic, but this seems to be as good a time as any to take a look at them.

It is a good idea to mention up front that these keywords are, for the most part, simple documentation. It is up to the tool (frequently a language design-time environment; occasionally a runtime) to read the type library and act upon the keywords. None of these keywords affects the marshaling code that is generated from the IDL description. The only code that *is* affected by some of these keywords is the Dispatch API that uses the type library description to implement the Automation side of a dual interface. It pays attention to a limited set of attributes, such as `restricted`.

Connectable Objects

As I explained in Chapter 2, the connectable object protocol is a general-purpose protocol for working with outgoing interfaces. An outgoing interface, in turn, is the OO equivalent of a callback function – it is called (rather than being implemented) by the object that declares it.

The connectable object protocol is a specific protocol (defined for the OLE control specification and Visual Basic) that allows a container to register sink interfaces with an object. There is no strong requirement to use the connection point protocol for sinks defined in your application, and, as a matter of fact, it introduces significant overhead to the registration process (although none to the actual callback, which is, after all, the more common operation). However, as mentioned earlier, there is a lot of tool support for this protocol and it is in widespread use; it can be an easy protocol to support, and IDL has a couple of keywords with that in mind.

The source Attribute

The `source` attribute is used to declare the outgoing interfaces of a class – more specifically, those that have been implemented using the connectable object protocol. It is used in this way:

```
coclass MyObject
{
    [default, source] DMyOutGoingInterface;
    [source] DMyOutGoingInterface2;
};
```

The declaration above indicates that `DMyOutGoingInterface` and `DMyOutGoingInterface2` are outgoing interfaces of the coclass called `MyObject` – in other words, the `MyObject` coclass makes calls on this interface.

In a sense, this information is redundant because a tool can always *query* for `IConnectionPointContainer`, the interface that allows the client to navigate all the outgoing interfaces supported by a class. However, by the same token you might just as well argue that there is no need to declare the incoming interfaces on a class, since they can be discovered indirectly via `QueryInterface()` (and an enumeration of all the interfaces known to man).

In addition, the *default* source interface is the one that is assumed to be the most important event set interface for the object – the interface that Visual Basic and other container tools 'associate' with the object. Visual Basic actually *only* associates the interface marked with the default keyword with an object (or the first one in the list if none is so marked).

Properties

The source attribute may also be applied to a property or a method of an interface. When this is done, the implication is that the property or method returns an object that sources events:

```
interface IFooBar
{
    [source, propget] HRESULT Foo([out, retval] IDispatch** a_ppDsp);
    [source] HRESULT Bar([out, retval] IMyObject** a_ppMO);
    [source] HRESULT Bar2([out, retval] VARIANT* a_pVnt);

    [propget] HRESULT NSFoo([out, retval] IDispatch** a_ppDsp);
    [propget] HRESULT NSBar([out, retval] IMyObject** a_ppMO);
};
```

The intent of all the source declarations is to optimize tools (such as the Visual Basic design-time environment) that have access to type information. Tools like this are warned at design time about situations where they need to check for connection points and go through the connection point protocol as necessary. In all other instances (where there is no associated source keyword), there is no need to incur the overhead of running the protocol.

The defaultvtable Attribute

There is a subtle issue that arises when a dual interface is exposed as a source interface: on which side of the dual interface should the invocation occur? There is no mechanism for the sink interface (generally implemented by the client) to express a preference in the matter. The rule, therefore, is that a dual source interface is *always* called on its Automation side. If it ever becomes desirable (I can think of no situation where it is *essential*) to change this behavior, the defaultvtable attribute can be used. For example, given the dual interface IDualFoo, this declaration:

```
coclass MyClass
{
    [default, source] IDualFoo;
};
```

would require that MyClass fire events on the dispatch side of IDualFoo, while this declaration:

```
coclass MyClass
{
    [defaultvtable, source] IDualFoo;
};
```

indicates that the interface will be fired on the vtable side. So far, so good, but what about the following (legal) declaration:

```
coclass MyClass
{
    [default, source] IDualFoo;
    [defaultvtable, source] IDualFoo;
};
```

How can this possibly work? How can the object fire on both sides of the interface during a single event? Wouldn't that double the number of events received by the sink? The answer, of course, is that it can't. Sinks that want to register expecting to be fired on the Automation side of `IDualFoo` actually register for the `IDispatch` connection point. The sinks that register for `IDualFoo` will get invoked on the vtable side. The object, of course, has to implement the `IDispatch` connection point in addition to the `IDualFoo` connection point.

A Simple Design Exercise

Let's say that I want to create a simple event object, `EventObject`, with one incoming interface called `IIncoming` and three source interfaces `IOutgoing`, `IEventSet` and `ISource`. `IOutgoing` should be a dual interface that is fired on its vtable side, `IEventSet` a vtable interface, and `ISource` an ordinary dual interface that's fired on its Automation side. This design, combined with the attributes introduced above, yields the following coclass declaration:

```
coclass EventObject
{
    [default] interface IIncoming;
    [defaultvtable, source] interface IOutgoing;
    [default, source] interface IEventSet;
    [source] interface ISource;
};
```

Property Notifications and Binding

One of the standard connectable object interfaces in the OLE control specification is the `IPropertyNotifySink` interface, which is typically implemented by an ActiveX control container in order to track changes to control properties. The interface has two methods:

Method	Description
OnChanged()	Called when a property value has changed.
OnRequestEdit()	Called in order to request a change to a property value. The sink can allow or disallow the edit by returning S_OK or S_FALSE.

Each of these parameters takes a single argument that identifies the DISPID of the property to be changed.

One of the most important applications of these property notifications is in the implementation of **data bound controls**. These are visual controls on a form whose contents reflect the values in some underlying dataset. The container uses the notifications to keep the dataset and its visual representation in sync. For this reason, the IDL property notification attributes involved are sometimes called (**data**) **binding attributes**.

The binding attributes must be associated with properties on Automation interfaces. They are also associated with *all* declarations to do with the property, so they should appear in the declarations of the `propget`, `propput` and `propputref` methods.

bindable

The `bindable` attribute is used to tag a property that fires the `OnChanged()` notification. It is the most basic binding attribute, and is used by the design-time environment to ensure that the client sink handles each property that is capable of notifying.

requestedit

The `requestedit` attribute tags a property that fires `OnRequestEdit()`. It is expected that the implementation will honor the return value of the method. Once again, the purpose of this attribute is to ensure that the client sink will handle the specified property.

The `requestedit` and `bindable` attributes can be specified together or in isolation; there is no dependency between them.

defaultbind

The `defaultbind` attribute is used to identify a particular `bindable` property on an interface. The intention is that the `bindable` property so indicated best represents the entire interface, and is for use by containers that have a user model where properties are not bound individually – conceptually, the entire object is bound.

This attribute is used in Visual Basic and Visual FoxPro for simple data binding. Also, Internet Explorer uses it for data binding to an `<OBJECT>`.

Visibility

There are a number of other attributes that are present merely as hints for the various browsing mechanisms that work with type information.

appobject

The `appobject` attribute is used in situations where the type library is being used to describe an application that follows the Microsoft guidelines for structuring the object model of user-interactive programs. (For an example of such an object model, just look at any of the Office applications.) Within this object model, there is a creation hierarchy that is rooted in the so-called `Application` object.

Should you choose to build applications that follow this object model, you need to decorate the coclass of the `Application` object with the `appobject` attribute, as follows:

```
[
    ...,
    appobject,
    ...
]
coclass MyAppClass
{
    ...
```

Certain browsers and tools don't require members of the appobject coclass to be explicitly qualified with the class name. To see what this means, imagine that MyAppClass *doesn't* have the appobject attribute, but *does* have a default interface called IFoo with a member named MyAppMethod1(). The following Visual Basic code needs to be written to access the method:

```
Dim mac as IFoo
Set mac = New MyAppClass
call Mac.MyAppMethod1
```

However, if MyAppClass *does* have the appobject attribute, and provided that the appropriate type library has been referenced, then the method may be invoked simply as:

```
call MyAppMethod1
```

uidefault

The uidefault attribute is used to tag interface members for use with Visual Basic. Only one property or method on an interface should be tagged with this attribute.

On an incoming interface, the property tagged with uidefault is the one that gets the initial focus when the Visual Basic property browser displays an instance of the interface (called an 'object' in Visual Basic).

Methods can only be tagged with uidefault on an outgoing interface. When an object is double clicked in Visual Basic, the environment displays the code corresponding to the uidefault method on the default outgoing interface of the object's coclass. This is the code that Visual Basic connects to the sink implementation of that method.

restricted

The restricted keyword is used to label libraries, coclass interfaces and members of interfaces or dispinterfaces. Its intent is to mark entities that should not be made visible to the end user – in other words, entities that are meant to be used by the system, a tool or a language environment.

Prior to the introduction of this keyword, the only way to restrict visibility of a name was to begin it with the underscore character (_). This is now a deprecated practice, but it explains the convention of having a member named _NewEnum in a collection class. This member was intended to be used by the Visual Basic environment to implement For loops, and not meant for direct use by the Visual Basic programmer.

Notice that this attribute is just a hint to the appropriate language environment (and to the programmer). You cannot count on the programmer not being able to use a member that has been decorated with it. However, the Dispatch API (at the time of writing) *does* pay attention to this keyword. It will not allow an Automation call to an interface member that has been marked restricted. This leaves you with the sole option of vtable access to the member.

nonbrowsable

The nonbrowsable attribute is used with properties, and indicates that a property should not be visible in a property browser (such as the property grid in Visual Basic). It will continue to be visible, however, in an object browser (such as the Visual Studio Object Browser). Once again, this is just a hint, and you cannot assume with certainty that the property will not be visible to the programmer.

noncreatable

The `noncreatable` attribute is applied to the `coclass` statement. A non-creatable coclass is one whose objects cannot be created using normal COM calls. Specifically, it means that the object's class factory either does not exist, or is not registered with COM. The only way to create such objects is by calling methods on some other object that *is* directly creatable.

In a way, the notion of a non-creatable coclass is of questionable meaning, since such a class is really only visible via its interfaces. However the declaration of such a coclass does serve to document the object model.

hidden

The `hidden` attribute, like the `restricted` attribute, is meant to suppress the visibility of libraries, interfaces and members. However, it is even more restrictive in intent: the purpose of marking a construct with `hidden` is to stop its display in all browsers. The most common uses for `hidden` are:

❑ To hide an interface that is only exposed as the default or default source interface of a single coclass. In this case, the interface members are already visible as the coclass members, and it would only confuse some programmers to show the interface in addition to the coclass.

❑ To hide a deprecated version of a library interface or member that has been substituted by a new and improved version. Typically, the older version cannot be deleted outright, since that would break existing code.

❑ To hide interfaces that cannot, or should not, be used by scripting languages. For example interfaces that are not Automation compliant, or members that are meant to be used by the system. For the latter usage, it is more appropriate to use the `restricted` keyword, although you will sometimes use both.

In a reversal of its behavior towards the `restricted` attribute, the Dispatch API ignores the `hidden` attribute.

displaybind

The `displaybind` attribute is used to decorate a `bindable` property, and indicates that the property should be displayed to the user as being a `bindable` property.

control

The `control` attribute can decorate a library or a coclass declaration. When used with a coclass, it indicates that class is a full (OCX-style) ActiveX control. When used with a library, it generally means that the library exposes one main class that happens to be an ActiveX control. This is done for the benefit of containers and tools that distinguish controls (objects with user interfaces) from non-visual objects.

Optimization Hints

immediatebind

The `immediatebind` attribute is used to identify those properties whose notifications are urgent and must be acted upon immediately. In a data-binding situation, a checkbox may need to have its changes reflected in the dataset straight away, whereas updates to a list box could perhaps wait until the box loses focus. It is up to the container to decide what it does with such notifications; the `immediatebind` attribute is merely a hint.

defaultcollelem

In Visual Basic, the ! operator is syntactic sugar for indexing into the default property (assumed to be a collection) of an interface. Thus, given these interface definitions:

```
interface IField : IDispatch
{
    ...
};

interface IFields : IDispatch
{
    ...
    [id(DISPID_VALUE), propget] Item([in] VARIANT, [out, retval] IField**);
    ...
};

interface IRS : IDispatch
{
    [id(DISPID_VALUE), propget] IFields* Fields;
};
```

the Visual Basic expression

```
Dim rs as IRS
rs!field5
```

is syntactic shorthand for

```
rs.Fields.Item("field5")
```

Since this involves two method invocations, there is room for optimization if the Fields collection of IRS has items with well-known names (such as the fields in a specific recordset). If this is the case, the well-known items can be made members of the IRS interface directly. In our example, this would mean the modification:

```
interface IRS : IDispatch
{
    [id(DISPID_VALUE), propget] IFields* Fields;
    [id(0x6002000), propget, defaultcollelem] IField* field5;
};
```

If Visual Basic detects a field named field5, tagged with the defaultcollelem keyword, in the IRS interface, the expression

```
rs!field5
```

will be translated to the alternative, optimized form

```
rs.field5
```

This is really an ad-hoc mechanism that was designed to make up for the fact that the Visual Basic syntax makes collection indexing appear to have the same performance characteristics as method invocation. It forces you to short circuit your object model unnaturally. An alternative that involves just a little bit more typing is:

```
Dim rs as IRS
Dim fds as Ifields
Set fds = rs.Fields

call fds "field5"
call fds "field4"
call fds "field1"
```

This code avoids the need for the `defaultcollelem` hack while having roughly the same performance characteristics (with any reasonable collection implementation). My advice? Don't use `defaultcollelem` if there's any way to avoid it. Educate your Visual Basic users with good sample code instead.

Help Related

It is possible to associate various pieces of help information with individual syntactic elements in an IDL file. There are a number of help related attributes that accomplish this. This information goes into the type library and is typically queried using various methods on the type information retrieval interfaces `ITypeLib`, `ITypeLib2`, `ITypeInfo` and `ITypeInfo2`. Typical applications that use this information are the various types of browsers, IntelliSense, etc.

helpfile()

The `helpfile()` attribute is associated with the `library` keyword and lists the name of a help file that is associated with the type library. All types in the library share the same help file.

helpcontext()

The `helpcontext()` attribute sets the help context ID (a 32-bit value that identifies a location in the help file) associated with the IDL element that it decorates.

helpstring()

The `helpstring()` attribute associates a short character string with the IDL element.

helpstringcontext()

The `helpstringcontext()` attributes a context ID for the help string.

helpstringdll()

In situations where the help file is a DLL (in localized applications, for example), the `helpstringdll()` attribute can be used to specify this DLL name. What this permits is the ability to provide localized documentation using a single (non-localized) version of the type-library. This documentation covers only the help-related information, not the interface and method names. Instead of including a `helpstring()` in English with each property, you pull it out of the DLL resource file that is identified by the attribute parameter.

Miscellaneous

licensed

The licensed attribute is applied to a coclass to indicate that it supports the COM licensing protocol. Such a class must be instantiated using the IClassFactory2 interface.

aggregatable

The aggregatable keyword, associated with a coclass, indicates that objects of the class can be aggregated. A word of warning here: despite the huge amount of attention that aggregation gets in the COM literature, it cannot be used across apartment boundaries and is of less general-purpose use than other alternatives.

Summary

In this chapter, I have provided further details on Automation-style and dual interfaces, including:

- ❑ The rules for creating DISPIDs, and the rationale for them
- ❑ The use of custom DISPIDs in place of IDL attributes
- ❑ The most commonly used predefined DISPIDs, such as DISPID_VALUE, DISPID_NEWENUM and DISPID_EVALUATE
- ❑ The concepts of interface extension and dynamic inheritance
- ❑ The constraints on the semantics of IDispatch
- ❑ The type library driven implementation of the Automation side of dual interfaces

In addition, we looked at the relatively new IDispatchEx interface and its use to implement JScript objects, and I provided a full explanation of the Automation-compatible data types, including the IDL code for BSTRs, SAFEARRAYs and VARIANTs. Furthermore, we discussed the use of Automation data types to support parameter type variation, variable parameter lists, optional parameters, and default values.

Later in the chapter, we saw the application of late binding and the Dispatch API to solving the problem of localizing type library information, and concluded with a round-up of the IDL attributes for tool support, including:

- ❑ The connectable object protocol
- ❑ Property notifications and binding
- ❑ Visibility of interface declarations in various user interface elements
- ❑ Optimization hints
- ❑ Help information

Design Implications

❏ Unless you need an extensible interface, there is no reason to choose an Automation interface over a dual interface. Dual interfaces are easier to implement than straight Automation interfaces because you can simply re-use a sophisticated boilerplate implementation of the `IDispatch` methods. If you really *need* an Automation-only, non-extensible interface, you can always implement it as a dual and hide the vtable part (although I can't imagine why you would need such a beast).

❏ Use an Automation-capable interface if you want to get the benefits of variable numbers of parameters, optional parameters or dynamic typing, and you don't want to re-invent the `SAFEARRAY` and `VARIANT` types. As you will see in Chapter 6, such interfaces are more easily used from scripting clients than from strongly typed clients.

❏ If your vtable interface uses only Automation-compatible types, label it explicitly as being `oleautomation` compatible. Try to use Automation-compatible types instead of custom types if at all possible, since there is a much greater likelihood of the various type information driven tools working with these.

❏ In keeping with the principle of least surprise, always have explicit declarations instead of relying on compiler defaults. In particular:

  ❏ Declare a dispatch ID explicitly if you can. Try to conform to the guidelines for generating dispatch IDs. Note that the Visual C++ Wizards do not create conforming IDs.

  ❏ Declare both the default exported and the default source interface explicitly. Some tools depend on these declarations.

❏ Be aware of the subtlety of firing on an outgoing vtable interface. Most Microsoft clients implement pure Automation sinks, so your source interfaces will probably have to be dual interfaces (for ease of implementation) at the very least.

What's Next?

We've come to the end of our coverage of the details of IDL. From now on, this book deals with its use in building real applications in the various Microsoft language environments. Chapter 5 deals with design issues, including a fairly comprehensive design dictionary and an approach to designing COM object models based on use case analysis. Chapter 6 deals with the client side bindings and the use of the specification object model from the various Microsoft clients. Finally, Chapter 7 deals with a number of server implementation issues.

Application Design

It took me a long time to start writing *good* COM applications. After I'd gone through the fundamental workings of COM – interfaces, classes and Automation – I still had very little idea how to design good COM architectures, or even how to organize small parts of the design using standard principles. Some of the ideas of the regular object-oriented paradigm translated well, whereas others didn't make too much sense. This chapter is my attempt to improve the situation for others, and it has two major parts:

- ❑ The first part consists of a collection of standard COM techniques (or idioms, or patterns, or whatever you like to call them). These techniques are organized into three sections by the phase of the life cycle that I believe they fall into – design, implementation, and optimization.

- ❑ The second part of this chapter consists of a 'live' case study in designing a COM application. Starting from a functional description of the problem, I will walk you through to the design of what I call the **specification model**. This is an object model that describes only the *interfaces* (and not the classes) exposed by the application, without going into any implementation details. The specification model is based largely on the results of use case analysis. On the way, I shall explain the development strategies that I utilize, as well as discussing some general notes about design.

I should point out that I regard the specification model to be identical to the object model exposed to script programmers. I urge you to keep this in mind as you read through this chapter. Some of the points that I raise are not terribly important if all your clients are programmed in C++, but almost critical if the client is programmed in a scripting language.

I distinguish a specification model from an **implementation model**. The latter is the object model that actually implements all the interfaces exposed in the specification model. The implementation model is what most C++ programmers think of when they're thinking of object models – it goes into all the details of classes and the interfaces that they implement. Chapter 7 goes into the details of designing and building COM implementation models.

Design Techniques

This section describes a number of idioms that can help you structure your COM designs. It outlines each of the major issues facing architecture developers, and lists the best-known approaches to them.

Functionality Navigation

A number of issues arise when you consider the various ways that you can allow clients to navigate the functionality exposed by your object model. The most basic COM technique for functionality navigation is, of course, `QueryInterface()`. As you'll see over the next few subsections, however, this may not always be the most appropriate way to provide such functionality.

Don't Expose Classes (or, the Hazards of QueryInterface)

Whisper it quietly, but it turns out that one of the central protocols of COM – functionality discovery via `QueryInterface()` – is not necessarily a great thing to expose to the users of your object model.

Why would I say such an extraordinary thing? Well, I would argue that the way `QueryInterface()` works is an implementation detail that should not be exposed in a specification model. The great beauty of interface based programming is that it de-couples clients and servers to a huge extent; clients can be written in terms of *capabilities*, rather than being wired to classes. Different classes can then be used polymorphically, via their capabilities.

`QueryInterface()` actually creates an extra degree of coupling between client and server by revealing the relationship between the interfaces implemented by a single COM object. While there are situations where this is desirable (see the section on `CoTypes` below), especially in implementation models, in many instances it is an over-specification of the specification model. Once the client code has been written to make use of the relationship, an extra assumption about your object model has been made. From that point on, you can no longer separate the two capabilities into two different objects. The client expects to find them together.

The alternative to this technique is to use methods that explicitly retrieve (as `out` parameters) the desired interfaces. For example, given this class structure:

```
[...]
interface IMySecondInterface : IUnknown
{
};

[...]
interface IMyMainInterface : IUnknown
{
    [...] HRESULT GetMySecondInterface([out, retval] IMySecondInterface**)
};

[...]
coclass MyImplementation
{
    [default] interface IMyMainInterface;
    interface IMySecondInterface;
};
```

the client has the option of either performing a `QI()` on `IMyMainInterface` or using a call to `GetMySecondInterface()` in order to retrieve an interface pointer to `IMySecondInterface`. The benefit of the second approach is that I can change the internal structure of the object model to the following without breaking any existing clients:

```
[...]
coclass MyImplementation
{
    [default] interface IMyMainInterface;
};

[...]
coclass MyImplementation2
{
    [default] interface IMySecondInterface;
};
```

However, this is contingent on the client not doing anything with `IMySecondInterface` that would give away its 'true' object identity, such as performing a `QI()` for some other interface through it. If the client does this and depends on the results, then the actual class implementation will be frozen in the manner described above.

There is a way to avoid this problem, and that is to have the initial implementation *prevent* any peeking via `QI()`. This is accomplished by having the following conceptual structure:

```
[...]
coclass MyImplementation
{
    [default] interface IMyMainInterface;
    interface IMySecondInterface;
};

[
    ...,
    noncreatable
]
coclass
{
    [default] interface IMySecondInterface;
};
```

From the client's perspective, there are now two separate classes, even though they are in all likelihood, physically implemented by the same code module. With this implementation, the client call to `GetMySecondInterface()` would actually return an object of the second, anonymous, class. This class doesn't expose any interfaces that are not part of the exposed object model.

While this may seem like unnecessary work, it has a big payoff. The integrity of the interfaces exposed by your object model is guaranteed – the client cannot peek into your implementation in any way. Moreover, as we'll see later in this chapter in the section on *Alternate Identity* (and in code examples in Chapter 7), it's actually possible to accomplish this with pretty minimal coding.

Property Get instead of QueryInterface()

One special case of the `QI()` elimination technique is the "Property as `QI()`" idiom used on Automation interfaces. You'll remember that straight Automation has a significant limitation: the only interface on an Automation object that is usable by a pure Automation client is the primary one – the `IDispatch` interface exposed by the object. Even if your design factors the object's functionality into several dual interfaces, only one of them can be exposed as `IDispatch`. For example, if you have the following architecture:

```
[...]
interface IMyDual1 : IDispatch
{
    // Members of IMyDual1
    ...
};

[...]
interface IMyDual2 : IDispatch
{
    // Members of IMyDual2
    ...
};

[...]
coclass MyClass
{
    [default] interface IMyDual1;
    interface IMyDual2;
};
```

and the implementation of `QueryInterface()` returns `IMyDual1` as the `IDispatch` interface on `MyClass`, the second interface `IMyDual2` is invisible to pure Automation clients.

One solution to this problem is to expose the functionality of all the interfaces on a single interface, leading to what I call the "kitchen sink" interface. You sometimes see this kind of thing on commercially available ActiveX controls; they look something like this:

```
[...]
interface IMyScript : IDispatch
{
    // Members of IMyDual1
    ...

    // Members of IMyDual2
    ...
};

[...]
coclass MyClass
{
    [default] interface IMyScript;
};
```

The only potential benefit of this approach is performance: it avoids one expensive Automation invocation. However, it does so at the expense of model cleanliness (which probably involves much higher long-term costs, such as increased maintenance costs and time to market).

Another solution is to have a top-level Automation interface that simply exposes all the internal dual interfaces as read-only properties. This solution looks as follows:

```
[...]
interface IMyScript : IDispatch
{
    [propget, id(1)] HRESULT IMyDual1([out, retval] IMyDual1**);
    [propget, id(2)] HRESULT IMyDual2([out, retval] IMyDual2**);
};

[...]
coclass MyClass
{
    [default] interface IMyScript;
};
```

Internally, the property implementations do the `QueryInterface()` that the Automation client is incapable of doing. This solution is much more elegant than the first, and in line with hiding `QI()` from the specification model user.

> For the above to work, you *must* declare the out parameter using the actual interface type (`IMyDual1` or `IMyDual2` in the example above). If you declare the out parameter using `IDispatch`, marshaling code will not work correctly.
>
> Also, as we'll see when we look at scripting clients in Chapter 6, there is a problem with using `QI()` to implement such methods, since many scripting clients re-query for the resulting interface for `IDispatch` anyway. A specific implementation technique, based on Alternate Identities, is required to solve the problem, and you'll see this in action in Chapter 7.

Functionality Evolution

You may have noticed a problem with trying to get rid of the need for `QueryInterface()`. What was the rationale for `QI()` in the first place? It allows the client and object to negotiate a common set of interfaces that they both understand, thus providing an approach to solving version problems. If you eliminate `QI()`, as in the approaches above, how do you gracefully evolve the functionality of your object model without forcing clients to be rewritten? There are several ways of thinking about this:

- ❑ You could have an explicit version number, or provide a version compatibility test. This could be available at the top-level interface of the model, allowing the client to fail gracefully as soon as it checks the object model. Alternatively, it could be made available at each interface. Since many interfaces would be unchanged from version to version, this would allow greater interoperability between client and server.

- ❑ You could decide that the specification model really should be an inflexible contract, and that clients should be rewritten when the model changes. This approach is sometimes called, "defining the problem out of existence," but there is no getting away from the fact that replacing `QI()` with interface parameters as suggested above *does* create version problems than you would not have in an object model that reveals object structure using `QI()`.

- ❑ Finally, you could replace `QI()` with a general interface protocol that does not reveal the object structure of the application. This is the approach taken by the service provider protocol, explained next. While this looks like it should be the preferred approach to eliminating `QI()`, it suffers from the shortcoming that it cannot be used from Visual Basic or the scripting languages (or indeed anything that doesn't understand UUIDs).

Protocol: Service Provider

Another alternative to `QueryInterface()` is the `IServiceProvider` protocol that can be implemented by an object to support flexible functionality discovery:

```
[...]
interface IServiceProvider : IUnknown
{
    HRESULT QueryService([in] REFGUID guidService,
                         [in] REFIID riid,
                         [out, iid_is(riid)] void** ppv);
};
```

For the purposes of the protocol, a **service** is a group of related interfaces identified by a **service identifier**, or SID (which is of course a UUID). The service protocol provides more flexibility in implementing and discovering interfaces than `QI()`.

❑ There is no requirement that the various interfaces in a service be exported by the same object
❑ The object that exports the `IServiceProvider` interface may itself export zero or more of the service interfaces
❑ An interface may belong to more than one service
❑ An object that implements a service interface may implement other interfaces that do not belong to the service

In short, the service provider protocol allows pretty much unconstrained participation in a service by interfaces exported by different objects. The interface has one method, `QueryService()`, that takes a SID and an IID as inputs and, like `QueryInterface()`, returns a pointer to the relevant interface if it is implemented as part of the service.

The `IServiceProvider` interface was originally created for implementation on containers that support ActiveX Designers, but it is now seeing more widespread use – it's included in the protocol for asynchronous monikers, for example. It is also used in Internet Explorers 3 and 4 to gain access to the HTML control interface `IWebBrowserApp`. You may even recall seeing it in the signature of `IDispatchEx::InvokeEx()` to allow objects that implement JScript 'expando' interfaces to gain access to the various services provided by the script engine (or container).

CoTypes

A `CoType` is used to describe a set of COM classes that must meet more stringent requirements than just exposing `IUnknown`. It indicates that an object of a class that conforms to the type *must* expose certain interfaces. In addition, the type declares a number of interfaces as being optional.

The `CoType` is used in situations where functionality has been factored into interfaces, but it is natural for these interfaces to be implemented together. The `CoType` *requires* that a `QI()` on the object must always return each of the mandatory interfaces, and *allows* it to return optional interfaces.

CoTypes have been formally used in the specification of the OLE DB interfaces. For instance, here is the declaration of the CoType called TMultipleResults:

```
CoType TMultipleResults
{
    [mandatory] interface IMultipleResults;
    [optional] interface ISupportErrorInfo;
};
```

This documents the minimum (and optional) requirements on any COM class that is to be an OLE DB multiple result class. The various OLE DB protocols that work with multiple result classes depend on the presence of the mandatory interfaces in order to function correctly. A creator of complex COM protocols can therefore use a CoType to document an object model whose classes are *required* to expose certain interfaces in combination.

> *The* CoType *syntax is not currently supported by MIDL, and currently its usage is restricted to documenting assumptions about the types in an object model.*

Some of the benefits of a CoType regarding the notion of functionality that is always implemented together may be derived by creating an interface to mimic the structure of the CoType. Such an interface exposes the mandatory interfaces of the CoType as properties. A class that wishes to conform to the CoType would then have to implement this interface. For the example above, we might want to have this interface, which represents the mandatory interfaces in TMultipleResults:

```
interface ITMultipleResults : IUnknown
{
    [propget] HRESULT IMultipleResults([out, retval] IMultipleResults**);
};
```

Composition/Re-use

If you've been following the developments at Microsoft over the past few years, you'll have noticed that many of the more popular (and heavily marketed) object models are Automation APIs designed for ease-of-use rather than high performance. This is not surprising, since there is a large domain of applications that consist of simple scripts attached to a form-based UI. Such applications generally do not have serious performance requirements.

Simplification via Façades

In some cases, the simpler set of interfaces are actually proxies that wrap a richer, more flexible, higher-performance (but more complex) set of interfaces. One such example is the ADO object model for universal data access. This is built on OLE DB, another object model for universal data access. The latter is the more flexible, but it's also more complicated, harder to use, and not Automation compliant.

Automation proxies, or **façades**, are by far the most common, since interfaces that need to be easy to use typically also have to be scriptable. Because of this, the use of façade interfaces is pervasive in COM. For example, the IUnknown interface on a client proxy of a distributed object is actually implemented in terms of another interface, called IRemUnknown. The latter is better suited for performing the IUnknown operations over the wire, but its usage is more complicated.

Creation

Object creation in COM looks very strange to the object designer. On the one hand, the COM creation mechanism, with its use of class factories, is very sophisticated. On the other hand, the mechanism has been so well hidden away by the `CoCreateInstance()` API that most users don't know how to take advantage of its sophistication.

Protocol: Class Factory

Interestingly, the **object factory** pattern, one of the classic object-oriented design patterns, is built into COM's standard creation mechanism for named, registered classes. The class factory protocol makes use of the `CoGetClassObject()` API call to retrieve the `IClassFactory` or `IClassFactory2` (derived from `IClassFactory`) interface on the class object (see below) associated with the CLSID you specify.

As shown in the figure below, this interface is used to create an object of the given class and return the requested interface on it (via its `CreateInstance()` method). These steps are normally (invisibly) carried out by the `CoCreateInstance()` API call. The real (as opposed to proxy) class object has to reside physically in the same address space as any objects that it creates.

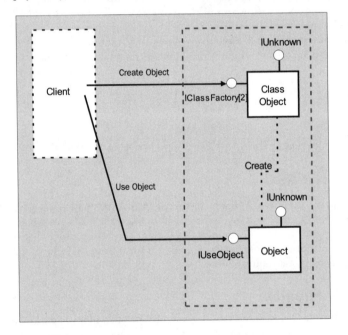

Initialization & Persistence

Historically, **initialization** and **persistence** have been related topics in the COM literature, and I will continue to treat them as such.

Initialization is particularly problematic in COM, since there is no equivalent of a 'custom' C++ constructor in the standard COM object creation protocol. All COM objects are initially created in an uninitialized (or standard or default) state. Any client-specific initialization must be carried out on an already-created object.

This is intended to be addressed in part by the use of "object construction strings" in COM+, the first step towards standard support for object initialization.

Constructor Interfaces on Class Objects

The closest approach to true construction semantics in COM is achieved by modifying the standard COM creation sequence. Instead of using CoCreateInstance() directly, we need to use CoGetClassObject() (or a class moniker – see below) to acquire an interface on the class object for the COM class.

The class object also needs to export a **constructor interface**, the goal of which is to expose a number of alternative methods to construct the object. Each of these methods not only creates the object, but also initializes its state based on the parameters passed into the method. This interface has to be used in the creation sequence in the place of the IClassFactory interface. The figure below shows this idea in use:

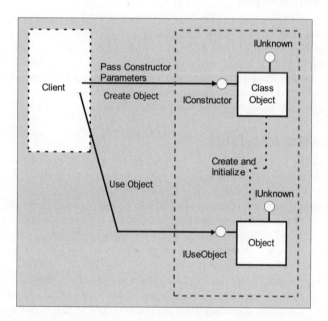

As so often, however, there is a potential problem with this. Certain users of COM services, such as MTS and some client languages, will *only* create objects using the standard class factory interfaces. In the case of MTS, this isn't a real problem because MTS objects are naturally 'stateless' and don't need construction. For languages that only support the standard creation mechanism, calls to the custom creation mechanism have to be hidden behind the specification model.

You also need to be aware that if you *remove* support for IClassFactory(2) when you add another constructor interface, you will need to implement IExternalConnection (see below) instead. This is because the COM run-time infrastructure still requires access to functionality equivalent to IClassFactory::LockServer(). It emulates this functionality by using the IExternalConnection::AddConnection() and IExternalConnection::ReleaseConnection() methods in the place of IClassFactory::LockServer(TRUE) and IClassFactory::LockServer(FALSE).

Initialization Interfaces on COM Objects

The simplest initialization technique of all is to define an **initialization interface** for your object. I think of this interface as the post-construction analog of the constructor interface that I just discussed.

A client that wishes to use your class creates an object, and then uses one of the methods on this interface to initialize its state. It is expected that only one of the methods on this interface will be called during the lifetime of the object (analogous to a C++ constructor only being called once per object), but it is up to the interface implementer to enforce this.

Note that unlike a constructor interface, which has to be called in order to create the object, there is no way to force a client to call an initialization interface. This means that an object that depends on an initialization interface to put it into a consistent state can still potentially get used in its uninitialized state.

Initialization via Automation

A technique that is similar in operational terms but very different in spirit is the use of various properties of an Automation object's primary Automation interface to initialize it. In this schema, the client creates the object and then uses its Automation interface to set properties and call methods that change its state. Unlike using an initialization interface, this activity can take several property invocations instead of being done in one shot (with the consequent performance degradation for remote objects). It is also hard to distinguish such initialization from normal state changing operations. This mechanism should only be used if there is no other option.

Protocol: Persistence Interfaces

COM has emphasized the importance of persistence interfaces from the earliest days of OLE 2. Traditional OLE persistence works like this:

❑ Persistence media are represented by interfaces that allow reading from and writing to them. The most pervasive of these interfaces are IStream (which represents a stream-like persistence medium), IStorage (which represents an OLE structured storage object) and IPropertyBag (which represents an unordered set of property-value pairs, used to persist various kinds of forms: Visual Basic, Visual C++ and HTML).

❑ Objects to be persisted export one or more persistence interfaces, such as IPersistStream(Init), IPersistStorage, IPersistFile, IPersistMemory, and IPersistPropertyBag. Each of these interfaces is used to persist to the appropriate type of persistence medium. The medium interface, in the form of an IStorage*, IStream* or IPropertyBag*, is passed as a parameter to the persistence interface methods.

The semantics of persistence and persistence medium interfaces are detailed as part of the COM/OLE specification. It is rare for an end user to have to implement the persistence medium interfaces, but quite common to implement the persistence interfaces. In fact, it's quite common for an object to implement *several* of these interfaces, giving its clients a choice of media in which to save. This is generally fairly inexpensive for the server implementer, since typically you have to implement only one interface (generally IPersistStreamInit) and re-use that implementation in the implementation of most of the others.

> IPersistStorage *is an occasional exception to this rule because of its semantics in low memory conditions.*

Persistence to Relational Databases

Database persistence is one of those hot button topics that can start religious wars among object-oriented designers. I don't have very strong opinions on the subject, but from a practical standpoint I've always used persistence with relational databases rather than object-oriented databases. The reason for this has always been exogenous to the technical requirements of the design: other people needed to get access to the same data, and they could only use relational tools. Another way of looking at it is that there are use cases that aren't part of the system being designed that have dictated using relational databases.

It's not really much harder to persist objects into a relational database than it is to persist into a stream. You make certain that there is a primary key in some table of the database that corresponds to the object class, and carry that primary key around as a (possibly hidden) member of the object. Beyond that, it's just a matter of making sure that you have the correct SQL query (preferably a stored procedure) to insert and extract the object from the database. However, there are a couple of things you should be aware of:

❑ As the system design changes (assuming that it is evolving), the object design and the data design will change independently of each other. The insertion and extraction queries will almost certainly need to change as well. These queries are best created and maintained using automated tools such as the OLE DB consumer Wizard in Visual C++ 6.0.

❑ Relational databases are designed for efficient manipulation of sets of rows. It is generally much more efficient to issue commands that simultaneously affect a large number of rows, than it is to manipulate individual rows. From a performance perspective, this makes it attractive to link object *collections* with databases, rather than individual objects.

I frequently use the following, simple rowset persistence interface, which is modeled on the other persistence interfaces mentioned above:

```
[...]
interface IPersistRowset : IUnknown
{
    HRESULT InitNew();
    HRESULT Load([in] IRowset* pRowset);
    HRESULT Save([in] IRowset* pRowset, [in] BOOL fClearDirty);
    HRESULT IsDirty();
};
```

One major point of departure from the other persistence interfaces is that this interface does not derive from `IPersist` (all the standard persistence interfaces do). The basic reason for this is that the interface is implemented on **collections** rather than individual objects, so the notion of a CLSID (which is what `IPersist` encapsulates) is not really relevant. In this sense also, it is quite different from the ordinary persistence interfaces.

You can see examples of the use of this interface in Chapter 7.

State Changes

You've now seen various COM idioms for construction, initialization and persistence. The logical next step is to look at idioms for changing the state of COM objects. The most straightforward way of changing state is to have properties or methods on an interface whose invocation affects the state of the object. Any state change operation, however, runs the risk of leaving the object in an invalid state. Although it is possible to have each state changing operation validate all its own inputs before committing to a new state, there are other approaches to the problem.

Validation Interfaces

The simplest approach to data validation is to have a validation interface that's similar to the initialization interface. The methods on this interface simply validate different combinations of input data, returning information on invalid parameter combinations. The methods on this interface are called prior to initializing the object or changing its state.

The problem, of course, is that out-of-apartment calls to the validation interface might result in performance-degrading network round trips. In this situation, it might be best to implement the validation interface, but have it called from the implementations of the state-change or initialization interfaces, rather than by the client. You would, of course, have to modify such state-change interfaces to return validation information on failure.

A validation interface tends to be a prime candidate for inclusion in a business logic layer.

Two-Phase Updates

Another approach to state change, and one that works well when the object's state is changed in a number of small increments over a longer period of time, or when the object's state is complex and dependent on the state of other entities, is to have a **transacted state**. Here, the new state of the object is built up over time, but not committed until an explicit 'commit' method is called. Just as with any other transactional capability, the state changes may be rolled back at any time to the previous state.

For an object to implement a simple transacted state, it is sufficient to export the following interface that I've defined, with the addition of error information functionality:

```
[...]
interface ITwoPhase : IUnknown
{
    HRESULT BeginTransaction();
    HRESULT Commit();
    HRESULT Rollback();
};
```

For more sophisticated transactions, it is best to use an established transaction infrastructure, such as that provided by the Microsoft Distributed Transaction Coordinator (DTC). The DTC is the transaction manager that is used by MTS, SQL Server, etc. to enable distributed transaction, but I will not be discussing it any further in this book.

Data Transfer

One of the issues that comes up very early in any real implementation of distributed objects is the question of how to transfer arbitrary user defined data between objects in the distributed system. We will look at several ways of approaching this issue.

Marshaled Interfaces

The simplest approach to data transfer is also the most obvious and the most general: use method parameters. Since method invocations are remotable via the mechanism of interface marshaling, this data transfer mechanism will work both in and out of apartment. It also allows the transfer of an arbitrary number and type of parameters, including user defined types and arrays. It requires that both the sender and receiver of data agree on the signature of the interface being used to transmit that data.

This mechanism is intended to be further improved in Windows 2000 by an extension of the RPC pipe mechanism to COM. COM pipes are designed to transfer large blocks of data of a specified type in any combination of synchronous/asynchronous and push/pull mode. The performance characteristics of pipes are potentially much better than passing the same data as an array parameter.

Automation Marshaling

A variation on the theme of data transfer by interface marshaling is the use of Automation interfaces to transfer data. Since an Automation interface looks like a user-defined data type (it has properties, for instance), data transfer by Automation marshaling *looks like* assignment to a remote, user-defined type. However, it is much less efficient than passing a true user defined type in a vtable interface, since each property and method invocation is marshaled individually.

Protocol: Data Objects

The **data object protocol** was designed to provide a polymorphic approach to data transfer, and to be more efficient than is data transfer via Automation interfaces. The goal of the protocol is to allow the producer and consumer of data to negotiate aspects of the transfer, such as data format and transfer medium. The basic interface used in the data object protocol is `IDataObject`; it is implemented by the data provider, and allows data transfers with the following features:

❑ The data provider lists a number of possible data formats in which it can provide data. The consumer can then select the format to receive in.

❑ The data consumer can specify one or more of a set of storage media types in which to receive the data. The media types include global memory, files, streams and storages.

❑ The data consumer is allowed to request notification from the provider when its data changes. The registration for this notification *doesn't* use the connectable object protocol. A simpler advise/unadvise scheme is used instead.

This protocol *has* to be used when your code needs to interact with other programs that use drag-and-drop, the clipboard (cut and paste) or other OLE Uniform Data Transfer technologies. It is also the protocol of choice if you are transferring data that fits naturally into the set of Windows clipboard data formats. The protocol is suited to large, complex data structures or documents that are associated with complete applications. In most other situations, it is not particularly applicable.

Serialized Object State

One of my favorite data transfer techniques is the use of **serialized object state**. The logic is simple and compelling:

❑ An object is the ultimate user-defined type.

❑ As part of their normal functionality, many objects support one or more of the standard persistence interfaces that allow their state to be serialized into persistence media. The data provider can create the serialized state of the object to be transferred.

❑ The persisted state can be interpreted as an array of bytes (or a `SAFEARRAY` of bytes) that can then be transferred between provider and consumer.

❑ The consumer can then use the same object's implementation to de-serialize the state and restore the original object.

Since the persistence interfaces are typically implemented already, this can be a fairly inexpensive way of performing very high performance data transfers.

The only practical problem with this approach is that if it uses the standard persistence interfaces, it is not completely general. The serialized state is usually at least architecture dependent, and frequently platform dependent as well (there's a reason why NDR was invented), which means that if the state crosses an architecture or platform boundary, its contents may be incorrectly interpreted.

However, if the serialization were to be based upon some architecture-neutral internal representation, it is actually a great approach. Such an internal representation could be NDR, or my personal favorite candidate, XML. Although the latter is less efficient than the former as a representation format, XML is already approximately object-oriented, has good (and growing) tool support, and has very broad application interoperability characteristics. For example, I can debug my persisted state by opening it in a text editor or specialized XML editor, transferring it into an XML-enabled database, etc.

Callbacks

As I mentioned in the discussion in Chapter 2, straightforward callbacks do not work in COM because they tend to have process affinity at the very least. Any COM callback protocol must be based on calling an interface method. The distinguishing characteristic of different callback mechanisms is in the way that they deal with aspects of registering clients with the source object.

Protocol: Connectable Objects

Refer to the discussion of the connectable object protocol in Chapter 2.

Protocol: Advise/UnAdvise/EnumAdvise

A more lightweight alternative to the connectable object protocol is a simpler and less general notification protocol that's used in a couple of different places in the COM technologies. I present my version of this protocol here, in which the notification interface is:

```
[...]
interface INotify : IUnknown
{
    Advise([in] REFIID a_pIID,
           [in, iid_is(a_pIID)] IUnknown* a_pIUnk,
           [out] DWORD * a_pdwCookie);

    UnAdvise([in] DWORD a_vdwCookie);
    EnumAdvise([in] REFIID a_pIID, [out, iid_is(a_pIID)] IUnknown** a_ppIUk);
};
```

This interface is used in situations where an object has a set of well-known source interfaces, so it is not necessary to discover the interfaces dynamically. The precise source interface being used is late bound (note the `iid_is()` attribute). The `Advise()` and `UnAdvise()` methods are used to register and unregister for notification, which means that the implementation must keep track of the collection of sink interfaces. The `EnumAdvise()` method is used to return a (late bound) enumerator interface (see the later section on enumerators) that iterates over a collection of the then-registered sink interfaces. The type of the actual items that are being enumerated is specified in the signature of the enumerator.

Errors and Exceptions

In Chapter 2, you saw the use and limitations of HRESULTs as a means of returning errors. I also pointed out that it is always possible to return arbitrary user defined error types (which can be base or Automation types) as out parameters instead of depending on the HRESULT return value. In addition, I showed you the standard COM exception protocol – COM error objects – that's used to transfer rich error information back to the client. At the same time, I stated that although there are performance benefits from doing so, there is no absolute requirement that you use this protocol. In this section, I want to take a closer look at some of the options.

Simple Status Codes as out Parameters

It is always possible to return simple status codes as an out parameter. For example, in the following interface declaration:

```
interface IFoo : IUnknown
{
    HRESULT Method1([in] long a_l1,
                    [in] long a_l2,
                    [out, retval] long* a_plStatus);

    HRESULT Method2([out, retval] long * a_plStatus);
};
```

Method1() and Method2() return a long retval as an out parameter. This value serves as your personal status code, with none of the restrictions that are placed on HRESULT values. It doesn't even have to be a long – as long as it's one of the base IDL or scripting types, it can be used from any COM client.

User Defined Error Types

We can take the "status code as return value" technique a step further and return an arbitrary, user-defined type as a status code. I can extend the above example by introducing a user-defined struct called Errortype, defined as:

```
typedef [public] struct
{
    long m_lStatus;
    BSTR m_strMessage;
} ErrorType;
```

and modifying the interface signature to the following:

```
interface IFoo : IUnknown
{
    HRESULT Method1([in] long a_l1,
                    [in] long a_l2,
                    [out, retval] ErrorType* a_petStatus);

    HRESULT Method2([out, retval] ErrorType* a_petStatus);
};
```

While this allows great flexibility in reporting errors and exceptions, it has the disadvantage that it is not accessible from all client languages (notably, scripting languages). Because it can only be used from languages that accept arbitrary method signatures, it is not even necessary to have the out parameter be the retval parameter. In fact, you can have more than one out parameter to store the status value.

Protocol: COM Error Objects

Refer to the discussion of the COM error objects in Chapter 2.

Protocol: OLE DB Error Objects

A more sophisticated version of the COM error object (CEO) protocol is the OLE DB error object (ODEO) protocol. There are three major differences between the two protocols:

❑   The ODEO protocol allows an object to return multiple error objects.
❑   The ODEO protocol explicitly allows a method call to return an error object even if the call returned a success status code.
❑   The ODEO protocol de-couples the detailed lookup of error information from the act of returning the error object. This allows the lookup of error information to be done in a lazy (on-demand) fashion, and also to be parameterized and localized easily.

An ODEO error object has to implement the IErrorInfo interface so that it appears as an 'ordinary' error object to a client that doesn't understand ODEO. In addition, however, it has to implement the IErrorRecords interface, which exposes the error information to be treated as a collection of error records. Finally, the IErrorLookup interface is used internally to implement the lookup of error information.

As seen from the client, the rest of the ODEO protocol follows the CEO protocol. The client queries the ISupportErrorInfo interface to check if any error object protocol is in use. If it finds the IErrorRecords interface, it gets the extra records associated with ODEO; otherwise it simply follows the CEO protocol.

Naming and Binding

One of the basic problems that needs to be solved by any distributed system of objects is the ability to find specific object instances. The easiest way to do so is to provide a name that uniquely identifies an object instance. The name typically has a persistent representation that may even be a human-readable string.

In a true distributed system, the object instance could actually be a replicated *object instance. In this case, there will be multiple physical implementations that all represent the 'same' object.*

The second functional requirement is that, given its name, the client must be able to 'find' the object and retrieve an interface on it. This process is generally termed **binding** to the name.

Finally, given the persistent representation of a name, the client has to decide what kind of name it is, and therefore what namespace it belongs to. The namespace typically determines what binding mechanism will be used.

There are various mechanisms that can be used to accomplish naming and binding. COM already has infrastructural support for the very important moniker protocol, but simpler options are possible as well, as we'll see later in the section.

Protocol: Monikers

The **moniker** is one of the most powerful concepts in COM. The purpose of a **moniker object** is to provide a name for another object that it uniquely identifies.

A moniker object – that is, an object that exports `IMoniker` – is an intelligent name. The moniker encapsulates the entire process of creating, initializing and connecting to a specific interface on the object that it names. The figure below shows a typical moniker usage scenario:

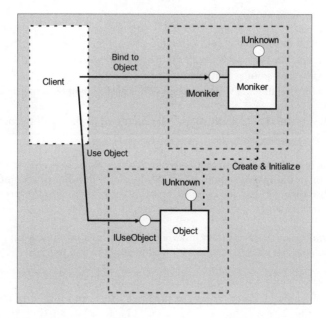

The client has a reference to an `IMoniker` interface on the moniker object. It uses this reference to instruct the moniker to **bind** to the object that it names. Binding is the process of connecting the client to a specified interface on the object. If the object is not currently loaded, the moniker will load it, initialize its state, and then return the requested interface. After the client has the object interface, it typically has no further use for the moniker.

All the details of binding are hidden behind the moniker implementation. The actual object may be created in a different apartment, and only a proxy to it returned by the binding method.

This may seem like a pretty obvious mechanism for object initialization, but its simplicity belies great abstraction power. It generalizes and encapsulates a large part of the object life cycle as seen by the client. For example, assume that the client simply wants to use the Automation interface on an object for which it has a persisted name. As long as the persisted name can be de-serialized into a moniker object, it doesn't matter if the object being named by the moniker is persisted in a file, a URL or a database. Furthermore, it doesn't matter what application is needed to serve the object. The client code is shielded from all these details. All the client code needs to know is how to create the moniker object, load it from its persisted state, and call the `IMoniker::BindToObject()` method. At the end of this call, it simply uses the Automation interface that is returned to it.

The IDL definition of this method is as follows:

```
interface IMoniker : IPersistStream
{
    ...

    [local] HRESULT BindToObject([in, unique] IBindCtx* pbc,
                                 [in, unique] IMoniker* pmkToLeft,
                                 [in] REFIID riidResult,
                                 [out, iid_is(riidResult)] void** ppvResult);
    ...
};
```

The parameters of this method are:

- ❑ A pointer to the bind context object to be used
- ❑ A pointer to the moniker that precedes this one in the composite
- ❑ The IID of the interface pointer requested
- ❑ The address of the output variable that receives the interface pointer requested

Don't worry if these parameters seem confusing at the moment, as they will become clearer in the following sections.

Obviously, the process of activating an object is dependent on the actual type of the object as well as its persistence format or initialization sequence. COM defines a number of commonly used base moniker types, and also a mechanism for composing monikers. This saves the programmer from having to create monikers for the most common situations.

You need an understanding of the various monikers to decide how to name your objects, and this is essentially a decision about the namespace to which your objects will belong.

File Monikers

A **file moniker** represents a name that is a path in the file system, and therefore identifies an object that is stored in its own file. The API function CreateFileMoniker() is used to create the moniker object, given a string containing a file name.

For example, the string "C:\\TEMP\\MYSHEET.XLS" names a path in the file system representing a Microsoft Excel Spreadsheet. A file moniker created from this string could be used to load the spreadsheet object that it represents.

A file moniker binds to its object in several steps. First, it uses the file extension to determine the class of the object (in this case, an Excel Spreadsheet). It then instantiates an object of the class (here it would launch Excel) and uses the IPersistFile interface (which the Excel object must export) to initialize the newly created object from its persisted state in the file.

A file moniker represents the file system namespace, and unless you're using UNC names in your file system, this suffers from a serious defect: it is workstation relative. This is not a good choice for a true distributed system.

URL Monikers

The **URL moniker** is a generalization of the file moniker to refer to *any kind* of URL (including a file system URL). The API function CreateURLMoniker() is used to create a URL moniker object given a string containing the URL.

Extending the above example, we could get the Excel spreadsheet from the URL ftp://ftp.wrox.com/pub/office/mysheet.xls. The URL moniker can be used to load the spreadsheet object that it represents.

A URL moniker binds to its object in a manner analogous to file moniker binding. First, the class of the object to be created has to be determined; this is associated with the MIME type of the URL. If no such class can be found, filename extension matching is performed instead. When the class has been determined, an object of the class is created. This object is loaded from its persisted state by using one of several persistence interfaces, in the following order of preference: IPersistMoniker, IPersistStream(Init) and IPersistFile. An object that can be instantiated by a URL moniker must support one of these interfaces.

Because of Microsoft's extension of the meaning of a URL to include all the other namespaces, a URL moniker can represent just about any namespace in the known Microsoft universe. If you restrict yourself to traditional URLs, such as web locations (http://-style URLs), you have a relatively good basis for naming distributed objects.

Item Monikers

So far, we've seen monikers that are associated with entire files or URLs. What about a moniker that is associated with a sub-object *within* a file, such as a paragraph within a document, or a range of cells in a spreadsheet?

An **item moniker** is used to identify such a sub-object within a containing object, and therefore only makes sense in the context of that containing object. An item moniker is created by calling the CreateItemMoniker() API function with a string that represents the item.

Continuing our spreadsheet example, the range of cells A1:B3 in the spreadsheet would be represented by the item string "A1:B3". Of course, the string only makes sense in the context of the spreadsheet.

An item moniker needs a containing object in order to bind to the sub-object that it names, and this containing object is named by the moniker that is passed in as another parameter of BindToObject(). The containing object must implement the IOleItemContainer interface. The item moniker calls the GetObject() method on this interface, passing it the item string. The containing object implementation is then responsible for interpreting the string and creating the sub-object that it refers to. In our example, the IOleItemContainer of the spreadsheet object instantiated from ftp://ftp.wrox.com/pub/office/mysheet.xls would be used to retrieve the sub-object represented by "A1:B3".

Composite Monikers

Consider the problem of naming a cell range within an Excel spreadsheet. The spreadsheet itself is usually named by means of a file or URL path. For example, I might have a spreadsheet stored in the file named "C:\\TEMP\\MYSHEET.XLS". The cell range itself is generally named using the Excel expression language – the range of interest may be "A1:B3". These two items can be represented as a file moniker and an item moniker respectively.

It's possible to combine these monikers using the `CreateGenericComposite()` method. This results in a **generic composite**, which has no special knowledge of its individual moniker types. If you're familiar with Microsoft Office naming conventions, you can probably guess that the string representation for this composite is the concatenation of the two individual strings with the `"!"` character in between – that is, `"C:\\TEMP\\MYSHEET.XLS!A1:B3"`. Using *this* moniker, the entire process of obtaining an interface on the cell range object can be carried out in what looks like one step to the client.

This is a simple example of **moniker composition** – creating a new moniker that is composed of two other monikers. Obviously, each member of a composite can itself be another composite, thus allowing arbitrarily long compositions of monikers. A composite moniker is parsed and bound from right to left – each moniker is bound with respect to the binding of the monikers to the left of it.

A generic composite binds to its object by recursively calling `BindToObject()` on its right hand moniker, passing in the pointer to the left hand moniker as the second parameter. In our example, the generic composite would bind by calling `BindToObject()` on the item moniker for `"A1:B3"`, passing in the file moniker for `"C:\\TEMP\\MYSHEET.XLS"` as a parameter. We've already seen how the item moniker handles this binding. The generic composite thus re-uses the binding mechanism provided by the monikers from which it is composed.

Class Monikers

Once the idea of a generic composite moniker has been introduced, a couple of other moniker types come in handy: class and anti monikers. A **class moniker** names the class object that is associated with a particular COM class. It allows the use of the moniker binding mechanism to create the class object associated with a class, rather than an actual object of the class itself. This is the only way to name and bind to a class object, since these objects do not have CLSIDs and are normally accessibly only by `CoGetClassObject()`.

In addition, the class moniker can be used in a composite moniker to create objects of a particular class. When composed to the left of a file moniker, the class moniker (rather than the file extension) determines the type of object that gets created. For example, the file `"C:\\TEMP\\MYWORD.DOC"` is associated with the Microsoft Word document type by its extension. If we wanted to open it using the WordPad application instead, we would compose the class moniker for WordPad with the file moniker for the document. The string representation of the composite moniker would be `"CLSID:73FDDC80-AEA9-101A-98A7-00AA00374959:C:\\TEMP\\MYWORD.DOC"`, where the first part of the string is the string representation of the class moniker.

Anti-Monikers

Moniker composition also leads to the notion of the **inverse** of a given moniker. A moniker A has an inverse A^{-1} such that the two in composition nullify each other. This is analogous to the effect of the `".."` directory name in a file path: it cancels out the directory name immediately preceding it. Each moniker can be queried for its inverse by calling `IMoniker::Inverse()`.

An **anti-moniker** is a **generic inverse moniker**. It applies to any file, URL, item, class, or pointer moniker. When composed to the right of any moniker it nullifies it, causing both monikers to be removed from the composition. This is useful in the situation where an object moves after a composite moniker has been created for it – you can't delete parts of the moniker, so instead you have to nullify them.

Pointer Monikers

A **pointer moniker** is a 'fake' moniker. In a situation where a client needs a moniker to an object that has no persisted representation, a pointer moniker can be created that connects to the actual object.

A pointer moniker binds trivially to its object, since the object is already in existence. It simply `QI()`s the object for the requested interface.

Custom Monikers

A **custom moniker** is a user-defined class that exports `IMoniker`. Effectively, what you do when you create a custom moniker is provide support for a new global naming scheme and global namespace. There are times when you may want to do this, but in most common situations you can achieve your objectives with the pre-defined moniker types. A custom moniker class must implement `IMoniker`, `IROTData` and `IClassActivator`.

Protocol: Display Names

Whew! That's a bunch of different kinds of monikers, isn't it? It almost seems like we're replacing one problem – creating and initializing an object from its persisted state – with another: creating the appropriate system or composite moniker, and initiating the binding process. It would seem that the client will have to incorporate a lot of intelligence (hence many lines of code) to do that.

Happily, this turns out to be unnecessary, by virtue of the fact that every moniker has an equivalent string representation. This string representation is what is actually seen by the client, rather than the composite moniker structure. The client makes one API call to the function `MkParseDisplayNameEx()` (or the deprecated `MkParseDisplayName()`), passing in the entire name string. As its name suggests, this function parses the string into its individual components and returns the `IMoniker` pointer to the moniker composite that is equivalent to the string.

Protocol: Running Object Table

Every workstation has a Running Object Table (ROT) associated with it. This table contains an entry for every COM object currently loaded in the workstation that can be identified by a moniker. It is up to the COM object's server to ensure that its named objects are registered in this table when they are loaded, and unregistered when they are unloaded. The server is also required to update the entry when the object's state changes.

Moniker implementations are required to check the ROT at the start of the binding process, to determine if the object is already loaded (the moniker is already registered), thus preventing possible duplication of the object.

Collections

A **collection** object is a single object that represents a group of objects. Hand in hand with the collection goes an **enumerator**, which is an object that allows the client to iterate over the individual elements of the collection.

Protocol: Collection

COM defines a **collection interface** that is recognized as such by Visual Basic. A collection interface is an Automation-capable interface with a type signature something like this one:

```
[...]
interface IFoo : IDispatch
{
    // Required Methods
    [propget, id(DISPID_VALUE)]
    HRESULT Item([in] LONG a_vlIndex, [out, retval] LONG* a_pl);

    [propget, id(DISPID_NEWENUM), restricted]
    HRESULT _NewEnum([out, retval] LPUNKNOWN* a_punk);

    [propget, id(1)]
    HRESULT Count([out, retval] LONG* a_pl);

    // Optional Methods
    [id(2)] HRESULT Add([in] LONG a_vlIndex, [in] LONG a_vl);
    [id(3)] HRESULT Remove([in] LONG a_vlIndex);

    // Additional Collection Methods
    ...
};
```

This interface defines a collection of LONG elements, indexed by a LONG value. More generally, a Visual Basic collection can have VARIANT elements indexed by VARIANT values. The required methods for any collection object are the first three methods in the interface:

- ❏ The Item() property, which must have an ID of DISPID_VALUE, returns an element of the collection given its index
- ❏ The _NewEnum() property, which must have an ID of DISPID_NEWENUM and should have the restricted attribute, returns an enumerator that can be used to iterate over the elements of the collection
- ❏ The Count() property returns a count of the number of elements in the collection

The collection may also have any other methods that make sense. For example, a collection that can be modified by the user by having elements added to and removed from it will typically have Add() and Remove() methods as well. The type signatures of the Add() and Remove() methods do not have to exactly match those provided here. For instance, you might have an Add() method that, instead of taking an item itself, takes parameters that can create the item and add it to the collection, returning a reference to the added item.

Protocol: Enumerator

The collection interface that we just saw is intended to allow general-purpose interactions with the collection and its elements. For the special case of iterating over collections, the COM standard is to use the so-called **enumerator interfaces**. The enumerator is really a template for a class of interfaces. For an enumeration over type Foo, the template would look like this:

```
[...]
interface IEnumFoo : IUnknown
{
    [helpstring("Try to fetch the next N elements")]
    HRESULT Next(
        [in] ULONG a_vulCount,
        [out, size_is(a_vulCount, 1), length_is(*a_pulFetched, 1)] Foo* a_abid,
        [out] ULONG* a_pulFetched);

    [helpstring("Skip over the next N elements")]
    HRESULT Skip([in] ULONG a_vulCount);

    [helpstring("Reset the enumeration to the beginning")]
    HRESULT Reset();

    [helpstring("Create a new enumerator with the same state")]
    HRESULT Clone([out] IEnumFoo** a_ppEnum);
};
```

Of these four methods, only two (Next() and Clone()) have signatures that are dependent on the type being enumerated over. Skip() and Reset() have the same signatures regardless of the underlying type.

❑ The Next() method attempts to fetch the next *n* elements in the enumeration, where *n* is specified by the first parameter to the method. The fetched elements are placed in the array pointed to by the second parameter. The third parameter simply returns the actual number of elements that were fetched.

❑ The Skip() method jumps over the next *n* elements in the enumeration.

❑ The Reset() method reinitializes the state of the enumeration so that the next call to Next() or Skip() will restart from the beginning of the enumeration.

❑ The Clone() method returns another enumerator object whose state is initialized to be the current state of this enumerator. This would be helpful in a situation where you have to place a bookmark in an enumeration and restart at that point if necessary.

Implementation Techniques

So far, I've examined idioms and techniques that are helpful for designing the functionality of the object model. Although the distinction might seem arbitrary at times, the following techniques are more applicable when getting into the nitty-gritty implementation details of building the model.

Composition/Re-use

The following techniques are various ways in which object functionality may be re-used. The most obvious re-use technique is the connection, which is what gets used in the vast majority of cases. All the other techniques have much more limited applicability, and I'm mentioning them largely because they have received so much exposure in the literature, and it is worth pointing out that they *should not* be used except in unusual situations.

Connection

A **connection** between two objects occurs when an object of class A holds a reference to an interface on an object of class B, as shown below:

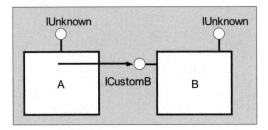

This means that object A is a client of (the interface ICustomB on) object B. As you can imagine, such simple connections, where an object is a client in addition to being a server, are quite common. This is the simplest way for one COM class to use the services of another COM class.

Containment

A special case of a simple connection is one where object B is not available to any client other than A. This is illustrated below – object A is the *only* client of (the interface ICustomB on) object B.

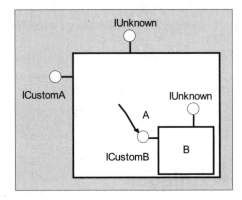

In this situation and the ones that are described below, the object B is **contained** by object A. In standard terminology, A is called the **outer object** and B the **inner object**. Interfaces on the inner object are typically used to assist in the implementation of the functionality of the outer object. The lifetime of the inner object is generally strictly enclosed within the lifetime of the outer object, and is under its control.

Delegation

Delegation is a constrained form of containment where an interface on the outer object is implemented by calls to the methods of the identical interface on the inner object. The figure on the following page shows the ICustomB interface on outer object A being implemented by delegating to the same interface on object B:

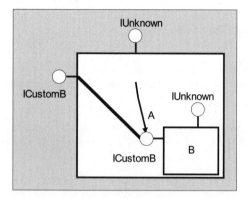

The delegated call to the method on the inner object may of course be preceded and followed by other code implemented by A. A delegated interface for which the outer object does nothing except forward the call to the inner object is sometimes called a 'trivially' delegated interface.

Trivial Delegators and Interception

Of late, **trivial** (also called **universal**) **delegators** have become all the rage. The concept, which I first saw proposed by Crispin Goswell in the *COM Programmer's Cookbook*, is very simple. A universal delegator is capable of delegating to *any* interface without advance knowledge of its definition. This generally requires manipulation of the stack in order to change a method invocation on the delegator to the equivalent invocation on the actual interface being delegated to.

Universal delegators can be used to build an interception framework, where calls to an interface are imperceptibly intercepted and hooked (generally to provide functionality such as authentication, auditing, transaction support, connection pooling, and other exogenous services).

Another way of building a universal delegator is to be aware of the signature of the interface being delegated to. This allows more sophisticated services such as just-in-time activation and connection pooling, and is the strategy used by MTS. This is also why MTS requires either a type library or an interpretive marshaler.

Aggregation

In COM, the term **aggregation** has a very specialized definition that is different from that used by many object theorists. It is a special case of containment where the actual interface from the inner object is exposed to a client of the outer object:

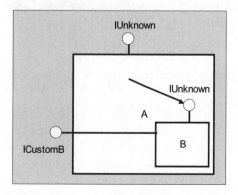

In the figure, the actual interface `ICustomB` on object B is exposed by the outer object A. There are a number of extra rules that must be followed for successful aggregation, and details of these rules are available in many introductory COM books.

> **Aggregation should be used very carefully in your designs, since it is not guaranteed to work when the outer object and inner object are in different apartments.**
>
> **Some of the introductory books do not provide all the constraints related to aggregation. Consult *Professional ATL COM Programming* if you're in doubt.**

Singletons

In the object-oriented community, a **singleton** is a class of which only one instance can ever be created. All clients of the class see the one-and-only instance when they try to create or access an object of this type. The implementation of singletons in COM is somewhat complicated by the fact that multiple instances of a COM server may be running simultaneously on a single machine, and almost certainly *will* be running simultaneously on a network.

How can multiple instances of a COM server be running on a single machine? There are two distinct ways in which this can happen:

- ❑ If the server is an in process DLL server, each executable that loads the DLL will get its own copy of the server.
- ❑ If the server is implemented by an EXE file, it is allowed to set instancing properties when registering its class factories. One of the possible values for this instancing property is `REGCLS_SINGLEUSE`, which allows a class factory to create only a single object of its class before it gets hidden from the client. A request for another object instance forces a new server process to be launched and its class factory used for the creation of the next object instance.

The second scenario, of a COM server running on different machines, is easier to imagine. In any case, the possibility of multiple simultaneous server instances complicates the implementation of singleton classes. There are several 'levels' of singletons in COM.

In general, the notion of a singleton in a true distributed system is not very robust. Having a true singleton, which is a single physical object, is asking for trouble, because it also becomes the single point of failure. What is much more acceptable is a logical singleton, which may be implemented by a replicated physical object. This is how high-traffic web-sites (probably the most scalable distributed systems in existence today) serve up URLs.

Server Singletons

A **server singleton** is a singleton class within a server process, meaning that only one instance of the class can ever be created within the same server process. This kind of singleton is actually relatively simple to implement:

- ❑ The class factory for the class should be a singleton factory – it never creates new objects, always returning interfaces on the one-and-only object created for the class.
- ❑ The `Release()` implementation only decrements the reference count; it never actually de-allocates resources when the reference count goes to zero.

In addition, the COM runtime has to ensure that DLL will never be loaded twice into a process to service a single CLSID.

Workstation Singletons

A **workstation singleton** is a singleton that is guaranteed on a single workstation. This is a little more complicated to achieve, but it can be done by using the Running Object Table that is part of the moniker binding protocol. As long as you can identify your singleton with an appropriate moniker, and only allow client access via the moniker binding mechanism, you can create a workstation singleton. You also need to make certain that the instancing properties of the class factories have been set appropriately.

Full Singletons

What the Running Object Table does for a workstation singleton is to provide a single, application-independent cache of pointers to named, currently active objects on a workstation. For a system-wide singleton object, we need an analogous system-wide cache:

❑ We need a way of uniquely identifying system-wide objects. This is the easy part, since COM transparently preserves object identity across the network.

❑ We need to implement the system-wide object as a workstation singleton on a single machine – that is, we need to ensure that only one workstation singleton ever runs at any time. In particular, this means that we have to make sure that our server always has its own security context, and cannot be launched on some other workstation. In addition, we need to ensure that a second attempt to launch the server, whether on the same or a different machine, will detect the first instance running. This depends on the naming mechanism outlined below.

❑ We need a naming mechanism that can find the unique, system-wide object that we are looking for. This naming system could be based on access to a common registration database, such as Active Directory, or a regular database server, or even some roll-your-own registration scheme based on files. The simplest (but least flexible) option is to set up the DCOM client configuration so that the server always runs on a single named machine. A more sophisticated approach might wrap the actual name registration mechanism in a custom moniker, to obtain the many benefits of monikers (see above).

Lifetime Management

Here are some techniques that are useful because of COM's reliance on reference counting for lifetime management. The most frequently useful of these is **weak identity**, which can be used in the majority of cases. The remaining cases can be resolved by using a combination of **object locking** and `IExternalConnection`.

The Reference Cycle Problem

Consider the figure below, which shows a reference cycle of interfaces IA, IB and IC:

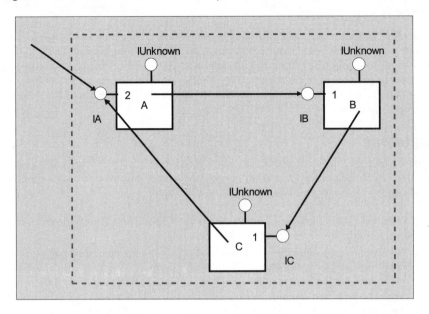

Each interface is labeled with the number of outstanding strong references to it – in other words, its reference count. The only reference external to the cycle is the one to IA, so when this reference is released, each of the objects in the cycle should be released as well. However, at this point, the new reference counts will be IA: 1, IB: 1 and IC: 1. For interface IA to be released, the object C must release it, which it only does when it de-allocates itself. This can only happen when IC's reference count goes to zero – that is, when B releases it. Of course B only releases IC in its own destruction sequence, which can only be triggered by the release of IB by A. This depends on IA's reference count going to zero, which is where we came in. The bottom line is that the resources for these objects can't be released.

Reference cycles can occur in a number of common situations. We've already seen that a reference cycle is involved in aggregation, but broken with a weak reference (see the next subsection). Another common scenario for a reference cycle is a hierarchical structure in which a parent node has references to its child nodes, and each child node has a reference back to its parent node. Having a generic solution to this problem is therefore quite important.

Weak References

The figure below shows one way to resolve the reference cycle problem:

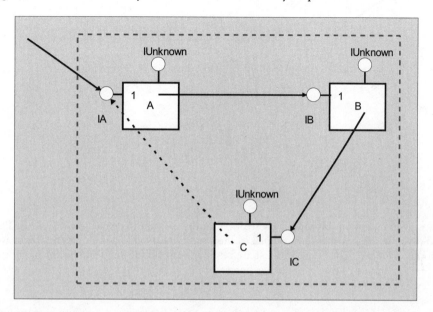

The last reference in the cycle (the cycle begins at the external reference) is a weak reference – one whose reference count is not incremented. In this scenario, when the external reference is released, IA's reference count *does* actually go to zero, causing A to self-destruct and triggering a cascade of destruction through the cycle. Obviously there has to be some ad-hoc or 'out-of-band' mechanism for informing object C that it is holding a weak reference to IA.

Of course, the problem with this solution is that it breaks one of the rules of COM: weak references are prohibited. As we saw in Chapter 3, a weak reference can break down when it crosses an apartment boundary.

Split or Weak Identity

The split identity technique permits an object to expose a **weak identity**. The strong identity of an object is an interface, which causes the object to begin its destruction sequence when its reference count goes to zero. A weak identity is an interface that, by contrast, does not cause the object to go into its destruction sequence when its reference count goes to zero. *Both* counts must be zero in order for the object destruction sequence to complete.

The next figure shows the same problem we've been addressing solved with a split identity:

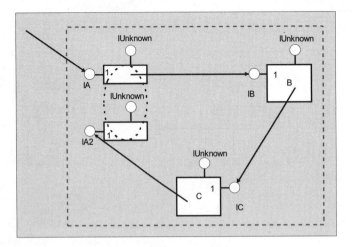

The object A now exposes two identities: its strong identity IA, and its weak identity IA2. The cycle is 'completed' by C holding a strong reference to the weak identity IA2 on A. There are no weak references in this scenario. There has to be some ad-hoc, out-of-band mechanism for passing the weak identity to object C, but once the identity has been passed, C can treat it as it would treat any other COM interface.

Now when the external reference to the strong identity IA is released, IA's reference count goes to zero, which triggers object A's destruction sequence. This sequence causes IB to be released, in turn triggering IC's release. Finally, the destruction sequence of C releases IA2, which causes its reference count to go to zero, thus enabling the completion of A's destruction sequence.

Alternate Identities

A variation on split identity is to have two different COM objects, each with its own *strong* identity. The objects share parts of their implementation, and the identities share a reference count. The object lifetimes are therefore dependent – neither can be de-allocated until both have had their reference counts go to zero. This scenario is shown below:

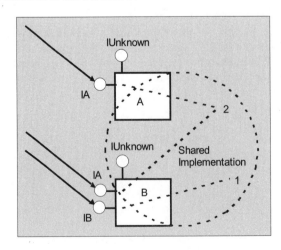

Essentially, a single 'object implementation' is representing itself as two different COM identities, A and B. These both export the interface IA, but B additionally exports IB. Notice how the IA reference count is shared by A and B. As far as the client is concerned, they are two *different* COM objects or identities whose lifetimes happen to be coincident.

Alternate identity is an extremely useful implementation technique that I've used in Chapter 7 to solve the problem of having a single 'object' implement several scripting interfaces.

Identity Navigation

Although not always desirable, there are situations where some clients need to be able to navigate between the different identities that share an implementation. I use the following interface for this purpose:

```
[...]
interface ICOMIdentity : IUnknown
{
    [id(1), helpstring("GetAlternateID")]
    HRESULT GetAlternateID([in] LONG a_vl,
                           [out, retval] IUnknown** a_ppuk);

    [id(2), helpstring("QIAltID")]
    HRESULT QIAltID([in] LONG a_vlid,
                    [in] REFIID a_riid,
                    [out, iid_is(a_riid), retval] IUnknown** a_ppuk);
};
```

The first method of the interface allows the IUnknown pointer of a specific alternate identity of the object to be returned. The second allows a QI() on a specific alternate identity.

Object Locking

We know that a COM object is only guaranteed to stay in memory for as long as there are strong references to it. However, there are certain complicated situations in object linking, involving multiple linking containers, where the *only* references to an object are weak references. In these situations, it may become necessary to 'lock' the object for a specified duration programmatically – that is, to force it to stay in memory by some means other than the interface reference counts.

One standard COM API call that's used for locking an object is the CoLockObjectExternal() function. Internally, this function works by calling AddRef() on the object (on its IUnknown interface), thus creating a strong reference on it. This may only be called on an *actual* object, so it should only be called by the object implementation, not by a client.

Other ways of locking provide explicit lock/unlock methods. These increment/decrement a lock count that is used by a Release() implementation in addition to the normal reference count. For example, an OLE embedded object is required to hold a lock on its container. This is necessary in the case when the embedded object is itself a link source into some other application.

Protocol: External Connections

The COM standard marshaling architecture keeps track of *all* marshaled interfaces for an object, regardless of whether they have been AddRef()'d or not. It also supports a protocol whereby the object itself can be informed of each marshaled interface. If the object supports the IExternalConnection interface, the AddConnection() and ReleaseConnection() methods are called by the COM infrastructure every time an interface on the object is marshaled. The object can use this to keep track of all external references, weak and strong, and to help lock it in memory until they are all released.

This protocol works because the stub manager (recall the standard marshaling architecture from Chapter 3) for an object that implements IExternalConnection will not destroy itself even if it no longer has live references to the object. Instead, the object must itself call the CoDisconnectObject() API function when it is ready to destroy itself. This function call communicates with the stub manager to cause a graceful release of the object as well as the stub manager.

Global Information and Operations

Recall from Chapter 2 that it is hard to associate 'global' information with COM objects and servers. For example, if your COM server is a DLL, you can't just use a regular DLL entry point to retrieve static information stored in the DLL, since the same DLL may be loaded independently by non-COM code.

This is not a serious obstacle, since there are various techniques to associate information with an entire class, or even an entire application. We will look at these in the following subsections.

Class Objects

There are many situations in which it is necessary to associate data and/or operations with *every* object of a class, rather than any specific object instance. For instance, something as simple as keeping track of the number of active instances of the class has to be done on a class-wide basis. In the object-oriented community, the standard pattern for doing this is the **class object**. As its name suggests, a class object is an object that is associated with an entire class.

COM has partial support for class objects as a consequence of its class factory mechanism. A COM server is required to expose a class object for each creatable class implemented by that server. This object can be accessed by the CoGetClassObject() API function that takes as a parameter the CLSID of the class for which a class object is desired.

The reason I consider this support to be limited is that the standard class object is a server singleton (see above) − it is associated with all objects of the class *that are created on the server that exposes the class object*. If another server instance is able to create the same class, there is a different class object for the objects that it serves up. Thus, the COM notion of a class object allows for multiple instances, each associated with a subset of all the objects of the class.

Despite these limitations, the COM class object works reasonably well in many situations, particularly in the class creation sequence where a server singleton is all that is needed. A class object needs to implement IClassFactory or IClassFactory2 if it is to use the CoCreateInstance() method, or some other constructor interface if it isn't.

Protocol: IClassActivate

In order to provide greater flexibility than is provided by the standard class object mechanism (`CoGetClassObject()`), the `IClassActivate` protocol has been added to the class moniker binding sequence.

In its binding process under this protocol, the class moniker no longer blindly calls `CoGetClassObject()` with the appropriate class ID. Instead, It first checks the object that is bound by the moniker to the left of it (in a composite moniker) for the `IClassActivate` interface. This interface has a member method `CoGetClassObject()` which can be substituted for the standard `CoGetClassObject()` call.

This mechanism allows the architect to replace `CoGetClassObject()` calls systematically, throughout the architecture, and thereby replace the standard COM class object with any other object as desired.

Application Objects

Just as class objects are needed in order to have a central coordination point for an entire class, **application objects** are needed as a central coordination point for an application. The IDL attribute `appobject` is used to decorate the class that represents the application.

In the OLE terminology, an application is a document based, user interactive program, such as Microsoft Word or Excel. The application object is required to be registered in the ROT using the API call `RegisterActiveObject()`. This registration mechanism ensures that the object is not duplicated on a workstation.

Optimization Techniques

The next series of techniques have to do with optimizing time or resources. It is best to introduce techniques such as these once you have a working implementation and know where the true performance bottlenecks are.

Resource Allocation

There are a number of standard COM optimization techniques that are variations on the theme of **lazy evaluation** – putting off a computation until the last possible moment before its results are actually needed.

Tear-Offs

An interface that is created only on demand and maintains a reference count independent of the rest of the object is called a **tear-off**. When this reference count goes to zero, the resources used to implement the interface are released. If another `QI()` comes in for the interface, a new set of resources are allocated, and a new interface pointer is exposed to the client. Typically, a tear-off interface is not created when the object is first created, but when the first `QI()` for it occurs.

> *Tear-offs are the reason why* `QI()` *doesn't guarantee that an interface pointer (except* `IUnknown*`*) will remain constant over the lifetime of an object.*

The tear off is a useful technique for implementing resource-intensive interfaces that are not commonly requested, or interfaces that are only required transiently. The resources are allocated on demand, and, as long as the tear-off is in-apartment, they are released when the reference count goes to zero. As mentioned in Chapter 3, out-of-apartment tear-offs do not release resources in quite such an optimized fashion.

Flyweights

There has been some confusion over the precise meaning of the term **flyweight** when applied to COM. The definition that seems to be currently accepted is that a flyweight is a COM interface that is created on-demand for a piece of program state (such as a C++ object) that is not normally a COM object.

The rationale is quite simple. Certain objects have so little state that converting every object of the type into a COM object adds an unacceptable amount of overhead. Consider making each cell in a spreadsheet a COM object, for example, or each character in a text document. In this situation, the storage cost of adding COM interfaces is prohibitively high. In Win32, each interface adds a storage cost of 4 bytes (the size of the vptr) per object. With even 4 or 5 interfaces, that adds up to 16 to 20 extra bytes just for interface *pointers*, which can easily (at least) double the size of a small object.

Using the flyweight technique, these bytes are not allocated until an interface is actually requested. This optimization works very well if most of the small objects are never actually used as COM objects. While similar in spirit to the idea of a tear-off, the implementation of flyweights is completely dependent on the specific situation in which they are to be used.

> *If you're a fan of the "Gang of Four" Design Patterns book, I should point out that even though the problem being solved is quite similar, their "flyweight" design pattern is not directly comparable to this technique.*

Lazy Initialization

The tear-off is a technique for creating the entire interface when first requested by QI(). A less drastic use of the same technique is to create the interface at object creation time, but to defer any time-consuming resource allocation or initialization to the first use of the interface. Initialization is initiated by the QI() implementation when the interface is first requested.

Lazy Re-use

By the same token, interfaces implemented by contained objects, whether delegated or aggregated, can delay inner object creation and initialization until the interface is actually requested or used.

Network Performance

Marshaling interface method invocations across the network generally has a serious impact on the performance characteristics of the interface. These performance characteristics are described by two factors: latency and bandwidth.

Latency is the minimum delay involved in setting up the communication channel between the proxy and stub. The latency of a cross-process call on the same machine can generally be measured in hundreds of machine instructions, which generally means microseconds of time. In contrast, the latency of a cross-network call can be measured in tenths of a second on the Internet, and sometimes even more than that.

The **bandwidth** of a data transfer is the rate at which data is transferred during the invocation. It can be in the multi-Mbytes per second range in a single machine cross process call, or less than a Kbyte per second across a busy wide area network.

To see what this can mean, consider a method invocation that transfers 10K of data as in arguments to a call. If the method were invoked across a process boundary on a single machine, it would take microseconds for the method to invoke. In contrast, a cross network invocation on the Internet could take up to 10 seconds. If this method were to be called 100 times, it would still take negligible amounts of time on a single machine, but be prohibitively expensive across a network. This highlights the performance issues that can arise when you take an interface that works just fine on a single machine and use it across a network.

Finally, you need to consider the performance characteristics of the ORPC protocol used by COM remote method calls. There is overhead of approximately 200 bytes per ORPC call for an unauthenticated call. Authentication requires a lot of additional traffic, and should be avoided where possible.

Passing Structures instead of Interfaces

Consider this Automation-capable interface:

```
[...]
interface IFoo : IDispatch
{
    [propget, id(2), helpstring("Price")]
    HRESULT Price([out, retval] LONG* a_pl);

    [propget, id(3), helpstring("Number")]
    HRESULT Number([out, retval] SHORT* a_ps);

    [propget, id(4), helpstring("Time")]
    HRESULT Time([out, retval] LONG* a_pl);
};
```

If a number of objects with this interface were being transferred across a process boundary in a single method invocation – in a call to this method, for example:

```
HRESULT Next(
        [in] ULONG a_vulCount,
        [out, size_is(a_vulCount, 1), length_is(*a_pulFetched, 1)] IFoo** a_ppfo,
        [out] ULONG* a_pulFetched);
```

the caller would receive not the actual interfaces, but proxies to them. This means that each 'property get' on the interface would result in a fresh remote method call that *also* crossed the process boundary. If the Next() method were used to fetch 100 IFoo interfaces at one go, and each of these interfaces was queried for all three of its numeric properties, how many remote method invocations would result? The answer is 301 (one invocation to get back 100 interfaces, and then three invocations on each of them).

If, instead of passing the Automation interface with three properties, we passed this structure:

```
typedef struct tagFoo
{
    LONG  m_vlPrice;
    LONG  m_vlTime;
    SHORT m_vsNumber;
} SFoo;
```

using this method:

```
HRESULT Next(
        [in] ULONG a_vulCount,
        [out, size_is(a_vulCount, 1), length_is(*a_pulFetched, 1)] SFoo** a_abid,
        [out] ULONG* a_pulFetched);
```

we would now,in the exact same scenario, have only 1 remote method invocation that transfers all the numeric data in an array of 100 pointers to `struct`s.

As you've seen, cross machine remote method calls are orders of magnitude slower than in-process or single machine invocations, so the technique of replacing interfaces with structures is well worth considering.

Smart Interface Proxies

Let's consider the same interface as before, `IFoo`. Further, let's assume that two of its three properties – say, `Number` and `Time` – are fixed once the object has been created. However, the third property, `Price`, is subject to change over time. The way COM standard marshaling works, each property lookup would result in a remote method call. There is currently no way of specifying that a property is a constant.

If you are willing to consider smart interface proxies, this is not hard to fix. Instead of using the standard COM proxy directly, we create a **smart proxy**. This is an object of an altogether different class that exposes the same interface (`IFoo`) as the actual object. It stashes away an interface pointerto the actual object, which is most probably `IFoo`, although it could use some other, optimized, interface. If the client looks up the `Number` or `Time` properties now, the smart proxy implementation only needs to query the remote object once (the first time the request comes in), and then cache the received data. On subsequent requests, it simply returns the cached value. Every request for `Price`, on the other hand, results in a remote method call, since its value is not a constant.

There is nothing special about smart proxies; they're just ordinary COM classes that use a variation on delegation to implement an interface. This makes them very easy to implement, and they cause no difficulties as long as there is no issue of object identity – that is, as long as the client does not request that the proxy do anything that only the real object could do. This essentially boils down to avoiding performing a `QI()` on the interface exposed by the smart proxy.

> **This is perhaps my biggest single reason for preferring application designs where the client never has to perform a `QI()`. It enables the easy integration of smart proxies when the application has to be distributed.**

Notice that these smart proxies are quite different from those used in custom and handler marshaling. The handlers used in *those* protocols are smart proxies that are integrated into the COM architecture (and have the advantage of respecting COM identity). Such handlers have to follow a very specific protocol that requires a fundamentally non-portable operation (persisting to an IStream), whereas our smart proxies are much simpler and completely portable (although they do not respect COM identity).

Custom Marshaling: Client Side Handlers

Referring back to the discussion of Chapter 3, custom marshaling has been used to implement various 'smart proxying' strategies. One of the most popular of these is the **marshal by value** (MBV) proxy that uses object state serialization to recreate the entire remote object in-process.

Note though, that if your object model doesn't require object identity (that is, QueryInterface()), there is absolutely no need to get into custom marshaling – ordinary smart proxies work very well indeed.

Minimize Transfer Data

An obvious optimization for network performance is to minimize the amount of data that needs to be transferred in a remote method call. For instance, if the method has an array parameter, it's a good idea to pass the minimum number of elements that will allow the server method to work correctly. As you saw in Chapter 3, the IDL attributes size_is(), first_is(), last_is(), etc. allow you to do this.

Aggregate Data Transfers

Another consequence of the network performance characteristics mentioned above is that five method invocations with five parameters apiece is frequently more expensive than a single method invocation with 25 parameters. This is because the client sees five individual latency periods in the five-transfer case, and only a single latency period in the one-transfer case. The time required to transfer the parameters is roughly equal in both cases.

This means that it is often better to have methods that take a large number of parameters for cross machine invocations. Thus, instead of setting/getting the three properties individually on a marshaled IFoo interface, it might be better to have a separate interface with this signature that allows aggregated sets/gets:

```
interface IRemFoo : IUnknown
{
    SetFoo(LONG, SHORT, LONG);
    GetFoo(LONG*, SHORT*, LONG*);
};
```

An aggregated interface of this kind could even be used by a smart proxy façade that exposed the simpler IFoo interface. This would work very well in conjunction with the interface ITwoPhase presented earlier for transactional updates. The client could set the properties on IFoo individually, and cause IRemFoo to be invoked by calling ITwoPhase::Commit() when the state update was complete.

Latency Hiding by Multithreading

A standard approach to dealing with latency is the **latency hiding** technique. This is based on the fact that delays caused by latency, unlike delays caused by limited bandwidth, are not intrinsically throughput limiting. As long as the client can do something useful while it is waiting for the connection to be made, there is no theoretical loss of throughput performance.

This fits very well with multithreaded applications, where both the client and the server have multiple threads performing useful activities. If any single thread is blocked waiting for a network transfer to continue, some other thread can take control and perform useful work. Since the COM runtime supports MTAs, the server only needs to implement MTA objects in order to take advantage of multithreading.

Limiting Multithreading

However, even multiple threads of control have disadvantages. Each thread consumes operating system resources, so if the number of threads becomes too large, the overall responsiveness of the kernel can drop dramatically. Since COM currently has no way of limiting the number of RPC threads in an MTA, this can be a problem if the server is receiving large numbers of requests.

> *There is a fix for this problem that involves controlling the STA in which your object is created. For details, check out* Professional ATL COM Programming *by Dr. Richard Grimes.*

An Online Auction System: A Case Study

For my examples, I will use an online auction system that I created for this book. The system is used by a fictitious Internet startup company, MajorDeals.Com, which has received a large round of venture capital on the basis of a demonstrated Internet auction market.

Functional Description

The application that I will develop in this book is an online auction site. A functional description of this application follows:

- ❑ A number of lots are offered for auction. Each lot consists of a number of identical items. Auction participants can visit the Internet site and search through the available lots to find items that interest them. At this point, a user can check on the status of the auction (see the current bidding on the item), and if they so choose, place their own bid as well. As the auction progresses, users are informed when their bids are displaced by better bids, as well as being informed if their bid is successful.

- ❑ The system will also have other users: the vendors that actually provide items for sale, and the customer service folks who have to respond to cranky user calls. It will also contain the transaction and order fulfillment systems that provide the back-end of the service.

- ❑ Certain aspects of the application need to be exposed through scripting interfaces for use by application programmers. The user interface for the application will be created separately using several client technologies.

Development Strategies

Our initial stab at the design of the application, presented in this chapter, models the first part of the functional description. It is a relatively straightforward translation of the use cases into a domain model described in terms of COM IDL interfaces. I will use the strategies in the following sections to develop the application over this and the next two chapters.

The most important meta-strategy is to make incremental changes to get from working prototype to full product. With a good initial design, this ensures that we are close to a fully functional/shippable application at all times, greatly reducing the development risk.

Feature Set Evolution

I shall begin by implementing the features in part 1 of the functional description above. As the requirements for the application become clearer over time, I will continue adding and refining features.

COM-based designs support such evolution extremely well, since new and refined functionality is simply exposed as new interfaces.

I will not actually implement part 2 of the specification in this book; it is present to remind you of the larger context within which our design has to work.

Distribution Evolution

I'll start by implementing the server as an STA in-process server. This allows me to get most of the code working without having to worry about issues concerning remoting. The application will then be implemented as an executable server running on the same machine, and finally as a fully distributed application running on multiple machines.

This strategy allows me to encapsulate distribution risk, because the bulk of my application code is debugged before I start the distribution. The issues that I need to consider at the point of distributing the application are:

- ❑ Class/interface design from the perspective of optimizing performance for inter-process and possibly inter-machine invocation
- ❑ Thread safety issues

Optimization Strategy

For optimization, I use the universal strategy: first get it working, then tune it. I will make no attempt at optimization in the early stages of the design and implementation. Once the application is working, I will identify potential trouble spots and tune only those areas.

Architecture Strategy

I will build a traditional, fat-client application that runs on one machine and uses a local ODBC data source and the file system for persistence. I will also show how the architecture allows easy evolution to a thin client, Web-based application.

Interface Design Strategy

The most important tradeoffs in interface design are ease of use vs. performance, and simplicity vs. power. I will start off by creating simple, easy-to-use interfaces. As the requirements and performance issues become clearer over time, I will add higher performance interfaces that will not necessarily be as easy to use. At this point, the simpler interfaces will be converted into façades that wrap the high performance interfaces. The user of the object model will then have the choice of using the simple interface or the more complex one.

Use Cases

In this book, I will not go through a formal object-oriented analysis and design process. However, I *will* walk through the more important use cases while designing the application. Here is the most important use case scenario:

- ❏   A user browses or searches through lot descriptions and finds an item that interests them
- ❏   They can then check the status of the ongoing auction: the bids that are currently active
- ❏   If they choose, they can place a bid of their own
- ❏   Finally, they are informed of the status of the auction after their bid

Designing for COM: Objects and Interfaces

This design leads us naturally to think of classes to represent the nouns in the use cases. These are:

- ❏   An individual lot
- ❏   A collection of lots
- ❏   An individual bid
- ❏   A collection of bids
- ❏   An auction user

However, COM designs never deal with objects directly – they all deal with interfaces. This is where COM design departs from traditional object design.

State and Capabilities

A COM interface represents an aspect of the behavior or capability of an object. The state of the object is never directly visible to a COM client; only that aspect of the state that is exposed by a specific behavior can be discovered.

Object-oriented Mixin Classes

As a matter of fact, this is not as foreign an idea as it might at first appear. Object-oriented programming has long had the notion of **mixin classes** and capabilities-based programming. Within this framework, an object is viewed as providing its functionality in sets of 'capabilities' (such as the capability to save itself to a stream) that are typically exposed by inheriting from a mixin class, which is frequently an abstract base class (or an implementation thereof). A client of the class sees it not as a whole, but in terms of the individual capabilities that it provides. This kind of programming needs a somewhat different mindset from the traditional object-as-state-and-behavior view of the world.

This idiom has never achieved mainstream stature in the C++ world, although it seems to have done so in Java. This is despite the fact that, at this point in its evolution, C++ has very good language support for programming with mixin classes: multiple inheritance and run-time type identification.

In C++, a mixin class is best described as a 'fully abstract' base class. A class that implements the capability identified by one or more mixins can do so by multiply inheriting from the abstract base classes. A client of the implementation class can then query for a capability by performing a `dynamic_cast()` from the implementation class to the capability base class. In some respects, this C++ idiom has a very COM-ish flavor – fully-abstract base classes and `QueryInterface()` style run-time functionality negotiation. Of course, the C++ solution is language dependent, while the COM solution is not.

Interfaces as Partial Objects

Another way of thinking about interfaces is as 'partial' objects, where each interface represents a subset of the object's full state and behavior. This is actually how Visual Basic clients view interfaces (which are called "objects" in this context).

Viewed in this fashion, all the standard object-oriented tools and techniques work very well if you substitute interfaces for objects. You can then design the functionality of each *interface* separately, and assign each interface to an object as is appropriate.

The one thing you have to be careful about during such design is that you're not making any assumptions about the complete object based on its state, or even on the other interfaces it exposes.

Design Patterns and Re-use

One of the most significant features of COM design is the amount of re-use that is possible. The earliest significant use of COM was in the development of the OLE and ActiveX technologies, and, as I mentioned earlier, OLE can be considered to be a set of completely specified design patterns for common paradigms of application interoperability. As much of your code will be solving the same problems, you can re-use the OLE interfaces.

For example, if your COM class needs the capability to save itself to a stream, you can simply implement (or re-use a boilerplate implementation of) `IPersistStream` on your class, even if it is not going to interact with any other ActiveX container or server. In most cases this is preferable to rolling your own persistence interface, since you are utilizing a large body of experience and code.

Designing Interfaces: The Specification Model

In this section, I will show you how to build up the specification model for your application by stepping through a use case analysis. After this is done, additional interfaces will be added to fill out the specification model.

Use Case Interfaces

I'll now step through each of the use cases that were identified earlier. I'll keep breaking each one down into its constituent cases until sub-division isn't possible. At that point I'll list the various interfaces that are required to fulfil the requirements of the 'atomic' use cases.

Use Case: Find an Item

A user browses or searches through lot descriptions and finds an item that interests them.

This use case can be decomposed into the following sections:

Find a Lot

The user requests a collection of lots that satisfies some criterion. If you've used a web search form, you know that there are usually several ways of finding an item of interest. The result of such a search is a list of possible matches. In our example, let us assume that each 'find' operation returns a list of toys. Here are the common ways in which such a list is generated:

❏ A simple search through the entire database looking for the occurrence of one or more search strings. Thus we might look for the search string `"Furby"` and find all lots that have a Furby for sale.

❏ A more sophisticated search with additional constraints on the search space, such as restricting the category of records to be searched. In addition, the search strings could be more complex, perhaps allowing Boolean predicates to combine phrases. To extend the example, if our search space had millions of records, we might want to constrain the search by restricting the category to **stuffed creature** in addition to the string `"Furby AND talk"`. As you can readily imagine, such search constraints or filters are highly domain-specific.

❏ Sometimes, the lists have been pre-selected by editorial staff to meet some criteria. For instance, a link on the home page of the auction site might suggest browsing for **hot toys**. Such lists are sometimes generated from the same database as the search results using a special filter that returns the relevant items. In other instances they may be in a different database, or even statically defined.

Additionally, it should be possible to cancel a long-running find operation on demand.

Notice that searching for an item is a very general capability – one that you'd expect to crop up in all sorts of applications. Is this an opportunity to re-use design? For databases that respond to ANSI SQL-style queries, Microsoft has defined the OLE DB interfaces. If we choose to implement our find function on top of a relational database, we will probably wind up using the OLE DB interfaces, anyway. Should I expose them to the user? The downsides to using OLE DB are:

❏ It is based on viewing data as hierarchies of rowsets
❏ It is a completely general and therefore rather complicated framework

Either of these points is sufficient to kill the idea of exposing OLE DB to the user. We need to present much simpler domain-specific abstractions instead. I'll keep the interface extremely simple to begin with. The user will be able to:

❏ Find lots based on a category
❏ Cancel the current find operation

In order to keep the sample complexity manageable I will leave these other two operations as exercises:

❏ Find lots based on a full text search
❏ Find lots based on a custom filter

From a design standpoint, however, these are not very different from the category-based find operation:

```
[...]
interface ILotFinder : IDispatch
{
    [id(1), helpstring("Cancel Current Find Operation")]
    HRESULT Cancel();

    [id(2), helpstring("Search Based on Category")]
    HRESULT SearchCategory([in] LONG a_vlCategory, [out, retval] ILots** a_pplt);
};
```

The `SearchCategory()` method performs a search based on a category ID. The result of the search is an interface pointer to `ILots`, which (as we'll discuss in a moment) represents a collection of lots. This return value is the collection of lots that belong to the specified category.

The `Cancel()` method is simple. It is intended to cancel the current search (whatever that may be) on the object exposing the interface. Note that this means that only one search can be active per `ILotFinder` interface instance. Also note that the `Cancel()` operation must be callable while the search operation is active, which implies that they have to be capable of being run on different threads.

Categories

Notice that the category search operation is using an integer to represent a category; this is the normal way to represent a finite number of options in any kind of searchable collection (such as a relational database). However, this is *not* a domain-specific abstraction. The user sees categories as descriptive strings that are mapped onto integers by the system. A simple way to maintain this mapping is as a collection of integer-string pairs, and we do this using the normal COM collection protocol, as follows:

```
[...]
interface ICategories : IDispatch
{
    [propget, id(DISPID_VALUE), helpstring("Item")]
    HRESULT Item([in] LONG a_vlIndex, [out, retval] BSTR* a_pstr);

    [propget, id(DISPID_NEWENUM), helpstring("_NewEnum"), restricted]
    HRESULT _NewEnum([out, retval] LPUNKNOWN* a_punk);

    [propget, id(1), helpstring("Count")]
    HRESULT Count([out, retval] LONG* a_pl);

    [id(2), helpstring("GetItemID")]
    HRESULT GetItemID([in] LONG a_vlIndex, [out, retval] LONG* a_pl);

    [id(3), helpstring("Category Lookup")]
    HRESULT ID2Category([in] LONG a_vl, [out, retval] BSTR* a_pstr);

    [id(4), helpstring("ID Lookup")]
    HRESULT Category2ID([in] BSTR a_pstr, [out, retval] LONG* a_pl);

    [id(5), helpstring("GetStringAndID")]
    HRESULT GetStringAndID([in] LONG a_vlIndex,
                           [out] LONG* a_pl,
                           [out] BSTR* a_pstr);
};
```

The first three methods above are standard for collections, so the only explanation required is of the precise types that were chosen for the various parameters:

❑ The Item() method takes a LONG index into the collection. This method returns the string part of the string-ID pair that is stored at the specified index. This is returned as a BSTR to keep the interface scripting-compliant.

❑ The _NewEnum() property returns the IUnknown pointer on an enumerator for the collection class.

❑ The Count() method returns the current size of the collection.

Because each item in the collection is a pair (consisting of the category string and its corresponding ID) the Item() method is not sufficient. We also need the GetItemID() method to return the ID stored at a specific index of the collection. There is also a method GetStringAndID() which returns both the ID and the string. This is the method of choice since it returns the pair in one shot, but Automation-only clients cannot deal with the non-retval, out-only parameters in its type signature (although they can still 'see' the method). This is the rationale for requiring both Item() and GetItemID() – their signatures are fully scripting-compliant.

Finally, the ID2Category() method is used to lookup the category of a given ID. It finds the category-ID pair in the collection and returns the category associated with that ID. The Category2ID() method goes the other way: it returns the ID associated with a specified category.

The category collection does not have Add() or Remove() methods (the other standard collection methods) because this collection is static – there is no use case for adding and removing category-ID pairs. Clearly, some exogenous mechanism is required to initialize the object implementing this interface.

Lot Collection

The result of a 'find' operation is a list of auction lots that match the selection criteria. This list will be modeled as a COM collection as well:

```
[...]
interface ILots : IDispatch
{
    [id(DISPID_VALUE), helpstring("Item")]
    HRESULT Item([in] LONG a_vlIndex, [out, retval] ILotScript** a_pplt);

    [propget, id(DISPID_NEWENUM), helpstring("_NewEnum"), restricted]
    HRESULT _NewEnum([out, retval] LPUNKNOWN* a_punk);

    [propget, id(1), helpstring("Count")]
    HRESULT Count([out, retval] LONG* a_pl);
};
```

This is also a pretty standard COM collection interface. The Item() method uses a LONG input parameter to index into the collection and returns an ILotScript interface pointer (which will be examined shortly).

Once again, this interface has no modification methods. The current use case (which is the basis for the interface design) does not permit modification of the collection, only iteration through it.

Lot Name

When the search operation is complete, the user is given a list of lot descriptions. Implicit in any such list is the idea that each description corresponds to a unique auction lot. This lot is uniquely identified by a handle or a name, which may or may not be made visible to the user.

At the end of a web search, for example, each search item is uniquely identified by a URL. For large database searches, this URL may consist of a generic prefix followed by arguments that identify the specific record or query result that generates the requested page. The user does not see the URL explicitly; it is looked up by the browser code when the user clicks on a hyperlink. The URL is typically displayed in the address edit box after the page has been fetched.

Clearly we can pick any reasonable naming scheme for lots. We will select the name type to be a string, and leave the binding details unspecified, because:

❑ This gives us great flexibility (remember moniker display names) to change the naming and binding mechanism later

❑ The 'true' name of the lot never needs to be visible to the end user

Lot Summary

When the auction users see listings for a lot, there is a certain minimum amount of descriptive information they expect to find. This description is used to decide whether they want to examine the bidding process for the lot, or see more detailed information about it. The description must therefore consist of the following minimum information:

❑ A one-sentence description of the item being auctioned
❑ The category to which the lot belongs
❑ The starting price for bids on the lot
❑ The increment by which the bid has to rise
❑ The time at which bidding stops
❑ The current lowest bid price
❑ The current highest bid price
❑ The time that the most recent bid was placed

Here is the interface that results from these criteria:

```
[...]
interface IAuctionInfo : IDispatch
{
    [propget, id(3), helpstring("Description")]
    HRESULT Description([out, retval] BSTR* a_pstrDescription);

    [propget, id(4), helpstring("Category")]
    HRESULT Category([out, retval] LONG* a_vlCatID);

    [propget, id(5), helpstring("Starting Price")]
    HRESULT StartPrice([out, retval] LONG* a_vl);

    [propget, id(6), helpstring("Bid Increment")]
    HRESULT BidIncrement([out, retval] LONG* a_vl);
```

```
        [propget, id(7), helpstring("Lo Bid")]
        HRESULT LoBid([out, retval] LONG* a_vl);

        [propget, id(8), helpstring("Hi Bid")]
        HRESULT HiBid([out, retval] LONG* a_vl);

        [propget, id(9), helpstring("Auction Closes At")]
        HRESULT ClosesAt([out, retval] DATE* a_vl);

        [propget, id(10), helpstring("Time of Last Bid")]
        HRESULT LastBidAt([out, retval] DATE* a_vl);
};
```

Note that this interface is simply a list of properties, one for each piece of information required in the summary. The description, being a string, is represented as a BSTR. The category is being represented by a LONG ID. The start price, bid increment, low bid and high bid are all stored as LONGs. The auction close time and time of last bid are both stored as the Automation DATE type.

This last decision is made for ease of use from scripting languages. As you'll see in the next chapter, it's possible to use other time formats from scripting languages, but at the cost of needing explicit conversion functions.

Use Case: Check Status

They can then check the status of the ongoing auction: the bids that are currently active

This use case breaks down as follows:

Bid Collection

The user receives a listing of the currently active bids on the lot. Typically, this listing will be sorted according to bid ranking. This should be fairly straightforward; the user just needs a collection of bid objects to iterate over. We will use a collection of bids for the purpose:

```
    [...]
    interface IBids : IDispatch
    {
        [id(DISPID_VALUE), helpstring("Item")]
        HRESULT Item([in] LONG a_vlIndex, [out, retval] IBid** a_ppbd);

        [propget, id(DISPID_NEWENUM), helpstring("_NewEnum"), restricted]
        HRESULT _NewEnum([out, retval] LPUNKNOWN* a_punk);

        [propget, id(1), helpstring("Count")]
        HRESULT Count([out, retval] LONG* a_pl);
    };
```

Once again, this is very similar to the other collections that you've seen. The only new type is the return value from the Item() method – it is an IBid pointer, which is discussed next.

Bid Information

For each bid in the list, the user can see basic information on the bid. This includes:

- ❏ Information about the user who placed the bid
- ❏ The price of the bid
- ❏ The number of items the user is bidding for
- ❏ The time at which the user placed the bid

This information is encapsulated in the following interface:

```
[...]
interface IBid : IDispatch
{
    [propget, id(1), helpstring("Bidder")]
    HRESULT Bidder([out, retval] IBidder** a_ppbdr);

    [propget, id(2), helpstring("Price")]
    HRESULT Price([out, retval] LONG* a_pl);

    [propget, id(3), helpstring("Number")]
    HRESULT Number([out, retval] SHORT* a_ps);

    [propget, id(4), helpstring("Time")]
    HRESULT Time([out, retval] LONG* a_pl);
};
```

Just as in the case of the lot information, this interface is implemented as a series of properties. `Price()`, `Number()` and `Time()` should be straightforward enough; `Bidder()` returns an `IBidder` pointer.

Bidder Information

The information on the bidder consists of the following basic information:

- ❏ The first name of the bidder
- ❏ The last name of the bidder
- ❏ The city of the bidder
- ❏ The state of the bidder

```
[...]
interface IBidder : IDispatch
{
    [propget, id(2), helpstring("First Name")]
    HRESULT FirstName([out, retval] BSTR* a_pstr);

    [propget, id(3), helpstring("Last Name")]
    HRESULT LastName([out, retval] BSTR* a_pstr);

    [propget, id(4), helpstring("City")]
    HRESULT City([out, retval] BSTR* a_pstr);

    [propget, id(5), helpstring("State")]
    HRESULT State([out, retval] BSTR* a_pstr);
};
```

Predictably, the interface is structured as a number of BSTR properties.

Use Case: Bid on an Item

If they choose, they can place a bid of their own.

This use case can be decomposed into the following steps:

Login

Typically, the user has to log in to the auction to establish that they are who they claim to be. For the purposes of the book, I will omit this step and assume that there is a list of members from which the user can select their identity. This is an obvious simplification to reduce the amount of code that needs to be explained.

For the purposes of satisfying our use cases, each user is identified by the IBidder interface identified earlier. We organize these into collections as follows:

```
[...]
interface IMembers : IDispatch
{
    [id(DISPID_VALUE), helpstring("Item")]
    HRESULT Item([in] LONG a_vlIndex, [out, retval] IMemberScript** a_pstr);

    [propget, id(DISPID_NEWENUM), helpstring("_NewEnum"), restricted]
    HRESULT _NewEnum([out, retval] LPUNKNOWN* a_punk);

    [propget, id(1), helpstring("Count")]
    HRESULT Count([out, retval] LONG* a_pl);
};
```

Notice that IBidder is not directly visible in this interface. For structural reasons that will become clearer over the next sections, I'm using another interface called IMemberScript that is related to a bidder.

Place a Bid

Once the user has logged in, they can place a bid by specifying a bid price and the number of items to bid for. This is encapsulated by the following interface:

```
[...]
interface IPlaceBid : IDispatch
{
    [id(1), helpstring("New Bid")]
    HRESULT CreateBid([in] IBidder* a_pmemMember,
                      [in] SHORT a_vsNumber,
                      [in] LONG a_vlPrice);
};
```

In our use case there is only a single way of creating a new bid. The CreateBid() method takes the different pieces of information that are required to do this.

Use Case: Notification

> *Finally, they are informed of the status of the auction after their bid.*

After the bid is placed, the user is automatically updated with the new status of the auction by the updated display of the bid collection.

If other users are placing bids at the same time, the new status of the auction will periodically appear to the user. Since the user may be connected to the auction using a web client, we cannot assume the use of asynchronous notifications. Therefore any status changes will become apparent only through synchronous polling.

Structural Interfaces

The use case interfaces of my application will probably wind up getting used by scripting programmers. In a conventional setting, these will also be the interfaces that will have the most code written to them. I have to plan on being able to evolve my implementation without breaking code that uses these interfaces. This has implications for how I expose my interfaces to the user; it indicates the following constraints:

- ❑ All interfaces in the design must be dual interfaces (currently a requirement for scripting clients).
- ❑ QI() must never be used for interface discovery. As mentioned earlier in the chapter, this is currently a restriction of scripting clients. It makes sense for use in the specification model, although there are problems with interface versioning as mentioned earlier.

The second restriction pretty much forces the 'property as QI()' idiom that was introduced at the beginning of the chapter. It also means that the application will be structured hierarchically.

The Interface Hierarchy

For conceptual simplicity, I decided to have a singly rooted hierarchy of interfaces. The figure below displays the interface hierarchy available to a script client, based on the use cases we've seen so far:

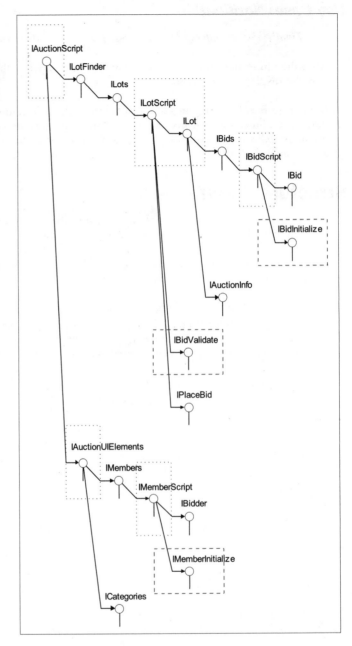

As you've seen, this hierarchy represents the navigational structure of the application – the access routes to various interfaces.

The bulk of the interfaces shown have already been introduced during the use case walkthrough. The remaining interfaces (drawn with boxes around them) are new. The ones with dashed boxes around them are utility interfaces, which are covered later. The ones with dotted boxes are there to aid the navigational structure of the interface hierarchy and are covered in the next few sections.

Top-level Interface

The top-level interface is the central interface from which all functionality discovery proceeds. It is defined as:

```
[...]
interface IAuctionScript : IDispatch
{
    [propget, id(2), helpstring("ILotFinder")]
    HRESULT ILotFinder([out, retval] ILotFinder** a_pplf);

    [propget, id(3), helpstring("IAuctionUIElements")]
    HRESULT IAuctionUIElements([out, retval] IAuctionUIElements** a_pplf);
};
```

This interface simply exposes two other interfaces as member properties; we've already seen the ILotFinder interface.

Functionality Grouping

The other interface exposed by IAuctionScript is an 'organizing' interface, and has this definition:

```
[...]
interface IAuctionUIElements : IDispatch
{
    [propget, id(1), helpstring("ICategories")]
    HRESULT ICategories([out, retval] ICategories** a_pplm);

    [propget, id(2), helpstring("property IMembers")]
    HRESULT IMembers([out, retval] IMembers** a_ppmm);
};
```

As you can see, IAuctionUIElements serves the purpose of gathering together the interfaces that will be used to create certain user interface elements. In this sense, it groups together a number of functionally related interfaces.

Note that these interfaces could have been directly exposed as members of the top-level IAuctionScript interface instead, resulting in a little less structure but one fewer method invocation for navigation. This design tradeoff is somewhat dependent on personal taste – mine is for more structure rather than less. The extreme case (zero structure) is the situation where the top-level interface exposes *all* the methods and properties of *all* the leaf and intermediate node interfaces in the hierarchy. I call this design the "kitchen-sink" interface, and it's not a desirable place to occupy in design space.

Interfaces Defining a 'Class'

Another form of organization is typified by the following interfaces:

```
[...]
interface ILot : IDispatch
{
    [propget, id(1), helpstring("LotInfo")]
    HRESULT Info([out, retval] IAuctionInfo** a_ppai);

    [propget, id(2), helpstring("Bids")]
    HRESULT Bids([out, retval] IBids** a_ppbd);

    [propget, id(3), helpstring("property IPlaceBid")]
    HRESULT IPlaceBid([out, retval] IPlaceBid** a_pppb);
};

[...]
interface ILotScript : IDispatch
{
    [propget, id(1), helpstring("property ILot")]
    HRESULT ILot([out, retval] ILot** a_pplt);

    [propget, id(2), helpstring("property IBidValidate")]
    HRESULT IBidValidate([out, retval] IBidValidate** a_ppbv);

    [id(3), helpstring("Save Lot object to the named file")]
    HRESULT Copy2File([in] BSTR FileName);
};
```

Together with `IBids`, `IAuctionInfo` and `IPlaceBid` (which we've already seen), these interfaces define the functionality associated with the auction lot class. The `ILot` interface gathers together the features of a lot that are of direct interest to the user – the auction information, the collection of bids, and the ability to place bids. The `ILotScript` interface gathers together additional features of a lot – the ones that aren't directly visible to the user as such. This includes bid validation as well as a persistence function.

This organization separates out the interfaces that were directly derived from the use case analysis (those in `ILot`) from those that are part of the 'implementation' (`ILotScript`). Once again, this reflects my personal taste for structure. It would be quite acceptable to merge the two into a single interface that exposed all the interfaces associated with the lot 'class'.

However, notice one very important fact. Although these interfaces, taken together, can be viewed as exposing the entire functionality of a lot class, we have *not* actually defined a lot class in the COM sense – they are not being navigated using `QI()`. This same structuring principle is in play in the following definitions:

```
[...]
interface IBidScript : IDispatch
{
    [propget, id(1), helpstring("IBid")]
    HRESULT IBid([out, retval] IBid** a_ppbd);

    [propget, id(2), helpstring("IBidInitialize"), hidden]
    HRESULT IBidInitialize([out, retval] IBidInitialize** a_ppbi);
};
```

```
[...]
interface IMemberScript : IDispatch
{
    [propget, id(1), helpstring("IBidder")]
    HRESULT IBidder([out, retval] IBidder** a_ppbr);

    [propget, id(2), helpstring("IMemberInitialize"), hidden]
    HRESULT IMemberInitialize([out, retval] IMemberInitialize** a_ppmi);
};
```

These are used to define the bid 'class' and the member 'class' respectively. You'll notice that the `IBidInitialize` and `IMemberInitialize` properties are both marked as `hidden`, reflecting their forbidden nature. Although they can be used from a scripting language, their definitions are not easily visible to the programmer.

Utility Interfaces

The remaining interfaces are miscellaneous utility interfaces that will be required in a real application for things like initialization and validation.

Validation Interfaces

The following validation interface will be required in a user interface that allows the user to enter new bids:

```
[...]
interface IBidValidate : IDispatch
{
    [id(1), helpstring("Validate Bid information")]
    HRESULT IsValid1([in] LONG a_vlPrice,
                     [in] SHORT a_vsNumber,
                     [in] DATE a_vdatTime,
                     [out, retval] VARIANT_BOOL* a_pb);

    [id(2), helpstring("Validate Bid information")]
    HRESULT IsValid2([in] LONG a_vlPrice,
                     [in] SHORT a_vsNumber,
                     [in] LONG a_vlTime);
};
```

The two methods do approximately the same thing, but the first is designed for use from a scripting language. It returns a `VARIANT_BOOL` to signify the validation results, which translates into the Boolean type of most client languages. It also takes a time parameter that is an Automation `DATE` type.

The second method is designed for calling from C++. It takes its time parameter as a simple `LONG`, the type used to represent time in the C runtime. It returns the validation result in the `HRESULT` return value.

In the complete interface hierarchy (based on *all* the use cases for the application), there would likely be validation interfaces for each 'class' that is exposed.

Initialization Interfaces

Strictly speaking, initialization interfaces should not be part of the scripting interface hierarchy, and in a production design I would frown upon their inclusion.

The reason for my disapproval is that initialization and persistence are both intrinsically related to object state, and therefore tied to the COM class itself. As such, exposing these sort of interfaces in the interface navigation hierarchy goes against the spirit, if not the letter, of the "No QI()" rule.

In a production system, all initialization should happen automatically in response to creation methods. For example, in our hierarchy the InsertBid() method of the IPlaceBid interface would create a bid 'object' and insert it into the lot. The scripting programmer would never have to create or initialize a bid 'object' using the IBidInitialize method.

It is, however, convenient to have these interfaces while the hierarchy is being developed and debugged, so I'm showing them to you, warts and all. In this example, we have two initialization interfaces:

```
[...]
interface IMemberInitialize : IDispatch
{
    [id(1), helpstring("Initialize object with Member information")]
    HRESULT Init([in] LONG a_vlMemberID,
                 [in] BSTR a_vstrFirst,
                 [in] BSTR a_vstrLast,
                 [in] BSTR a_vstrCity,
                 [in] BSTR a_vstrState);
};

[...]
interface IBidInitialize : IDispatch
{
    [id(1), helpstring("Initialize object with Bid information")]
    HRESULT Init([in] IBidder* a_pmem,
                 [in] LONG a_vlPrice,
                 [in] SHORT a_vsNumber,
                 [in] LONG a_vlTime);
};
```

Incidentally, you will notice that these interfaces are exposed as hidden properties of the IMemberScript and IBidScript interfaces, again reflecting the forbidden nature of these properties.

Class Design

You'll surely have noticed that as yet I've not said a word about class design. I've designed the entire scripting interface relevant to the use cases without once talking about objects or state, or showing a single line of code!

COM classes are not part of the design of a COM specification model, since it may be desirable to change the class structure as the application is tuned. (You'll recall that this separation is the rationale for avoiding QI() in the scripting interface.) In a sense, therefore, we are now getting into implementation rather than design issues. However, the class design is a relatively high-level activity, so we are not straying too far.

The goal of class design is to group the interfaces into classes. At this point it is impossible to avoid the notion of state, since the location of an interface on a class is best determined by figuring out what state is required to implement the interface. Here is a first cut at this exercise, which reflects a partitioning of only those interfaces that we have seen so far. As we will see later, additional interfaces will need to be defined for implementation purposes.

The final class structure will only become apparent as we complete the design of the implementation model in Chapter 7.

Application Class Structure

The Application Class

The application object is the one that implements the root interface of our hierarchy, and is the only object in our application that has to be directly creatable by clients of the application. All other objects are created indirectly to satisfy method invocations. This is the declaration of the application object:

```
[
    ...,
    appobject
]
coclass Auction
{
    [default] interface IAuctionScript;
    interface ILotFinder;
    interface IAuctionUIElements;
    interface ISupportErrorInfo;
};
```

Notice that in addition to the root `IAuctionScript` interface, this class also implements the `ILotFinder` and `IAuctionUIElements` interfaces. The basis for the grouping is the likelihood of the interfaces sharing state.

Furthermore, it implements the `ISupportErrorInfo` interface, indicating support for COM error objects. The default interface for this object is `IAuctionScript`.

Collection Classes

There's a class to expose each of the collection interfaces, so we have the following class declarations:

```
[
    ...,
    noncreatable
]
coclass Bids
{
    [default] interface IBids;
    interface IPlaceBid;
    interface ISupportErrorInfo;
};
```

The `Bids` class represents the collection of bids, and exposes the `IBids` interface. It is also the natural place to put the `IPlaceBid` interface, since that needs access to the state of the bid collection.

The remaining collection classes are pretty unremarkable; they expose the corresponding collection interfaces:

```
[
    ...,
    noncreatable
]
coclass Lots
{
    [default] interface ILots;
    interface ISupportErrorInfo;
};

[
    ...,
    noncreatable
]
coclass Members
{
    [default] interface IMembers;
    interface ISupportErrorInfo;
};

[
    ...,
    noncreatable
]
coclass CategoryCache
{
    [default] interface ICategories;
    interface ISupportErrorInfo;
};
```

Note that *all* the classes above expose ISupportErrorInfo. In addition, they are decorated with the noncreatable attribute – since the application client never has to create these classes directly; the creation is done by the appropriate interface implementation. All the rest of our classes will have the same characteristics.

Other Classes

The remaining classes are those that correspond to an individual bid, lot or user:

```
[
    ...,
    noncreatable
]
coclass Bid
{
    [default] interface IBidScript;
    interface IBid;
    interface IBidInitialize;
    interface ISupportErrorInfo;
};
```

```
[
    ...,
    noncreatable
]
coclass Lot
{
    [default] interface ILotScript;
    interface ILot;
    interface ILotInitialize;
    interface IBidValidate;
    interface IAuctionInfo;
    interface ISupportErrorInfo;
};

[
    ...,
    noncreatable
]
coclass Member
{
    [default] interface IMemberScript;
    interface IBidder;
    interface IMemberInitialize;
    interface ISupportErrorInfo;
};
```

Class Structure vs. Interface Structure

There are several noteworthy features of the interface design when compared with the class design. First, notice that there are only eight classes implementing the 18 interfaces in the design (and there are more that we haven't seen as yet). This gives some idea of the effect of **interface factoring** – there are many more entities. Well-designed object-oriented projects typically have a proliferation of small classes; in a way, this increase in the number of entities is the cost of client-server de-coupling.

The classes that we wound up with *do* correspond closely to the list of nouns that we derived from a coarse-grained examination of the use cases. Each class corresponds to a noun in the use case, while each interface corresponds to a capability of each noun.

Finally, although the allocation of interfaces to classes was straightforward for the most part (closely corresponding to the 'classes' of the interface hierarchy), there were a few unusual allocations. For example, recall that the `IPlaceBid` interface logically belonged to the `Lot` 'class' in the interface hierarchy (property of `ILot`). It is natural to expect that it would be physically implemented on the corresponding COM class. However, there is a separate `Bids` class that encapsulates the actual state that is modified by `IPlaceBid`. This `Bids` class is where the interface winds up being implemented.

IDL Naming Conventions

A few points about the naming conventions used in this book. The names that I use follow C++ naming conventions rather than scripting conventions, but the reason for this is simple: I'm a big consumer of my own IDL. Even when I'm writing Visual Basic/script code, I like to know the 'real' type that I'm dealing with, so I like the Hungarian prefixes on parameters. However, when the audience is pure script programmers, these prefixes are considered confusing, since the equivalent scripting data type is generally visible to the programmer.

With this in mind, here are the IDL naming conventions sanctioned by Microsoft – for the most part, they make a great deal of sense:

❑ Classes and interfaces should have plain English names. In particular, interfaces should *not* be prefixed with an I. (This is the guideline that I have the most trouble with – the C/C++ COM naming conventions for interfaces are just so deeply rooted by now!)

❑ Don't use leading underscore characters in names if possible. Before the introduction of the hidden attribute, a leading underscore was the mechanism used to hide a name from an object browser. This mechanism is now deprecated.

❑ A ProgID should have the format <TypeLibraryName> <CoClassName>. In our example, all the ProgIDs should have the prefix WroxAuction.

❑ Method parameter names are visible in the object browser. Try to avoid using Hungarian prefixes.

❑ Constants and enumerator types should be mixed case, with a leading capital.

❑ Enumerator values should be mixed case with a prefix indicating the enumerator type (remember that enumerator values are injected into the global namespace). The prefix should begin with a lower case letter.

Summary

This chapter attempted to do the following things:

❑ Provide a list of standard COM idioms and techniques along with guidelines on when to use them

❑ Present a case study on the design of an actual COM-based application

The goal of the first half was to introduce you to specific COM design techniques. You should now be familiar with:

❑ The reasons why it may be best not to use QueryInterface() for functionality navigation in a specification model

❑ The alternatives to QI(): output parameters in methods and read-only properties

❑ The problems that arise when you avoid QI()

❑ The IServiceProvider interface, and how it avoids the problems associated with QI()

❑ The use of CoTypes for documentation

❑ How to simplify interfaces by the use of façades

❑ The use of class factories in the COM creation process

❑ How to use alternative constructor interfaces on COM class objects to create and initialize new COM objects

❑ Using initialization interfaces to initialize an already-created COM object

❑ The problems associated with using Automation interfaces for initialization

❑ The various predefined persistence interfaces, and how they are used

❑ The various issues that arise when persisting data into relational databases

❑ Both the usefulness and potential pitfalls associated with validation interfaces

❑ Using transacted state changes – having an explicit 'commit' operation to make the new state 'stick'

❑ Why ordinary interface remoting is one of the best ways to transfer data between client and server

❑ The issues that arise concerning the use of Automation properties to transfer data

❑ The data object protocol, and what it's good for

❑ The power of using object state serialization to transfer data
❑ The use of custom callback mechanisms
❑ Using simple and user-defined types as error return values
❑ The OLE DB extension to the COM error object protocol
❑ Monikers, and their use in naming and binding
❑ The running object table, and how it is used with monikers
❑ COM collection and enumerator interfaces
❑ COM composition patterns, such as connection, containment, delegation and aggregation
❑ Issues related to singleton objects, and the design limitations of COM singletons
❑ The reference cycle problem, and various approaches and protocols for solving it
❑ Details of the COM alternate identity mechanism
❑ Various details of class and application objects
❑ Resource optimization techniques such as tear-offs, flyweights, lazy initialization and lazy re-use
❑ The performance characteristics of a network, and how this affects COM remote method calls
❑ Why it makes sense to remote structures rather than interfaces
❑ How to achieve superior performance using smart proxies
❑ Custom marshaling and its use to create smart proxies
❑ How and why to aggregate data transfers
❑ Why multithreading improves performance
❑ Why you might want to limit multithreading

The second part of this chapter provided you with a case study of a real COM object model. The case study began with a functional description of the problem, an online auction system. As we progressed, you should have seen:

❑ The development strategies that were used to structure the system implementation
❑ The general issues that come up when performing COM design as opposed to traditional OO design
❑ The details of designing a specification model for the system by a careful analysis of the use cases
❑ How the specification model is actually specified in terms of COM interfaces
❑ The ease with which the specification model is turned into a scripting model

What's Next?

In this chapter, I have shown you a number of COM design techniques and idioms. I also walked you through the design of a specification model for a COM object model.

In Chapter 6, we'll see how various clients use this specification model. We begin with a look at the COM bindings of various client languages – the abstraction that each language layers on top of COM in order to use it.

After we've seen these bindings, we'll build a UI based client of our specification model. Exactly the same client will be built in each of the languages, which will give you a way of seeing exactly how the object model gets used from the various languages, each with their idiosyncrasies and strengths.

Chapter 7 will describe the C++/ATL bindings, the design of the implementation model and the details of realizing that model in ATL.

6

Client Side Bindings

In this chapter, we will look at the consumers of the IDL that we used to define our system architecture. Such consumers are generally termed **clients** of the COM/IDL services. Any program can be a client of a COM server, including another server.

Since COM and IDL are standards that are independent of language and development tool, it's important for you to know how the COM services that you develop will be used in other environments, even if you do all your own work in C++. This chapter will show you exactly that.

❑   First, I shall describe the tools in each language that support COM development, especially the rapid application development (RAD) features designed for ActiveX (that is, visual) controls.

❑   Second, I'll show you the language correspondence between the data types in the IDL and the data types in the various client languages.

❑   Third, I'll show you the language constructs that are associated with COM classes, interfaces, object creation, `QI()`, `AddRef()`, `Release()`, memory allocation, errors, events and all of the other common COM features. This correspondence will give you a complete picture of the COM support in each language.

❑   Finally, I'll show you an application – a simple forms-based user interface to the auction server. I'll implement it in each major Microsoft development language: Visual Basic, Java, C++ and HTML/script. In addition to using the auction services, this user interface will also employ a couple of ActiveX controls.

By the end of this process, you will have a complete picture of how COM components of all kinds are actually used to build real applications. It is my hope that you'll have enough understanding of the issues to be able to design object models that can be used from any environment.

You may also appreciate the fact that if you encapsulate your code in COM services and design the IDL in your object model correctly, you can use just about any RAD tool to build user interfaces. Visual Basic no longer enjoys the compelling advantage that it once had.

Tool Support

If you've programmed in Visual Basic, you may be wondering exactly what it has to do with IDL, but I'm sure I can convince you that there's a strong connection. After all, the Visual Basic equivalent of a C header file is the type library, which can be supplied stand-alone or 'baked' into a DLL, OCX or EXE as a resource. Type libraries are now universal, and the Microsoft development environment for each language has tool support for incorporating type libraries into a project.

For simple COM objects, all you need are the appropriate header files, but ActiveX controls require rather more information in order to be incorporated in your projects. You need toolbar bitmaps and the like, and a bunch of other interfaces so they can be used by visual container applications and tools that 'understand' the OCX specification. In this case, the development environment needs to create the ActiveX control and use its various support interfaces, rather than simply translating IDL into a format understood by the language processor.

Such support exists, and not surprisingly the various Microsoft development environments use very similar mechanisms for incorporating ActiveX controls into forms-based applications.

Visual Basic

Visual Basic is the granddaddy of the Microsoft RAD tools. As such, it originated many of the ideas that have now been incorporated into all the other development environments. In fact, one of the conclusions of this chapter is that RAD in Visual Basic no longer enjoys the kind of productivity edge that it once did. In particular, Visual C++ 6.0 now gives almost the same RAD ease-of-use, while retaining all the benefits of C++ programming.

Visual Basic Forms

"Visual" development in Visual Basic is supported by allowing the programmer to draw controls onto the surface of a form that represents the appearance of the running code.

During design time, the programmer selects a control from a toolbar and draws it onto a form. Visual Basic adds a variable representing this control as a data member of the Visual Basic object corresponding to the form. The variable is then used at runtime to manipulate the control programmatically. At design time, the various properties of the object can be set by direct manipulation via the property window or property sheets.

Objects and values that do not correspond to visual controls may be explicitly declared and used by a programmer. The types of variables may be determined at compile time (strong typing) or left unspecified till runtime (weak typing).

Each form object has code associated with it, as well as a description of its layout (the type and position of various controls) and starting state (control properties that were set at design time).

Setting a Reference to a Type Library

In Visual Basic, it is not necessary to incorporate a type library explicitly at compile time. This is Visual Basic in its weak or dynamically typed flavor. When in this mode, only Automation objects and interfaces can be used by Visual Basic. In order to use a vtable interface, Visual Basic must have the signatures of the interface methods available at compile time, and that means setting a reference to a type library. Most entities within the library can then be used by Visual Basic.

Type Libraries of ActiveX Components

In order to be able to use an ActiveX control at design time, it must first be incorporated into Visual Basic. This is done by adding its type library to the list of components that are available to a project. Once this is accomplished, the control is made available to the programmer in a manner that is indistinguishable from that of 'native' controls.

Visual J++

Visual J++ is the most recent of the Microsoft RAD tools. While having been designed from the ground up to inter-operate with the HTML page and site design features of Visual InterDev (in fact, the IDE is identical to the Visual InterDev IDE) it uses the design metaphor of the older RAD tools.

Java Forms

In Visual J++, a form is a specific class (`com.ms.wfc.ui.Form`) that corresponds to a top-level window. At design time, programmers can drag and drop controls from the toolbar and manipulate their properties, just as they could in Visual Basic. One difference, however, is that in Visual J++ the layout of the form is stored as a sequence of Java statements that initialize an object of the class.

The form designer adds member variables to the form class for each control on the form. This is similar to what goes on in Visual Basic, except that the variable declaration is like any other Java variable declaration, and therefore visible to the programmer. (In Visual Basic this declaration is implicit, a property of the control on the form.)

Adding a COM Wrapper

The objects and interfaces in a type library are made available to a Java project by invoking the Add COM Wrapper command. This invokes the `jactivex` program to generate a Java package corresponding to the type library. This package can be used by any Java code in the project. Typically, a Java `import` statement is also used to make possible the use of abbreviated names for the classes.

Customizing the Toolbox

An ActiveX control is included into a project by adding it to the Java toolbox; the process automatically generates the COM wrapper classes for all the entities present in the type library of the control. Typically, this includes the default incoming and outgoing interfaces of the control (both of which must be Automation capable), as well as all supporting enumerations.

Visual C++

The support for forms-based application development in C++ is less homogeneous than it is in Visual Basic and Visual J++. Up to the present time, full support for such development is available only in projects with MFC support. However, it is becoming clear that forms-based development in ATL (based on composite controls and dialog windows) is evolving in such a way that full tool support can only be a matter of time, although even then it may remain a control creation framework rather than an application development framework. To complicate matters further, it is now possible to build forms-based projects using DHTML as the underlying template instead of using a dialog resource, and you'll see an example of how to use such a form later in the chapter, and how to build one in Chapter 7.

In this section, I'm talking about traditional forms-based development using MFC and dialog resources.

C++ Dialog Resources

C++ forms-based development uses a Windows dialog resource to describe the layout and initial state of the form. Additional state for ActiveX controls is stored in a DLGINIT resource in binary form. The dialog editor is used to edit the form visually.

> *This state is typically created at design time by calling the* Save() *method on the appropriate persistence interface, and loaded at runtime by calling* Load() *on the same persistence interface. If the resource does not exist,* InitNew() *is called instead and you get the default state for the control.*

ClassWizard is used to associate member variables with controls on the dialog; these variables are created as data members of the C++ class associated with the dialog resource. Unlike the situation in Visual Basic and Visual J++, not every control on the dialog has an associated variable (the underlying Win32 Dialog API can be used to get at *anything* in the dialog, regardless of MFC).

#import of a Type Library File

In Visual J++, you invoke a tool to create a wrapper class for a simple type library, but Visual C++ has a preprocessor extension – #import – that serves much the same function. It reads a type library and creates C++ wrapper code that corresponds to the various entities in it.

The #import directive is similar to #include, except that it takes the name of a type library as its argument rather than the name of a C++ header. It translates the type library into a pair of header files with extensions .tlh and .tli. The effect of the #import statement is identical to generating the header files and then silently #include'ing them; We will look at the contents of these header files a little later in the chapter.

Inserting an ActiveX Control into a Project

For projects in which this is allowed, you can insert an ActiveX control into a form in one of two ways:

- ❑ Insert one of the Registered ActiveX Controls from the Components and Controls Gallery. This will add the control to the dialog editor's Controls toolbar. Subsequently, you can work with the control just as you would with a native control.
- ❑ Use the Insert ActiveX Control... item from the context menu in the dialog editor. This will insert the control into the current dialog, but not add it to the control toolbar.

In each case, a wrapper class will be created (in the second case, on demand) for the control; this will be similar in spirit to the #import generated wrappers, but it will work only with Automation interfaces (it is based on COleDispatchDriver).

Visual InterDev

At the time of writing, the Visual InterDev environment is the same as the Visual J++ environment. However, the options available for DHTML applications are similar, but not identical, to the options for a Java application.

DHTML Based Forms

The beauty of HTML-based forms is that they can be created using a very wide variety of editing tools. If aesthetic considerations are paramount, you probably want to create the functionality of your application in Visual InterDev, and then transplant the form elements to a page designed using one of the numerous HTML page layout programs (and preferably by a graphic designer, rather than by a programmer!).

The basic form elements available in HTML are very limited, but thanks to Java applets, WFC controls, ActiveX controls and even DHTML scriptlets, a wide variety of visual plug-in elements can be inserted into HTML forms. In addition, ordinary non-visual Automation objects can be used within a DHTML form too. These form elements and controls are programmed using a scripting language (the only choices I'm aware of right now are JScript and VBScript).

This makes DHTML the richest, most flexible way to develop forms based applications. I knew there had to be a reason why there are now more web-based software applications (you may have seen them; they're called "web sites") than all the other kinds put together.

Scripting is Dynamically Typed

Scripting languages are intrinsically dynamically typed. Therefore, there is no need to import or reference a type library explicitly. In this respect, scripting languages are very similar to interpreted Visual Basic (which started as a pure scripting language and evolved over time into a strongly typed language). As a matter of fact, VBScript is exactly that: an untyped, stripped down version of the Visual Basic language.

Type Library Browsers and IntelliSense

Let me finish this section with a quick word about type library browsers. There are a couple of different browsing tools that let you inspect the contents of a type library. The OLE/COM Object Viewer (`Oleview.exe`) lets you open up specific type libraries and look at the IDL corresponding to different entities in them (it reverse engineers the ASCII version from the binary version), while the object browser gives a user-friendly, iconic view of the type library stripped of IDL syntax.

All the Microsoft development tools now have IntelliSense built in; this is marketing-speak for the ability to have variable names completed for you automatically as you type. Sophisticated text editors have supported rudimentary completion for years (I was using it in Emacs a decade ago), but the mechanism built into the visual tools is far more mature, and provides completion for method names and parameters in addition to completion for member variables and functions.

You need to be aware that the IDL code you write will show up both in the browsers and in the completion suggestions offered by IntelliSense. In particular, you should pay close attention to the documentation-related aspects of IDL, such as naming conventions and help strings.

Data Type Mappings

This section examines the mappings from various languages onto the base IDL and Automation data types. For the most part, these bindings are quite straightforward, the exceptions being the structured types `BSTR`, `SAFEARRAY` and `VARIANT`.

Base Type Mappings

To begin with, let us take a quick look at the base IDL types and their mappings in various languages. Recall that each base IDL type is characterized by the range of permissible values – by the data width, and signed-ness. The table below lists the mappings from IDL types to C/C++, VBScript, Visual Basic and Java types.

Unsigned	Bits	IDL	C/C++ (Win32)	Scripting Client	VB6	Java
Yes	8	boolean	(unsigned) char	-	-	char
-	8	byte	unsigned char	-	Byte	byte
Yes	8	char	(unsigned) char	Yes	-	char
No	8	small	char	-	-	char
Yes	16	wchar_t	(unsigned) short	-	Integer	short
No	16	short	short	Yes	Integer	short
No	32	long	long	Yes	Long	int
No	64	hyper	__int64	-	-	long
-	32	float	float	Yes	Single	float
-	64	double	double	Yes	Double	double

There are only a few points worthy of note:

❑ Visual Basic does not support all the basic IDL types, but for the most part this is not a problem. The lack of support for the boolean type, for example, is not very significant because Visual Basic has one of its own. The only potential problem is the lack of a 64-bit integer.

❑ C/C++ is obviously capable of supporting the full range of types.

❑ Java also supports the full range of basic IDL types. The only noteworthy fact here is that the Java long is 64 bits wide. It also uses signed types to hold the unsigned IDL types.

Automation Type Mappings

This brings us to the next issue: the use of the Automation-compliant VARIANT types. Automation-compatible types include the basic IDL types that are supported by Visual Basic, as well as a few extra ones. These are listed in the next table:

IDL	C/C++ (Win32)	Scripting Client	VB6	Java
VARIANT_BOOL	VARIANT_BOOL	Variant	Boolean	boolean
CURRENCY	CURRENCY	Variant	Currency	long
DATE	DATE	Variant	Date	double

Table Continued on Following Page

IDL	C/C++ (Win32)	Scripting Client	VB6	Java
BSTR	BSTR	Variant	String	java.lang. String
SAFEARRAY(type)	SAFEARRAY	Variant	type()	com.ms.com. SafeArray
VARIANT	VARIANT	Variant	Variant	com.ms.com. Variant
IUnknown*	IUnknown*	Variant	Unknown	com.ms.com. IUnknown
IDispatch*	IDispatch*	Variant	Object	java.lang. Object

The VARIANT_BOOL Type

Here is the definition of VARIANT_BOOL from wtypes.idl:

```
typedef short VARIANT_BOOL;
```

The only interesting fact about VARIANT_BOOL is that VARIANT_TRUE has the value –1, and VARIANT_FALSE has the value 0.

Note that there are 3 different Boolean types that are used in IDL: the 8-bit boolean, *the 16-bit* VARIANT_BOOL *and the 32-bit* BOOL.

The CURRENCY Type

The CURRENCY type is defined as:

```
typedef struct tagCY
{
    LONGLONG int64;
} CY;
```

In other words, it's a 64-bit integer.

The DATE Type

The DATE type is defined as:

```
typedef double DATE;
```

Scalar Automation Types

The VARIANT_BOOL, CURRENCY and DATE types are not very interesting except for the fact that they are treated specially by Visual Basic, and they have specific interpretations as Boolean, currency or time values. Fundamentally, they are simple, numeric types (although the currency might be defined as a struct, depending on the architecture).

The next three types are more interesting because they are intrinsically non-scalar and of variable length. They comprise the BSTR, the SAFEARRAY and the VARIANT.

The BSTR Type

We looked at the definition and layout in memory of BSTRs in Chapter 4, and I'd refer you back to the that discussion now if you want a quick refresher before heading into the new material I'm about to present about the BSTR API.

Memory Allocation

The BSTR data type is the only base Automation type that requires heap allocation using a special heap API that I will outline here. All the allocation operations initialize the allocated memory to a given, null-terminated string.

SysAllocString() creates a BSTR that's a copy of a given, null-terminated wide character string. Thus, the string cannot have any embedded null characters.

SysAllocStringLen() allocates a BSTR of the given length, and copies up to that number of wide characters from the input wide character string. Strings created this way *can* have embedded null characters.

SysAllocStringByteLen() is a function that can be used to copy a binary buffer into a BSTR. It accomplishes this by doing a string copy without performing an ANSI to Unicode conversion.

SysFreeString() releases the memory that was allocated for a BSTR. For legacy reasons, a null pointer is equivalent to an empty BSTR – that is, a BSTR whose first character is the null character and whose length is 0. This is useful because it means you can safely call SysFreeString() on an empty BSTR.

SysReAllocString() and SysReAllocStringLen() are the equivalents for SysAllocString() and SysAllocStringLen() in the situation where you want to assign a new value to an existing BSTR. These methods release the previously allocated memory.

Since BSTRs are pointers, the rules for memory ownership of pointer parameters to remote method invocation are applicable to them as well. However, instead of using the COM Task Memory Allocator, you are required to use the API just outlined above. In Chapter 7, we'll see how this is done.

Other Operations

SysStringLen() and SysStringByteLen() respectively return the number of characters and the number of bytes in a string, *excluding* the final null character. Note that there may be more than one null character in a BSTR, so this represents the fully allocated length, rather than a strlen()-type value.

String Conversions

Naturally, there are a large number of conversions that are required between the various character types. In general, Visual C++ uses macros for this purpose; you can find a list of these in the MSDN Library by searching the index for string conversion macros.

BSTR Language Bindings

It turns out that there is little need to deal with the BSTR API directly. At this point, each of the major Microsoft language implementations has seamless support for BSTRs.

Visual Basic Strings

The BSTR is exactly the same as the Visual Basic String primitive type (this is not surprising, since that's where the BSTR came from in the first place).

Java Strings

The Microsoft Virtual Machine converts BSTR types directly into Java native strings – that is, java.lang.String.

C++/ATL Support: CComBSTR and _bstr_t

The C++ _bstr_t wrapper around the C API simply integrates the BSTR API into the normal C++ operations of construction, assignment and destruction. The appropriate C API is called without requiring explicit thought on the part of the programmer. In addition, these APIs also give you a first class string object, rather than the C-style pointers.

> *The* CComBSTR *class is more lightweight than* _bstr_t; *the latter uses a reference counted, copy-on-write string implementation.*

Each wrapper also has attach/detach functionality to associate a C++ string object with (and unlink it from) an existing BSTR. In addition, the _bstr_t class converts error returns into thrown C++ exceptions.

Note that neither class is actually *derived* from BSTR, so neither can seamlessly replace a BSTR, particularly when you need an out parameter in a function call. Instead, each has conversion operators that return various kinds of C-style strings, and these can be used for dealing with in-only parameters. Although the conversions are well designed and intuitive for the most part, it pays to look at the reference material if you're doing anything unusual. For more details on using these classes, see Dr. Richard Grimes' *Professional ATL COM Programming*.

The SAFEARRAY Type

A SAFEARRAY is a self-descriptive, multidimensional vector type that was originally introduced by Visual Basic. It is defined as follows:

```
typedef struct tagSAFEARRAYBOUND
{
    ULONG cElements;
    LONG  lLbound;
} SAFEARRAYBOUND, *LPSAFEARRAYBOUND;

typedef struct tagSAFEARRAY
{
    USHORT cDims;
    USHORT fFeatures;
    ULONG  cbElements;
    ULONG  cLocks;
    PVOID  pvData;
    SAFEARRAYBOUND rgsabound[];
} SAFEARRAY;
```

The code you can see consists of a descriptor structure that includes a specification (using the ancillary SAFEARRAYBOUND structure) of the dimensionality and extents (bounds in each dimension) of the array, Visual Basic type, element size, reference count and a pointer to the actual data stored in the array.

The array data is stored in column major order (as in Basic and Fortran), rather than row major order (as in C and C++), so an index conversion calculation is generally needed when accessing the data from C/C++. SAFEARRAYs are manipulated using an array API that allows for the creation, destruction, descriptor manipulation and data manipulation of these arrays.

Creation and Destruction

SafeArrayCreate() is a function that creates a new array descriptor, and then creates and initializes the data for the array. It works only with element types that are base Automation types, although it can't deal with arrays.

SafeArrayDestroy() destroys an array previously allocated by SafeArrayCreate(), along with all the data in it. It's clever enough to do the proper clean up and resource de-allocation for Automation types.

The SafeArrayRedim() function allows the least significant dimension of an array to be resized. Like the 'Create' and 'Destroy' methods, the 'Redim' method allocates and initializes new elements, or de-allocates extraneous elements as necessary.

So far, then, we've seen the methods that are restricted to work with Automation data types. For the most part, these are the methods of interest, since the SAFEARRAY type is largely used to work with Automation compliant interfaces. However there *are* API functions that allow more flexible patterns of array creation, including creation of arrays of non-Automation types. They are SafeArrayAllocDescriptor(), SafeArrayAllocData(), SafeArrayDestroyData() and SafeArrayDestroyDescriptor().

When you're creating arrays of non-VARIANT types, remember that there is no way for the SAFEARRAY API to know how to initialize or de-allocate these elements, so no resource initialization or clean up is possible. In practice, this severely restricts the scope of SAFEARRAYs of non-VARIANT types, and in general I would recommend that you don't use them. Of course, there are ways of converting non-VARIANT types to VARIANT types (check out the section on Data Transfer in Chapter 5), but they tend to be either non-portable or inefficient.

Controlled Access

SafeArrayGetElement() and SafeArrayPutElement() are functions that allow access to array elements. The 'Get' retrieves a copy of the array element, while the 'Put' copies the element into the array. For Automation data types, resource allocation, initialization and cleanup are performed as necessary. The position in the array is specified by a vector of indices, one for each dimension.

Reference Counting

Like other COM entities, a SAFEARRAY is reference counted so that it cannot be freed (or re-dimensioned) while it is in use. The SAFEARRAY API itself makes sure that locks are appropriately managed. However there are situations when the user wants direct access to the underlying data instead of using the API – when performance is critical and it becomes necessary to copy blocks of the array, for example.

To this end, a pointer to the array data is stored in the `pvData` member of the `SAFEARRAY` structure. However, the user needs to call `SafeArrayLock()` and `SafeArrayUnlock()` around any direct manipulation of the `pvData` member, to ensure that the array data is not released during such access.

Index Calculation for Raw Access

How about the situation where the user is trying to get access to the underlying data of a multidimensional array? There are several features of SAFEARRAYs that make index calculations non-intuitive for people used to C-style arrays:

- ❑   SAFEARRAYs are arranged in column-major order (as in Basic and Fortran), rather than row-major (as in C)
- ❑   Array bounds (or extents) can be defined by any range of integers (as in Visual Basic) rather than being zero-based (as in C)
- ❑   A multidimensional array is contiguous in memory, rather than being an array of pointers to an array of pointers to... as it is in C

The `SafeArrayPtrOfIndex()` function can be used to take a vector of indices and gain access to the memory address at which that index element is kept. Direct index calculations are also possible, but must take the above differences from C arrays into account.

Copying

The `SafeArrayCopy()` function makes a complete copy of an existing array. For Automation data types, the appropriate copying semantics are used.

`SafeArrayCopyData()`, on the other hand, is used to copy an existing array into another existing array. Resources in the destination array will be released if necessary. The only point to bear in mind here is that Visual Basic allows the declaration of 'static' arrays, whose dimensionality and extents cannot be changed. In the situation where the destination array is static, the 'CopyData' function imposes the appropriate constraints on the copy semantics.

Descriptor Querying

There are several functions in the SAFEARRAY API that wrap the retrieval of information from the array descriptor. These include the `SafeArrayGetDim()` and `SafeArrayGetElemsize()` functions that are used to query for the dimensionality of the array and the size of a single memory element respectively. The `SafeArrayGetLBound()` and `SafeArrayGetUBound()` functions are used to get the extents of a specific dimension of an array.

SAFEARRAY Language Bindings

It can't have escaped your attention that SAFEARRAYs are awkward things to deal with, and that some help to manipulate them would be nice. If you were expecting some kind of language support for SAFEARRAYs, you'd be two-thirds right.

Visual Basic Arrays

As with other Automation data types, the `SAFEARRAY` type is identical to the Visual Basic array. Arrays in Visual Basic may be declared and subsequently changed dynamically as follows:

```
Dim Static x(1 to 5, 4, 8 to 12) as Integer    ' Static array
Dim y()                                          ' Dynamic array
ReDim y(3, 4, 5)                                 ' Allocate new extents
ReDim Preserve y(3, 4, 12)                       ' Redimension existing array
```

Arrays may also be used in the declaration of a function that can be called with a variable number of arguments. In this case, the type name `ParamArray` (which is a dynamic array of variants) is used.

Java Arrays

The `SAFEARRAY` in Java is represented by the new Microsoft class `com.ms.com.SafeArray`, and the various pieces of the SAFEARRAY API are hidden behind methods of this class.

Java SAFEARRAYs are *not* reference counted, which means that unlike other Java types, the user has to be aware of memory allocation rules, especially the normal COM memory allocation rules relating to method parameters.

Since Java is a completely type-safe language with no `void` pointer type, there need to be get/set class members for every possible element type.

There are problems with extracting `IDispatch*` and `IUnknown*` values from SAFEARRAYs if the objects they represent are not free threaded. This is a special case of the general problem of integrating the apartment model into the Java Virtual Machine.

No Standard C++ Support

At the time of writing, there is no standard C++/ATL wrapper around SAFEARRAYs. There *is* an old MFC wrapper called `COleSafeArray`, but it's not based on templates, and must be considered outdated for new, non-MFC code. However, it's not hard to create a custom wrapper class of your own if this kind of manipulation is going to be a big part of your application.

The VARIANT Type

Automation also defines the overarching `VARIANT` data type that is a union of all the other Automation data types, the most interesting of which are `BSTR`, `SAFEARRAY`, `IUnknown*` and `IDispatch*`. These are the types that are associated with dynamically allocated resources, and therefore require careful handling.

Here is the definition for a `VARIANT` (I have removed some lines that apply to `VARIANTARG`, which is similar but not quite identical to a `VARIANT`, as I shall explain shortly):

```
struct tagVARIANT
{
  union
  {
    struct __tagVARIANT
    {
      VARTYPE vt;
      WORD    wReserved1;
      WORD    wReserved2;
      WORD    wReserved3;
      union
      {
        LONG      lVal;        /* VT_I4    */
        BYTE      bVal;        /* VT_UI1   */
        SHORT     iVal;        /* VT_I2    */
        FLOAT     fltVal;      /* VT_R4    */
        DOUBLE    dblVal;      /* VT_R8    */
```

```
            VARIANT_BOOL  boolVal;      /* VT_BOOL        */
            SCODE         scode;        /* VT_ERROR       */
            CY            cyVal;        /* VT_CY          */
            DATE          date;         /* VT_DATE        */
            BSTR          bstrVal;      /* VT_BSTR        */
            IUnknown *    punkVal;      /* VT_UNKNOWN     */
            IDispatch *   pdispVal;     /* VT_DISPATCH    */
            SAFEARRAY *   parray;       /* VT_ARRAY       */
            CHAR          cVal;         /* VT_I1          */
            USHORT        uiVal;        /* VT_UI2         */
            ULONG         ulVal;        /* VT_UI4         */
            INT           intVal;       /* VT_INT         */
            UINT          uintVal;      /* VT_UINT        */
            struct __tagBRECORD
            {
                PVOID           pvRecord;
                IRecordInfo * pRecInfo;
            } __VARIANT_NAME_4;         /* VT_RECORD      */
          } __VARIANT_NAME_3;
        } __VARIANT_NAME_2;

      DECIMAL decVal;
    } __VARIANT_NAME_1;
};
```

As you can see, the VARIANT type is a discriminated union of all the base Automation types. As is the case for BSTRs and SAFEARRAYs, there exists an API that performs the allocation and release of resources when VARIANTs are initialized, copied, converted and destroyed.

A VARIANTARG type is distinct from the VARIANT type, and can contain either a VARIANT value or a reference (pointer) to a VARIANT value. This is specified by OR-ing the VT_BYREF flag with the tag, vt. VARIANTARG is the actual type used in the parameters that are passed into IDispatch::Invoke().

Initialization and Cleanup

The VariantInit() function is used to initialize raw memory into the VT_EMPTY value, since many functions will not work with a VARIANT that has a garbage tag.

The VariantClear() function is used to clean up an existing VARIANT value, or to *re*-initialize it to the empty value. The current contents of the existing value are released correctly before this is done. VariantClear() should be used before assigning a new value to a VARIANT variable to ensure appropriate cleanup of the data.

Assignment

VariantCopy() makes a copy of the source variable. The old value in the destination variable is released correctly before the new value is assigned. Deep copy semantics are used in the process, so new resources would be allocated for strings and arrays.

However, VariantCopy() does *not* work in the situation where the source value is a *reference* to a VARIANT – that is, a VARIANTARG. Instead, the VariantCopyInd() function is defined to work with VARIANTARGs, and it also uses deep copy semantics – it de-references a VT_BYREF value.

Type Conversion

There exist natural conversions between many of the VARIANT types, such as short to long, long to double, etc. To take advantage of these conversions without having to do all the type checking and translation in user code, you need to use the VariantChangeType() and VariantChangeTypeEx() functions.

VariantChangeType() takes source and destination VARIANTARGs and a target VARIANT type, and attempts to coerce the source VARIANTARG into a VARIANT of the requested type. The result is placed in the destination VARIANTARG (which can be the same as the source, in which case the conversion happens in-place).

VariantChangeTypeEx() extends VariantChangeType() with a target locale ID, so the conversion also attempts to tailor the result to a specific locale. The conversions to strings are especially interesting, since DATEs, CURRENCYs, etc. all get converted to the correct format. These functions will both automatically de-reference a VT_BYREF source type.

The strangest aspect of these functions is that a source VARIANT of object type (IDispatch*) is automatically converted into its value (the property with a DISPID of DISPID_VALUE). The automatic conversion can be disabled by passing the VARIANT_NOVALUEPROP flag into the call, but this is officially discouraged.

There also exist a number of one-to-one data type conversion routines that you can use to go from one specific type to another specific type. These routines are used internally by the higher-level routines, and for the most part there is no reason to use them directly.

VARIANT Language Bindings

Given the importance of VARIANT types, it will come as no surprise that each of the client languages has good support for VARIANTs. They're built into Visual Basic and VBScript, and have great wrapper classes in Java and C++.

Visual Basic Variants

The Variant is the data type used by Visual Basic whenever a variable is not explicitly typed. It can also be used explicitly to declare variables:

```
Dim x as Variant
Dim a(3,4) as Variant
```

Java

In Java, the VARIANT type is encapsulated by the com.ms.com.Variant class. This is a fairly unremarkable class, consisting largely of a number of get/set/to style conversion functions for the various VARIANT subtypes.

C++/ATL Support: CComVariant and _variant_t

The CComVariant and _variant_t classes both encapsulate the VARIANT type and make calls to the appropriate API functions within the C++ construction/assignment/destruction sequence.

As was the case with BSTR support, one of the classes (_variant_t) converts errors into thrown exceptions, and the other does not. Unlike the BSTR wrappers, however, the VARIANT wrappers *are* actually derived from the VARIANT struct, and are therefore layout-compatible with VARIANTs — they can be substituted seamlessly for them. As with the BSTR classes, the CComVariant class is the more lightweight of the two and is used more often in server code.

Class and Interface Mappings

I'll now examine the various client bindings for creating classes and using interfaces: method invocations, error returns, QI(), memory allocation and event handling. To compare the various languages, we'll use a variation on the design from the previous chapter. Here are the relevant IDL definitions:

```
coclass Lot
{
    [default] interface ILotScript;
    interface ILot;
    interface ILotInitialize;
    interface IBidValidate;
    interface IAuctionInfo;

    [default, source] interface ILotEvents;

    interface ISupportErrorInfo;
};
```

I begin with the Lot coclass, augmented with a source interface called ILotEvents for the purposes of this example. The relevant interface declarations are:

```
interface ILotInitialize : IDispatch
{
    [id(1), helpstring("Initialize object with basic Lot information")]
    HRESULT InitAuctionInfo([in] LONG a_vlStartPrice,
                            [in] LONG a_vlBidIncrement,
                            [in] LONG a_vlClosesAt,
                            [out, retval] BSTR* a_vstr);
};

...

interface ILotEvents : IDispatch
{
    [id(1), helpstring("Some Other User Added a Bid")] HRESULT BidsChanged();
};

...

interface ILot : IDispatch
{
    [propget, id(1), helpstring("LotInfo")]
    HRESULT Info([out, retval] IAuctionInfo** a_ppai);
    [propget, id(2), helpstring("Bids")]
    HRESULT Bids([out, retval] IBids** a_ppbd);

    [propput, id(2), helpstring("Bids")]
    HRESULT Bids([in] IBids* a_pbid);
};
```

Raw C++

As a baseline for comparison, let us look at some 'raw' C/C++ client code:

```cpp
ILot* g_pILot = 0;

HRESULT LotInitialize()
{
    if(g_pILot)
        g_pILot->Release();

    HRESULT hr = CoCreateInstance(
        CLSID_Lot, NULL, CLSCTX_ALL, IID_ILot, reinterpret_cast<void**>(&g_pILot))
    if(SUCCEEDED(hr))
    {
        ILotInitialize* pILotInitialize = 0;
        hr = g_pILot->QueryInterface(
                IID_ILotInitialize, reinterpret_cast<void**>(&pILotInitialize));
        if(SUCCEEDED(hr))
        {
            BSTR out = 0;
            hr = pILotInitialize->InitAuctionInfo(45, 3, 8, &out);
            pILotInitialize->Release();
            SysFreeString(out);
            if(FAILED(hr))
            {
                HRESULT hrOld = hr;
                ISupportErrorInfo* pISEI = 0;
                hr = g_pILot->QueryInterface(
                        IID_ISupportErrorInfo, reinterpret_cast<void**>(&pISEI));
                if(FAILED(hr))
                    return hrOld;

                hr = pISEI->InterfaceSupportsErrorInfo(IID_ILotInitialize);
                pISEI->Release();

                // If the call failed, S_FALSE is returned,
                //   so we cannot use the SUCCEEDED() macro
                if(hr == S_OK)
                {
                    IErrorInfo* pIErrorInfo = 0;
                    hr = GetErrorInfo(&pIErrorInfo);
                    if(hr == S_OK)
                    {
                        // Process the error info.
                        ...
                        pIErrorInfo->Release();
                    }
                }
                return hrOld;
            }
            else if(hr != S_OK)
            {
                // Non-S_OK success code
                return S_OK;
            }
        }
    }
    return hr;
}
```

This code is doing almost nothing. It creates a new lot, initializes it, and stores a reference to it in the global g_pILot variable. If there is an error, it does some (unspecified) error processing. However, the code itself needs to take care of a number of little details that are part of the COM idiom.

Creating an Object

There is an explicit check to release the current interface in the global variable if it has already been initialized.

A new object is created using CoCreateInstance(), and a pointer to its ILot interface (the type of the global) is requested. If successful, the interface will be returned in the global.

Interface Use

If the creation code succeeded, we then request the ILotInitialize interface on the object.

If this interface was successfully returned, we can initialize the object using the InitAuctionInfo() method of the interface.

Once we are done using it, we release the ILotInitialize interface.

Memory Allocation

When we've finished using the output string value, we have to free it. Since this is a BSTR, we use the SysFreeString() API call (in most cases we would need to use the COM task allocator API).

Error Handling

If there was an error, we check whether the interface supports the COM error objects, eventually getting the appropriate IErrorInfo interface on the current error object. This is then processed in some unspecified fashion.

Eventually, we return the value of the HRESULT code.

Event Handling

I have not yet shown you the raw code for handling events. You'll recall that the client needs to expose the appropriate interface for handling the event, and then register with the server to be informed of the event. Since we are doing a cross language comparison, and script does not permit custom event registration protocols, I will demonstrate code for the connectable object protocol.

Creating the Sink

Here is the code that implements the event handler object.

```cpp
class CEventHandler : public ILotEvents
{
    CEventHandler() : m_dwRef(0), m_dwEvtCount(0)
    {
    }

    HRESULT __stdcall QueryInterface(REFIID a_riid, void** a_ppv)
    {
        if(a_ppv == NULL)
            return E_POINTER;

        *a_ppv = NULL;
        if(a_riid == IID_ILotEvents)
        {
            *a_ppv = static_cast<ILotEvents*>(this);
        }
        else if(a_riid == IID_IUnknown)
        {
            *a_ppv = static_cast<IUnknown*>(this);
        }
        else
            return E_NOINTERFACE;

        (static_cast<IUnknown*>(a_ppv))->AddRef();
        return S_OK;
    }

    ULONG __stdcall AddRef()
    {
        return InterlockedIncrement(&m_dwRef);
    }

    ULONG __stdcall Release()
    {
        if(InterlockedDecrement(&m_dwRef) == 0)
        {
            delete this;
            return 0;
        }
        return m_dwRef;
    }

    HRESULT __stdcall BidsChanged()
    {
        InterlockedIncrement(&m_dwEvtCount);
        return S_OK;
    }
private:
    DWORD m_dwRef;
    DWORD m_dwEvtCount;
};
```

As you can see, most of this code is a boilerplate implementation of a COM object, with a standard `QueryInterface()`, `AddRef()` and `Release()`. The only added functionality is the implementation of the `BidsChanged()` method of the `ILotEvents` interface. The implementation simply increments a counter.

Registering the Sink

Now we need to see the code that implements the connectable object protocol. This code would be implemented on each client that needs to register a sink.

```
DWORD g_dwCookie = 0;

BOOL ConnectToLot(ILot* pILot, IUnknown* pIUnk)
{
    // No Existing Connection
    _ASSERTE(0 != g_dwCookie);

    IConnectionPointContainer* pICPC = 0;
    HRESULT hr = pILot->QueryInterface(
               IID_IConnectionPointContainer, reinterpret_cast<void**>(&pICPC));
    if(FAILED(hr))
       return FALSE;

    IConnectionPoint* pICP = 0;
    hr = pICPC->FindConnectionPoint(IID_ILotEvents, &pICP);
    pICPC->Release();
    if(FAILED(hr))
       return FALSE;

    hr = pICP->Advise(pIUnk, &g_dwCookie);
    pICP->Release();
    if(FAILED(hr))
       return FALSE;

    return TRUE;
}

BOOL DisconnectFromLot(ILot* pILot)
{
    // Connection Must Exist
    _ASSERTE (0 == g_dwCookie);

    IConnectionPointContainer* pICPC = 0;
    HRESULT hr = pILot->QueryInterface(
               IID_IConnectionPointContainer, reinterpret_cast<void**>(&pICPC));
    if(FAILED(hr))
       return FALSE;

    IConnectionPoint* pICP = 0;
    hr = pICPC->FindConnectionPoint(IID_ILotEvents, &pICP);
    pICPC->Release();
    if(FAILED(hr))
       return FALSE;

    hr = pICP->Unadvise(&g_dwCookie);
    pICP->Release();
    if(FAILED(hr))
       return FALSE;

    return TRUE;
}
```

Once again, this code is close to boilerplate – it maintains a single connection to the event interface on the lot object. The `ConnectToLot()` method establishes this connection given a lot object, while the `DisconnectFromLot()` method revokes the connection.

Visual Basic

Now, here's the same client code in Visual Basic:

```
Private WithEvents gLot as Lot
Private glEvtCount as Long

Sub LotInitialize()
On Error GoTo ErrHandler
    Set gLot = New Lot

    Dim ili As ILotInitialize
    Set ili = gLot
    Dim str As String
    str = ili.InitAuctionInfo 45, 3, 8
    Exit Sub

ErrHandler:
    ...
    Err.Raise
End Sub

Sub gLot_BidsChanged()
    glEvtCount = glEvtCount + 1
End Sub
```

I don't know about you, but that looks a lot simpler to me! Here are the important points.

Creating an Object

In its strongly typed flavor, Visual Basic has language support for creating objects. Once the type library has been added to the project references, Visual Basic recognizes all classes (`coclass` statements) declared in the library. An object is created by using the `New` operator and assigning it to an interface variable. In Visual Basic, a variable declared as an object is, in reality, declared to be the type of the default interface of the object class.

Alternatively, the `CreateObject()` function can be called with a string representing the ProgID of the object being created, although this is not shown in the above code.

Any object that has been created on a form using the Visual Basic form builder is automatically created when the form is loaded. A name can be assigned to this object in the **Properties** window for the object.

All these techniques correspond to a call to `CoCreateInstance()` that returns (unless otherwise specified, as mentioned below) the default interface of the class.

You can only create instances of a coclass, never an instance of an interface. Put another way, `New` and `CreateObject()` only work with coclass names and ProgIDs, not interface names. This makes sense, since it is always an *object* that is created, even though you only ever manipulate it through interfaces.

Interface Use

When strong typing is in force, interfaces as well as objects can be declared directly in Visual Basic. Adding the type library to the project references results in Visual Basic recognizing all the interfaces declared therein. A Visual Basic variable declared as an interface can be used to invoke methods on that interface.

You can assign things to an interface variable by placing it on the left-hand side of a Set statement. The Visual Basic runtime silently QI()s the interface on the right-hand side to retrieve an interface of the same type as the variable on the left-hand side.

The same QI() protocol is followed when the assignment is implicit, such as when you pass an interface as an argument into a function or a subroutine whose parameters are strongly typed. If the QI() fails, a Visual Basic error is raised. Visual Basic doesn't have any explicit type casting statements.

A method on the interface is called by using the Visual Basic dot notation (the pointer is automatically de-referenced for you), like this:

```
str = ili.InitAuctionInfo 45, 3, 8
```

Visual Basic is now capable of using the vtable of a dual interface rather than making an Automation call – in fact, it even supports vtable-only interfaces. The runtime transparently wraps all actual method invocations. An interface method called from Visual Basic seems to return not an HRESULT, but the parameter decorated with the out and retval attributes.

Visual Basic automatically calls Release() on an interface when that interface is going out of scope. Release() is also called when an interface variable is being assigned a new value: the old value is released. This is why we don't need to check the value of gLot when assigning a new lot to it. If you need it, Visual Basic also provides a mechanism for explicitly calling Release() on an interface pointer: you just Set the variable to the value Nothing.

Memory Allocation

The Visual Basic runtime is aware of the IDL memory allocation conventions, and calls the appropriate heap operators when storage needs to be released.

Error Handling

The COM error object protocol is built into the Visual Basic runtime. When an interface returns a failure code, the runtime kicks into the error protocol. The returned IErrorInfo interface is used to create an Err object, which then becomes visible in Visual Basic's own exception handling mechanism.

Event Handling

The connectable object protocol is also built into the Visual Basic runtime, and event sink interfaces are created by the Visual Basic runtime for a number of different types of objects. For a start, when a strongly typed object is declared with the WithEvents keyword, a sink is created for its default outgoing interface. In addition, all objects that live on forms have sinks created for their default outgoing interfaces. The programmer can implement Visual Basic subroutines to handle some or all of the methods on the sink interface; the method implementation on the sink created by Visual Basic delegates to the programmer's method (if one exists), otherwise it does nothing.

Connecting the Sink

The connection between the Visual Basic sink and the programmer's code is made by a special naming convention. Programmer-defined event sink methods must have names with the structure `<objectname>_<eventmethod>`. The subroutine must also have the appropriate type signature for the event. In our example, the `gLot_BidsChanged` subroutine will be called to handle the `BidsChanged()` method on the default `ILotEvents` source interface of the `Lot` class.

> **This means that Visual Basic is only set up to connect to an object's default source interface. At present, it cannot connect to any other interface.**

So that Visual Basic can look up the default source interface, either the type library of the object must be available or (if it is embedded on a form) the object must implement `IProvideClassInfo(2)`. In turn, this means that you must declare your source interfaces as such. The information Visual Basic finds is then used to construct the appropriate sinks.

Registering the Sink

The Visual Basic runtime registers all sinks automatically with the appropriate object.

Other Notifications

As you saw in Chapter 4, Visual Basic recognizes attributes in the type library that specify property change notifications.

Late Binding

The above example showed early bound (strongly typed) Visual Basic code. As we've seen, Visual Basic also allows objects to be dynamically typed, when the type of the object is not known until runtime. For a COM object to be dynamically typed, it *must* implement an `IDispatch` or dual interface. A dynamically typed object can be used like this:

```
Dim gLot as Object
Set gLot = CreateObject("Auction.Lot")

Dim ili As ILotInitialize
Set ili = gLot
```

An `Object` variable is exactly equivalent to a variable declared as `IDispatch`. (Or it would be, if Visual Basic actually allowed the use of `IDispatch` in a variable declaration!)

Visual Basic and CLSIDs

The `UUID` type is a restricted type in Visual Basic 6, and therefore it cannot be used in user code. This prevents Visual Basic users from using the parts of the COM API that require UUIDs directly – `CoCreateInstance()`, for example, cannot be called without a UUID. The simplest solution to this problem is the creation of a wrapper function.

Whenever you have a DLL entry point that uses a type that isn't allowed in Visual Basic, you can write a wrapper function (in another language) to hide the offending parameter. Essentially, the wrapper function has a type signature in which the 'bad' parameter is replaced by one of a type that *is* compatible with Visual Basic. Internally, the wrapper function translates the new parameter's value into a value of the original parameter type, and then calls the actual API function involved. The new entry point must be made available to Visual Basic through a `module` entry in a registered type library.

For example, I could write a wrapper for `CoCreateInstance()` called `CCI()` that takes a single string argument that is the string representation of a UUID. The wrapper function would convert this string into the 128-bit UUID value, call `CoCreateInstance()` internally with this value, and then return the resulting interface to Visual Basic. The `module` declaration would look like this:

```
library MyLibrary
{
    [dllname("MYWRAPPR.DLL")]
    module MYWRAPPR
    {
        [helpstring("CCI"), entry("CCI")]
        HRESULT CCI([in] LPCOLESTR a_pstr, [out, retval] IDispatch** a_ppdp);
    };
};
```

This assumes that the wrapper is implemented by the `CCI()` entry point of the DLL called `Mywrappr.dll`.

IDL enums and structs

It used to be the case that Visual Basic (prior to version 5) couldn't use user-defined types at all – and for our purposes, that means IDL `structs`. With the advent of Visual Basic 6 and Windows NT4 SP4's new system marshaler, however, there is no longer a problem. Visual Basic can also use `enums` from a type library without difficulty.

Parameter Type Restrictions

Visual Basic allows two kinds of parameters: those passed by value, and those passed by reference. These have very specific mappings onto the IDL directional attributes. Parameters passed by value map onto the `in` attribute. Parameters passed by reference map onto the `in`, `out` attribute. This basically means that there is no Visual Basic parameter passing mechanism that maps onto `out`-only parameters.

The trouble with this is that even though it can now use type information, Visual Basic still allows calls to Automation interfaces that do not have any, and this highlights a known problem with `out`-only parameters of method invocations. An initialized variable should not be passed into an `out`-only parameter, since the server expects it to be empty and might overwrite it, resulting in a memory leak on the client. However, without type information, a scripting language (like Visual Basic in its weakly typed mode) has no way of distinguishing an `out`-only parameter from any other kind.

The only exception to this rule is an `out`, `retval` parameter, which is treated as a separate entity by `IDispatch::Invoke()`, and is clearly distinguishable from the other parameters. This is an awkward restriction on method type signatures, since it means that all parameters that return values must be `in`, `out` (recall the painful semantics of marshaling `in`, `out` parameters). Happily, Visual Basic in its strongly typed mode has no restrictions of this kind.

Java

We've seen it in C++ and Visual Basic, so now let's look at the same code in Java:

```
import auctsrvr;

class Sample
{
    ILot g_ILot;

    void LotInitialize() throws ComException
    {
        g_ILot = (ILot)new Lot();
        ((ILotInitialize)g_ILot).InitAuctionInfo(45, 3, 8);
    }
}
```

Pretty short, isn't it? It doesn't look like it could get any easier! Here's what's happening.

Creating an Object

Once a COM wrapper has been created for the type library, Java can use COM objects and interfaces exactly as if they were native Java objects and interfaces. The COM wrapper tool creates a number of Java classes that are proxies to the actual COM classes. These proxies have the same names as the corresponding IDL entities.

The command line equivalent of the COM wrapper tool is jactivex.exe.

In particular, you can use the Java new operator to create (a Java proxy to) a COM object. Technically, this is a Java object (not an interface) whose methods you can invoke directly.

In this sense, the Java proxy of a COM class actually represents the class itself, rather than the default interface of the class (which was the case in Visual Basic). However, it goes against the COM idiom to invoke methods in this fashion, and there are no clear benefits from doing so. There are also problems with name clashes when multiple interfaces on the object implement methods with the same name. This is why I immediately cast the newly created class to an interface, rather than stashing it as a Java object.

Interface Use

An interface variable can be declared in Java using the proxy class representing the interface. Since Java has no notion of pointers (all variables, except basic types, are pointers by implication), you don't need to de-reference the variable explicitly in order to invoke a method.

Type conversions in Java need to be performed using explicit type casts. The casting mechanism in Java does the QueryInterface() required when assigning an interface variable of one type to an interface variable of another type. If the dynamic cast fails, a Java exception is thrown. The Java instanceof operator may also be used to test for the presence of an interface explicitly before casting.

The Java VM has a built-in garbage collector, and the Microsoft implementation recognizes COM objects and calls Release() on them when appropriate. The programmer does not need to call Release() explicitly. This also permits us the luxury of using a very 'functional' style when calling the InitAuctionInfo() method. We can use the temporary (ILotInitialize) variable for the invocation, since the variable doesn't need an explicit call to Release().

At the time of writing, there are known bugs in the interaction of COM threading models and the garbage collector, so COM memory leaks can occur if you rely on the garbage collection mechanism. Use the `com.ms.com.ComLib.release` *method to release a COM object forcibly. This method releases* all *references held by the Java proxy, so it is semantically different from* `Release()` *'ing an individual interface.*

Memory Allocation

The garbage collector in the Java Virtual Machine deals with *all* memory; it is simply extended to cover the case of COM memory. At the time of writing, there is a known issue with garbage collection in apartment-threaded objects, a consequence of the fact that the Java VM is not fundamentally driven by a Windows message pump. There is also a known issue with the garbage collection of SAFEARRAYs.

Error Handling

The proxy interface method wraps the actual method invocations. Just as in Visual Basic, a method called on the proxy returns not an HRESULT, but the parameter decorated with the out and retval attributes.

The HRESULT is used by the VM to convert COM error codes and rich error information transparently into a Java run-time exception that's derived from `com.ms.com.ComException`. If the VM detects an unsuccessful result code, it sets the properties of the exception object using the HRESULT code and any available COM rich error information. It then throws an exception that needs to be handled using Java exception handlers.

The ComException class hierarchy has mechanisms to support discovery of the actual HRESULTs returned by the invocation, as well as to distinguish success codes that are not S_OK. In this respect, it provides more information about the underlying COM method invocation than the Visual Basic runtime does.

Event Handling

The Microsoft Java VM has classes that support building and registering event sink interfaces. The procedure for event handling in Java consists of the following steps:

- ❑ Create the Java interface that corresponds to the COM event interface
- ❑ Create a multicasting delegator sink
- ❑ Implement the sink methods on an appropriate object
- ❑ Associate the event methods with the multicaster

Currently, the environment generates code that supports event handling only for ActiveX controls, rather than arbitrary COM objects. If you want to respond to events from COM objects that are not ActiveX controls, you need to re-create the class infrastructure manually.

Java Interfaces from COM Interfaces

Java has a notion of interfaces that is very similar in spirit to the COM interface. However, the physical invocation mechanism is *not* identical to that of a COM interface. In order to expose a Java interface as a sink object, some translation must be done. This is accomplished by a COM-aware proxy that the Java VM creates for any Java interface that needs to be exposed to COM. Event sink interfaces are one situation where Java objects need to be exposed to COM.

The COM import tool generates the Java interface class corresponding to the COM event interface. In our example, this would look like the following snippet (I have deliberately omitted some other information generated by jactivex that's peripheral to this example):

```
public interface ILotEvents extends IUnknown
{
    public void BidsChanged();
}
```

Multicasting Delegator Sink

The rest of the jactivex-generated code is associated with the Java class that is proxying the event source class.

The event wrapper classes take a multicasting approach to sink interfaces. A single interface is registered with the source object as usual, but *this* single interface is actually a multicasting delegator – that is, it forwards the event that it receives from the event source onto a number of other interfaces. These interfaces are registered with the multicaster instead of being registered directly with the source object. The architecture makes sense, because it's cheaper for a Java interface to be invoked from within Java (from the multicaster) than from outside (from the source object).

Past this point, the tools actually support two different event-handling architectures. Depending on how the COM wrappers are generated (directly on a type library, or indirectly via inclusion in the toolbox), one architecture or the other is generated for you.

Implementing the Entire Sink

The first architecture requires the programmer to implement the entire sink interface; the tool-generated classes simply support registration of the appropriate sink interfaces. In this architecture, there are three Java classes of interest: the COM class proxy, the multicasting delegator, and an event listener class that is simply the 'pure' Java interface that's equivalent to the COM/Java interface.

> *The COM/Java interface has "@com" annotations that cause it to be treated differently by the Java Virtual Machine than a straight Java interface.*

The multicasting delegator has this type signature:

```
class LotEventMulticaster implements ILotEvents, com.ms.com.NoAutoScripting
{
    Vector _jcommem_listeners;
    public void BidsChanged();
}
```

And the main proxy class has this signature (only the relevant members):

```
public class Lot extends com.ms.activeX.ActiveXControl
{
    private LotEventMulticaster _jcommem_eventmulticaster1;

    public synchronized void enableEvents();
    public void addLotEventListener(LotEventListener listener);
    public void removeLotEventListener(LotEventListener listener);
}
```

The methods `enableEvents()`, `addLotEventListener()` and `removeLotEventListener()` in the `Lot` class are used to turn event handling on (by going through the connection point protocol with the underlying object), to add new listeners to the multicast, and to remove listeners from the multicast.

The programmer is responsible for implementing the sink interface and adding it to the multicast. The programmer is also responsible for calling `enableEvents()` to turn events on – that is, to register the sink.

The Delegator Architecture

The second architecture supported by the tools is a delegator architecture. Here, the multicasting sink interface calls only a single method that is implemented on an object known as a **delegator object**. In our example, the multicasting sink has this type signature:

```
class LotEventMulticaster implements ILotEvents,
                                com.ms.com.NoAutoScripting,
                                com.ms.com.NoAutoMarshaling
{
    LotEventMulticaster(Lot _jcom_parent);
    public void BidsChanged();
}
```

The relevant members of the main proxy class look like this:

```
public class Lot extends com.ms.wfc.ui.AxHost
{
    private LotEventMulticaster _jcommem_eventmulticaster1;
    EventHandler onBidsChanged;

    protected synchronized void createSink();
    protected synchronized void detachSink();
    protected synchronized void attachInterfaces();

    public synchronized void addOnBidsChanged(EventHandler handler);
    public synchronized void removeOnBidsChanged(EventHandler handler);
}
```

Here, `onBidsChanged` is the member variable of `Lot` that represents the delegator. When the 'invoke' method on the delegator is called, all methods that have been registered with this delegator get called in turn.

The programmer implements methods that have the appropriate signature to respond to the event method invocation. Such a method is registered with the delegator by using `addOnBidsChanged()`, and unregistered with the method `removeOnBidsChanged()`.

The `attachInterfaces()` method actually creates the multicaster object, while the `createSink()` and `detachSink()` methods are used to register with the COM source object by going through the connectable object protocol.

Architecture Differences

Clearly, the second architecture is the more flexible and abstract, since it allows the programmer to create handlers for only those interface methods that are of interest. In the first architecture, the programmer has to implement the entire sink interface, but it is very clear exactly how the method is being called.

Bare Bones Connectable Objects

If you need to work with an object that is not an ActiveX control, you will need to replicate at least some of the code that we've just seen manually. The underlying mechanism to register a Java interface with a COM event source is accomplished by the com.ms.com.ConnectionPointCookie class that encapsulates an event connection. You can use this method directly to create any sink architecture that you choose.

IDL enums and structs

Java is not quite as good at dealing with user defined types as Visual Basic 6/NT4 SP4. Some kinds of structs and unions can be automatically imported from IDL into Java, while other user defined types can be supported by providing custom marshaling and Java-specific type information. An example of mapping a Java class to an IDL struct is given below.

Java has special difficulty with pointers to objects, since it doesn't really have the notion of a pointer, but it recognizes enums straight out of the type library.

Notes

Java has support for UUIDs, as well as a mechanism (J/Direct) for calling the Win32 API from Java. This means that many useful functions from the COM API are directly callable from Java.

Java/COM Mapping: The @com Directives

If you've examined the jactivex-generated Java classes that proxy the equivalent COM classes, you've probably seen the commented areas with @com directives. These directives are used by the Microsoft Java VM to map the Java constructs onto the equivalent COM constructs at runtime. There are several such directives, as you can see in this example:

```
/** @com.class(classid=2F7EBD35-368D-11D2-A5F0-000086056448, DynamicCasts)
    @com.interface(iid=07CBBCA1-470D-11D2-A641-000086056448,
                                           thread=AUTO, type=DUAL) */
public class Member implements IUnknown,
                           com.ms.com.NoAutoScripting,
                           auctsrvr.IMemberScript,
                           auctsrvr.IBidder,
                           ...
{
   /** @com.method(vtoffset=4, dispid=1, type=PROPGET, name="IBidder",
                                                  addFlagsVtable=4)
      @com.parameters([iid=2F7EBD34-368D-11D2-A5F0-000086056448,
                                  thread=AUTO,type=DISPATCH] return) */
   public native auctsrvr.IMemberInitialize getIMemberInitialize();
   public static final com.ms.com._Guid iid = new com.ms.com._Guid(
          (int)0x7cbbca1, (short)0x470d, (short)0x11d2,
          (byte)0xa6, (byte)0x41, (byte)0x0, (byte)0x0,
          (byte)0x86, (byte)0x5, (byte)0x64, (byte)0x48);

   ...
};
```

This example declares a Java COM Proxy class called Member. Here is a quick listing of the directives that are relevant for Java/COM clients; there are some other directives that are relevant only to Java/COM servers.

@com.class is a directive that declares that a Java class represents or proxies a COM class. In this example, the directive is associating the Java class with the COM coclass with the given CLSID. Normally, ordinary Java inheritance information is used to detect if a COM wrapper class supports a COM interface. However, the DynamicCasts argument specifies that if an interface is not found in the inheritance list, a QI() should be performed to discover it.

@com.interface is a directive that marks an interface as being a COM interface. When applied to a class as above, it refers to the default interface of the class, in this case IMemberScript. The thread argument indicates whether a method call to the interface should be marshaled or not, while the type indicates the type of the interface.

@com.method declares a method as being a COM method and, in conjunction with the @com.parameters directive, specifies a translation from the Java types to the IDL types. In this example, you can see that the directive is specifying a vtable offset, a DISPID, the interface name, and other information that you would expect to see. The following example shows the directives that map Java types to C++ structs:

```
/** @com.struct(noAutoOffset) */
public final class tagBidder
{
  /** @com.structmap([offset=0, type=STRING] m_vstrFirstName) */
  public String m_vstrFirstName;

  /** @com.structmap([offset=4, type=STRING] m_vstrLastName) */
  public String m_vstrLastName;

  /** @com.structmap([offset=8, type=STRING] m_vstrCity) */
  public String m_vstrCity;

  /** @com.structmap([offset=12, type=STRING] m_vstrState) */
  public String m_vstrState;
}
```

@com.struct declares that the Java class maps onto a C++ struct. The noAutoOffset argument indicates that each member will have its offset explicitly specified.

@com.structmap provides information about the mapping from each member in the class to the corresponding C++ struct member. It provides information about the offset as well as the C++ type that is involved.

Java Summary

We've seen that COM support is very tightly integrated with the Java language. In fact, COM classes and interfaces are mapped almost seamlessly onto Java classes and interfaces. This is made possible because:

❑ Java classes and interfaces are actually very similar in spirit to COM classes and interfaces
❑ Java is an interpreted language with a virtual machine that can hide all the translation details of going from COM to Java

The only problems with the integration show up in places where the Java VM does not mesh well with the Windows architecture:

❏ In the interaction of STA threads and apartments with Java native threading
❏ In the interplay of the garbage collector with apartments and with the SAFEARRAY type

Visual C++

We've now seen Visual Basic and Visual J++ client code that made our earlier attempt at communication using C++ look extremely clumsy, but we really weren't comparing like with like. Let's look now at some C++ client code that uses the COM support built into Visual C++. Here it is:

```
#import "auctsrvr.tlb" no_namespace;

ILotPtr g_spILot;

void LotInitialize() throw(_com_error)
{
    g_spILot = ILotPtr(__uuidof(Lot));
    bstr_t vstr =
            (static_cast<ILotInitializePtr>(g_spILot))->InitAuctionInfo(45, 3, 8);
}
```

Now *that* looks every bit as simple as the Java code! What's happened here? Has C++ suddenly acquired an all-powerful runtime, or a VM that we haven't been told about?

As it turns out, we're almost exclusively using perfectly normal C++ language constructs here. There just happens to be a very powerful combination of template classes, tool support and a couple of teensy-weensy Microsoft compiler extensions at work. Let's look at each of these before we look at the COM operations.

Creating an Object

The COM object is created inside the call to the constructor of ILotPtr, an instance of the smart pointer template class _com_ptr_t<>, which is responsible for much of the simplification you see in the code above.

The CLSID for the call to CoCreateInstance() is associated with the identifier Lot (which represents the class) by a Visual C++ compiler extension that can associate UUIDs with a class. This extension consists of the pair of operators __uuidof() to query a class UUID, and __declspec(uuid) to associate a UUID with a class. The COM support classes are designed so that this feature is optional – that is, it doesn't depend on a compiler that supports these extensions. I believe this to be a useful innovation, and it's also simple enough that it shouldn't be too hard for other compiler vendors to incorporate it into their products.

Interface Use

The _com_ptr_t<> smart pointer class does all the painful work of keeping track of the reference count, and has a lot of other COM interface 'intelligence' built into it. QueryInterface(), for example, is squirreled away within a templatized assignment operator and constructor that permit conversion between smart pointers encapsulating different interface types. These C++ methods make it possible to *cast* from one interface smart pointer type to another, instead of having to call QI().

Many people have problems with smart pointers, saying that a smart pointer is neither an object nor a true pointer. It provides certain methods of its own, but implements the functionality of the underlying pointer by delegating via an overloaded -> operator. This can confuse programmers who start thinking of it as a real pointer, and don't realize that it has constructors, destructors and overloaded assignment operators that are being implicitly substituted by the compiler. The templatized assignment operator allowing assignment between different interface pointers can be especially confusing.

My own response to this issue is to use the Hungarian prefix sp rather than p when declaring smart pointers. I believe that this gets rid of 95% of the confusion surrounding the use of these beasts; the remaining 5% is then the price to be paid for their convenience.

`AddRef()` and `Release()` are called as parts of the "big three" C++ lifetime operations: the copy constructor, the assignment operator, and the destructor. The destructor enables interface smart pointers to be returned as expression values – anonymous variables that can be used to invoke methods. For example, if we hadn't had the global variable in the above snippet, the two lines in the function might have been abbreviated to

```
bstr_t vstr = (static_cast<ILotInitializePtr>(
                        ILotPtr(__uuidof(Lot))))->InitAuctionInfo(45, 3, 8);
```

Interface methods can be called by using the overloaded -> operator of the smart pointer class. This gives access to the actual underlying interface.

`#import` generates a C++ class that, in addition to the pure virtual functions corresponding to the interface methods, has non-virtual functions that wrap calls to the pure virtuals. These non-virtual functions do the following:

❑ The HRESULT from the call to the pure virtual function is tested, and any error returns converted into a call to _com_issue_errorex(). This function, which you can override if you really must, checks for the availability of error objects, converts it into a _com_error (a class that encapsulates the COM error object) and then throws it.

❑ Instead of the HRESULT, which is converted into an exception, the return value is the underlying parameter with the out and retval attributes. If there is no such parameter, the HRESULT is returned. This is what makes the method call in the client code above look so much like the Java and Visual Basic equivalents.

❑ Parameters of type BSTR and VARIANT in the underlying pure virtual function are substituted by parameters of the _bstr_t and _variant_t classes we looked at earlier. Parameters that are interface pointers are substituted by parameters whose types are the equivalent smart pointers.

In our example, the wrapper method for `InitAuctionInfo()` has this declaration:

```
inline _bstr_t ILotInitialize::InitAuctionInfo(
                    LONG a_vlStartPrice, LONG a_vlBidIncrement, LONG a_vlCloseAt)
{
    BSTR _result;
    HRESULT _hr = get_Description(&_result);
    if(FAILED(_hr))
        _com_issue_errorex(_hr, this, __uuidof(this));

    return _bstr_t(_result, false);
}
```

The description above represents the transformation of a vtable interface, and the tool works in a very similar way with Automation interfaces. Instead of wrapping a call to a virtual function, the generated functions wrap calls to `IDispatch::Invoke()`. All the other transformations are the same as for a COM interface.

> **Names generated by #import:**
>
> The proxy C++ class that is generated from an interface uses the interface name from the type library. This name can be used to call methods directly by using the pure virtual functions, or indirectly by calling the wrappers.
>
> By default, the names generated for the non-virtual wrapper methods are the same as the underlying IDL method names. The 'real' pure virtual methods are given names prefixed by `raw_`.
>
> By default, properties are represented by a pair of non-virtual wrapper methods with the IDL names prefixed by `Get` and `Put`. The underlying pure virtual functions are prefixed with `get_` and `put_`. The same naming conventions are followed for Automation interfaces.
>
> The smart pointer classes are `typedef`'d to names that add the suffix `Ptr` to the IDL name for the interface.
>
> The injection of all these names into the global namespace can be confusing, since it is often not clear how they got there, and also due to the possibility of name clashes (in IDL, the 'real', unique name of an entity is its UUID, not its ASCII identifier). To resolve this issue, the code generated by #import is wrapped in a C++ namespace that has the same name as the type library itself.

Memory Allocation

The wrapper methods generated by the proxy do some of the memory allocation grunge work as well. Take a look at the last line of the wrapper function that I displayed earlier — the one that constructs a _bstr_t that is to be used as the return value. The first parameter is the BSTR that is returned from the method invocation, while the second parameter (`false`) specifies that this BSTR is not copied into the _bstr_t during construction (the default behavior), but rather that it is 'attached'. The normal lifetime mechanisms of the _bstr_t will ensure that this attached value is released when necessary.

Of course, if you're using a type that isn't understood by the #import directive (such as a user-defined type with embedded pointers), or if for some reason you're using a raw BSTR value, the programmer is still responsible for memory allocation operations.

Error Handling

As we saw earlier, the COM error object protocol is encapsulated in the call to the _com_issue_errorex() function, which creates a _com_error value from the rich error information and throws it. You can override this function if you choose; situations in which you might wish to do so include error logging or sending the error to a debug stream.

Event Handling

Visual C++ does provide some client support for event handling, but it's fairly old and not completely consistent with the new architectural direction taken by ATL. In fact, it is part of the standard MFC messaging and event framework that can respond to events fired by ActiveX controls (not COM objects in general).

> *The pure ATL support for connection point clients requires the creation of ATL objects, and is covered in the next chapter.*

Trying to perform event handling without MFC or ATL support boils down to doing something like the 'raw' C++ code I showed you at the beginning of this section.

Notes

The UUID association mechanism isn't the only language extension that Visual C++ has made to C++; there is another one that can look quite strange from the perspective of the traditional C/C++ programmer.

This extension allows the declaration of 'virtual' data members in a C++ class. These 'members' are implemented by pairs of get and set member functions, allowing the writing of code that seems to assign a value to (and retrieve it from) a data member. The compiler silently generates code that substitutes a call to the appropriate member of the get/set pair.

From a semantic perspective, this is odd. A data member that takes up no space in the class layout? A data member whose use in an expression might result in an exception being thrown? As far as I can see, its only benefits are:

❑ A slight abbreviation compared with writing out the full method syntax for the Get and Put methods
❑ The fact that the object browser and IntelliSense representations of an interface will show a property icon in addition to the get/put methods.

I recommend against the use of virtual properties. They are confusing enough that in the absence of a clear benefit, it's best to forego their use.

VBScript

Let's look at the same example one more time using a scripting language. Here it is in VBScript:

```
Private gLot

Sub LotInitialize()
    Set gLot = CreateObject("Auction.Lot")

    Dim ili
    Set ili = gLot.ILotInitialize
    ili.InitAuctionInfo 45, 3, 8
End Sub
```

This code has one very significant point of departure from all our previous examples. There is no support for COM's QueryInterface() within the language!

Creating an Object

Objects in VBScript can be created in one of two ways:

❑   By using the `CreateObject()` function, just as in the dynamically bound version of Visual Basic.

❑   By creating an object using the HTML `<OBJECT>` tag within the page in which the script is executing. You can name the object using the `ID` parameter of the tag. This is very similar to objects created on Visual Basic forms. At present, only objects served by in-process servers can be loaded using the `<OBJECT>` tag.

Interface Use

Like Visual Basic in its early days, VBScript is dynamically typed – it doesn't support compile-time typing of variables. This means that VBScript cannot use *a priori* unknown COM interfaces. The only interface that it knows how to call is `IDispatch`, and so even if it *could* request a different interface type (by using some appropriately-proxied call to `QueryInterface()`), it wouldn't be able to use the resulting interface. This has two related consequences:

❑   Every interface that needs to be used from a scripting language must be a dispinterface or a dual interface (in practice, I always use dual interfaces for ease of ATL implementation).

❑   Since scripting languages cannot request an interface other than `IDispatch`, the default `IDispatch` interface of the object must also fulfill the function of `QueryInterface()`; it must allow the scripting language to gain access to other interfaces exposed by the object.

An alternative that is very commonly used is to provide all the functionality of the object in one gigantic `IDispatch` interface. While this addresses the issue of scripting language clients, it does so at the cost of seriously compromising the cleanliness of the design for use from other platforms.

The solution that I am proposing here addresses the same issue while maintaining a better factored and therefore more re-usable design.

Just as in Visual Basic, the runtime transparently wraps all actual method invocations. An interface method called from VBScript seems to return not an `HRESULT`, but the parameter decorated with the `out` and `retval` attributes. Furthermore, the runtime automatically calls `Release()` on an interface when the interface is going out of scope. `Release()` is also called when an interface variable is being assigned a new value; the old value is released.

VBScript also allows explicit calls to `Release()` by `Set`'ing the variable to the `Nothing` value.

Memory Allocation

As in the case of Visual Basic, the runtime performs all the necessary memory allocation. You might wonder how the runtime can do this in the absence of a type library (how does it know the types of parameters?), but this is exactly why VBScript only allows `VARIANT` types.

Also, as explained in the earlier section on Visual Basic *Parameter Type Restrictions*, the type signature of VBScript-callable methods allows only one `out`-only parameter: the one that is marked `retval` and serves as the return value of `IDispatch::Invoke()`. The allocation policy for in and in, out parameters looks the same from the standpoint of the runtime, so that distinction is not an important one.

Error Handling

Just as in Visual Basic, the VBScript runtime automatically calls the COM error object protocol and populates the `Err` object. However, at the time of writing, the VBScript language only supports a subset of the Visual Basic error handling mechanism (it doesn't support `On Error GoTo`, for example).

Event Handling

VBScript event handling is a restricted version of that provided by Visual Basic. The essential differences are:

❑ The VBScript runtime can catch events thrown by objects that are embedded in HTML, just as Visual Basic can catch events thrown by objects on forms.

❑ Since VBScript does not (yet) have support for type libraries, the object must somehow provide information on its event interface so that the runtime can provide suitable sink objects. This is done via the `IProvideClassInfo2` interface, which must be exported by all objects that have to fire events into scripts.

❑ Unlike Visual Basic, VBScript does not support the `WithEvents` keyword that allows programmatically created objects to fire events that the runtime can catch.

VBScript uses the same naming convention as Visual Basic to connect handlers to sinks (`<objectname>_<handlername>`), and VBScript can only connect to the default source interface; it cannot connect to any others.

IDL enums and structs

Currently, VBScript has no support for IDL `struct`s or even IDL `enum`s.

Parameter Type Restrictions

Just as in Visual Basic, with the exception of the `retval` parameter, VBScript can only use `in` and `in, out` parameters.

Naïve "Property Get as QI()" Doesn't Work

The situation with respect to VBScript only being able to call the `IDispatch` interface is worse than it might seem. *Every* assignment of an object to a variable actually results in a `QI()` for `IDispatch`. To see how this can cause a serious problem, read on.

In our example, all the "Lot" interfaces are dual interfaces and therefore are scriptable. Recall also that the `ILotScript` interface is the navigational interface of the lot object – that is, it allows access to the other interfaces via the "Property as `QI()`" idiom. For this reason, `ILotScript` is exposed as the primary `IDispatch` interface on the `Lot` object:

```
interface ILotScript : IDispatch
{
    [propget, id(1), helpstring("ILot")]
    HRESULT ILot([out, retval] ILot** a_pplt);

    [propget, id(2), helpstring("IPlaceBid")]
    HRESULT IPlaceBid([out, retval] IPlaceBid** a_pppb);
```

```
    [propget, id(3), helpstring("ILotInitialize")]
    HRESULT ILotInitialize([out, retval] ILotInitialize** a_ppli);

    [id(4), helpstring("Save Lot object to the named file")]
    HRESULT Persist2File(BSTR FileName);
};
```

`ILotScript` is replicating the functionality of `QueryInterface()` by providing access to the other dual interfaces provided by the `Lot` object. Since `ILotScript` is the `IDispatch` interface on the lot class, it is the interface that is returned by the call to `CreateObject()` in the example above.

There is only one problem with exposing interfaces in this fashion instead of using `QI()`: it may not work! Most simple Automation controllers (and that includes current scripting languages) will not recognize a dual interface returned to them as being a usable `IDispatch` interface. Instead, the language runtime will `QI()` the returned interface for `IDispatch`. This means that if two different interfaces on a single COM object are being exposed via "property get", then *at most* one is actually usable by a scripting client – the one that is the 'real' `IDispatch` of the object.

> *This is not done with complete consistency. I've seen some versions of the scripting engines that seem to accept some dual interfaces as being "Automatable", but request* IDispatch *from others. In general, it is wisest to assume that this will not work; you may be able to tell that I've been bitten by this behavior.*

This implies that it is not possible to implement multiple scriptable interfaces on a 'single' COM object. If this were true, it would be a serious nuisance. You'll recall that in the previous chapter we grouped interfaces together whose implementations required access to a common state; these groups were COM classes. If only one interface on each class can be made visible to a scripting client, we're in serious trouble. We'll have to implement each interface on its own object, and then have the objects somehow share each others' states.

There is, of course, a better solution: that of **alternate** or **dependent identities**. We'll see this in action in the next chapter.

JScript

Other than minor differences in syntax, JScript is quite similar to VBScript. Here is the corresponding JScript code:

```
var gLot

function LotInitialize()
{
    gLot = new ActiveXObject("Auction.Lot")
    var ili
    ili = gLot.ILotInitialize
    ili.InitAuctionInfo(45, 3, 8)
}
```

Creating an Object

In JScript, COM objects can be created in one of two ways:

❑   By using the `ActiveXObject()` construct function in conjunction with the JScript `new` operator.

❑   By creating an object using the HTML `<OBJECT>` tag within the page in which the script is executing. You can name the object using the `ID` parameter of the tag.

Interface Use

Like VBScript, JScript is dynamically typed, so it does not support compile-time typing of variables. All the comments on VBScript interface use apply to JScript, with the following differences:

❑   The JScript runtime can call the `IDispatchEx` interface (see Chapter 4) in addition to `IDispatch`.

❑   JScript does not have a `Nothing` value, but the effect of calling `Release()` on an interface can be achieved by assigning the `null` value to the interface.

❑   The JScript runtime provides a stock implementation of `IDispatchEx` for the addition of new methods and properties to dynamically created JScript interfaces (see Chapter 4 for an example). It is likely that some such capability will be made available in VBScript in the future.

Memory Allocation

Like Java, JScript uses a garbage collector for memory allocation, so there is no need for per-method memory cleanup.

Error Handling

At present, JScript provides no error catching mechanism. It is intended that the next version will introduce a `try-catch` language construct.

Event Handling

Event handling in JScript has the same restrictions as VBScript, with a single difference caused by syntax. Instead of the `<objectname>_<handlername>` convention, there is an explicit addition to the `<SCRIPT>` HTML tag to do the association:

```
<SCRIPT LANGUAGE=javascript FOR=objectname EVENT=handlername>
actualhandler();
</SCRIPT>
```

The above tag associates a call to the function `actualhandler()` with the `handlername` method of the default source interface on `objectname`. In turn, `objectname` must be the `ID` value on an object declared using the `<OBJECT>` tag.

Recap

We've now examined the COM client bindings in the various Microsoft-supported languages. The range of COM abstractions is fairly large.

❑ Raw C/C++ reveals all the details of the native COM architecture and plumbing.

❑ The COM protocols were built into, and grew out of, Visual Basic. COM classes and interfaces can be used directly out of a referenced type library, and Visual Basic has support for almost any COM interface in addition to its traditional support for Automation interfaces. Visual Basic loses some power because of its 'one-size-fits-all' approach towards exceptions and events. It is also unable to use certain types (including UUIDs), and it loses access to HRESULT return values.

❑ Java is a curious thing. Its language abstractions, such as classes and interfaces, are *semantically analogous* to COM classes and interfaces (as indeed are C++ classes and interfaces). Unlike C++, however, the fact that Java has a virtual machine makes it possible to make the classes and interfaces appear *semantically identical* to COM classes and interfaces by having the VM act as a translation layer between Java and COM.

Because of this translation, once the Java proxy classes have been set up, COM usage becomes ordinary Java usage. Pretty much all of COM is accessible via the translation layer, although Java does have a few problems with COM apartments and garbage collection of SAFEARRAYs, does not yet have full support for all structs, and has problems with pointers.

❑ C++ with COM client support is an excellent balance of abstraction and power. The new COM client support includes seamless #import'ing of type libraries, smart pointers, interface wrappers, C++ COM Automation support classes, and conversion of error objects to C++ exceptions. However, the C++ support *is* only a convenience (albeit an enormous one), and doesn't prevent programmers from getting their hands dirty by using the underlying infrastructure directly.

❑ VBScript and JScript, like earlier versions of Visual Basic, only support late-bound Automation interfaces, specifically IDispatch. They also suffer from an inability to use types other than VARIANT types, have the same limited event support as Visual Basic and do not have full exception support.

Building a User Interface for the Auction Server

We'll now begin a detailed examination of a simple client for our auction server that I'll build using every one of the client-side programming languages that I've discussed in this chapter. My purposes in doing so are manifold.

The exercise of building a reasonably-sized, UI-based application illustrates a number of practical details of client side IDL bindings, such as how to pass optional arguments, how to deal with different time formats, and so forth. It provides a realistic basis for comparing how the same design is implemented in various languages. With the right interface design, however, the client code is pretty similar in each case, being simple glue code that ties together separately implemented COM objects that encapsulate the major pieces of functionality.

As a server implementer, I hope that the exercise will give you a better sense of the context within which your IDL designs get used, with the intention of refining your design sense.

I also hope to convince the skeptical that in this era of multi-tier systems, user interface implementation can be effectively done in any of the development environments. All of Microsoft's "visual" tools are capable of creating forms-based UIs extremely quickly and efficiently. If anything, my feeling is that C++ and Java now have the edge because their stronger typing allows earlier detection of bugs. Script is the hardest to debug, but HTML provides the nicest looking interfaces. You pays your money and you takes your choice.

Design Constraints

You'll see that the client code for the different languages is almost identical in terms of the module and control structure of the code, right down to the level of individual lines. This not an accident: the high level design is deliberately constrained to maximize re-use potential, and to flatten learning curves.

- ❑ A forms-based approach is taken towards building the client code, which is the approach that most RAD environments take towards UI development.
- ❑ The high-complexity business logic is encapsulated in the auction server. This functionality is made available through a set of interfaces (an object model) that are identical on all clients. No business logic is implemented in the UI.
- ❑ The high-complexity visual functionality is encapsulated in a couple of ActiveX controls – the Microsoft FlexGrid and ListView controls – instead of using controls that are language specific (WFC controls, Visual Basic controls, or MFC classes). Since ActiveX controls expose functionality via COM interfaces, the exposed functionality is guaranteed to be identical in all client languages, making translation a relatively mechanical matter. Similarly, the design time features are exposed in very similar fashion by all the visual environments.
- ❑ We only use environment-specific visual controls for simple items such as buttons or edit boxes whose interfaces are so simple that there is no learning curve.

This means that most of the work on the client side is visual form design (which is operationally very similar in all the RAD environments) and writing glue code that makes calls to the appropriate COM interfaces. Out of interest, I built the Visual Basic client first, and then did a hand translation of all the code into the other clients.

You'll notice that many of the functions are grouped into logical units based on the business object they work with. The reason why the functions aren't encapsulated into objects is mostly because of the way that the Wizards generate code; they don't allow you to create objects of a finer granularity than the entire form to represent subsets of elements on the form. If there were complex visual representations that were clearly associated with business objects, it might make sense eventually to encapsulate them in an ActiveX control for reusability. Doing so in Visual Basic, or Visual J++ or MFC didn't make too much sense.

Other than some familiarity with the IDE of each environment, the only thing that you need to accomplish this translation is an understanding of how COM objects are instantiated, invoked and cleaned up in each language, and that's exactly what we've covered in this chapter.

The User Interface

I'll show you a screenshot of how the user interface looks at the beginning of each client language project, but in general the primary user interface for the application consists of a main form with:

❑ A group of static text and edit controls representing information associated with the member currently logged on.

❑ A list view control that displays all the members. If a new member is selected and the 'change' button pressed, the new member becomes logged on, displacing the current member. This is meant to simulate the login process (which you'll recall wasn't one of the use cases in our server design).

❑ Another list view control that displays a list of categories that you can use to constrain your search. A new 'find' operation is initiated by selecting a new category and clicking the appropriate button.

❑ A grid control (Microsoft FlexGrid) that displays the results of the find operation, each line containing information about one lot that matches the search criteria. Upon double clicking on a lot in the grid, further information about the lot is made visible in *another* grid on the form that displays the list of currently active bids for that lot.

❑ A group of static text and edit controls that display auction information associated with the currently selected lot.

❑ An 'add bid' button that allows a user to place a new bid on the lot.

A secondary UI, also form-based, is a modal dialog that allows a bid price and quantity to be entered. This form is brought up when the user presses the 'add bid' button. If the form is successfully dismissed, a new bid appears in the grid of bids. In the DHTML application, this UI is implemented as a control on the primary form that appears and disappears on demand.

Application Structure

This application runs on a single computer, but the code is structured to be completely oblivious about the actual location of various objects. This is accomplished by adhering to some simple constraints:

❑ The UI code has no knowledge of the location of any of its services or data. No filenames (or any other identifiers) are generated by the UI; this is all done within the objects of the auction service. The UI only ever deals with pointers to interfaces.

❑ The UI code never calls `QueryInterface()`. This has two consequences:

    ❑ It makes the glue code more portable, since the `QI()` mechanism is invoked differently in different languages (and is not even available in the scripting languages).

    ❑ The user interface code cannot be dependent on COM object identity – it has no way of verifying whether it is talking to the real object or to a proxy. As I pointed out in the previous chapter, this provides much more flexibility when the time comes to distribute the object.

❑ I do not use any bound objects (such as data bound grids). Instead, there are separate procedures, invoked at the appropriate times, which keep the contents of the grid in sync with the underlying data. Although bound objects are wonderful in terms of simplifying the code for database queries, using them has some unfortunate consequences:

    ❑ It makes the design very data-centric, based on recordset manipulation rather than object manipulation. This makes it almost impossible to change the design if you move to an alternative collection metaphor.

    ❑ It encourages fat clients, persistent connections and hard-to-maintain code (especially if stored procedures aren't used), because the database querying code is scattered over a number of applications rather than being centralized in one place.

The level of coding detail in the application is fairly realistic. The user interface design is a reasonable one, without an over-reliance on modal dialogs for input. Issues such as data validation are dealt with in a sensible (though not completely comprehensive) fashion. The major changes required to ready this code for production are:

❑ Improved error checking and handling. I am not checking for any errors or handling exceptions. This would be completely unacceptable in production code.

❑ Working out the details of user interaction to a finer level of granularity.

❑ A transacted user interface, with an undo facility for changes.

❑ More sophisticated UI elements for some of the data. For example, the time fields could have been represented using a date/time picker, the numbers by masked edit controls, and so on.

❑ An auto-save feature for the lot object.

I have left these details out to reduce the amount of code that I show (and the amount I needed to write!).

Recapping the Specification Model

The client code shown in this chapter is based on the specification model that was developed in Chapter 5, so this would be a good time to refresh your memory with a look at the *Specification Model* and *Class Design* sections in the last chapter.

I should point out before we begin that I shall only show you *all* the code for the Visual Basic client. For the remaining clients, I will show only enough code to illustrate significant aspects of using the COM infrastructure, and the similarities and differences between the various languages. Complete versions of all the clients are, of course, available from the Wrox web site at http://www.wrox.com.

The Visual Basic Client

Here's the user interface of the application we're building, with all the various controls labeled. The two controls at the top are ListViews; the two large display areas are MS FlexGrid controls.

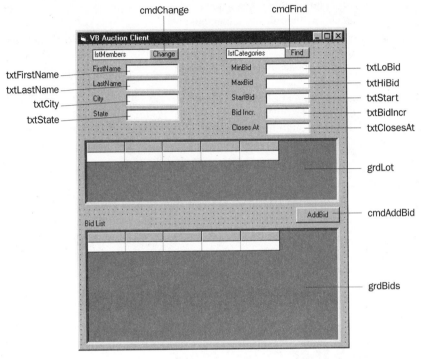

Global Variables

The main form needs a number of variables that represent the current state of the application, and are available from various methods in the application. This includes variables such as the current ILotScript interface, the current ILot interface, the current IBidder interface, etc. Although there is a certain element of redundancy in the choice of interfaces (you can always find the current ILot given the current ILotScript, for example), the redundancies serve the purpose of caching frequently used values.

```
' Variables used by other forms
Public m_lot As WroxAuction.Lot               ' Current ILotScript
Public m_ilot As WroxAuction.ILot             ' Current ILot
Public m_ibidder As WroxAuction.IBidder       ' Current IBidder
Public m_iauct As WroxAuction.Auction         ' Current IAuctionScript

' Cached interfaces
Private m_ilots As WroxAuction.Lots           ' Current ILots
Private m_ibids As WroxAuction.Bids           ' Current IBids

Private m_icl As WroxAuction.CategoryCache     ' Current ICategories
Private m_imm As WroxAuction.Members          ' Current IMembers

Private m_tm As TimeUtil.COMTime              ' Current ICOMTimeScript

Private Const PfxTitle As String = "VB Auction Client"
```

The only one of the interfaces here that didn't appear in the analysis of the last chapter is `ICOMTimeScript`, which is contained in the `TimeUtil.COMTime` variable. It is an interface for converting between time formats whose design is described at the end of this chapter.

Initialization

The form is initialized by a call to its `Form_Load()` subroutine, which in turn invokes the `AuctionInitialize()` method. This method creates the `COMTime` and `Auction` objects, each of which is the root object of its own hierarchy. Given the design of our object model, we will not have to create any other objects directly, thus encapsulating inner object creation from the object model user. Finally, `AuctionInitialize()` invokes the `UIInit()` method.

```
Private Sub Form_Load()
    Caption = PfxTitle
    AuctionInitialize
End Sub

Sub AuctionInitialize()
    Set m_tm = New TimeUtil.COMTime
    Set m_iauct = New WroxAuction.Auction
    Set m_icl = m_iauct.IAuctionUIElements.ICategories
    Set m_imm = m_iauct.IAuctionUIElements.IMembers

    UIInit
End Sub
```

`UIInit()` sets up aspects of the user interface, such as the member list control and the category list control. Since we don't want to hard-wire either of these aspects into the UI, the values for these lists come from our object model, specifically from the `IAuctionUIElements` interface, which provides the `ICategories` and `IMembers` collection interfaces.

```
Sub UIInit()
    CategoryLoad
    MemberLoad
    grdLot.Enabled = False
    cmdAddBid.Enabled = False
End Sub
```

The category list is loaded by the `CategoryLoad()` subroutine, while the member list is loaded by the `MemberLoad()` routine. Here is the implementation of `CategoryLoad()`:

```
Sub CategoryLoad()
    Dim i As Long
    Dim itm As ListItem
    i = 0
    Do While i < m_icl.Count
        Set itm = lstCategories.ListItems.Add
        itm.Text = m_icl.Item(i)
        itm.ListSubItems.Add
        itm.ListSubItems(1).Text = m_icl.GetItemID(i)
        i = i + 1
    Loop
    lstCategories.SelectedItem = lstCategories.ListItems(1)
End Sub
```

As you can see, it iterates over the category collection presented by m_icl, retrieving individual categories. The method gets the category string and corresponding ID, and stores the pair in consecutive items of the lstCategories list view control. Since a list view control can only accept the string as an item, the ID has to be stored as a sub-item at index 1. Finally, the current selection in the list is set to be the first item (remember that Visual Basic array indexing starts at 1 by default).

One point to note here is that many of the list view methods take optional arguments. In Visual Basic, it is very easy to specify that arguments at the end of a parameter list are missing: we just leave them out! The runtime fills in the appropriate 'missing parameter' VARIANT value.

The MemberLoad() subroutine is almost identical to CategoryLoad(), except that it fills the list view control that displays members. The routine iterates over the current list of members, adding the member names (and IDs) to the list view control.

```
Sub MemberLoad()
    Dim i As Long
    Dim idx As Long
    Dim m As Member
    Dim itm As ListItem
    i = 0
    Do While i < m_imm.Count
        Set itm = lstMembers.ListItems.Add
        Set m = m_imm.Item(i)
        itm.Text = m.IBidder.FirstName & " " & m.IBidder.LastName
        itm.ListSubItems.Add
        itm.ListSubItems(1).Text = m.IBidder.MemberID
        i = i + 1
    Loop
    lstMembers.SelectedItem = lstMembers.ListItems(1)
    Set m_ibidder = m_imm.Item(0).IBidder
    MemberRefresh m_ibidder
End Sub
```

When this is done, the current bidder is set to the first bidder in the collection, and MemberRefresh() is called. Notice that although the IMembers collection returns IMemberScript interfaces, we are really interested in the IBidder interface that contains member details. We retrieve this interface by calling the IBidder "property as QI()"-style method, instead of performing a QI(). As pointed out in the previous chapter, this hides object identity from a non-intrusive client.

Updating the UI

The code that refreshes the user interface is fairly straightforward. MemberRefresh() simply takes properties of the current IBidder interface (passed in as a parameter) and displays them in the corresponding edit controls:

```
Sub MemberRefresh(mem As IBidder)
    txtFirstName.Text = mem.FirstName
    txtLastName.Text = mem.LastName
    txtCity.Text = mem.City
    txtState.Text = mem.State
End Sub
```

The `InfoRefresh()` and `BidsRefresh()` functions are responsible for displaying information that is associated with a single lot, and as such they are never called until a lot is actually selected by being double-clicked upon. The functions are therefore called from event handlers, as shown later.

`InfoRefresh()` is similar in intent to `MemberRefresh()` but a little more complicated, since it needs to check that the high and low bids actually exist, and to display blanks if there are no outstanding bids. It does this by comparing the bid values to the `auctAIBSNoBid` constant, which is defined in the type library.

```
Sub InfoRefresh(info As IAuctionInfo)
    If info.LoBid = auctAIBSNoBid Then
        txtLoBid.Text = ""
    Else
        txtLoBid.Text = info.LoBid
    End If

    If info.HiBid = auctAIBSNoBid Then
        txtHiBid.Text = ""
    Else
        txtHiBid.Text = info.HiBid
    End If

    txtStart.Text = info.StartPrice
    txtBidIncr.Text = info.BidIncrement
    txtClosesAt.Text = info.ClosesAt

    frmLot.Caption = PfxTitle & " : Bidding on Lot: " & info.Description
End Sub
```

The most interesting UI code is in the `LotsRefresh()` and `BidsRefresh()` subroutines. Here is the first of these, which displays attributes of the current collection of lots. The function is called when a search has been completed, and the search results need to be displayed in the grid.

```
Sub LotsRefresh(lots As ILots)
    grdLot.Clear
    grdLot.Rows = lots.Count + 1

    ' Set the column headers
    grdLot.FormatString = "<Closes At |<Description          " _
                        & " |<Category |<Min Price    |<Bid Increment"

    Dim lot As ILot
    Dim i As Long
    i = 1
    Do While i < grdLot.Rows
        Set lot = lots.Item(i - 1).Ilot

        grdLot.TextArray(faIndex(i, 0, grdLot)) = lot.info.ClosesAt
        grdLot.TextArray(faIndex(i, 1, grdLot)) = lot.info.Description
        grdLot.TextArray(faIndex(i, 2, grdLot)) = lot.info.Category
        grdLot.TextArray(faIndex(i, 3, grdLot)) = lot.info.StartPrice
        grdLot.TextArray(faIndex(i, 4, grdLot)) = lot.info.BidIncrement
        i = i + 1
    Loop

    grdLot.Enabled = True
    cmdAddBid.Enabled = False
    grdBids.Clear
    grdBids.Rows = 1
End Sub
```

This subroutine completely clears the `grdLot` variable that holds the 'lot' grid control. It resets the column headers and the refills the grid from the data made available by the `IAuctionInfo` member of the `ILot` interface. When the grid has been repopulated, it enables the grid control, disables the 'add bid' button, and clears the 'bids' grid (since there is no currently selected lot, there is no current bids collection).

Note in particular the unusual assignment performed on the `TextArray`, which is a parameterized property that takes a single argument in addition to its property value. The `faIndex()` function is used to calculate a one-dimensional index position (the `TextArray` only takes a single index parameter) from the two-dimensional (row, column) coordinate. It is a utility function declared as:

```
Function faIndex(row As Long, col As Long, ctrl As Object) As Long
    faIndex = row * ctrl.Cols + col
End Function
```

In the code as presented, the grid is being used in 'dumb' mode – it only serves to display the values in the collection of bids. Sorting is implicit in the order of items returned from the `ILots` interface, and is not performed by the grid object.

Now examine the code that refreshes the bids grid:

```
Sub BidsRefresh(bids As IBids)
    grdBids.Clear
    grdBids.Rows = bids.Count + 1

    ' Set the column headers
    grdBids.FormatString = "<Member        |<Location       |<Price" _
                    & " |<Quantity |<Time                          "

    Dim b As Bid
    Dim bid As IBid
    Dim i As Long
    i = 1
    For Each b In bids
        Set bid = b.IBid
        grdBids.TextArray(faIndex(i, 0, grdBids)) = bid.Bidder.FirstName _
                                        & " " & bid.Bidder.LastName
        grdBids.TextArray(faIndex(i, 1, grdBids)) = bid.Bidder.City _
                                        & ", " & bid.Bidder.State
        grdBids.TextArray(faIndex(i, 2, grdBids)) = bid.Price
        grdBids.TextArray(faIndex(i, 3, grdBids)) = bid.Number
        m_tm.ICOMTime.ToTimeT bid.Time
        grdBids.TextArray(faIndex(i, 4, grdBids)) = m_tm.ICOMTime.AsOleDate

        i = i + 1
    Next b

    cmdAddBid.Enabled = True
End Sub
```

This subroutine works in a very similar fashion to `LotsRefresh()`, which I described earlier. It clears and then repopulates the bids grid with the current bids collection. It iterates over this collection one item at a time, and fills the grid one row at a time.

There are a couple of new features in this sample. First, recall from the declaration of the `IBid` interface (bid is declared to be an `IBid`) that the placement time of a bid is returned as a `long` (or `time_t`) value rather than as a `DATE`. Visual Basic doesn't know how to interpret `long` values as `DATE`s, and so I've provided a COM utility class called `IComTimeScript` to provide conversions between favored time formats in different languages. The global member variable `m_tm` contains this interface, and has been used here to convert from a `time_t` to the equivalent `DATE` format. Some details about this interface are presented in the final section of this chapter.

The second feature of interest is that I use Visual Basic iteration in this example, rather than explicit looping over the items in the collection. Note the expression in the `For` loop: it is not testing against a high index value, but iterating over the collection without requiring an index. The big benefit of this idiom is that it reduces the possibility of erroneous index computation and guarantees a single pass over the collection. It requires that the collection make available (not export) an enumeration interface called `IEnumVARIANT`.

Constraining User Input

If you use the Visual Basic client, you will notice that various features of the user interface are disabled when not required. For instance, it is not possible to interact with the lot grid until it has been initialized. Similarly, the 'add bid' button is disabled until a lot is selected. These features are turned on and off at the appropriate times in the application's operation.

Finding a Lot

Clicking on the 'find' button causes the lot search function to get invoked, by way of the event handler. Like all event handlers in Visual Basic, the name reflects the `<objectname>_<eventname>` syntax:

```
Private Sub cmdFind_Click()
    Set m_ilots = m_iauct.ILotFinder.SearchCategory( _
                                lstCategories.SelectedItem.ListSubItems(1))
    LotsRefresh m_ilots
End Sub
```

As you can see, this code calls the `SearchCategory()` method on the `ILotFinder` interface made available by the auction object model. The search is passed a single integer parameter that indicates the category to search on. This value is extracted from the auxiliary information associated with the currently selected item in the category list.

`SearchCategory()`, which is implemented by the auction server, returns a collection of lots that is then passed into the redraw routine for the lot grid. Note that the previous value of the `m_ilots` variable is released when the new assignment takes place.

Viewing the Bids

By default, no lot is selected when a find operation completes. The user needs to double click on a row of the grid in order to select a lot. When a lot *is* selected, the bids associated with the lot are displayed. If the selection is changed by double clicking once more, the bids associated with the new lot are displayed. This is accomplished by the double-click event handler for the lot grid.

```
Private Sub grdLot_DblClick()
    Dim i As Long
    i = grdLot.row
    Set m_lot = m_ilots.Item(i - 1)
    Set m_ilot = m_lot.ILot
    InfoRefresh m_ilot.info
    BidsRefresh m_ilot.bids
End Sub
```

This handler changes the current lot selection by indexing into the appropriate item of the current lots collection. It then forces a UI update of information associated with the lot, including the bid information and the auction information.

Changing the Current User

Since changing the current user wasn't really one of our use cases, we use a very simple mechanism to change users: we simply select a new user from the user list and then click on the 'change' button. This invokes the following event handler:

```
Private Sub cmdChange_Click()
    Dim idx As Long
    idx = lstMembers.SelectedItem.Index
    Set m_ibidder = m_imm.Item(idx - 1).IBidder
    MemberRefresh m_ibidder
End Sub
```

The handler indexes into the collection of members at the currently selected index, the bidder interface is retrieved from the newly selected member, and the UI for the member is then refreshed.

Adding a New Bid

Clicking on the 'add bid' button launches a new modal input form to accept a bid price and quantity for the current user. The form is launched by the click event of the 'add bid' button.

```
Private Sub cmdAddBid_Click()
    frmBidInput.m_viPrice = 0
    frmBidInput.m_viQuantity = 0
    frmBidInput.Show 1
End Sub
```

The event initializes the form's state and then displays it. Once the form is visible, the user can change the bid price, the bid quantity or both, and finally dismiss the form with either the OK or the Cancel button. This is the form's initialization code:

```
Public m_viQuantity As Long
Public m_viPrice As Long

Private Sub Form_Load()
   BidInitialize m_viQuantity, m_viPrice
End Sub

Sub BidInitialize(a_vsQuantity As Long, a_viPrice As Long)
   txtQuantity.Text = a_vsQuantity
   txtPrice.Text = a_viPrice
End Sub
```

The **OK** button is where the interesting action takes place; here's the event handler:

```
Private Sub OKButton_Click()
   Dim ibv As IBidValidate
   Set ibv = frmLot.m_lot.IBidValidate
   If ibv.IsValid1(txtPrice.Text, txtQuantity.Text, Now) Then
      Dim plcbid As IPlaceBid
      Set plcbid = frmLot.m_ilot.IPlaceBid
      plcbid.InsertBid frmLot.m_ibidder, txtQuantity.Text, txtPrice.Text
      frmLot.InfoRefresh frmLot.m_ilot.info
      frmLot.BidsRefresh frmLot.m_ilot.bids

      Unload frmBidInput
   End If
End Sub
```

The handler needs to validate the current inputs before attempting to place a new bid, and this is accomplished by the `IsValid1()` method on the `IBidValidate` interface. If the validation is successful, the `InsertBid()` method of the `IPlaceBid` interface is used to place the new bid on the lot. The UI refresh code of the main form is then called, and the current form is unloaded.

If the bid is invalid, the form doesn't get unloaded, but no error messages are generated. This is probably the wrong behavior, but I didn't want to complicate the code by adding a universally accessible UI for status messages. In production code, this would obviously be fixed. As a matter of fact, it's extremely unlikely that I would use *any* modal dialogs in production code.

The **Cancel** button simply dismisses the modal dialog:

```
Private Sub CancelButton_Click()
   Unload frmBidInput
End Sub
```

The Working Client

The following screenshot shows the Visual Basic client in action:

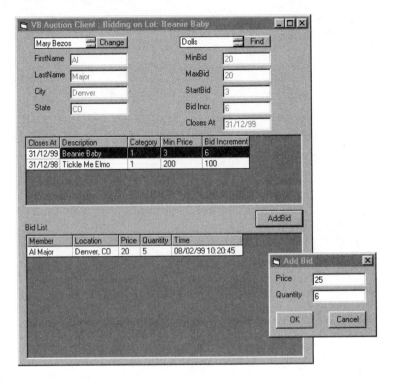

Java Client

Since the Java client is so similar in structure to the Visual Basic client, I will simply show you a few snippets of code that illustrate the similarities and differences, rather than doing a complete walkthrough of the entire application. Apart from the mechanism for using modal dialogs, the module structure of the code in the two languages is identical.

Global Variables

We declare the same variables that we had in the Visual Basic client as Java class globals:

```
private ILots m_ilots;
private IBids m_ibids;

private ICategories m_icl;
private IMembers m_imm;
private ICOMTime m_tm;
private IBidder m_ibdr;
```

Initialization

Let's begin by looking at the Java code for AuctionInitialize():

```
private void AuctionInitialize()
{
    m_tm = new COMTime();
    m_iauct = new Auction();
    m_icl = m_iauct.getIAuctionUIElements().getICategories();
    m_imm = m_iauct.getIAuctionUIElements().getIMembers();
    UIInit();
}
```

Notice the use of the Java new operator to create the root COM objects COMTime and Auction. The great thing about the Java support for COM is that it *looks* like all the code is dealing directly with native Java classes and interfaces. The tool-generated proxy classes and interfaces hide all the details of the plumbing between the Java VM and COM.

Next, let's take a look at MemberLoad(). In order to make the code easier to read, I've removed the module prefixes (strings such as com.ms.com) from type names.

```
private void MemberLoad()
{
    IMemberScript m;
    IListItem itm;
    for(int i = 0; i < m_imm.getCount(); i++)
    {
        itm = lstMembers.getListItems().Add(
                       vtMissing, vtMissing, vtMissing, vtMissing, vtMissing);
        m = m_imm.getItem(i);
        itm.setText(m.getIBidder().getFirstName() +
                               " " + m.getIBidder().getLastName());
        itm.getListSubItems().Add(
                       vtMissing, vtMissing, vtMissing, vtMissing, vtMissing);
        itm.getListSubItems().getItem(vtOne).setText(
                              String.valueOf(m.getIBidder().getMemberID()));
    }

    lstMembers.setSelectedItem(lstMembers.getListItems().getItem(vtOne));
    m_ibdr = m_imm.getItem(0).getIBidder();
    MemberRefresh(m_ibdr);
}
```

A few points can be made about this code:

❑ It is almost a line-by-line facsimile of the Visual Basic code.

❑ As mentioned earlier, Java proxy classes replace properties with a pair of get/set methods. This replaces assignments to property values in Visual Basic with function calls in Java.

❑ Java has a very strong type system with no automatic type conversion as in Visual Basic. This requires explicit programmer intervention in several places:

    ❑ Java has no support for optional parameters. In a Java call with IDL optional parameters, an actual substitution must take place. This is accomplished by the variable vtMissing, which holds the VARIANT value indicating a missing parameter. The declaration for this variable is shown below.

❑ In addition, in order to make parameters optional, the IDL for the list view control (as defined by its developers) declares all parameters to be of type VARIANT rather than a more specific type. Thus, for instance, the getItem() method actually takes a VARIANT parameter rather than a long. This is not a problem in Visual Basic, which simply does the conversion in the runtime, but Java's stronger type system requires that an actual VARIANT must be passed. This is the purpose of the constants vtOne and vtZero, which hold the VARIANT values for 0 and 1 respectively. Their declarations are also shown below.

❑ There is no automatic conversion from integers to strings. Thus, setting a string property to a numeric value requires a conversion from number to string. Fortunately, the standard Java classes come with such conversion operators (see String.valueOf() in the code above).

In case you're wondering, here are the declarations of the Variant values:

```
private final Variant vtMissing = new Variant();
private final Variant vtOne = new Variant(1);
private final Variant vtZero = new Variant(0);
```

vtMissing also needs to be initialized, as follows:

```
vtMissing.noParam();
```

This sets it to the 'missing' variant value.

Updating the UI

Next, let's take a look at the code that refreshes the user interface. Once again, we will look at only one method, BidsRefresh():

```
private void BidsRefresh(IBids bids)
{
    int iCount = bids.getCount();

    grdBids.Clear();
    grdBids.setRows(iCount + 1);
    grdBids.setFormatString("<Member          |<Location        |<Price"
                    + " |<Quantity |<Time                        ");

    for(int i = 0; i < iCount; i++)
    {
        IBid bid = bids.getItem(i).getIBid();
        grdBids.setTextArray(faIndex(i + 1, 0, grdBids),
            bid.getBidder().getFirstName() + " " + bid.getBidder().getLastName());
        grdBids.setTextArray(faIndex(i + 1, 1, grdBids),
                bid.getBidder().getCity() + ", " + bid.getBidder().getState());
        grdBids.setTextArray(faIndex(i + 1, 2, grdBids),
                                        String.valueOf(bid.getPrice()));
        grdBids.setTextArray(faIndex(i + 1, 3, grdBids),
                                        String.valueOf(bid.getNumber()));
        Date vdat = new Date(1000 * (long)bid.getTime());
        grdBids.setTextArray(faIndex(i + 1, 4, grdBids), m_sdf.format(vdat));
    };
    cmdAddBid.setEnabled(true);
}
```

It's remarkable how similar is this code to the Visual Basic code. You've already seen the difficult part – knowing the exact semantics of the grid control methods – in the Visual Basic example, so all that's happened here is a translation to the equivalent Java invocations.

As in the earlier section, the strong typing in Java leads to more explicit specification of conversions than was needed in Visual Basic; the other two noteworthy facts are:

❑ The Java runtime does not support the IEnumVARIANT interface directly, and therefore there is no automatic way to use the enumerator interface provided by the server. Instead, we fall back on the collection interface and explicit indexing through the collection.

❑ Java uses a Date class as its native date/time type. However, this class has a constructor that takes a value that's 1000 times bigger than a time_t value (that is, the granularity of the Java time_t is in milliseconds instead of the CRT's seconds). This makes conversion from time_t to Date very simple. The m_sdf.format() method converts a Date into a String; this variable has the following declaration:

```
private final SimpleDateFormat m_sdf = new SimpleDateFormat();
```

Finally, for conversion from the Automation DATE type to a time_t, I provide these utility methods:

```
private synchronized int Ole2TimeT(double od)
{
   m_tm.ToOleDate(od);
   return m_tm.AsTimeT();
}

private synchronized long Ole2JTime(double od)
{
   return 1000 * (long)Ole2TimeT(od);
};
```

The return value from Ole2JTime() can go directly into a Date constructor.

Finding a Lot

Here is the code that responds to a click of the 'find' button.

```
private void cmdFind_click(Object source, Event e)
{
   String str =
     lstCategories.getSelectedItem().getListSubItems().getItem(vtOne).getText();
   int i = Integer.valueOf(str).intValue();
   m_ilots = m_iauct.getILotFinder().SearchCategory(i);
   LotsRefresh(m_ilots);
}
```

Once more, the structure of the Visual Basic code is echoed here, although there is a new conversion idiom to change from a String to an int, using a Java integer as an intermediate step. This turns out to be the simplest way to convert the string representation of an integer into a Java int. Unlike int, which is a base type, Integer is a Java *class*, and therefore has associated conversion methods.

Although the event procedure is named here with the `<objectname>_<eventname>` format, in Java this is a matter of convention rather than a requirement. The name is not significant to the environment in the way it is in Visual Basic. The actual code that hooks up this method to the Java delegation mechanism can be found in the form initialization code:

```
cmdFind.addOnClick(new EventHandler(this.cmdFind_click));
```

This associates the named method with the delegator of the click event on the variable:

```
Button cmdFind = new Button();
```

Note that the `Button` is actually a Java control rather than an ActiveX control, but that the same delegator mechanism is used to handle Java events. In the next section, you'll see that the code for handling events from the grid ActiveX control is almost identical.

Viewing the Bids

Here is the code that responds to a double click on the lot grid:

```
private void grdLot_DblClick(Object source, Event e)
{
    int i = grdLot.getRow();
    m_iLotScript = m_ilots.getItem(i - 1);
    m_ilot = m_iLotScript.getILot();
    InfoRefresh(m_ilot.getInfo());
    BidsRefresh(m_ilot.getBids());
}
```

Since there are fewer explicit type conversions, the structural similarity to the Visual Basic code is even stronger than in our previous examples. Let's take a look at how the event is hooked up to the grid control. As in the case of the button, the name of the handler is irrelevant. The hookup occurs in the initialization code at:

```
grdLot.addOnDoubleClick(new EventHandler(this.grdLot_DblClick));
```

Which associates the methods with events from the control:

```
grdLot = new MSFlexGrid();
```

You'll remember from the section on Java events earlier in the chapter that this is using the 'delegate' mechanism for sink construction.

Adding a New Bid

Let's see how the business objects are manipulated in Java – what the IDL interface calls look like. Here's the code that adds a new bid, which is invoked as the event handler for the click event on the 'add bid' button.

```
private void cmdAddBid_click(Object source, Event e)
{
    frmAddBid frm = new frmAddBid();
    frm.m_viPrice = 0;
    frm.m_vsQuantity = 0;
    if(frm.showDialog(this) == DialogResult.OK)
    {
        IBidValidate ibv = m_iLotScript.getIBidValidate();
        Date vdatNow = new Date();
        if(ibv.IsValid2(frm.m_viPrice, frm.m_vsQuantity,
                                      ((int)(vdatNow.getTime() / 1000))))
        {
            m_ilot.getIPlaceBid().InsertBid(
                                    m_ibdr, frm.m_vsQuantity, frm.m_viPrice);
            InfoRefresh(m_ilot.getInfo());
            BidsRefresh(m_ilot.getBids());
        }
    }
}
```

This is one method whose structure *doesn't* exactly match that of the Visual Basic code. In Java, it's easier to handle the dismissal of a modal dialog from the code that popped it up, rather than in an event handler within the modal form. Therefore, the code that was in the OK button handler in Visual Basic has been moved into this method. However, other than the difference in native time format, the overall control flow is very close to the Visual Basic code.

The C++ Client

Let us now take a look at the C++ client, which I decided to build as an MFC dialog-based application for speed. You will notice strong structural similarities to the Visual Basic code, and near identity with the Java code, enabling me to keep the explanations in this section quite brief. Once again, I will present only snippets of code; head for the Wrox web site for a complete example.

Global Variables

Here are the C++ class member variables that keep the current state of the user interface. Notice the use of the smart interface pointer types.

```
class CMainForm : public CDialog
{
    // Wizard code omitted for brevity

public:
    IAuctionScriptPtr  m_spIAuctionScript;
    ILotPtr            m_spILot;
    ILotScriptPtr      m_spILotScript;

private:
    IBidderPtr         m_spIBidder;
    ICOMTimePtr        m_spICOMTime;
    ICategoriesPtr     m_spICategories;
    IBidsPtr           m_spIBids;
    ILotsPtr           m_spILots;
    IMembersPtr        m_spIMembers;

    // More omitted code
}
```

Initialization

Let's begin by taking a look at the COM creation code that creates the root COM objects:

```
void CMainForm::AuctionInitialize()
{
    m_spICOMTime = ICOMTimePtr(__uuidof(COMTime));
    m_spIAuctionScript = IAuctionScriptPtr(__uuidof(Auction));
    m_spICategories =
                m_spIAuctionScript->GetIAuctionUIElements()->GetICategories();
    m_spIMembers = m_spIAuctionScript->GetIAuctionUIElements()->GetIMembers();

    UIInit();
}
```

As you can see, the objects are created in the constructors of the appropriate smart pointers, and the other assignments look very much like the Java code. Just as in Java, the tool-created smart pointer wrapper methods completely hide the grungy details of accessing interface pointers. In particular, the two interface 'properties' actually return smart pointers instead of returning plain interfaces.

Next, look at the `MemberLoad()` method:

```
void CMainForm::MemberLoad()
{
    IMemberScriptPtr m;
    CListItem itm;

    for(LONG i = 0; i < m_spIMembers->GetCount(); i++)
    {
        itm = m_lstMembers.GetListItems().Add(&vtMissing, &vtMissing,
                                        &vtMissing, &vtMissing, &vtMissing);
        m = m_spIMembers->GetItem(i);
        itm.SetText(m->GetIBidder()->GetFirstName() +
                                        " " + m->GetIBidder()->GetLastName());
        itm.GetListSubItems().Add(&vtMissing, &vtMissing, &vtMissing,
                                        &vtMissing, &vtMissing);
        CString str;
        str.Format("%ld", m_spICategories->GetItemID(i));
        itm.GetListSubItems().GetItem(&vtOne).SetText(str);
    }

    _variant_t vtStr(m_lstMembers.GetListItems().GetItem(&vtOne));
    m_lstMembers.SetSelectedItem(&vtStr);
    m_spIBidder = m_spIMembers->GetItem(0)->GetIBidder();
    MemberRefresh(m_spIBidder);
}
```

Just as in the Java code, we can see the effects of strong type checking at work. We need a `vtMissing` value (supplied with COM client support) to pass as an argument into a function that has optional parameters specified in IDL, and we also need `vtOne` and `vtZero` values. These are declared as

```
_variant_t vtOne(1L);
_variant_t vtZero(0L);
```

We also wind up using the MFC `CString` class to provide string formatting functionality.

Updating the UI

Here's the code that updates the 'bids' grid:

```
void CMainForm::BidsRefresh(IBidsPtr& a_spIBids)
{
   LONG iCount = a_spIBids->GetCount();

   m_ctlBids.Clear();
   m_ctlBids.SetRows(iCount + 1);
   m_ctlBids.SetFormatString(_T("<Member          |<Location        "
                      " |<Price |<Quantity |<Time                      "));

   for(LONG i = 0; i < iCount; i++)
   {
      IBidPtr spIBid = a_spIBids->GetItem(i);
      m_ctlBids.SetTextArray(faIndex(i + 1, 0, m_ctlBids),
                      (LPCTSTR)(spIBid->GetBidder()->GetFirstName() +
                         " " + spIBid->GetBidder()->GetLastName()));
      m_ctlBids.SetTextArray(faIndex(i + 1, 1, m_ctlBids),
                      (LPCTSTR)(spIBid->GetBidder()->GetCity() +
                         ", " + spIBid->GetBidder ()->GetState()));

      CString str;
      str.Format("%d", spIBid->GetPrice());
      m_ctlBids.SetTextArray(faIndex(i + 1, 2, m_ctlBids), (LPCTSTR)(str));
      str.Format("%d", spIBid->GetNumber());
      m_ctlBids.SetTextArray(faIndex(i + 1, 3, m_ctlBids), (LPCTSTR)(str));

      COleDateTime datBid = TimeT2Ole(spIBid->GetTime());
      m_ctlBids.SetTextArray(faIndex(i + 1, 4, m_ctlBids),
                      (LPCTSTR)(datBid.Format("%m/%d/%Y %h:%M:%S %p")));
   }
   m_ctlAddBid.EnableWindow (TRUE);
}
```

Other than string and date formatting features (dates are handled with the MFC `COleDateTime` class), and a difference in enabling MFC window controls, this is identical to the Java code.

Finding a Lot

Here is the code for searching for a lot, which really only differs from the Java in the formatting code:

```
void CMainForm::OnButtonfind()
{
   CString str =
      m_lstCategories.GetSelectedItem().GetListSubItems(). \
                                     GetItem(&vtOne).GetText();
   LONG i;
   sscanf(str, "%ld", &i);
   m_spILots = m_spIAuctionScript->GetILotFinder()->SearchCategory(i);
   LotsRefresh(m_spILots);
}
```

I am not going to get into the event model for MFC applications here because it is not COM specific. Rather, it's based on the MFC command-handling framework that encapsulates COM event sinks.

Viewing the Bids

The event handler for the double click event on the lot grid is also just like the Java code:

```
void CMainForm::OnDblClickLotgrid()
{
    LONG i = m_ctlLot.GetRow();
    m_spILotScript = m_spILots->GetItem(i - 1);
    m_spILot = m_spILotScript->GetILot();
    InfoRefresh(m_spILotScript->GetILot()->GetInfo());
    BidsRefresh(m_spILotScript->GetILot()->GetBids());
}
```

Adding a New Bid

As is the code that handles the 'add bid' button click:

```
void CMainForm::OnButtonaddbid()
{
    CAddBidDlg dlg;

    dlg.BidInitialize(0, 0);
    if(dlg.DoModal() == IDOK)
    {
        IBidValidatePtr spIBV = m_spILotScript;
        time_t t;
        time(&t);
        if(spIBV->IsValid2(dlg.m_vsQuantity, dlg.m_vsQuantity, t))
        {
            m_spILot->GetIPlaceBid()->InsertBid(
                              m_spIBidder, dlg.m_vsQuantity, dlg.m_vlPrice);
            InfoRefresh(m_spILot->GetInfo());
            BidsRefresh(m_spILot->GetBids());
        }
    }
}
```

The Working Client

Coming after our examination of the Java client, the C++ client has thrown up few surprises – the structural similarity between the two is very strong. This reflects not just the syntactic closeness of the languages, but the fact that the C++ COM wrappers behave in quite a similar fashion to the Java COM proxy classes.

The following picture shows the MFC client in action. You'd be hard-pushed to tell it apart from the Visual Basic client I showed you earlier on, but then, that's exactly what we're trying to achieve.

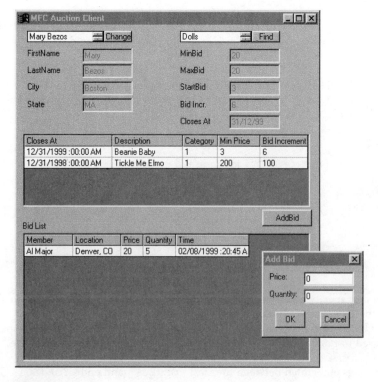

The DHTML Client

The DHTML client is the one that looks and feels a little different from the other clients that we have seen so far, and there are two reasons for this:

❑   The form layout language is HTML, a much more flexible page description language, with much better tool support, than the form designers built into the other languages.

❑   I decided not to use a modal dialog box for the input of new bids. This is primarily because traditionally, HTML interfaces do not pop up modal dialog windows – they either display the dialog in a completely new page, or they include it as a sub-form on the current page. However, there is a third option that is also the hardest to do: have the sub-form appear and disappear on demand within the same page. I picked this option, since it makes for a superior example.

We are limited to using VBScript and JScript for our coding. Despite the restrictions of these scripting languages (no `QI()` and exclusive use of `IDispatch`), the code in our script example has exactly the same structure as our Visual Basic code. However, this is only possible because of the care that I took in the design of the object model (Chapter 5), and its implementation (coming up in Chapter 7).

Incidentally, I picked my terminology carefully. This is *not* a web client (it doesn't interact with a web server); it is a DHTML client. It uses DHTML to build a forms-based front end to our COM services.

HTML Page Design

With one small change, I used exactly the same HTML page description for both the VBScript and JScript clients. The page was designed in Visual InterDev 6, but could have been designed in any HTML-capable editor that allows embedded objects.

The specifics of the HTML are not very important, but let me quickly introduce by example a few HTML tags that affect the programmability of the interface. I will assume that you are familiar with the basics of HTML.

The <OBJECT> Tag

Here is an example of the `<OBJECT>` tag in use:

```
<OBJECT classid=clsid:BDD1F04B-858B-11D1-B16A-00C0F0283628 id=1stMembers
    height=24 style="HEIGHT: 24px; LEFT: 0px; TOP: 0px; WIDTH: 121px" width=121>

<PARAM NAME="_ExtentX" VALUE="3201">
<PARAM NAME="_ExtentY" VALUE="635">

</OBJECT>
```

The tag is used to specify an ActiveX object embedded in the HTML page. From a programming perspective, the most important attributes of this tag are `CLASSID` and `ID`. The `CLASSID` attribute specifies the CLSID of the object that will be embedded, while the `ID` attribute specifies the name that will be used to refer to this object by any script that is embedded in the page.

The `<PARAM>` tags embedded between the start `<OBJECT>` and end `</OBJECT>` tags are used to initialize the object. The entire collection of these is used to create a **property bag** (an unordered set of attribute-value pairs). The property bag is used by a newly created instance of the object to load its persistent state using the `IPersistPropertyBag` interface.

The <SCRIPT> Tag

Here is an example of the `<SCRIPT>` tag in use:

```
<SCRIPT LANGUAGE="vbscript">
<!--

Private Sub window_onload()
   ScptltStow
   AuctionInitialize
End Sub

-->
</SCRIPT>
```

Unsurprisingly, the `<SCRIPT>` tag is used to embed script into the page. Frequently, the script is embedded within HTML comment delimiters `<!--` and `-->` nested within the script begin and end tags. The purpose of the comment is to ensure that HTML browsers that don't support this tag don't show the script as text.

The ID Attribute

The ID attribute that we saw used with the <OBJECT> tag actually has broader usage. It can be used with many HTML tags to identify a DHTML entity that can be manipulated by a script. For example, this tag:

```
<INPUT id=cmdAddBid type=button value="Add Bid">
```

identifies the button labeled Add Bid with the script named cmdAddBid. The button can then be scripted using this name.

Event Attributes

You may recall from earlier in the chapter that JScript required special HTML tags to associate events with specific objects (those created by the <OBJECT> tag). For other scriptable elements (those that are not embedded objects) there are **event attributes**, one for each event associated with that element. The <BODY> tag, for example, might have an event called onload that is fired when the body finishes loading. This would be represented by including the onload attribute in the <BODY> tag, as follows:

```
<body onload="window_onload()">
```

Note that this syntax is only required for JScript, and even then it can be avoided by suitable labeling of the tag with an object ID, and using the normal JScript syntax for associating script with events.

The Add Bid Control

We'll look now at one of the interesting features of the DHTML client: the 'add bid' control being used to replace the modal dialog box that we've been employing so far. What we need is an ActiveX control that has the following features:

- ❑ It will have edit controls for price and quantity. The values from these controls can be extracted from the script.
- ❑ It will have OK and Cancel buttons that fire corresponding events to the script.
- ❑ It will have the ability to show and hide itself upon request from the script.

In the next chapter, we will look at how this control is implemented; it turns out to be easiest to build it as a DHTML control. What we're doing now is designing the interfaces that this UI object should have.

The Control Interface

For now, let us concentrate on the client interface exposed by the control, which needs to export the following interface to the script:

```
interface IAddBid : IDispatch
{
    [propget, id(1), helpstring("property Quantity")]
    HRESULT Quantity([out, retval] short *a_ps);

    [propput, id(1), helpstring("property Quantity")]
    HRESULT Quantity([in] short a_vs);

    [propget, id(2), helpstring("property Price")]
    HRESULT Price([out, retval] long* a_pl);
```

```
    [propput, id(2), helpstring("property Price")]
    HRESULT Price([in] long a_vl);

    [propget, id(3), helpstring("property Enabled")]
    HRESULT Enabled([out, retval] BOOL* a_pb);

    [propput, id(3), helpstring("property Enabled")]
    HRESULT Enabled([in] BOOL a_vb);
};
```

The `Quantity` and `Price` properties allow the values in the edit control to be set, and the `Enabled` property can be used to make the control visible or invisible.

The Event Interface

What about the OK and Cancel events? Should we define a new event interface to fire them? Well, we could do so, but for now let's try a little interface re-use, if only to see how it's done. Since our control is a little bit like a scriptlet (all right, maybe I'm pushing my luck, but indulge me), we'll re-use the scriptlet event interface `DWebBridgeEvents` from the scriptlet type library (`mshtmlwb.dll`). Here it is:

```
dispinterface DWebBridgeEvents
{
properties:
methods:
    [id(1), helpstring("Indicates that the control script has raised an event")]
    HRESULT onscriptletevent([in] BSTR name, [in] VARIANT eventData);

    [
        id(0xffffffd9f),
        helpstring("Indicates that the readyState property has changed")
    ]
    void onreadystatechange();

    [id(0xffffffda8)]
    VARIANT_BOOL onclick();

    [id(0xffffffda7)]
    VARIANT_BOOL ondblclick();

    [id(0xffffffda6)]
    void onkeydown();

    [id(0xffffffda4)]
    void onkeyup();

    [id(0xffffffda5)]
    VARIANT_BOOL onkeypress();

    [id(0xffffffda3)]
    void onmousedown();
    [id(0xffffffda2)]
    void onmousemove();

    [id(0xffffffda1)]
    void onmouseup();
};
```

We'll overload the generic method `onscriptletevent()` to have the following semantics:

"If the `name` parameter to `onscriptletevent()` is `"addbid"`, the **OK** button was clicked. If the parameter has the value `"cancel"`, then the **Cancel** button was clicked."

This allows us to overload a single method to correspond to two different events.

VBScript Code

Here is the truly remarkable thing. Except for the fact that variables are not typed, and the code for adding a bid has changed to reflect the new user interface, my VBScript code is *identical* to the Visual Basic code. I don't mean, "looks identical," or, "close to identical," or, "structurally similar," as I've been saying so far in this chapter. I mean, "*is* identical."

Again, this is not a coincidence. Essentially, I took my Visual Basic code and translated it into VBScript (in other words, I removed all the types from it). Apart from a couple of errors in translation, the code ran out of the box. This happens to be my favored way of writing complicated VBScript; writing in pure VBScript straight away is hard because of its primitive debugging environment.

Of course, I needed to ensure that all my form objects had the same names in the HTML form as they did in the Visual Basic form, but this was relatively easy to do. Just as an example, I'll show you a couple of snippets of code to illustrate the identity.

Global Variables

Here are the declarations of the VBScript variables:

```
Public m_lot            ' Current ILotScript
Public m_ilot           ' Current ILot
Public m_ibidder        ' Current IBidder
Public m_iauct          ' Current IAuctionScript

' Cached interfaces
Private m_ilots         ' Current ILots
Private m_ibids         ' Current IBids

Private m_icl           ' Current ICategories
Private m_imm           ' Current IMembers

Private m_tm            ' Current ICOMTimeScript
```

You'll notice that these are the same as the Visual Basic declarations, except that they've been stripped of the type specifiers. As mentioned earlier, all VBScript variables are VARIANTs.

Initialization

The only VBScript routine that isn't identical to the Visual Basic code is `AuctionInitialize()`, which has to create the root objects. Since VBScript doesn't have the Visual Basic `New` operator, we need to use `CreateObject()` here.

```
Sub AuctionInitialize()
    Set m_tm = CreateObject("TimeUtil.ComTime")
    Set m_iauct = CreateObject("WroxAuction.Auction")
    Set m_icl = m_iauct.IAuctionUIElements.ICategories
    Set m_imm = m_iauct.IAuctionUIElements.IMembers

    UIInit
End Sub
```

The rest of the VBScript code is identical to the Visual Basic code. Here is the `CategoryLoad()` function for VBScript.

```
Sub CategoryLoad()
    Dim i
    Dim itm
    i = 0
    Do While i < m_icl.Count
        Set itm = lstCategories.ListItems.Add
        itm.Text = m_icl.Item(i)
        itm.ListSubItems.Add
        itm.ListSubItems(1).Text = m_icl.GetItemID(i)
        i = i + 1
    Loop
    lstCategories.SelectedItem = lstCategories.ListItems(1)
End Sub
```

If you compare this with the Visual Basic code, you'll find that it is identical except for the lack of type in the `Dim` statements.

Adding a New Bid

The only extra piece of code here is the process of adding a bid using the new 'add bid' control, and here's the code that does that:

```
Private Sub cmdAddBid_onclick()
    ScptltRstr
End Sub
```

Recall that events in VBScript work just like they do in Visual Basic. The name of the function determines the object and the event method it is responding to. This function responds to the click event on the `cmdAddBid` button.

The event handler simply calls the `ScptltRstr()` function, which makes the 'add bid' control display itself by setting its enabled property to 1, as follows (the name of the 'add bid' control is `sctAddBid`):

```
Private Sub ScptltRstr()
    sctAddBid.Enabled = 1
End Sub
```

At this point, the 'add bid' control is visible. The user may type values into the 'price' and 'quantity' controls, and then finally click on OK or Cancel. This is handled by the event handler declared as:

```
Private Sub sctAddBid_onscriptletevent(ByVal txtEvent, ByVal evtData)
   If txtEvent = "addbid" Then
      Dim ibv
      Set ibv = m_lot.IbidValidate
      If ibv.IsValid1(sctAddBid.Price, sctAddBid.Quantity, Now) Then
         Dim plcbid
         Set plcbid = m_ilot.IPlaceBid
         plcbid.InsertBid m_ibidder, sctAddBid.Quantity, sctAddBid.Price
         InfoRefresh m_lot.ILot.Info
         BidsRefresh m_lot.ILot.Bids
         ScptltStow
      End If
   ElseIf txtEvent = "cancel" Then
      ScptltStow
   End If
End Sub
```

Note that the both parameters are declared as ByVal, and this is required because the IDL for the method specifies that these are in-only parameters. By default, Visual Basic and VBScript both assume that parameters are passed by reference – that is, as in, out parameters.

As you can see, the code that handles the OK and Cancel events is virtually identical to the Visual Basic code that handled the OK and Cancel buttons: it validates the bid and then inserts it into the lot. The one new line of code is the call to ScptltStow(), which is declared as:

```
function ScptltStow()
{
   sctAddBid.Enabled = 0;
}
```

This resets the enabled property of the 'add bid' control, thus causing it to become invisible.

Window Initialization

Finally, we need to look at the code that initializes the HTML page when it has loaded. The loaded state is signaled by the firing of the onload event from the window object. In VBScript, this is handled by the method:

```
function window_onload()
{
   ScptltStow();
   AuctionInitialize();
}
```

As you can see, this causes the 'add bid' control to hide itself at initialization. It then initializes the rest of the application.

The Working Client

The next picture shows this client in action. Isn't it pretty? Seriously though, the use of HTML allows forms that have much better graphical designs than anything you can do with the other form builders. It may seem strange from a technical perspective, but these are the kinds of factors that will force us all into building forms-based applications in HTML.

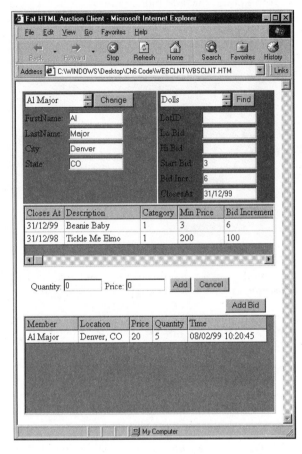

Our next example is actually very similar, but we substitute JScript for VBScript.

JScript Code

As mentioned earlier, JScript interacts with COM in almost exactly the same way as VBScript. Since the syntax is just a little different, though, I'll show you enough JScript code that you can appreciate where problems may arise. If you want to make a detailed comparison, look at the working code from the Wrox web site.

Global Variables

Here are the equivalent JScript global variable declarations:

```
var m_lot;
var m_ilot;
var m_ibidder;
var m_iauct;

var m_ilots;
var m_ibids;
```

```
var m_icl;
var m_imm;

var m_tm;
```

Other than the replacement of the `Dim` (or `Public` or `Private`) keyword with `var`, the code is the same.

Initialization

Here is the initialization sequence for the root object. As you can see, JScript requires the use of the `ActiveXObject()` constructor with the `new` keyword, instead of the VBScript `CreateObject()`.

```
function AuctionInitialize()
{
    m_tm = new ActiveXObject("TimeUtil.ComTime");
    m_iauct = new ActiveXObject("WroxAuction.Auction");
    m_icl = m_iauct.IAuctionUIElements.ICategories;
    m_imm = m_iauct.IAuctionUIElements.IMembers;

    UIInit();
}
```

The syntax for declaring and calling functions is also different from VBScript, and ordinary assignment is used. As another example, take a look at the `CategoryLoad()` function.

```
function CategoryLoad()
{
    var i;
    var itm;
    i = 0;
    for(i = 0; i < m_icl.Count; i = i + 1)
    {
        itm = lstCategories.ListItems.Add();
        itm.Text = m_icl.Item(i);
        itm.ListSubItems.Add();
        itm.ListSubItems(1).Text = m_icl.GetItemID(i);
    }
    lstCategories.SelectedItem = lstCategories.ListItems(1);
}
```

Other than the syntactic differences (look at the `for` loop; it's like a C-style loop), it looks the same as VBScript.

Window Initialization

Window initialization is a little different in JScript:

```
function window_onload()
{
    ScptltStow();
    AuctionInitialize();
}
```

Although a very similar function is called as in VBScript, we need to have an explicit attribute in an HTML tag to associate the method with the appropriate sink interface. It turns out that a reasonable place to put this is in the `onload` attribute of the `<BODY>` tag.

```
<body onload="window_onload()">
```

The Working Client

The JScript client *looks* indistinguishable from the VBScript client, and I'm sure that you don't need to see the same screenshot again! These identical results mean that choosing between VBScript and JScript is purely a matter of personal preference.

Which Language is Best?

Having now seen the exact same application built in all the languages, it would be reasonable for you to ask the question, "Which one is best?" Unfortunately, there is no easy answer. What I will do instead is discuss the strengths and weaknesses of each language.

❑ Visual Basic has great support for simple COM usage – developing small COM applications is painless. The environment has been optimized over the years, and the generated client code is small and fast. For larger projects however, Visual Basic's ad-hoc type system becomes apparent and certain classes of errors are not caught until runtime. Also, as mentioned earlier, Visual Basic does not allow completely flexible use of COM functionality.

❑ Java also has great COM support by virtue of its seamless integration into the VM. Once the COM proxy classes have been generated by `jactivex`, you are working and thinking Java. Java also has a great standard class library, with a very clean, modern object-oriented design that makes it a cinch to re-use standard code, and makes application structure clean and intuitive. The Java idiom is also very COM friendly. Java's extremely strong type system (exceptions are part of a method signature) is delightfully effective at catching errors. However, the programming environment is still new, and the code optimizer does not seem to be working too well as yet.

❑ Visual C++ is a little odd. On the one hand, it is now just as COM friendly as Java, and better than Visual Basic. The new COM support is wonderful – it has all the benefits of abstraction (in my opinion it's every bit as good as Java), while still leaving the expressive power of C++ at the programmer's disposal. On the other hand, MFC is beginning to show its age, at least in comparison with the standard Java packages. If you're already familiar with MFC, you can make it do anything you want it to, but the Java learning curve is shorter and the structure of Visual J++ applications is more intuitive. If Visual C++ had a standard class library of design quality comparable to that of Java (such as an object-oriented companion to ATL), it would be superior in every respect. Right now, I would still tilt the scales in its favor, for performance reasons as well as the quality and maturity of the environment and tools.

❑ The scripting languages are easy to evaluate. They're horribly difficult to debug, and writing large pieces of new code in a scripting language is a time sink that is best avoided. If you're using VBScript, then do as I do: write in Visual Basic and then port to VBScript. If you're careful about how your object model is designed and you write very stylized Visual Basic code, this works remarkably well. If you're programming JScript, the same procedure is possible, but a little more painful. However, HTML is likely to become the standard for all forms-based UIs of the future, and script is currently the only way of programming HTML.

A Time Conversion Utility Class

If you have built COM classes for use in different language environments, you've probably noticed a problem with the way I defined the interfaces for the auction services: I used a mixture of 'date' types. In some cases I used the Automation DATE, while in others I used a time_t (LONG). There are several problems with this:

❑   The use of a time_t will certainly cause a Year 2038 problem, and though I will finesse this issue in the book, you probably don't want to do so in production code.

❑   You probably don't want to mix time formats in a single interface. Pick one and go with it; I'm breaking the rules in order to illustrate some inter-operability issues.

❑   Each environment has its own notion of time. The use of a LONG (time_t) to represent time instants has a very CRT flavor; Visual Basic uses a variant DATE type; Java uses a 64-bit value (which thankfully is 1000 times the time_t value) or the Date class; Win32 uses the FILETIME and SYSTEMTIME structs.

The variety of different time APIs within the Microsoft environment is a source of some annoyance to people who need to write code that works with different Microsoft systems. However, the fix isn't hard – I've provided a COM class called COMTime that provides an interface ICOMTime to do conversions between the various representations. Here is the interface:

```
interface ICOMTime : IDispatch
{
    [id(1), helpstring("Set value to a CRT 'time_t'")]
    HRESULT ToTimeT([in] LONG a_vl);

    [id(2), helpstring("Get value as CRT 'time_t'")]
    HRESULT AsTimeT([out, retval] LONG* a_pl);

    [id(3), helpstring("Set value to a DATE variant")]
    HRESULT ToOleDate([in] DATE a_vdat);

    [id(4), helpstring("Get value as a DATE variant")]
    HRESULT AsOleDate([out, retval] DATE* a_pdat);

    [id(5), helpstring("Set value to a UTC string")]
    HRESULT ToUTCString([in] BSTR a_vstr);

    [id(6), helpstring("Get value as a UTC string")]
    HRESULT AsUTCString([out, retval] BSTR* a_pstr);

    [id(7), helpstring("Set individual date/time fields")]
    HRESULT ToDateTime([in] SHORT a_vsYear,
                       [in] SHORT a_vsMonth,
                       [in] SHORT a_vsDay,
                       [in] SHORT a_vsHour,
                       [in] SHORT a_vsMinute,
                       [in] SHORT a_vsSecond,
                       [in] SHORT a_vsMilli);
```

```
    [id(8), helpstring("Get individual date/time fields")]
    HRESULT AsDateTime([out] SHORT* a_psYear,
                       [out] SHORT* a_psMonth,
                       [out] SHORT* a_psDay,
                       [out] SHORT* a_psHour,
                       [out] SHORT* a_psMinute,
                       [out] SHORT* a_psSecond,
                       [out] SHORT* a_psMilli);

    [id(9), helpstring("Set to current time")]
    HRESULT ToCurrentTime();
};
```

As you can see, it consists of pairs of get/set functions that are capable of getting/setting the value of a COMTime object using any time type as the output/input parameter. The supported types are LONG, DATE, BSTR, and individual date/time fields. Setting to and getting from a DATE, for example, are accomplished by the ToOleDate() and AsOleDate() methods respectively.

The COMTime object can also be set to the current time, rather than to a specific time value, and this is accomplished with the ToCurrentTime() method.

Summary

In this chapter I have showed you the IDL client bindings for the various Microsoft languages. At this point, you should understand:

❑ The RAD support for COM and ActiveX that is built into each of the Microsoft IDEs, including the basics of:
    ❑ Building the actual forms-based user interfaces
    ❑ Including regular COM components in such a user interface using a type library
    ❑ Including ActiveX controls using the toolbox
❑ How type libraries are incorporated into the IDE, and a general understanding of IntelliSense
❑ Data type mappings from IDL to each of the client languages for the base types
❑ Data type mappings from IDL to each of the Automation types
❑ How the more complex Automation types (BSTR, SAFEARRAY and VARIANT) map onto native language classes/types that encapsulate the data, as well as the API governing the types
❑ How classes and objects are created and used in each language
❑ How interfaces are mapped onto each language, including the constraints on scripting languages
❑ How parameter types may be constrained by the language in use
❑ How error/exception handling maps onto each language
❑ How events are dealt with
❑ Memory allocation policy
❑ For Java and C++, the structure of the proxy classes and wrappers that are generated by the Wizards from the descriptions in the type library

❑ General design techniques for building a forms-based user interface that utilizes COM object models and ActiveX controls, including:

> ❑ Design constraints that help you if you ever need to port your code
>
> ❑ The criteria to use when selecting UI elements
>
> ❑ Overall principles for structuring your application

I have also provided an example of building a real, forms-based application based on COM/ActiveX, including the nitty-gritty details of using COM classes, interfaces, different data types, errors and exceptions. Finally, we examined the pros and cons of each language's support for COM interfaces and COM-based RAD design.

Implied Guidelines for Interface Design

Use the strongest possible typing for interface declarations. If a parameter is an enum, declare it as an enum rather than an integer type. If a parameter is a dual interface, declare it as one rather than as an IDispatch – Automation controllers will still be able to use it correctly. Use a VARIANT parameter only if different data types can be passed in that parameter (although this should be suspicious in itself). You gain the benefits of type checking in strongly typed languages, and lose nothing in scripting languages (assuming that your IDispatch implementation does VARIANT conversions correctly, as described in Chapter 4).

Define enumerations and constants wherever it makes sense to do so. Enumerations serve as language-independent #defines that are supported by IntelliSense.

Visual Basic expects a default interface on your object, so provide one. If you don't, it guesses (it picks the first one in the type library generated from your IDL), which may not be what you want.

Client Side Proxies and Wrappers

Be aware of how the type library is used to generate wrapper methods in the different programming environments. Parameters marked out, retval generally become return values of wrapper functions.

Scripting Languages

Be aware that current scripting languages have no way to do a QueryInterface(). They are also restricted to using Automation interfaces exclusively, so design your object model accordingly. The design that I use – the "property as QueryInterface()" idiom – is a good way of avoiding scripting issues. There are also some subtleties of implementation that are described in the next chapter.

Visual Basic and the scripting clients expect you to identify the default source interface for a scripting client explicitly, since that is the *only* outgoing interface they can see. This is the only way they can create a sink that is type-compatible with your outgoing interface.

If you want events to be visible to a scripting client, your object needs to implement IProvideClassInfo and IProvideClassInfo2. This is the only way that scripting clients can currently find type information.

Connection Points

Source interfaces are best implemented as pure dispinterfaces. Languages like Visual Basic (prior to version 6) and the scripting languages cannot receive events on vtable interfaces. You can implement your outgoing interface as a dual interface for ease of implementation, but be careful only to fire an event using the Automation side of the interface.

Type Restrictions

Scripting languages support only Automation-capable interfaces and VARIANT types. Remember that VBScript and Visual Basic (when it's using Automation) have restrictions on non-retval, out-only parameters.

Java does not have complete access to arbitrary user-defined types, although it does provide a form of custom marshaling to gain such access.

Only C++ provides completely unrestricted type support, so be mindful of complex structures that go into your interface design. They may not be visible from other client languages.

Environment Support

Be aware that your IDL is beginning to show up in more and more places in the programming environment – from IntelliSense, to object browsers, to the debugger. Use descriptive help strings to document your interfaces, coclasses, enumerations and every other entity in the type library. Consider shipping a help file with your IDL, and use help contexts in the IDL in that case.

Exceptions and Error Handling

All COM client environments have support for the COM error object protocol. Whenever possible, declare your classes as supporting the ISupportErrorInfo interface that interacts with the rich error reporting mechanism. Also ensure that you prove a help string, a help file and a help context when you return an error.

What's Next?

The final chapter covers the details of implementing the object model that exposes the specification model we have seen in use here. We will see the server side C++/ATL bindings, and the practical application of a large number of the design techniques that were outlined in Chapter 5.

7

Server Bindings, Design and Implementation

At some stage in your COM education, when you've started building relatively complicated object models, you come to a point where COM seems to break down, and you start considering out-of-band, non-COM techniques to meet the requirements of sophisticated implementations. This is the point at which you start to need many of the more sophisticated techniques that I showed you in Chapter 5.

The only problem with the approach in Chapter 5 is that the techniques don't have any meat when discussed in isolation. Idioms are all well and good, but what are they really useful for? Unfortunately, it's hard to come up with a small object model that really exhibits a need for these techniques, and therefore they're often not discussed in any meaningful way in COM books. Programmers learn these techniques by working on larger COM projects, preferably with someone else who's already figured them out. Shortening the learning curve can save large amounts of time and money.

That is what I hope to do with this chapter. A very large part of this very long chapter is devoted to implementing the specification object model that was developed in Chapter 5. The implementation model is large enough, and has enough interesting twists to it, that it displays many of the most valuable techniques from Chapter 5 in a real down-and-dirty, flesh-and-blood implementation. It begins with the detailed design of an implementation model, and goes on to display real code in C++/ATL (with some of my own ATL extensions, which are detailed in Appendix B), and is an example of very sophisticated use of the ATL.

The chapter begins, however, by detailing the server bindings associated with an IDL description. Since I focus on the use of C++/ATL to build COM servers, I shall only examine the C++/ATL server bindings. I will then proceed to show you the large implementation I just described. There are also a couple of smaller server implementations that are demonstrated in this chapter:

❏ The first example focuses on method implementations that employ user defined types (UDTs) with embedded pointers. Of particular interest is the code that's needed to support memory management of arbitrary UDTs. We'll look at how UDTs can be used to replace one of the Automation interfaces in our example, and measure the performance improvements.

❏ Second, I will present some code that adds monitoring functionality to the COM task memory heap API, and that is capable of detecting memory leaks.

❏ Finally, I'll show you the implementation of the embedded DHTML form control that I used in the DHTML client in Chapter 6.

C++ Server Bindings

Let's return to the example that we used for client bindings and see how those bindings work on the server. If you need to, take a look the client-side IDL declarations in Chapter 6 for reference.

Files

The interface declarations used on the server are the ones generated by MIDL. In principle, any tool could be used to generate the headers, and it's possible that in the future the `#import` directive will be used for this purpose instead.

The important difference between the MIDL-generated headers and the `#import` headers is that the former do not contain any wrapper classes. The declarations generated are base C data types and raw interfaces.

As shown in Chapter 2, the files used for compilation of the server (which are generated by the IDL compiler from the `foo.idl` file) are the ones named `foo.h` and `foo_i.c`.

Data Type Bindings

The C data type bindings on the server side are the same as those for C clients, and this is not surprising when you consider that in the simplest case, client and server are actually communicating through an ordinary in-process method invocation.

There are also some C++ data type wrappers that are used on the server side, although they are not referenced in the MIDL-generated header files. These wrappers are very similar to the ones used on the client. However, on the server side, the preferred wrapper classes are those that do not throw C++ exceptions (`CComPtr<>`, `CComBSTR` and `CComVariant`), rather than the exception throwing ones (`_com_ptr_t`, `_bstr_t` and `_variant_t`).

This may strike you as odd. After all, isn't exception handling a desirable feature in a server, to guarantee against abnormal termination? As a matter of fact it is, but there are some other factors in play here.

As has been pointed out by Tom Cargill and others, the semantics of exception handling can be trickier than is immediately obvious. The semantics of status codes, on the other hand, are fairly straightforward, and although it is more tedious to write such code, it is more likely to be demonstrably correct.

The situation could be improved if C++ compilers, like their Java counterparts, *enforced* exception specifications. This would force programmers (and library writers) to pay more attention to exceptions in their code.

Exception handling imposes a 10-15% increase in code size, which is potentially damaging when you consider that unless an exception occurs, this code is never actually executed. However, this figure is less meaningful than it might be, since measurements of overhead use code that does *no* error handling as a comparison, rather than code that handles errors using status codes.

In reality, there are always going to be situations where you 'know' that certain operations are guaranteed to be error-free, so you don't actually need to check the status code (although you should at least add an ASSERT). In such cases, you may decide not to incur the size overhead that exception-handling code would impose.

On Win32 platforms, C++ (or synchronous) exception handling does not mesh well with the C-style (or asynchronous) Win32 structured exception mechanism. They cannot both be used within a single function.

I'll now provide a little more detail on some of the data types that were less visible in the section on client-side data bindings.

UUIDs

UUIDs are mapped to a C/C++ struct named _GUID. This is a peculiar-looking struct with a number of members that taken together define the 128 bits of storage that are required for a UUID:

```
typedef struct _GUID             // size is 16
{
    DWORD Data1;
    WORD  Data2;
    WORD  Data3;
    BYTE  Data4[8];
} GUID;

typedef GUID IID;
typedef GUID CLSID;
```

In our example, the `foo.h` file containing the definition of the `ILotInitialize` interface has the following declaration for its IID:

```
EXTERN_C const IID IID_ ILotInitialize;
```

The coclass `Lot` has this generated variable to hold its CLSID:

```
EXTERN_C const CLSID CLSID_Lot;
```

And the library itself is identified by the following LIBID:

```
EXTERN_C const IID LIBID_LOTLib;
```

The corresponding variable definitions are present in the C/C++ file `foo_i.c`:

```
const IID IID_ILotInitialize =
    {0xA5C2C850,0x3825,0x11d2,{0xA5,0xFC,0x00,0x00,0x86,0x05,0x64,0x48}};
const CLSID CLSID_Lot =
    {0x2F7EBD30,0x368D,0x11D2,{0xA5,0xF0,0x00,0x00,0x86,0x05,0x64,0x48}};
const IID LIBID_LOTLib =
    {0xE98F70A7,0x40C8,0x11D2,{0xA6,0x1E,0x00,0x00,0x00,0x00,0x00,0x00}};
```

The definitions essentially create storage for and initialize the variables declared in the headers. Note that you will not find `foo_i.c` in a typical ATL project file listing; this is because the file is `#include`'ed into the main CPP file, rather than being treated as an independent compilation unit.

One reason for this is that the difficulty that would otherwise ensue regarding pre-compiled header sections. In particular, you would have to turn them off for the `_i.c` file.

IDL enums

The different IDL data abstraction keywords generate the intuitively obvious C/C++ equivalents. For example, this IDL enum:

```
typedef enum OLECMDF
{
    OLECMDF_SUPPORTED       = 0x00000001,
    OLECMDF_ENABLED         = 0x00000002,
    OLECMDF_LATCHED         = 0x00000004,
    OLECMDF_NINCHED         = 0x00000008,
} OLECMDF;
```

generates this C enum:

```
typedef enum OLECMDF
{
    OLECMDF_SUPPORTED = 0x1,
    OLECMDF_ENABLED   = 0x2,
    OLECMDF_LATCHED   = 0x4,
    OLECMDF_NINCHED   = 0x8
} OLECMDF;
```

IDL structs

This IDL `struct`:

```
typedef struct tagMSG
{
    HWND    hwnd;
    UINT    message;
    WPARAM  wParam;
    LPARAM  lParam;
    DWORD   time;
    POINT   pt;
} MSG, *PMSG, *NPMSG, *LPMSG;
```

generates this C `struct`:

```
typedef struct tagMSG
{
    HWND    hwnd;
    UINT    message;
    WPARAM  wParam;
    LPARAM  lParam;
    DWORD   time;
    POINT   pt;
} MSG;

typedef struct tagMSG __RPC_FAR* PMSG;
typedef struct tagMSG __RPC_FAR* NPMSG;
typedef struct tagMSG __RPC_FAR* LPMSG;
```

IDL unions

In a slight variation on the trivial cases above, this IDL encapsulated union:

```
typedef union _userHMETAFILE switch(long fContext)
{
    case WDT_INPROC_CALL: long       hInproc;
    case WDT_REMOTE_CALL: BYTE_BLOB* hRemote;
    default:              long       hGlobal;
} userHMETAFILE;
```

generates this C `struct`, which encapsulates both the union and its discriminator:

```
typedef struct _userHMETAFILE
{
    long fContext;
    /* [switch_is] */ /* [switch_type] */ union __MIDL_IWinTypes_0004
    {
        /* [case()] */ long hInproc;
        /* [case()] */ BYTE_BLOB __RPC_FAR* hRemote;
        /* [default] */ long hGlobal;
    } u;
} userHMETAFILE;
```

On the other hand, an IDL non-encapsulated union, like this one:

```
typedef struct tagTYPEDESC
{
    [switch_type(VARTYPE), switch_is(vt)] union
    {
        [case(VT_PTR, VT_SAFEARRAY)] struct tagTYPEDESC* lptdesc;
        [case(VT_CARRAY)] struct tagARRAYDESC* lpadesc;
        [case(VT_USERDEFINED)] HREFTYPE hreftype;
        [default];
    };
    VARTYPE vt;
} TYPEDESC;
```

generates this C `struct`:

```
typedef struct tagTYPEDESC
{
    /* [switch_is][switch_type] */ union
    {
        /* [case()] */ struct tagTYPEDESC __RPC_FAR* lptdesc;
        /* [case()] */ struct tagARRAYDESC __RPC_FAR* lpadesc;
        /* [case()] */ HREFTYPE hreftype;
        /* [default] */  /* Empty union arm */
    };
    VARTYPE vt;
} TYPEDESC;
```

Note that the MIDL-generated header file doesn't contain any code corresponding to coclass or library declarations, other than declaring the appropriate UUIDs.

Interface Bindings

Next, let's take a look at interface bindings. You'll recall that on the C++ client side, we used #import to generate an (exception throwing, type translating) interface wrapper and a smart pointer class to that wrapper. A client that uses these wrappers sees the signatures of the wrapper methods, rather than the signature of the actual interface methods.

On the server side, we work *directly* with the interface methods rather than the Wizard-generated wrapper, since we have to implement the interface as it is specified in the IDL file.

IDL custom and dual interfaces generate code that creates the correct vtable structure for the interface. The generated code is guarded by preprocessor conditions that insert different declarations into the source, depending on whether it is a C++ or a C file.

C++ Bindings

For each interface, the generated C++ code is an abstract base class with a pure virtual method corresponding to each IDL method. In our example, the `ILotInitialize` interface generates this C++ declaration:

```
MIDL_INTERFACE("E454BE82-95AA-11D2-A6FF-000086056448")
ILotInitialize : public IDispatch
{
public:
    virtual /* [helpstring][id] */ HRESULT STDMETHODCALLTYPE InitAuctionInfo(
            /* [in] */ LONG a_vlStartPrice,
            /* [in] */ LONG a_vlBidIncrement,
            /* [in] */ LONG a_vlClosesAt,
            /* [retval][out] */ BSTR __RPC_FAR *a_vstr) = 0;
};
```

Notice that the IDL attribute decorations make it into the C++ file as comments. The
`MIDL_INTERFACE(x)` macro expands out to:

```
struct __declspec(uuid(x)) __declspec(novtable)
```

You may remember that the first use of `__declspec()` here is a compiler extension that associates a
UUID with the `struct` declaration. The second occurrence, in which `novtable` is passed as an
argument, is used to specify that no vtable is generated for this class (a C++ `struct` is just a class
with default public membership), even though it has a virtual function. I will have more to say on this
subject in a short while.

A Subtle Trap

There is a subtle trap inherent in the IDL inheritance syntax. The C++ bindings for an IDL interface
hierarchy mirror that hierarchy by using C++ inheritance in the place of IDL inheritance. This means
that, within the context of C++, it is possible to *up*-cast along the interface hierarchy. Consider, for
example, the IDL hierarchy implied by these declarations

```
[...]
interface ISequentialStream : IUnknown
{
    ...
};

[...]
interface IStream : ISequentialStream
{
    ...
};
```

This structure would be reflected in these C++ bindings:

```
class ISequentialStream : IUnknown
{
    ...
};

class IStream : ISequentialStream
{
    ...
};
```

Now, given these two C++ declarations:

```
IStream* pIStream;
ISequentialStream* pISequentialStream;
```

The following code would be legal:

```
pISequentialStream = static_cast<ISequentialStream*>(pIStream);
```

What this code is doing is giving you access to the ISequentialStream methods *as they are implemented by* IStream. It is *not* giving you the ISequentialStream interface implemented on the same object (they are not guaranteed to be the same, even in the in-apartment case).

This is a particularly dangerous example of up-casting, and it is not a legitimate way to negotiate COM interfaces. If the COM object did indeed implement both these interfaces, QueryInterface() would be the correct mechanism to retrieve one interface from the other. If the C++ hierarchy were not based on C++ inheritance, the potential for this kind of error would be greatly diminished.

C Bindings

The C definition of the same interface looks like this:

```
interface ILotInitialize
{
    CONST_VTBL struct ILotInitializeVtbl __RPC_FAR* lpVtbl;
};

typedef struct ILotInitializeVtbl
{
    BEGIN_INTERFACE
    HRESULT(STDMETHODCALLTYPE __RPC_FAR* QueryInterface)(
        ILotInitialize __RPC_FAR* This,
        /* [in] */ REFIID riid,
        /* [iid_is][out] */ void __RPC_FAR* __RPC_FAR* ppvObject);

    ULONG(STDMETHODCALLTYPE __RPC_FAR* AddRef)(
        ILotInitialize __RPC_FAR* This);

    ULONG(STDMETHODCALLTYPE __RPC_FAR* Release)(
        ILotInitialize __RPC_FAR* This);

    HRESULT(STDMETHODCALLTYPE __RPC_FAR* GetTypeInfoCount)(
        ILotInitialize __RPC_FAR* This,
        /* [out] */ UINT __RPC_FAR* pctinfo);

    HRESULT(STDMETHODCALLTYPE __RPC_FAR* GetTypeInfo)(
        ILotInitialize __RPC_FAR* This,
        /* [in] */ UINT iTInfo,
        /* [in] */ LCID lcid,
        /* [out] */ ITypeInfo __RPC_FAR* __RPC_FAR* ppTInfo);
```

```
        HRESULT(STDMETHODCALLTYPE __RPC_FAR* GetIDsOfNames)(
            ILotInitialize __RPC_FAR* This,
            /* [in] */ REFIID riid,
            /* [size_is][in] */ LPOLESTR __RPC_FAR* rgszNames,
            /* [in] */ UINT cNames,
            /* [in] */ LCID lcid,
            /* [size_is][out] */ DISPID __RPC_FAR* rgDispId);

        /* [local] */ HRESULT(STDMETHODCALLTYPE __RPC_FAR* Invoke)(
            ILotInitialize __RPC_FAR* This,
            /* [in] */ DISPID dispIdMember,
            /* [in] */ REFIID riid,
            /* [in] */ LCID lcid,
            /* [in] */ WORD wFlags,
            /* [out][in] */ DISPPARAMS __RPC_FAR* pDispParams,
            /* [out] */ VARIANT __RPC_FAR* pVarResult,
            /* [out] */ EXCEPINFO __RPC_FAR* pExcepInfo,
            /* [out] */ UINT __RPC_FAR* puArgErr);

        /* [helpstring][id] */ HRESULT(STDMETHODCALLTYPE __RPC_FAR* InitAuctionInfo)(
            ILotInitialize __RPC_FAR* This,
            /* [in] */ LONG a_vlStartPrice,
            /* [in] */ LONG a_vlBidIncrement,
            /* [in] */ LONG a_vlClosesAt,
            /* [retval][out] */ BSTR __RPC_FAR* a_vstr);
    END_INTERFACE
} ILotInitializeVtbl;
```

As you can see, the C declaration has to lay out a vptr and a vtable explicitly, and it must pass a `This` pointer into the interface methods explicitly as well. In addition, it needs to specify the `IDispatch` and `IUnknown` methods that were generated automatically by the C++ compiler via inheritance.

The `BEGIN_INTERFACE` and `END_INTERFACE` macros expand out to vtable adjustments for different C/C++ compilers.

> **The direct correspondence between COM interfaces and C++ vtables is an artifact of the way that the Visual C++ compiler lays out vtables. The C++ language itself does not mandate any specific vtable structure. Indeed, it doesn't even require that virtual functions be implemented using vtables.**

In some senses, the C type signature is the most accurate definition of the interface, since it makes the binary vptr and vtable layouts explicit (the C compiler lays out `structs` exactly as specified by the programmer). With the C++ declaration, you have to know that the compiler will do the appropriate transformations to create the vtable.

Class Bindings

Given the nature of the data type and interface bindings that we have seen, it is natural to wonder if there is a coclass binding from IDL to C++ as well. However, it turns out that there is *no* single correct binding. Given the nature of the COM binary standard, there is no restriction on how COM classes are implemented in either C or C++. As long as the appropriate `QI()` rules are followed, any implementation is a coclass binding.

There are however, a few standard techniques for implementing COM classes in C++. A C++ implementation of a COM interface always begins by inheriting from the interface and implementing the methods on it. This is the easiest way to get a conformant vtable structure, and it works for a single interface. However, when an object has to expose multiple interfaces, there are many ways of approaching the situation:

❑ Have a single object multiply inherit from all interfaces
❑ Have a master object that contains sub-objects that individually implement single interfaces
❑ Have a master object that creates a sub-object that individually implements a single interface

The Active Template Library

All the above are legitimate techniques in the COM/C++ design space, but instead of going into various examples of each, I will restrict myself in this chapter to using the C++ ATL framework for building COM objects. So, before going any further, let me give you a super-quick summary of ATL.

❑ ATL COM classes are implemented by creating a C++ class that inherits multiply from the required interfaces and one or more ATL support classes. The support classes provide boilerplate implementations to be used by the `IUnknown` and `IDispatch` interfaces, and by the class factory. There are also support classes that provide boilerplate implementations of a number of other standard interfaces.

❑ ATL code accesses the interface declarations by `#include`'ing the MIDL-generated header and C file that I discussed in the previous section.

❑ ATL also supports other forms of C++/COM implementation. For example, it supports the creation of tear-off interfaces by deriving from a 'templatized' tear-off class.

❑ ATL has support for dual interfaces. Internally, ATL actually uses the Dispatch API, a type library driven implementation of the `IDispatch` methods. This system-supplied Dispatch API implementation looks up information in the type library to figure out how to translate a call to `IDispatch::Invoke()` to a call to the appropriate method on the custom side of your dual interface.

❑ ATL has built in support for implementing various COM server functions, such as self-registration, exposing appropriate class factories, etc.

❑ ATL provide several helper classes to help with common COM data types – these are the `CComPtr<>`, `CComBSTR` and `CComVariant` classes mentioned earlier.

❑ Finally, ATL has been built from the ground up with support for the COM threading models. By `#define`'ing the appropriate symbols and choosing the correct template parameters for `CComObjectRootEx<>`, you automatically get the safest and most efficient implementation for the threading model that you're trying to support.

A Server Implementation in ATL

Let's start with a simple, example implementation of a class that implements the `ILotInitialize` interface defined earlier. This is a fairly straightforward ATL class, so if you're familiar with ATL you might want to speed over this sub-section. The basic skeleton of this class (I've called it `CLot`) is an ordinary-looking ATL C++ class declaration:

```
class ATL_NO_VTABLE CLot :
   public CComObjectRootEx<CComSingleThreadModel>,
   public CComCoClass<CLot, &CLSID_CLot>,
   public ISupportErrorInfo,
   public IConnectionPointContainerImpl<CLot>,
   public CProxyILotEvents<CLot>,
   public IDispatchImpl<ILotInitialize, &IID_ILotInitialize, &LIBID_LOTLib>
{
public:
   CLot()
   {
   }

DECLARE_REGISTRY_RESOURCEID(IDR_LOT)
DECLARE_NOT_AGGREGATABLE(CLot)
DECLARE_PROTECT_FINAL_CONSTRUCT()

BEGIN_COM_MAP(CLot)
   COM_INTERFACE_ENTRY(ISupportErrorInfo)
   COM_INTERFACE_ENTRY(IConnectionPointContainer)
   COM_INTERFACE_ENTRY(IDispatch)
   COM_INTERFACE_ENTRY(ILotInitialize)
END_COM_MAP()

BEGIN_CONNECTION_POINT_MAP(CLot)
   CONNECTION_POINT_ENTRY(IID_ILotEvents)
END_CONNECTION_POINT_MAP()

// ISupportsErrorInfo
   STDMETHOD(InterfaceSupportsErrorInfo)(REFIID riid);

// ICLot
public:

// ILotInitialize
   STDMETHOD(InitAuctionInfo)(LONG, LONG, LONG, BSTR*);

private:
   CComPtr<IInitHelper> m_spIInitHelper;
};
```

IUnknown

Part of the implementation of IUnknown is provided by the base class CComObjectRootEx<> of class CLot. This is the ATL support class that's responsible for the implementation of reference counting – that is, the AddRef() and Release() methods.

The BEGIN_COM_MAP() and END_COM_MAP() macros bracket the declaration of the COM map, an array of structures that is used in a table-driven implementation of QueryInterface(). Each row in the array describes one interface that is implemented by our class. The actual code for QI() is present in the templatized class CComObject<CLot> that is derived from CLot. As a matter of fact, actual objects of the COM class are of type CComObject<CLot> (or related classes such as CComObjectEx<>), rather than being of type CLot.

ATL_NO_VTABLE

This last fact also explains another oddity. The ATL_NO_VTABLE macro in the class declaration expands out to __declspec (novtable), specifying that the compiler should not generate a vtable for this class. This is acceptable because no objects of the class are ever created; only objects of the derived class CComObject<CLot> are.

The one thing to be careful about is *never* to call a virtual function in the constructor of CLot. If you have to call such a virtual function, do it in the FinalConstruct() method, which is called after the vtable has been built.

Method Implementation

In this class, just about the only method that we need to implement ourselves is the InitAuctionInfo() member of ILotInitialize. Examine this (completely illustrative) implementation:

```
STDMETHODIMP CLot::InitAuctionInfo(LONG a_vlStartPrice,
                        LONG a_vlBidIncrement, LONG a_vlClosesAt, BSTR* a_vstr)
{
    if(a_vstr == NULL)
        return E_POINTER;
    *a_vstr = NULL;

    if(a_vlBidIncrement > 500)
        return LOT_E_HIGHINC;

    HRESULT hr = m_spIInitHelper->InitAuctionInfo(
                        a_vlStartPrice, a_vlBidIncrement, a_vlClosesAt);

    if(SUCCEEDED(hr))
    {
        *a_vstr = SysAllocString(OLESTR("Hello World"));
        return S_OK;
    }
    else
        return hr;
}
```

Preparing out Parameters

The first thing you'll notice is the test to see if the value of a_vstr is NULL. Recall from the IDL that a_vstr is a top-level out pointer. Now, from Chapter 3 we know that a top-level out pointer has to be a ref pointer, meaning that its value can never be zero. We need to test for this possibility right away.

Second, the value of the pointer is being set to 0. This is being done to prepare for the eventuality of an error return. Again, recall from Chapter 3 that all out pointers should be set to zero in the event of an error. By performing the assignment at function entry, we avoid having to do an explicit assignment later.

Custom HRESULTs

Next, notice that we are returning a custom failure code LOT_E_HIGHINC after checking a condition, and in doing so we must remember to conform to the rules set out in Chapter 2. The HRESULT must be in FACILITY_ITF, and it must have a value greater than 0x1ff.

There is an easy way to create custom HRESULTs in C. The MAKE_HRESULT() macro takes a severity code, a facility code and a status code, and creates a failure code. You can even use this macro from an IDL file, as follows:

```
#include "winerror.h"
...
typedef enum LOTHRESULTS
{
    LOT_E_HIGHINC = MAKE_HRESULT(SEVERITY_ERROR, FACILITY_ITF, 0x200)
} LOTHRESULTS;
```

This will declare the failure code as an enum value in the type library, thus making it available to all type library-aware clients.

Avoiding HRESULTs Altogether

Before you get too fancy with custom HRESULTs, recall that some clients cannot see them. In particular, Visual Basic and the scripting clients have no way to access the HRESULTs returned by a method invocation.

If you need to create universally available custom status codes, there is an excellent alternative to HRESULTs that is guaranteed to work: you pass a custom status code as an out parameter of your method. This has the advantage that it is accessible from all languages, and there are no restrictions on the allowed range of values. There is, however, a small additional marshaling cost.

Transforming HRESULTs

Now take a look at the rest of the code. It turns out that we're using a helper interface called IInitHelper that's stashed away in the smart pointer m_spIInitHelper in order to implement the method. We call the InitAuctionInfo() method of this helper interface.

Why not just return the value from the method invocation directly, instead of the two-step test that I perform here? That is, why not have the following line as the last line of code in the method:

```
return m_spIInitHelper->InitAuctionInfo(
                        a_vlStartPrice, a_vlBidIncrement, a_vlClosesAt);
```

The reason why you can't do this has to do with interface contracts. Recall that success result codes are part of the interface contract, but that failure codes are not. If we were to return the value directly, our method invocation would wind up having the same success codes in its contract as IInitHelper::InitAuctionInfo(). This *might* be what was intended, but if it's not, the first alternative is better. Also, choosing the second alternative makes you dependent on the implementer of IInitHelper not violating *its* contract (by changing the documented success codes), which would in turn cause you to violate yours. With the first, as I presented it originally, you are insured against this possibility.

On the other hand, passing *failure* codes without transformation is quite acceptable, and does not violate the interface contract.

Dual Interfaces

Notice that the ILotInitialize interface shows up in the inheritance list for CLot as a parameter to the IDispatchImpl template class. This class, which also takes an IID and a LIBID as parameters, is the class that performs the type library implementation of the dual interface. Notice that both ILotInitialize and IDispatch are present in the COM map.

COM Error Objects

ATL provides excellent boilerplate support for COM error objects, making them trivial to use. The `ISupportErrorInfo` interface is included in the multiple inheritance list, and the Object Wizard generates an implementation for its `InterfaceSupportsErrorInfo()` method as follows:

```
STDMETHODIMP CLot::InterfaceSupportsErrorInfo(REFIID riid)
{
    static const IID* arr[] = {&IID_ILotInitialize};
    for(int i = 0; i < sizeof(arr) / sizeof(arr[0]); i++)
    {
        if(InlineIsEqualGUID(*arr[i], riid))
            return S_OK;
    }
    return S_FALSE;
}
```

This method returns `S_OK` or `S_FALSE` depending on whether its IID parameter specifies an interface whose implementation provides rich error information or not. The method is table driven, so you only need to provide a list of IIDs (in the array `arr`) of interfaces that do support rich error information.

The second part of this support involves making the methods of the identified interface actually create error objects when they encounter an error. The code that we just saw for `ILotInitialize` did not actually do this – I deliberately kept it simple in order to make the various points related to HRESULTs. Here is the modified code that actually *does* use error objects:

```
STDMETHODIMP CLot::InitAuctionInfo(LONG a_vlStartPrice,
                        LONG a_vlBidIncrement, LONG a_vlClosesAt, BSTR* a_vstr)
{
    SetErrorInfo(0, NULL);

    if(a_vstr == NULL)
        return Error(OLESTR("a_vstr is a ref pointer and cannot be zero"),
                                            IID_ILotInitialize, E_POINTER);
    *a_vstr = NULL;

    if(a_vlBidIncrement > 500)
        return Error(OLESTR("The Bid Increment is too high"),
                                            IID_ILotInitialize, LOT_E_HIGHINC);

    HRESULT hr = m_spIInitHelper->InitAuctionInfo(
                        a_vlStartPrice, a_vlBidIncrement, a_vlClosesAt);

    if(SUCCEEDED(hr))
    {
        *a_vstr = SysAllocString(OLESTR("Hello World"));
        return S_OK;
    }
    else
        return Error(OLESTR("Error in IInitHelper"), IID_ILotInitialize, hr);
}
```

Note the initial call to `SetErrorInfo(0, NULL)`, ensuring that the error object on the current logical thread is released. This can never cause a problem. If the method returns an error, it resets this error object to a newly created one. If the method is successful, the stale error object has already been released.

The call to `SetErrorInfo()` may be wasteful in the standard error object protocol, because the client shouldn't actually check the error object unless an error `HRESULT` is returned. However, this is not the case in the OLE DB error protocol, which specifies that a method may set the error object even on a successful `HRESULT`. This means that stale error objects must *always* be released upon entry to an interface method that supports the OLE DB error object protocol. My suggestion is to bite the bullet and call this function on entry if you think you're ever going to support OLE DB error objects.

As you can see, some key support is provided by the `Error()` method. This polymorphic method is made available by the ATL template `CComCoClass<>`, and calls a subroutine that sets the error object appropriately. In its different polymorphic forms it supports all combinations of information that can be supplied to the error object.

Connectable Object Protocol

ATL also supports the connectable object (CO) protocol, to which end it provides two support classes `IConnectionPointContainerImpl<>` and `IConnectionPointImpl<>` that provide boilerplate implementations of the CO protocol. The former is present in the class inheritance list, and works with the connection point map that's declared between the `BEGIN_CONNECTION_POINT()` and `END_CONNECTION_POINT()` macros to provide access to the individual connection points.

The individual connection points are implemented by `IConnectionPointImpl<>` which appears in the inheritance list *indirectly* through `CProxyILotEvents<>`, a Wizard-generated class. This class has wrapper functions conforming to the signatures of the actual events that cause events to be fired on all connected sinks. Thus, in our example, `CProxyILotEvents<>` has to provide support for firing the `ILotEvents::BidsChanged()` method. It does precisely that, as you can see from this declaration of the `CProxyILotEvents<>` class:

```
template <class T>
class CProxyILotEvents :
    public IConnectionPointImpl<T, &IID_ILotEvents, CComDynamicUnkArray>
{
    // Warning: this class may be recreated by the Wizard.
public:
    HRESULT Fire_BidsChanged()
    {
        HRESULT ret;
        T* pT = static_cast<T*>(this);
        int nConnectionIndex;
        int nConnections = m_vec.GetSize();
```

```
        for(nConnectionIndex = 0;
                            nConnectionIndex < nConnections; nConnectionIndex++)
        {
          pT->Lock();
          CComPtr<IUnknown> sp = m_vec.GetAt(nConnectionIndex);
          pT->Unlock();
          ILotEvents* pILotEvents = reinterpret_cast<ILotEvents*>(sp.p);
          if(pILotEvents != NULL)
              ret = pILotEvents->BidsChanged();
        }
        return ret;
      }
    };
```

As you can see, this is just a thin wrapper around `IConnectionPointImpl<>`. All it does in addition is provide a wrapper function called `Fire_BidsChanged()` that runs through all the sinks, calling `BidsChanged()` on each of them.

The only thing your code needs to do when an event needs to be fired is to call the `Fire_BidsChanged()` method as supplied by this proxy. This is about as simple as event firing can get. The connectable object protocol is handled by the two 'Impl' classes, and a Wizard generates the iterative firing code.

Auction Server Design

In Chapter 5, I showed you what I call the analysis or specification object model (SOM), which was the object model that grew out of an analysis of the use cases. In Chapter 6, I showed you how this object model was used to build a user interface for the auction server.

Now I'm going to show you the actual implementation of the SOM. From this point on, we're dealing with a concrete example, and the best way for you to follow along is to download the source code for this book from the Wrox Press web site at http://www.wrox.com. The project being built for the majority of this chapter is called `AuctSrvr`.

In this project, there is another object model at work that is quite apart from the SOM – I call it the **implementation object model** (IOM). There is one major characteristic that distinguishes specification and implementation models in my mind. The SOM, as a matter of conscious design, does not expose any classes at all, only interfaces. A client of the SOM is not expected to know, or to care about, the actual objects exposing the various interfaces. The implementation model, on the other hand, has to expose its class structure.

Initial Class Structure

Let us start with the class structure that I outlined at the end of the use case analysis. The figure below shows the application class structure as a box-spoon diagram with UML style relationships between the classes:

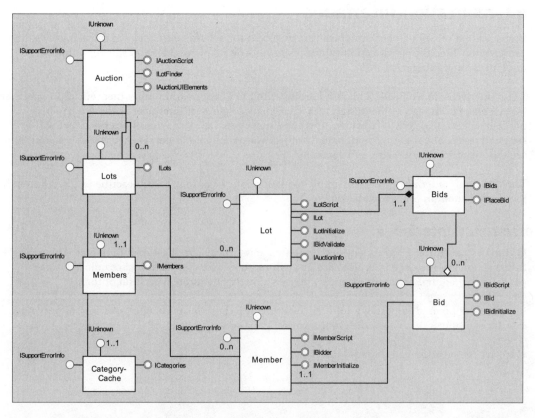

This structure is derived directly from the IDL that was shown in Chapter 5. The relationships have been derived from the functional specification. Here is a list of these relationships:

- ❑ An `Auction` object is associated with zero or more `Lots` objects
- ❑ An `Auction` object is composed of exactly one `Members` object
- ❑ An `Auction` object is associated with exactly one `CategoryCache` object
- ❑ A `Lots` object is associated with zero or more `Lot` objects
- ❑ A `Lot` object is composed of exactly one `Bids` object
- ❑ A `Bids` object aggregates zero or more `Bid` objects
- ❑ A `Bid` object is associated with exactly one `Member` object
- ❑ A `Members` object is associated with zero or more `Member` objects

If your UML is a little rusty, recall that **association** is simply a relationship between classes and objects. Their lifetimes may or may not be related, although obviously they must overlap. **Composition** is a very strong form of association, where the lifetime of the composed object is coincident with the lifetime of the composing object. The UML (not COM) term **aggregation** is less strictly defined; I use it to mean a relationship where the aggregated object's creation and destruction is controlled by the aggregator, and where the aggregated object's lifetime falls strictly within that of the aggregator.

Implementation Interfaces

We've started off with a class structure that maps out the relationship between the classes we'll be using, onto which the specification interfaces have been mapped. Next, let's begin to look at implementation interfaces.

What interfaces do we need? This is a hard question to answer from purely theoretical premises, and we've come far enough in the design that it's difficult to guess at interfaces without a concrete implementation to refer to. However, there are some general categories of interface that will be required in just about any system, namely **object construction** and **persistence** interfaces, and these are described in the following sub-sections.

The remaining interfaces are 'pure' implementation interfaces that I will describe as I step through the implementation process with you.

Persistence Interfaces

Of the two categories I have identified, persistence interfaces are the easier to define. The reason for this is simple: persistence interfaces are not tailored to object classes; they are tailored to the persistence medium. Thus, for example, there is exactly one implementation of the `IPersistStreamInit` interface, which can be used to persist a bid to a stream. Exactly the same interface can be used to persist a lot if necessary, but I chose to implement a variety of persistence interfaces to illustrate various different forms of persistence.

Here are the persistence interfaces that I use:

```
interface IPersistStream;
interface IPersistStreamInit;
interface IPersistFile;
interface IPersistPropertyBag;
```

These are all standard persistence interfaces that persist to streams, files, and property bag objects respectively, and I will not repeat their definitions here. In addition, I used the very useful `IPersistVariant` interface, as defined by Jonathan Pinnock in his book *Professional DCOM Application Development*. Since this is likely to be less familiar, I'll show you the definition:

```
[...]
interface IPersistVariant : IDispatch
{
    [id(1)] HRESULT GetClassID([out, retval] BSTR* pbstrCLSID);
    [id(2)] HRESULT IsDirty([out, retval] VARIANT_BOOL* pbDirty);
    [id(3)] HRESULT Save([in] VARIANT_BOOL bClearDirty,
                         [out, retval] VARIANT* pvar);
    [id(4)] HRESULT Load([in] VARIANT var);
};
```

The original design goal for this interface was to create a persistence interface that was available from scripting languages, but as you'll see later, I found it useful for another reason.

Finally, let me refresh your memory with the definition of the rowset persistence interface that I described in Chapter 5. This interface was designed for persisting to and from relational databases (actually, any OLE DB data source):

```
[...]
interface IPersistRowset : IUnknown
{
    HRESULT InitNew();
    HRESULT Load([in] IRowset* pRowset);
    HRESULT Save([in] IRowset* pRowset, [in] BOOL fClearDirty);
    HRESULT IsDirty();
};
```

This is modeled on the standard persistence interfaces.

Construction Interfaces

Construction interfaces are harder to define because the specific construction methods only become clear as implementation proceeds. In this case, although I am showing you the interfaces at this point to give you an overview of the implementation, be aware that they were actually defined (and refined) while writing the code, in response to the needs of the implementation.

There is one particular point to note about the construction methods: each one takes a number of parameters that represent *one way* of constructing the object, and returns an interface on the constructed object. Instead of returning a specific interface, however, the interface that is returned is the one specified in an IID parameter passed into the method, cast to `IUnknown**`. This technique mirrors the action of the default COM constructor API, `CoCreateInstance()`, but provides an extra degree of freedom to the user by allowing the return of any interface accessible through the object. This is quite helpful, because any constructed COM object is assumed to have one or more implemented interfaces. The idiom mirrors `QI()` in the sense that construction returns a specific requested interface, saving the need for an extra `QI()` after the object is constructed.

First up, a new `Lot` object is created by passing the basic auction information, a unique lot identifier, and a moniker to the `CreateLot()` method of `ILotConstruct`:

```
interface ILotConstruct : IDispatch
{
    [id(1), helpstring("Construct Basic Lot")]
    HRESULT CreateLot([in] LONG a_vlLotID,
                      [in] BSTR a_vstrDescription,
                      [in] LONG a_vlCategory,
                      [in] LONG a_vlStartPrice,
                      [in] LONG a_vlBidIncrement,
                      [in] LONG a_vlClosesAt,
                      [in] BSTR a_vstrNameString,
                      [in] REFIID a_riid,
                      [out, iid_is (a_riid), retval] IUnknown** a_ppuk);
};
```

Similarly, a new `Bid` object is created by calling the `CreateBid()` method on the `IBidConstruct` interface:

```
interface IBidConstruct : IUnknown
{
    [id(1), helpstring("Construct an object with Bid information")]
    HRESULT CreateBid([in] IBidder* a_pmem,
                    [in] LONG a_vlPrice,
                    [in] SHORT a_vsNumber,
                    [in] LONG a_vlTime,
                    [in] REFIID a_riid,
                    [out, iid_is(a_riid), retval] IUnknown** a_ppuk);
};
```

Likewise, an empty `Bids` collection is constructed by calling the `CreateBids()` method on `IBidsConstruct`. The parameters will become clearer when you see the implementation:

```
interface IBidsConstruct : IUnknown
{
    [id(1), helpstring("Construct an object with Bids information")]
    HRESULT CreateBids([in] IUnknown* a_puk,
                    [in] REFIID a_riid,
                    [out, iid_is (a_riid), retval] IUnknown** a_ppuk);
};
```

Finally, the `IMemberConstruct::CreateMember()` method is used to create a `Member` object:

```
interface IMemberConstruct : IUnknown
{
    [id(1), helpstring("Initialize object with Member information")]
    HRESULT CreateMember([in] LONG a_vlMemberID,
                    [in] BSTR a_vstrFirst,
                    [in] BSTR a_vstrLast,
                    [in] BSTR a_vstrCity,
                    [in] BSTR a_vstrState,
                    [in] REFIID a_riid,
                    [out, iid_is (a_riid), retval] IUnknown** a_ppmm);
};
```

Why Expose Implementation Interfaces in IDL?

An argument can be made that these constructor interfaces are not really necessary. Remember that these interfaces are *not* exposed by the SOM, which is what scripting clients see, and according to this rationale, object construction is an implementation detail that does not need to be exposed as a COM interface.

I am (obviously!) not completely convinced by this argument. As I've already indicated, there are really two object models: the specification object model, which satisfies the requirements of the use case analysis, and the implementation object model, which provides all the down-and-dirty details required to build servers that can satisfy the specification model. However, such a server does not necessarily have to be built in a single programming language or within a single executable (as is done in this chapter). To get the full benefit of an object oriented design, it must be assumed that the object model can be implemented in pieces, in various languages and executables. In order for this to work, important areas of functionality such as construction and persistence should be made available through COM interfaces.

If the cost of this flexibility were very high, I would advise foregoing it. However, as you will see, implementing generic constructor interfaces is not that much harder than building C++ constructors. In situations where the default constructor interfaces are sufficient, this cost is zero. In any case, it is a technique that you should be familiar with, even if you question its specific utility in this object model.

New Classes

We've seen some of the interfaces introduced by implementation requirements; let's take a look now at the *classes* that are required because of implementation considerations.

Class Objects

Consider the construction interfaces that I just described. As mentioned in Chapter 5, the natural place to implement these interfaces is on the class object for the coclass – after all, that's where the default COM constructor interfaces IClassFactory and IClassFactory2 are implemented.

Unfortunately, a class object cannot be described in IDL because it is an anonymous class – it doesn't have a UUID associated with it, and consequently cannot be created by the standard COM CoCreateInstance() mechanism. If anonymous classes *were* allowed in IDL, this is what the definitions of various class objects would look like:

```
[...]
coclass COLot
{
    [default] ILotConstruct;
    interface IClassFactory;
};

[...]
coclass COBids
{
    [default] IBidsConstruct;
    interface IClassFactory;
};

[...]
coclass COBid
{
    [default] IBidConstruct;
    interface IClassFactory;
};

[...]
coclass COMember
{
    [default] IMemberConstruct;
    interface IClassFactory;
};
```

I've named each class object coclass by prefixing the name of the class it represents with CO. Notice that each class object coclass continues to implement IClassFactory in addition to implementing the specific constructor that was defined for the class. The interface is not strictly required, but in order to avoid it we would need to implement IExternalConnection (as outlined in the section on constructor interfaces on class objects in Chapter 5). It turns out to be simpler just to re-use the boilerplate IClassFactory implementation in ATL.

Remember that *every* creatable COM class has an anonymous class object that implements
`IClassFactory`. In our object model, these classes have the trivial declarations:

```
[...]
coclass COAuction
{
    interface IClassFactory;
};

[...]
coclass COLots
{
    interface IClassFactory;
};

[...]
coclass COMembers
{
    interface IClassFactory;
};

[...]
coclass COCategoryCache
{
    interface IClassFactory;
};
```

Singleton Class Factories

Sometimes, the semantics of a class indicate that only one object of the class needs to exist – that is,
all objects of the class will behave identically, so it is possible for there to be multiple references to
this single object. This is the **singleton class** I described in Chapter 5.

In such situations, the class factory can be modified so that it always returns exactly the same object.
This results in a *server* singleton, rather than a workstation or true singleton. In our example, the
`Auction`, `Members` and `CategoryCache` classes can be implemented as singletons.

Alternate Identities

Now let me show you another kind of anonymous class that shows up in the implementation. Recall
that the specification model exposes interfaces to the user as read-only properties of other interfaces –
the user is not expected to try to find out what the true identity of the object is. There are a couple of
problems with this:

❑ Scripting languages re-query the received interface for `IDispatch` even if the exposed interface
is a dual interface. In this sense, the scripting language is forcing the true identity of the object to
be revealed.
❑ A malicious (or nosy) client can break the encapsulation of the specification object model by
`QI()`'ing the exposed interface for other interfaces, specifically `IUnknown`.

Ideally, what we want to happen is for a nosy client to see a different COM object for each interface
that is exposed by the 'real' object. There is a simple solution to this problem, and that is to use the
alternate identity technique described in Chapter 5.

Each interface returned by the SOM is wrapped in its own independent COM identity (with its own implementation of `IUnknown`). This identity is not directly creatable by COM, so it is an anonymous COM class as well. For example, the `Lot` class is declared as:

```
[...]
coclass Lot
{
    [default] interface ILotScript;
    interface ILot;
    interface ILotInitialize;
    interface IBidValidate;
    interface IAuctionInfo;

    interface ISupportErrorInfo;
};
```

Under the scheme I'm proposing, `ILot` would actually have an additional identity for each interface that it exposes through the SOM (remember, this *isn't* legal IDL, because the classes are anonymous):

```
[...]
coclass IDILot
{
    [default] interface ILot;
    interface IDispatch;

    interface ISupportErrorInfo;
};

[...]
coclass IDILotInitialize
{
    [default] interface ILotInitialize;
    interface IDispatch;

    interface ISupportErrorInfo;
};

[...]
coclass IDIBidValidate
{
    [default] interface IBidValidate;
    interface IDispatch;

    interface ISupportErrorInfo;
};

[...]
coclass IDIAuctionInfo
{
    [default] interface IAuctionInfo;
    interface IDispatch;

    interface ISupportErrorInfo;
};
```

The box-spoon diagram for Lot would then look like the figure below. The dashed rectangles represent the other anonymous identities of the Lot object that are exposed via the SOM:

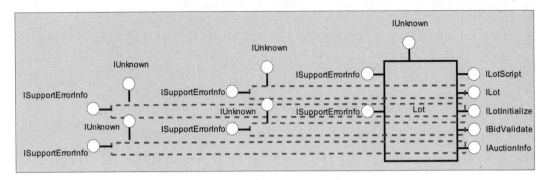

At first glance, this is likely to seem confusing. How is it any different from implementing each of these interfaces in a separate COM object? In a way, it's not: the client really does see separate identities. The point of using alternate identities, however, is that the same real 'state' is servicing all these identities, and the lifetimes of the different identities are coincident. This last fact is what makes these interfaces alternate COM identities with the same state, rather than just independent identities that happen to share state.

As you'll see when we get to the ATL implementation, a single C++ class is used to implement all the alternate COM identities.

Alternate Identities and Persistence

An interesting question comes up when a client holds a pointer to an alternate identity of an object. What happens if the client persists this identity, and then reloads it? Which identity does it get back, the original identity or the alternate? The answer is that it *must* get back the alternate identity, otherwise the encapsulation mechanism is broken.

The simplest solution to this problem is to forbid persistence from alternate identities, but if this is not possible, there has to be a mechanism for discovering which identity was in effect when the object was persisted.

Split Identity

It turns out that the Lot class also needs a weak identity (see Chapter 5). For reasons that will become clear when we look at the implementation code, the Bids object associated with a Lot object needs a back pointer to the Lot object. Since the Lot object actually composes the Bids object, this sets up a classic part-whole reference cycle. Recall that the safe way to deal with such a situation is to create a separate weak identity for the object, as illustrated below:

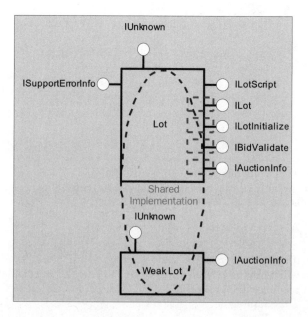

A weak identity is very similar to an alternate identity, the primary difference being that releasing the weak identity cannot initiate object destruction; only releasing a strong identity can do that. To keep the picture simple, I have shrunk the alternate identity boxes in size and removed the `IUnknown` and `ISupportErrorInfo` interfaces from them.

The lower box in the diagram represents the weak identity of the Lot class, and as you can see, not all its interfaces need to be exposed here. In this case, the client of the weak identity (the Bids class) only requires `IAuctionInfo` (and one other interface that I will describe later).

Enumerator Objects

The final class of objects that is not visible in this diagram are those that correspond to the enumerator interfaces. Each enumerator interface is *actually* implemented by an anonymous COM class that maintains the state of the enumeration. Each collection object in our class structure has an associated enumerator interface, and therefore an (anonymous) enumerator class. Here is the pseudo IDL describing the situation:

```
[...]
coclass EnumBids
{
    [default] interface IEnumVARIANT;
};

[...]
coclass EnumLots
{
    [default] interface IEnumVARIANT;
};
```

```
[...]
coclass EnumMembers
{
    [default] interface IEnumVARIANT;
};

[...]
coclass EnumCategories
{
    [default] interface IEnumVARIANT;
};
```

As you can see, each class exports the one interface (IEnumVARIANT) that is expected of an enumerator class. Since enumerator classes have such a trivial structure, they are frequently not mentioned as separate entities.

Class Persistence

Finally, let me explain how I intend to persist the various classes in my hierarchy. Some of the data associated with the auction will be made available in a SQL database (an Access database in this implementation). This information will be accessed by the OLE DB interfaces, so that the data repository can be changed in the future.

In particular, the list of categories, the list of members and the lot search parameters are natural candidates for storage in a database. Thus, the Categories and Members classes will each be loaded from a rowset that has the agreed upon columns. The Lots class is also loaded from a rowset of appropriate format, the results of a find operation.

Each of these classes implements the IPersistRowset interface. In practice, I use stored procedures to populate the rowset that is passed into IPersistRowset. This further encapsulates the object model from the data model.

The Lot class does not need a persistence interface of its own, since Lot objects are always persisted into the database as part of the persistence of a Lots object. The bid information on a lot, however, will be stored *outside* the database. In a real-world situation, it's unlikely (but not impossible) that we would do this, since bid information is also a natural for inclusion in a database. However, I am trying to illustrate several persistence models, so I will ignore this objection.

As a result of this decision, the Bids class will implement all the non-rowset persistence interfaces that I mentioned earlier. In turn, these will depend on the Bid object knowing how to persist itself to a stream, and so the Bid class will implement the IPersistStream(Init) interfaces, and just to make a point we will implement the IPersistPropertyBag interface as well.

Finally, it will turn out that the persistence implementation of the Bid class depends on the persistence of the Member class, requiring the latter to implement the same persistence interfaces as Bid. Here, then, is the IDL showing the persistence interfaces implemented by the IOM:

```
[...]
coclass CategoryCache
{
   ...
   interface IPersistRowset;
   ...
};

[...]
coclass Members
{
   ...
   interface IPersistRowset;
   ...
};

[...]
coclass Lots
{
   ...
   interface IPersistRowset;
   ...
};

[...]
coclass Bids
{
   ...
   interface IPersistFile;
   interface IPersistStream;
   interface IPersistStreamInit;
   interface IPersistPropertyBag;
   interface IPersistVariant;
   ...
};

[...]
coclass Bid
{
   ...
   interface IPersistStream;
   interface IPersistStreamInit;
   interface IPersistPropertyBag;
   ...
};

[...]
coclass Member
{
   ...
   interface IPersistStream;
   interface IPersistStreamInit;
   interface IPersistPropertyBag;
   ...
};
```

Implementation Class Diagram

The figure below displays the static implementation class diagram after I have inserted all the new classes and interfaces described so far:

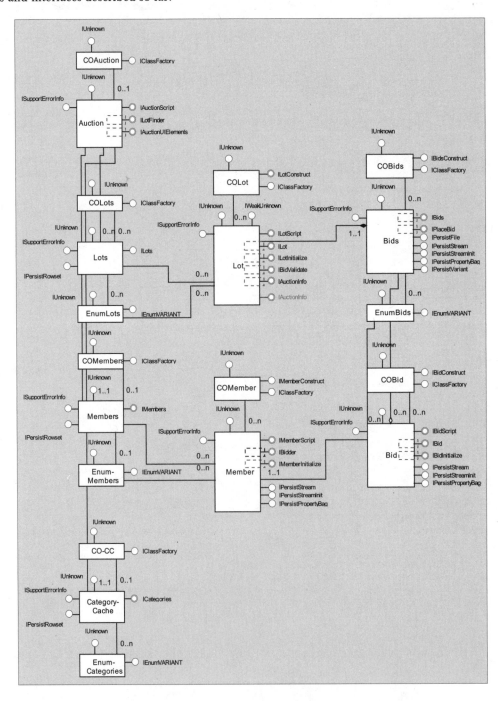

Alternate identities are represented by dashed gray rectangles, and I have abbreviated these by not showing their `IUnknown` or `ISupportErrorInfo` interfaces. One alternate identity that is of special interest is `IBidder` on the `Member` class. Note that this is surrounded by a black (instead of gray) dashed rectangle. This indicates that this alternate is a *persistable* identity.

There is a single weak identity interface in this diagram, and that's `IAuctionInfo` on the `Lot` class – it is depicted in gray. Note that there is a strong (black) `IAuctionInfo` interface as well. The other features of this diagram are the UML relationships:

- Except for singleton classes, each class object is associated with zero or more objects of its class. The singleton classes have class objects that are associated with zero or one objects of the class.
- Each collection object is associated with zero or more objects of the enumerator class.
- Each enumerator object is associated with zero or more objects of the class that it is enumerating.

It doesn't need me to tell you that this is a fairly complicated class diagram, and this is an object model that results from just one relatively small use case for the auction system. However, this is not really surprising – some of the complexity (and therefore the cost) of this implementation comes from providing a completely general and robust implementation of an object model that can be used from any client language in a uniform manner.

Auction Server Implementation

I'll now step you through an ATL implementation of the object model that I outlined in the previous section.

I should say that this is a fairly sophisticated ATL implementation that uses several advanced techniques and a few of my own ATL extensions. However, there is nothing fundamentally 'hard' about it. With some study and practice, these techniques will become clear and part of your own repertoire. In the mean time, hang in there and get a feeling for the general principles, even if the details are initially unclear.

Before getting into the details of the code, I would like to say a couple of things about it. Although I've made every effort to keep the code robust, especially the samples that are displayed in the book, this is *not* production quality code. Error checking is not always exhaustive, successful HRESULT transformations are not always performed, failure HRESULT transformations are almost never performed, and the `Error()` method is not always used to provide rich error information.

To some extent, this is due to a desire to keep the code short so that the main points being made are obvious. This is the reason I've avoided using the `Error()` method, which expands one line of code to three without being of much instructional value. To a greater extent, it is due to the fact that it would have taken much more time and effort to write production-quality code, without adding much to the essential knowledge that I am trying to transmit.

This is not an excuse that you can rely on when it comes to writing code that has to be shipped to customers. The best thing you can do to reduce the pain and long-term costs of supporting software is to write robust code.

The Auction Class

That out of the way, we'll begin by looking at the class that implements the top-level interface in the SOM, the `Auction` class. You'll recall its declaration:

```
coclass Auction
{
    [default] interface IAuctionScript;
    interface ILotFinder;
    interface IAuctionUIElements;

    interface ISupportErrorInfo;
};
```

The Auction Database

As I mentioned earlier, the persisted state of the auction lives in a database. For this version of the system, this is a Microsoft Access database. However, the design of the system makes it trivial to move the persisted state to some other database system, provided that it also is an OLE DB data source. I'll now outline this design.

Encapsulating the Database Connection

The auction data is accessed via the ODBC DSN `Wrox Auction`, which has been set up as a system DSN to point at the auction database file. However, the code could also be rewritten to permit DSN-less connections (since DSNs can be a pain to administer on the client side).

The use of an ODBC connection allows me to change the location of the data. It also permits me to change the underlying database server if necessary. If I had to migrate the auction data to SQL Server (providing the rest of the code needed no changes), I could do so simply by changing the DSN.

Encapsulating the Data Model

There are three classes in my object model that persist to the database: `Lots`, `Members` and `CategoryCache`. For each class, there is a query that returns the appropriate set of records for the type. The important elements of the query from the perspective of the code are:

❑ The data type of each field (or column) and parameter of the query
❑ The name of each field and parameter, or
❑ The ordering of the fields and parameters

As long as these elements remain the same, the actual query being used by the implementation can be replaced seamlessly.

The Member Recordset

This is a parameterless query with these output fields:

Name	Type
MemberID	Long
FirstName	char[50]
LastName	char[50]
City	char[50]
State	char[50]

The CategoryCache Recordset

This is another parameterless query. It has these output fields:

Name	Type
CatID	Long
CatDescription	char[50]

The Lots Recordset

This query takes a single parameter: a Long value named CatID. It has these output fields:

Name	Type
CatID	Long
LotID	Long
Description	char[255]
CatDescription	char[50]
Moniker	char[255]
StartPrice	Long
Increment	Long
ClosesAt	date/time

Encapsulating the DataSource Type

Finally, let's take a look at the code that is used to access these records. I decided to use OLE DB for this purpose for a couple of reasons:

- ❑ It is a COM-based approach to database clients, so it's a natural fit with the code and the subject of the book
- ❑ Visual C++ 6 has good support for creating OLE DB clients (or **consumers**, as they are called)

The OLE DB consumer Wizard in Visual C++ 6 (it is one of the ATL Object Wizard selections, even though it doesn't generate a COM object) runs against a stored procedure or table in a database. For each such recordset, it generates two C++ classes: an accessor class and a rowset class. The accessor class encapsulates an OLE DB accessor, an object that binds to the fields of a recordset and allows programmatic access to the individual fields. The rowset class encapsulates an OLE DB rowset. The rowset class is responsible for establishing a database connection, running the appropriate query, and giving access to the underlying recordset as an OLE DB rowset.

As an example, here is the accessor class that is generated by the Wizard for the Lots recordset. Compare this to the definition of the Lots recordset above:

```
class CLotAccessor
{
public:
    LONG m_prmCatID;
    LONG m_colCatID;
    LONG m_colLotID;
    TCHAR m_colDescription[256];
    TCHAR m_colCatDescription[51];
    TCHAR m_colMoniker[256];
    LONG m_colStartPrice;
    LONG m_colIncrement;
    DBTIMESTAMP m_colClosesAt;

BEGIN_PARAM_MAP(CLotAccessor)
    COLUMN_ENTRY(1, m_prmCatID)
END_PARAM_MAP()

BEGIN_COLUMN_MAP(CLotAccessor)
    COLUMN_ENTRY(1, m_colCatID)
    COLUMN_ENTRY(2, m_colLotID)
    COLUMN_ENTRY(3, m_colDescription)
    COLUMN_ENTRY(4, m_colCatDescription)
    COLUMN_ENTRY(5, m_colMoniker)
    COLUMN_ENTRY(6, m_colStartPrice)
    COLUMN_ENTRY(7, m_colIncrement)
    COLUMN_ENTRY(8, m_colClosesAt)
END_COLUMN_MAP()

DEFINE_COMMAND(CLotAccessor, _T("{ CALL LotDA (?) }"))

// You may wish to call this function if you are inserting a record and wish
// to initialize all the fields, if you are not going to explicitly set all
// of them.

    void ClearRecord()
    {
        memset(this, 0, sizeof(*this));
    }
};
```

As you can see, this class simply defines a number of member variables, one for each parameter and field of the corresponding recordset. The data types of the member variables correspond to the data types of the equivalent field or parameter.

The class also has a column map (delimited by the BEGIN_COLUMN_MAP() and END_COLUMN_MAP() macros) that associates each member variable with the corresponding field. As you can see, this association is done with the position of the field, rather than the name – m_colLotID, for example, is associated with field two, not with the field named LotID. Similarly, the parameter map (between the BEGIN_PARAM_MAP() and END_PARAM_MAP() macros) maintains an association between member variables and query parameters.

Finally, the accessor class contains a string representation of the SQL parameterized query that generates the recordset; it therefore encapsulates the query, its parameters and its fields.

Next, take a look at the Wizard-generated C++ class that is the rowset class for this recordset:

```cpp
class CLotDA : public CCommand<CAccessor<CLotAccessor> >
{
public:
    HRESULT Open()
    {
        HRESULT hr;
        hr = OpenDataSource();
        if(FAILED(hr))
            return hr;
        return OpenRowset();
    }

    HRESULT OpenDataSource()
    {
        HRESULT hr;
        CDataSource db;
        CDBPropSet dbinit(DBPROPSET_DBINIT);
        dbinit.AddProperty(DBPROP_AUTH_PERSIST_SENSITIVE_AUTHINFO, false);
        dbinit.AddProperty(DBPROP_INIT_DATASOURCE, OLESTR("Wrox Auction"));
        dbinit.AddProperty(DBPROP_INIT_PROMPT, (short)4);
        dbinit.AddProperty(DBPROP_INIT_LCID, (long)1033);
        hr = db.Open(_T("MSDASQL"), &dbinit);
        if(FAILED(hr))
            return hr;
        return m_session.Open(db);
    }

    HRESULT OpenRowset()
    {
        return CCommand<CAccessor<CLotAccessor> >::Open(m_session);
    }

    CSession m_session;
};
```

As you can see, this class takes the accessor class as a template parameter – it is actually derived indirectly from CLotAccessor. The few methods that you can see are used to establish a connection to the database, and this is the place where the DSN value is stored.

The rowset class encapsulates the database name and a database session. It is also capable of performing functions that correspond purely to rowsets. However, we will not be using this more advanced functionality, sticking only to its connection-establishing abilities.

There are analogous accessor and rowset C++ classes for the remaining recordsets – the Members recordset and the CategoryCache recordset.

Let us now take a look at the code that uses these OLE DB consumer classes. Within the Auction class, database code is needed to perform the find operation that returns a Lots object. It is also needed to initialize the CategoryCache object and the Members object.

Object State

In all my descriptions of object implementations, I'll begin by describing the mutable state of the object – that is, its member variables. The CAuction class only has two of these: m_spICategories and m_spIMembers:

```
CComPtr<ICategories> m_spICategories;
CComPtr<IMembers> m_spIMembers;
```

As you can see, these variables are smart pointers. They are used to cache the ICategories and IMembers interfaces returned by the functions of IAuctionUIElements, in order to reduce database loading time.

ILotFinder

The ILotFinder interface was defined as follows:

```
interface ILotFinder : IDispatch
{
    [id(1), helpstring("Cancel Current Find Operation")]
    HRESULT Cancel();

    [id(2), helpstring("Search Based on Category")]
    HRESULT SearchCategory([in] LONG a_vlCategory, [out, retval] ILots** a_pplt);
};
```

To simplify the implementation and stick to the main concepts, we do not implement the Cancel() operation at this time. When a method is not implemented, it simply returns the E_NOTIMPL result code, as follows:

```
STDMETHOD(Cancel)()
{
    return E_NOTIMPL;
}
```

Let's now look at the SearchCategory() method. Recall that this method has to return all the lots that belong to a specific category. Here is the implementation:

```
STDMETHOD(SearchCategory)(LONG a_vlCategory, ILots** a_pplt)
{
    if(a_pplt == NULL)
        return E_POINTER;
    *a_pplt = NULL;

    CLotDA lda;
    lda.m_prmCatID = a_vlCategory;
    lda.Open();
    CComPtr<IRowset> spIRowset(lda.GetInterface());
    CComPtr<IPersistRowset> spIPersistRowset;
```

```
      HRESULT hr;
      hr = spIPersistRowset.CoCreateInstance(CLSID_Lots);
      if(FAILED(hr))
         return hr;

      hr = spIPersistRowset->Load(spIRowset);
      if(FAILED(hr))
         return hr;

      hr = spIPersistRowset.QueryInterface(a_pplt);
      if(FAILED(hr))
         return hr;

      return S_OK;
   }
```

As usual, the first three lines are testing and preparing the out-only parameters to the method. The next few lines create an instance called 1da of the Lots rowset class I described earlier. The single parameter required by the query is the search category, and this is set by assigning the input parameter a_vlCategory to the member variable m_prmCatID of 1da. The Open() method is then called on 1da. This establishes a connection to the database, executes the query, and binds the accessor to the resulting recordset.

I now depart from the normal use of the OLE DB templates. Typically, we would now use 1da to iterate over the rows in the result recordset, but what we do instead is:

❑ Extract an IRowset interface from the 1da variable. This is possible because 1da is a C++ proxy to the underlying OLE DB interfaces. The GetInterface() method gives access to the rowset interface being wrapped by the proxy.

❑ Create an object of the Lots class. We use the standard CoCreateInstance() sequence to accomplish this (only I use the smart pointer method).

❑ Get the IPersistRowset interface on this object. A smart pointer is used to wrap the proxy.

❑ Pass our OLE DB rowset into the Load() method of IPersistRowset. This will cause the Lots object to load itself from the rowset, rather than requiring us to know how to load it.

❑ Remembering that we need to return an ILots interface from this method, we query for it, and return.

> You may be wondering why I use CoCreateInstance() to create the Lots object. Isn't that just another C++ class in the same executable? Why not 'new' the C++ class directly, and save a few cycles? A more sophisticated version of this question is the following: why not use the CreateInstance() function that is implemented by the CComObjectXXXX<>-derived class?
>
> The answer to the first part is that direct creation of the C++ object doesn't perform proper initialization of that object (for instance, the FinalConstruct() method will not get called). While these objections disappear with the use of the appropriate CreateInstance() function, there are additional problems.

If you should ever decide in the future to implement the Lots class in a different executable, *this* code will not need any modifications. The CreateInstance()-style code *would* need to be rewritten, since it depends on the object being implemented by the same ATL executable.

There may be additional constraints on object creation that are imposed by the semantics of the class factory. For instance, the class factory may be a singleton, or it may be a custom class factory that performs some default initialization. By using CComObjectXXXX<>::CreateInstance(), you would bypass these constraints, possibly violating some system invariant.

Besides, as you've probably heard by now, cycles are cheap compared to programmers.

IAuctionUIElements

Here is the declaration of IAuctionUIElements:

```
interface IAuctionUIElements : IDispatch
{
    [propget, id(1), helpstring("ICategories")]
    HRESULT ICategories([out, retval] ICategories** a_pplm);

    [propget, id(2), helpstring("IMembers")]
    HRESULT IMembers([out, retval] IMembers** a_ppmm);
};
```

Getting ICategories

Here is the implementation of the ICategories propget method:

```
STDMETHOD(get_ICategories)(ICategories** a_ppct)
{
    if(a_ppct == NULL)
        return E_POINTER;
    *a_ppct = NULL;

    if(!m_spICategories)
    {
        CCategories cda;
        cda.Open();
        CComPtr<IRowset> spIRowset(cda.GetInterface());
        CComPtr<IPersistRowset> spIPersistRowset;

        HRESULT hr;
        hr = spIPersistRowset.CoCreateInstance(CLSID_CategoryCache);
        if(FAILED(hr))
            return hr;

        hr = spIPersistRowset->Load(spIRowset);
        if(FAILED(hr))
            return hr;
```

```
            hr = spIPersistRowset.QueryInterface(a_ppct);
            if(SUCCEEDED(hr))
            {
                m_spICategories = *a_ppct;
                return S_OK;
            }
            else
                return hr;
        }
        else
            return m_spICategories.CopyTo(a_ppct);
    }
```

Notice the extraordinary similarity to the code that fetched the Lots recordset. We just substitute the CCategories C++ rowset class for the CLotDA class. The categories query doesn't have any parameters, so we can call Open() on cda right away.

The one point of departure is that this method caches the resulting category interface in the smart pointer variable m_spICategories. The next time the request is made, we return the cached interface instead of re-loading the categories from the database. This optimization works well if the category records in the database do not change often. Depending on your application, you may want your list to be refreshed from the database on every 'get'.

Getting IMembers

Here's the propget code for the IMembers property. Once again, you'll notice that it is very similar to the code for loading categories, right down to the cached interface:

```
    STDMETHOD(get_IMembers)(IMembers** a_ppmm)
    {
        if(a_ppmm == NULL)
            return E_POINTER;
        *a_ppmm = NULL;

        if(!m_spIMembers)
        {
            CMemberDA mda;
            mda.Open();
            CComPtr<IRowset> spIRowset(mda.GetInterface());
            CComPtr<IPersistRowset> spIPersistRowset;

            HRESULT hr;
            hr = spIPersistRowset.CoCreateInstance(CLSID_Members);
            if(FAILED(hr))
                return hr;

            hr = spIPersistRowset->Load(spIRowset);
            if(FAILED(hr))
                return hr;
```

```
        hr = spIPersistRowset.QueryInterface(a_ppmm);
        if(SUCCEEDED(hr))
        {
            m_spIMembers = *a_ppmm;
            return S_OK;
        }
        else
            return hr;
    }
    else
        return m_spIMembers.CopyTo(a_ppmm);
}
```

Implementing Alternate Identities

Before I show you the next interface, let me introduce the general technique that I'll be using to implement alternate identities.

What constitutes a COM identity? According to the rules of COM, it is the IUnknown pointer. At a minimum, therefore, we need a separate IUnknown pointer for each identity. Is this sufficient? Clearly not, since the QI() for each identity can only reveal the interfaces that belong to that identity, *not* all the interfaces that are implemented by the object. We therefore need a separate QI() implementation for each identity. Also, every interface exposed by that identity has to have the same, separate QI() implementation. This implies that we actually require a vtable per interface per identity. Thus, if the interface IA belongs to the primary identity (which is numbered zero), as well as alternates one and three, we'll need three vtables for IA, one to accommodate the QI() for each identity it appears in.

How about AddRef() and Release()? Are there any requirements here? Actually there is one: All identities have to access the *same* reference count to avoid premature deletion of the object.

The simplest way to accommodate all these requirements within the ATL framework is to create a separate interface per identity. Each identity has its own QI() implementation, but they all share the same AddRef() and Release() implementations.

Let me show you how these ideas actually play out in ATL by displaying the CAuction class. Recall from my class diagram that the Auction COM class consists of a primary identity and two alternate identities, one each for the ILotFinder and IAuctionUIElements interfaces. In the following code, the highlighted areas correspond to my ATL extensions for alternate identities (see Appendix B). The remaining portions constitute a standard ATL implementation of the primary identity of the class:

```
DEFINE_AUCTIONUIELEMENTS(1)
DEFINE_LOTFINDER(2)

class ATL_NO_VTABLE CAuction :
    public CComObjectRootEx<CComSingleThreadModel>,
    public CComCoClass<CAuction, &CLSID_Auction>,
    public ISupportErrorInfo,
    public IDispatchImpl<
        IAuctionScript, &IID_IAuctionScript, &LIBID_WroxAuction>,
    public IDispatchImpl<ILotFinder, &IID_ILotFinder, &LIBID_WroxAuction>,
    public IDispatchImpl<
        IAuctionUIElements, &IID_IAuctionUIElements, &LIBID_WroxAuction>,
```

```
      public ISupportErrorInfoID1,
      public IDispatchImpl<
         IAuctionUIElementsID1, &IID_IAuctionUIElements, &LIBID_WroxAuction>,

      public ISupportErrorInfoID2,
      public IDispatchImpl<ILotFinderID2, &IID_ILotFinder, &LIBID_WroxAuction>
   {
   public:
      CAuction()
      {
      }

   DECLARE_NOT_AGGREGATABLE_MI(CAuction, CComObjectID2)
   DECLARE_CLASSFACTORY_SINGLETON_EX(CAuction, 2)

   DECLARE_REGISTRY_RESOURCEID(IDR_AUCTION)
   DECLARE_PROTECT_FINAL_CONSTRUCT()

   BEGIN_COM_MAP(CAuction)
      COM_INTERFACE_ENTRY2(IDispatch, IAuctionScript)
      COM_INTERFACE_ENTRY(IAuctionScript)
      COM_INTERFACE_ENTRY(ISupportErrorInfo)
      COM_INTERFACE_ENTRY(ILotFinder)
      COM_INTERFACE_ENTRY(IAuctionUIElements)
   END_COM_MAP()

   BEGIN_COM_MAP2(CAuction,1)
      COM_INTERFACE_ENTRY2(IDispatch, IAuctionUIElementsID1)
      COM_INTERFACE_ENTRY(IAuctionUIElementsID1)
      COM_INTERFACE_ENTRY(ISupportErrorInfoID1)
   END_COM_MAP2(1)

   BEGIN_COM_MAP2(CAuction,2)
      COM_INTERFACE_ENTRY2(IDispatch, ILotFinderID2)
      COM_INTERFACE_ENTRY(ILotFinderID2)
      COM_INTERFACE_ENTRY(ISupportErrorInfoID2)
   END_COM_MAP2(2)

   BEGIN_IDENTITY_MAP(2)
      COM_IDENTITY_ENTRY(1)
      COM_IDENTITY_ENTRY(2)
   END_IDENTITY_MAP
```

Declaring the Interfaces

The first highlighted area consists of two macros; each is declaring an alternate identity for an interface. Thus:

```
DEFINE_AUCTIONUIELEMENTS(1)
```

is declaring the interface IAuctionUIElementsID1, the variant on IAuctionUIElements that is designed to work with alternate identity 1. Similarly:

```
DEFINE_LOTFINDER(2)
```

declares ILotFinderID2, the version of ILotFinder that works with alternate identity 2. No variant on ILotfinder is declared that will work with identity 1. Likewise, there is no variation of IAuctionUIElements that will work with identity 2.

For more information on (and expansions of) these particular macros, see the section in Appendix B under the heading *Interface Declarations*.

Adding the Interfaces to the Alternate Identity List

The next highlighted area shows how these interfaces have been included in the inheritance list for the ATL class. Essentially, each identity requires its interfaces to be included in this list. This is required to generate the appropriate vtable entries.

Declaring the Class Object

The following highlighted area shows the declaration of the class factory. Essentially, a new variant on CComObject<> has to be created that works with objects implementing alternate identities. Ordinarily this would be sufficient, but because the implementation of singleton class factories in ATL is a little different from other class factories, we need to specialize the declaration of singleton class factories to work with alternate identities. Again, the details of this can be found in Appendix B.

Multiple COM Maps

Here's the part that makes life easy and allows for multiple implementations of QI(). Each identity has its own COM map. To allow for this, I've created the _COM_MAP2() macros. BEGIN_COM_MAP2() and the END_COM_MAP2() each take an extra parameter (over the equivalent regular COM_MAP() macros) that specifies the identity whose COM map is being created.

The individual entries in each COM map look exactly like the individual entries in the primary COM map. There is one entry for each interface that will be exposed by QI(). Thus:

```
BEGIN_COM_MAP2(CAuction, 1)
    COM_INTERFACE_ENTRY2(IDispatch, IAuctionUIElementsID1)
    COM_INTERFACE_ENTRY(IAuctionUIElementsID1)
    COM_INTERFACE_ENTRY(ISupportErrorInfoID1)
END_COM_MAP2(1)
```

indicates the COM map for alternate identity 1. It consists of the versions of interfaces IAuctionUIElements and ISupportErrorInfo for identity 1, and it also implements IDispatch by exposing IAuctionUIElements. (This was the original reason for the use of AI: to expose different IDispatch interfaces to script clients, even though they were implemented on the same object).

The next COM map then declares the interfaces for alternate identity 2, and as usual the details of how this works can be found in Appendix B.

The Identity Map

Finally, there is a new map – the identity map – that has an entry identifying each alternate identity that is being exported by this object. In this case, it specifies that the object has two alternate identities.

> You'll notice that I've implemented my ATL extensions in the same spirit as ATL itself – as table-driven implementations with "MAGIC_MACROS". This is in keeping with the philosophy of attribute-based programming upon which ATL (and previously MFC) is based.

I do believe that the table driven approach simplifies the implementation of boilerplate functionality. However, I do *not* believe that it can be used blindly, and in particular I do not believe it is the correct approach to enable neophyte programmers to create working code (Visual Basic/VBScript is a much better option if that is the goal). I think of it as a way of enabling experienced programmers to be more productive.

Exposing Alternate Identities

If you use this class to implement a COM object, and then access this object using the usual COM mechanisms (`CoCreateInstance()` or `CoGetClassObject()`), you will never see any of the alternate identities. The only identity that is normally visible is the primary identity of the object. This is as it should be.

By the same token, if you have an alternative identity, there is no way of getting to any other identity, including the primary identity. Again, this is as it should be.

Special steps need to be taken to expose alternate identities from the implementation. Let me illustrate this by showing you the implementation of `IAuctionScript`.

IAuctionScript

Here is the declaration of the default interface on `Auction`:

```
interface IAuctionScript : IDispatch
{
    [propget, id(2), helpstring("ILotFinder")]
    HRESULT ILotFinder([out, retval] ILotFinder** a_pplf);

    [propget, id(3), helpstring("IAuctionUIElements")]
    HRESULT IAuctionUIElements([out, retval] IAuctionUIElements** a_pplf);
};
```

Recall that the individual properties of this interface are a mechanism for exposing the corresponding interfaces to scripting clients, one of the primary motivators for using alternate identities. It is clear that we need to expose the alternate identities when these properties are called. How do we do this? Let's examine the implementation of the `ILotFinder` propget method:

```
STDMETHOD(get_ILotFinder)(ILotFinder** a_pplf)
{
    if(a_pplf == NULL)
        return E_POINTER;

    HRESULT hr = QueryInterface2(
                        IID_ILotFinder, reinterpret_cast<void**>(a_pplf));
    ATLASSERT(SUCCEEDED(hr));
    return hr;
}
```

All this does is perform a `QI()` for the `ILotFinder` interface. However, instead of using straight `QI()`, it's using a method called `QueryInterface2()`. This method is the `QI()` that is associated with identity 2 of the object, the identity on which `ILotFinder` is the `IDispatch` method. If `QI2()` requests an interface that is not part of ID 2, it will fail.

In a similar fashion, the implementation of the `IAuctionUIElements` propget method:

```
STDMETHOD(get_IAuctionUIElements)(IAuctionUIElements** a_ppau)
{
   if(a_ppau == NULL)
      return E_POINTER;

   HRESULT hr = QueryInterface1(
                     IID_IAuctionUIElements, reinterpret_cast<void**>(a_ppau));
   ATLASSERT(SUCCEEDED(hr));
   return hr;
}
```

simply uses `QueryInterface1()`, the `QI()` associated with identity 1 to return the `IAuctionUIElement` interface associated with that identity.

The CategoryCache Class

Now, let's move on to the next class in the implementation. This is the `CategoryCache` class, with this declaration:

```
coclass CategoryCache
{
   [default] interface ICategories;
   interface IPersistRowset;

   interface ISupportErrorInfo;
};
```

This is a collection class that holds a collection of categories and their associated IDs. It exposes the collection via the `ICategories` interface and persists itself to a rowset using `IPersistRowset`.

Object State

The only member variable in the `CCategoryCache` class is:

```
vector<DescAndID> m_cIDD;
```

This is an STL `vector<>` designed to hold the collection of strings and IDs. Each element of the vector has the type:

```
struct DescAndID
{
   LONG       m_vlID;
   CComBSTR m_vstrDescription;
};
```

ICategories

Here is the declaration of ICategories:

```
interface ICategories : IDispatch
{
    [propget, id(DISPID_VALUE), helpstring("Item")]
    HRESULT Item([in] LONG a_vlIndex, [out, retval] BSTR* a_pstr);

    [propget, id(DISPID_NEWENUM), helpstring("_NewEnum"), restricted]
    HRESULT _NewEnum([out, retval] LPUNKNOWN* a_punk);

    [propget, id(1), helpstring("Count")]
    HRESULT Count([out, retval] LONG* a_pl);

    [id(2), helpstring("GetItemID")]
    HRESULT GetItemID([in] LONG a_vlIndex, [out, retval] LONG* a_pl);

    [id(3), helpstring("Category Lookup")]
    HRESULT ID2Category([in] LONG a_vl, [out, retval] BSTR* a_pstr);

    [id(4), helpstring("ID Lookup")]
    HRESULT Category2ID([in] BSTR a_pstr, [out, retval] LONG* a_pl);

    [id(5), helpstring("GetStringAndID")]
    HRESULT GetStringAndID(
                    [in] LONG a_vlIndex, [out] LONG* a_pl, [out] BSTR* a_pstr);
};
```

Let's look at the implementation of each of these members. First up is the propget method of the Item property:

```
STDMETHOD(get_Item)(LONG a_vlIndex, BSTR* a_pstr)
{
    if(a_pstr == NULL)
        return E_POINTER;
    *a_pstr = 0;

    if(a_vlIndex < 0 || a_vlIndex >= m_cIDD.size())
        return E_INVALIDARG;
    return m_cIDD[a_vlIndex].m_vstrDescription.CopyTo(a_pstr);
}
```

As you can see, after checking that the index is valid, the method simply returns a copy of the string that is at the requested index in the STL vector<>. Why a copy? Because the a_pstr parameter is out-only. As I said in Chapter 3, this means the caller is required to free the returned memory. If the *original* string were to be returned, the caller (or stub) would free it, thereby creating a dangling-pointer problem on the server.

The _NewEnum propget method is not implemented, largely because it doesn't serve any instructional purpose to do so here. Don't worry: I'll get into enumerator interfaces in gory detail shortly, in another context.

```
STDMETHOD(get__NewEnum)(LPUNKNOWN* a_punk)
{
    return E_NOTIMPL;
}
```

Here is the implementation of the propget method for the Count property. As you can see, it simply returns the current size of the STL vector<> that holds the collection:

```
STDMETHOD(get_Count)(LONG* a_pl)
{
    if(a_pl == NULL)
        return E_POINTER;

    *a_pl = m_cIDD.size();
    return S_OK;
}
```

The GetItemID() method is very similar to the propget method for the Item property, except that it retrieves the item ID rather than the item string:

```
STDMETHOD(GetItemID)(LONG a_vlIndex, LONG* a_pl)
{
    if(a_pl == NULL)
        return E_POINTER;

    if(a_vlIndex < 0 || a_vlIndex >= m_cIDD.size())
        return E_INVALIDARG;
    *a_pl = m_cIDD[a_vlIndex].m_vlID;
    return S_OK;
}
```

The ID2Category() and Category2ID() methods are quite similar to each other. They each iterate through the collection looking for a match and returning the requested category or ID:

```
STDMETHOD(ID2Category)(LONG a_vl, BSTR* a_pstr)
{
    if(a_pstr == NULL)
        return E_POINTER;

    vector<DescAndID>::iterator pIDD;
    for(pIDD = m_cIDD.begin(); pIDD < m_cIDD.end(); pIDD++)
    {
        if(pIDD->m_vlID == a_vl)
        {
            pIDD->m_vstrDescription.CopyTo(a_pstr);
            return S_OK;
        }
    }
    return E_INVALIDARG;
}
```

```
STDMETHOD(Category2ID)(BSTR a_vstr, LONG* a_pl)
{
    if(a_pl == NULL)
        return E_POINTER;

    vector<DescAndID>::iterator pIDD;
    for(pIDD = m_cIDD.begin(); pIDD < m_cIDD.end(); pIDD++)
    {
        if(pIDD->m_vstrDescription == a_vstr)
        {
            *a_pl = pIDD->m_vlID;
            return S_OK;
        }
    }
    return E_INVALIDARG;
}
```

Notice the use of STL iterators to iterate over STL vectors. Other than this, these are pretty straightforward methods.

Finally, the `GetStringAndID()` method is a combination of the `propget` method for `Item` and the `GetItemID` method:

```
STDMETHOD(GetStringAndID)(LONG a_vlIndex, LONG* a_pl, BSTR* a_pstr)
{
    if(a_pl == NULL || a_pstr == NULL)
        return E_POINTER;

    *a_pstr = 0;
    if(a_vlIndex < 0 || a_vlIndex >= m_cIDD.size())
        return E_INVALIDARG;

    *a_pl = m_cIDD[a_vlIndex].m_vlID;
    return m_cIDD[a_vlIndex].m_vstrDescription.CopyTo(a_pstr);
}
```

What makes these methods almost trivial to implement is the STL `vector<>` data member. All the hard work of maintaining the collection is being done by STL; we simply use the results. This is very much as it should be.

IPersistRowset

Here is the declaration of `IPersistRowset`:

```
interface IPersistRowset : IUnknown
{
    typedef IPersistRowset* LPPERSISTROWSET;

    HRESULT InitNew(void);
    HRESULT Load([in] IRowset* pRowset);
    HRESULT Save([in] IRowset* pRowset, [in] BOOL fClearDirty);
    HRESULT IsDirty(void);
};
```

Recall that this is the interface we used to initialize our `Categories` object from the database. In the current implementation, I only implement the `Load()` method, since that is the only one required by the use case. Here it is:

```
STDMETHOD(Load)(IRowset* pRowset)
{
    USES_CONVERSION;
    HRESULT hr;

    IAccessor* pAccessor;
    hr = pRowset->QueryInterface(
                        IID_IAccessor, reinterpret_cast<void**>(&pAccessor));
    pAccessor->Release();
    if(FAILED(hr))
        return hr;

    CAccessor<CCategoriesAccessor> acc;
    hr = acc.BindColumns(pRowset);
    if(FAILED(hr))
        return hr;

    CRowset rs(pRowset);
    rs.SetAccessor(&acc);

    hr = rs.MoveFirst();
    if(FAILED(hr))
        return hr;

    long i = 0;
    for(; hr == S_OK; i++)
    {
        DescAndID idd;
        idd.m_vlID = acc.m_CatID;
        idd.m_vstrDescription = T2W(acc.m_CatDescription);
        m_cIDD.push_back(idd);
        hr = rs.MoveNext();
        if(FAILED(hr))
            return hr;
    }
    return S_OK;
}
```

This code is fairly interesting because I'm combining the Wizard-generated OLE DB code with some undocumented (but public) functionality of the ATL OLE DB support classes.

To begin with, the code extracts the `IAccessor` interface of the incoming `IRowset` parameter to ensure that the interface is implemented. This interface is then bound to the Wizard-generated C++ accessor class (I'll show that to you in a minute) using its `BindColumns()` method. This code would fail if the incoming rowset were not compatible with the accessor, and that's the reason for the above check. Of course, we *know* that this will be OK here because we've seen the client code, but in general that wouldn't be the case.

Next, we associate the rowset with the ATL `CRowset` class, and associate the ATL accessor class with `CRowset`.

Finally, we can use the CRowset methods MoveFirst() and MoveNext() to iterate over the rows one at a time – the accessor is bound to the fields of the current row in the rowset. The values in these fields are copied into the accessor's member variables (m_CatID and m_CatDescription), and they are then bundled together and inserted into the m_cIDD member vector. I should point out that the T2W() macro (whose use is enabled by the USES_CONVERSION macro earlier in the code) converts TCHAR strings to the WCHAR strings expected by the CComBSTR<> constructor.

To finish off, let's take a quick look at the Wizard-generated accessor class for Categories:

```
class CCategoriesAccessor
{
public:
    LONG m_CatID;
    TCHAR m_CatDescription[51];

BEGIN_COLUMN_MAP(CCategoriesAccessor)
    COLUMN_ENTRY(1, m_CatID)
    COLUMN_ENTRY(2, m_CatDescription)
END_COLUMN_MAP()

// You may wish to call this function if you are inserting a record and wish
// to initialize all the fields, if you are not going to explicitly set all
// of them.
    void ClearRecord()
    {
        memset(this, 0, sizeof(*this));
    }
};
```

Unsurprisingly, this is very similar to the accessor class for Lots that I described earlier on.

The Members Class

The Members class is another collection class that can be loaded from an OLE DB rowset. Here is its declaration:

```
coclass Members
{
    [default] interface IMembers;
    interface IPersistRowset;

    interface ISupportErrorInfo;
};
```

Object State

Like the CategoryCache class that we just looked at, the CMembers class maintains its collection as an STL vector. In this case, since the class is a collection of COM interfaces, the type of the vector is a smart pointer to IMemberScript (the default interface of the Member class). Here is the declaration of the member variable:

```
vector<CComPtr<IMemberScript> > m_cmem;
```

IMembers

The collection interface of the `Members` class is `IMembers`. Here is its declaration:

```
interface IMembers : IDispatch
{
    [propget, id(DISPID_VALUE), helpstring("Item")]
    HRESULT Item([in] LONG a_vlIndex, [out, retval] IMemberScript** a_pstr);

    [propget, id(DISPID_NEWENUM), helpstring("_NewEnum"), restricted]
    HRESULT _NewEnum([out, retval] LPUNKNOWN* a_punk);

    [propget, id(1), helpstring("Count")]
    HRESULT Count([out, retval] LONG* a_pl);
};
```

The implementation of the methods is very similar to that shown for the `CategoryCache` class. The only member that is of some interest is the `propget` method for the `Item` property, since it is returning a COM interface rather than a value. Here is its implementation:

```
STDMETHOD(get_Item)(LONG a_vlIndex, IMemberScript** a_ppms)
{
    if(a_ppms == NULL)
        return E_POINTER;
    *a_ppms = 0;
    if(a_vlIndex < 0 || a_vlIndex >= m_cmem.size())
        return E_INVALIDARG;

    return m_cmem[a_vlIndex].CopyTo(a_ppms);
}
```

As you can see, there is a `CopyTo()` method on the smart pointer class. This returns the interface after calling `AddRef()` on it, thus incrementing the reference count.

The remaining methods are close enough to their counterparts in `ICategories` that it isn't worth showing them here.

IPersistRowset

Next, let's take a look at the implementation of `IPersistRowset`. This is somewhat similar to the implementation of `IPersistRowset` on the `CategoryCache` class, but the construction of objects adds enough additional complexity to make it worth a second look. Once again, `Load()` is the only method that is implemented:

```
STDMETHOD(Load)(IRowset* pRowset)
{
    USES_CONVERSION;
    HRESULT hr;
    IAccessor* pAccessor;
    hr = pRowset->QueryInterface(
        IID_IAccessor,
        reinterpret_cast<void**>(&pAccessor));
    pAccessor->Release();
    if(FAILED(hr))
        return hr;
```

```
CAccessor<CMemAccessor> acc;
hr = acc.BindColumns(pRowset);
if(FAILED(hr))
    return hr;

CRowset rs(pRowset);
rs.SetAccessor(&acc);

CComPtr<IMemberConstruct> spIMemberConstruct;
hr = CoGetClassObject(
    CLSID_Member,
    CLSCTX_SERVER,
    NULL,
    IID_IMemberConstruct,
    reinterpret_cast<void**>(&spIMemberConstruct));
if(FAILED(hr))
    return hr;

hr = rs.MoveFirst();
if(FAILED(hr))
    return hr;

long i = 0;
for(; hr == S_OK; i++)
{
    CComPtr<IMemberScript> spIMemberScript;
    CComBSTR first(T2W(acc.m_FirstName));
    CComBSTR last(T2W(acc.m_LastName));
    CComBSTR city(T2W(acc.m_City));
    CComBSTR state(T2W(acc.m_State));
    hr = spIMemberConstruct->CreateMember(
        acc.m_MemberID,
        first,
        last,
        city,
        state,
        IID_IMemberScript,
        reinterpret_cast<IUnknown**>(&spIMemberScript));
    if(FAILED(hr))
        return hr;

    m_cmem.push_back(spIMemberScript);

    hr = rs.MoveNext();
    if(FAILED(hr))
        return hr;
}
    return S_OK;
}
```

The OLE DB wrapper functionality in this example is almost identical to that in the previous section. The accessor is extracted from the rowset and bound to the Wizard-generated C++ accessor class. A CRowset object is then created and bound to this accessor, and the rowset is iterated over using the MoveFirst() and MoveNext() methods.

What's new about this method is that it is constructing new Member objects, which are COM objects rather than scalar values. In order to construct these objects, the method requests the IMemberConstruct constructor interface on the class object for the Member class. This interface is then used within the loop to construct (create and initialize) a number of Member objects, using the values extracted from records in the rowset. After the object is created, its IMemberScript interface is added to the collection vector.

Note the use of the CComBSTR variables to extract BSTR values from the accessor. You might want to pass the BSTR values directly into the constructor call to save some cycles, but I've separated the operation into two steps to keep the code structure simple. The Wizard-generated C++ accessor to the Members collection is called CMemAccessor, but its structure is so similar to the accessors you've already seen that I shall say no more about it here. If you want to take a look, it's defined in the memDA.h header file that comes with the source code.

The Lots Class

The Lots class is very similar to the Members class in its implementation:

```
coclass Lots
{
    [default] interface ILots;
    interface IPersistRowset;

    interface ISupportErrorInfo;
};
```

ILots

In fact, the implementation of the collection interface:

```
interface ILots : IDispatch
{
    [propget, id(DISPID_VALUE), helpstring("Item")]
    HRESULT Item([in] LONG a_vlIndex, [out, retval] ILotScript** a_pplt);

    [propget, id(DISPID_NEWENUM), helpstring("_NewEnum"), restricted]
    HRESULT _NewEnum([out, retval] LPUNKNOWN* a_punk);

    [propget, id(1), helpstring("Count")]
    HRESULT Count([out, retval] LONG* a_pl);
};
```

is so similar to the Members collection implementation that I will not display it.

IPersistRowset

You're probably used to this pattern by now. The only implemented method of IPersistRowset is Load(), and once again it has a few noteworthy differences from the method in Members of the same name:

```
STDMETHOD(Load)(IRowset* pRowset)
{
    USES_CONVERSION;
    HRESULT hr;
    IAccessor* pAccessor;
```

```
hr = pRowset->QueryInterface(
   IID_IAccessor,
   reinterpret_cast<void**>(&pAccessor));
pAccessor->Release ();
if(FAILED(hr))
   return hr;

CAccessor<CLotAccessor> acc;
hr = acc.BindColumns(pRowset);
if(FAILED(hr))
   return hr;

CRowset rs(pRowset);
   rs.SetAccessor(&acc);

CComPtr<ILotConstruct> spILotConstruct;
hr = CoGetClassObject (
   CLSID_Lot,
   CLSCTX_SERVER,
   NULL,
   IID_ILotConstruct,
   reinterpret_cast<void**>(&spILotConstruct));
if(FAILED(hr))
   return hr;

hr = rs.MoveFirst();
if(FAILED(hr))
   return hr;

long i = 0;
for(; hr == S_OK; i++)
{
   CComPtr<ILot> spILot;
   CDateTime dt(acc.m_colClosesAt);
   CComBSTR desc(T2W(acc.m_colDescription));
   CComBSTR name(T2W(acc.m_colMoniker));
   hr = spILotConstruct->CreateLot(
      acc.m_colLotID,
      desc,
      acc.m_colCatID,
      acc.m_colStartPrice,
      acc.m_colIncrement,
      static_cast<time_t>(dt),
      name,
      IID_ILot,
      reinterpret_cast<IUnknown**>(&spILot));
   if(FAILED(hr))
      return hr;

   m_clot.push_back(spILot);

   hr = rs.MoveNext();
   if(FAILED(hr))
      return hr;
}
return S_OK;
}
```

The OLE-DB interfaces are being used in a familiar way. Just as in the Load() method of Members, we use the "constructor interface on class object" technique. The retrieved constructor interface is used to crank out a number of objects that are initialized to the persisted state stored in the database.

One new thing that we have to deal with in this example is the SQL date type, which is used to store the auction close time for the lot. It is returned as a variable of OLE DB type DBTIMESTAMP. Within the server, I have used a modified version of the CDateTime class, which was first implemented by Sing Li and Panos Economopoulos in *Professional COM Applications with ATL*, although my version allows a few more conversions than the original.

The Lot Class

The Lot class is probably the single most complex class in the server implementation. Here is its declaration:

```
coclass Lot
{
    [default] interface ILotScript;
    interface ILot;
    interface ILotInitialize;
    interface IBidValidate;
    interface IAuctionInfo;

    interface IFinishInit;

    interface ISupportErrorInfo;
};
```

Since the design stage, I've added one additional interface – IFinishInit – that is required for implementation. This is a sink interface for the composed Bids object to signal completion of initialization.

You may recall from the design discussion that the Lot class had to expose not just alternate identities, but also a weak identity.

Object State

It shouldn't come as any surprise that a Lot object has a fairly substantial object state. It implements the following member variables:

```
public:
    unsigned              m_bRequiresSave:1;

private:
    CComPtr<IUnknown>   m_spBidsIUnknown;
    CComPtr<IBidsInfo>  m_spIBidsInfo;

    // Auction Info
    LONG                 m_vlLotID;
    LONG                 m_vlCategory;
    LONG                 m_vlClosesAt;
    LONG                 m_vlStartPrice;
    LONG                 m_vlBidIncrement;
    CComBSTR             m_vstrDescription;
    CComBSTR             m_vstrNameString;
```

The `m_bRequiresSave` field is required by various ATL persistence interfaces. In addition, `m_spBidsIUnknown` and `m_spIBidsInfo` are used to keep track of the `Bids` collection that's associated with the `Lot` object.

The remaining member variables are used to keep track of various auction parameters of the lot; they are typically exposed via the `IAuctionInfo` interface.

The Class Factory

Let me begin the examination of the `Lot` class by looking at how it is constructed. The constructor interface for the `Lot` class is `ILotConstruct`:

```
interface ILotConstruct : IDispatch
{
   [id(1), helpstring("Construct Basic Lot")]
   HRESULT CreateLot (
      [in] LONG a_vlLotID,
      [in] BSTR a_vstrDescription,
      [in] LONG a_vlCategory,
      [in] LONG a_vlStartPrice,
      [in] LONG a_vlBidIncrement,
      [in] LONG a_vlClosesAt,
      [in] BSTR a_vstrNameString,
      [in] REFIID a_riid,
      [out, iid_is (a_riid), retval] IUnknown** a_ppuk);
};
```

This interface only has one constructor. In the general case, you would expect to find more methods in this interface, one corresponding to each set of construction parameters.

Rather than being implemented by the `Lot` class itself, this interface is implemented by the class object for the `Lot` class. Since it implements a custom constructor interface, the class object is implemented by the following ATL class, derived from `CComClassFactory<>`:

```
class CLotCO :
   public CComClassFactory,
   public IDispatchImpl<ILotConstruct, &IID_ILotConstruct, &LIBID_WroxAuction>
{
public:
BEGIN_COM_MAP(CLotCO)
   COM_INTERFACE_ENTRY(IClassFactory)
   COM_INTERFACE_ENTRY(IDispatch)
   COM_INTERFACE_ENTRY(ILotConstruct)
END_COM_MAP()

   STDMETHOD(CreateLot)(
      LONG a_vlLotID,
      BSTR a_vstrDescription,
      LONG a_vlCategory,
      LONG a_vlStartPrice,
      LONG a_vlBidIncrement,
      LONG a_vlClosesAt,
      BSTR a_vstrNameString,
      REFIID a_viid,
      IUnknown** a_ppuk)
   {
```

```
        if(a_ppuk == NULL)
            return E_POINTER;
        *a_ppuk = NULL;

        HRESULT hr;
        hr = CreateInstance(NULL, a_viid, reinterpret_cast<void**>(a_ppuk));
        if(FAILED(hr))
            return hr;

        CComPtr<ILotInitialize> spILotInitialize;
        hr = (*a_ppuk)->QueryInterface(
                IID_ILotInitialize, reinterpret_cast<void**>(&spILotInitialize));
        ATLASSERT(SUCCEEDED(hr));

        return spILotInitialize->InitAuctionInfo(
            a_vlLotID,
            a_vstrDescription,
            a_vlCategory,
            a_vlStartPrice,
            a_vlBidIncrement,
            a_vlClosesAt,
            a_vstrNameString);
    }
};
```

As you can see, it creates a `Lot` object by calling the `CreateInstance()` method of the underlying class factory class. This method creates the `Lot` object and returns the requested interface on it. The returned interface is then used to obtain the `ILotInitialize` interface on the newly created object. The `InitAuctionInfo()` method is then used to initialize the object to its constructed state.

Notice that the actual initialization is performed by the `ILotInitialize` interface. Couldn't the user have called it directly? Absolutely! In general, if you don't want the extra work of implementing a custom construction interface on the class object, you can force the client to call an initialization interface such as `ILotInitialize`. However, construction is the safer idiom, since it cannot be misused unintentionally.

ILotInitialize

Here's the declaration for the `ILotInitialize` interface, which currently has only a single initialization method. Just as with constructor interfaces, you would expect an initialization interface to have several initialization methods in the general case:

```
interface ILotInitialize : IDispatch
{
    [id(1), helpstring("Initialize object with basic Lot information")]
    HRESULT InitAuctionInfo(
        [in] LONG a_vlLotID,
        [in] BSTR a_vstrDescription,
        [in] LONG a_vlCategory,
        [in] LONG a_vlStartPrice,
        [in] LONG a_vlBidIncrement,
        [in] LONG a_vlClosesAt,
        [in] BSTR a_vstrNameString);
};
```

Notice that the method signature is almost identical to that in the constructor interface. Typically, you should expect a close correspondence between the initialization and constructor interfaces – the latter are frequently implemented using the former. Here is the implementation of the single method:

```
STDMETHOD(InitAuctionInfo)(
    LONG a_vlLotID,
    BSTR a_vstrDescription,
    LONG a_vlCategory,
    LONG a_vlStartPrice,
    LONG a_vlBidIncrement,
    LONG a_vlClosesAt,
    BSTR a_vstrNameString)
{
    if(m_spBidsIUnknown)
        return E_UNEXPECTED;

    m_vlLotID             = a_vlLotID;
    m_vlCategory          = a_vlCategory;
    m_vlStartPrice        = a_vlStartPrice;
    m_vlBidIncrement      = a_vlBidIncrement;
    m_vlClosesAt          = a_vlClosesAt;
    m_vlLotID             = a_vlLotID;
    m_vstrDescription     = a_vstrDescription;
    m_vstrNameString      = a_vstrNameString;

    HRESULT hr;
    CComPtr<IBidsConstruct> spIBidsConstruct;
    hr = CoGetClassObject(
        CLSID_Bids,
        CLSCTX_SERVER,
        NULL,
        IID_IBidsConstruct,
        reinterpret_cast<void**>(&spIBidsConstruct));
    if(FAILED(hr))
        return hr;

    hr = spIBidsConstruct->CreateBids(
        reinterpret_cast<IUnknown*>(
            static_cast<IUnknownWeak*>(
                static_cast<IAuctionInfoWeak*>(this))),
        IID_IUnknown,
        reinterpret_cast<IUnknown**>(&m_spBidsIUnknown));
    ATLASSERT(SUCCEEDED(hr));
    return S_OK;
}
```

The initialization begins by testing the value of m_spBidsIUnknown. The default value of this member is null; a non-null value indicates that the object has already been initialized, which causes the method to return the E_UNEXPECTED error.

Memory Allocation for [in] BSTRs

The method then carries out a number of assignments of parameters to member variables. The only interesting point here is that two of the member variables are CComBSTRs that are assigned the incoming BSTR parameters. Recall that memory allocation/release for in parameters is the client's responsibility, which means that BSTR assignment to member variables involves creating a new copy of the string (since the incoming BSTR is in memory owned by the caller). This is what happens during the assignment of a BSTR to a CComBSTR. We could also have chosen to implement our member variables as BSTRs instead of CComBSTRs, but in that case the assignment would have required an explicit call to SysAllocString(), with a corresponding call to SysFreeString() in the destructor. The CComBSTR class greatly simplifies the usage of BSTR variables on the server by doing the 'right thing' in most situations.

Constructing a Part/Whole Relationship

The next section of code is also quite interesting, because it illustrates how to construct a part/whole relationship. Referring back to the class diagram, a Lot object is composed of a Bids object.

Normally, such composition would be relatively straightforward: the Lot object would have a member variable that held an interface on the Bids object. Within the ATL framework, the work of creating the Bids object and caching an interface on it would normally occur in the FinalConstruct() method.

However, the FinalConstruct() method is *not* conceptually an appropriate place for this initialization if the object has a construction/initialization interface. This is because FinalConstruct() is called as part of the CreateInstance() sequence, which cannot take any extra parameters that might be required to initialize the sub-object.

In this instance, the creation of the Bids object doesn't really require these extra parameters, so it *could* have been performed in FinalConstruct(). However, I chose to place it in the initialization interface to keep the design 'conceptually' clean. Note that there is no performance penalty for making this choice.

The other twist in this situation is that the Bids object needs a back pointer to the Lot object. (We'll see why this is the case in the next section.) This results in a reference cycle: the Lot object holds a pointer on Bids, and the Bids object holds a pointer on Lot. The best solution for this kind of cross-dependency, as we've seen, is to pass a weak identity to the Bids object.

The next section of code illustrates the construction of this relationship. The Bids object is constructed by the Lot object in the usual way – by means of a constructor interface on the Bids class object. This constructor interface, IBidsConstruct, has a single method called CreateBids() that takes as its first parameter a back pointer to the weak identity of the Lot object. In the next section, we'll see how a weak identity is created.

Implementing a Weak Identity

What are the requirements of implementing weak identities? Just as with alternate identities, we need (at a minimum) a separate IUnknown pointer for the weak identity. This IUnknown will require its own QI(), just as each alternative identity does. Moreover, the weak identity *also* requires its own implementation of AddRef() and Release(). Why is that?

In Chapter 5, we decided that a weak identity must maintain an independent reference count. For the object to destroy itself, both the strong and weak reference counts must be zero. The object initiates its destruction sequence when the strong count goes to zero, and completes it when the weak count goes to zero. Therefore, there have to be separate `AddRef()` and `Release()` implementations to maintain the weak reference count.

This is beginning to look very similar to the situation we had with alternate identities: we need a separate `QI()`, `AddRef()` and `Release()` implementation for the weak identity. Also, every interface exposed by that identity has to have the same, separate `IUnknown` implementation. Once again, this means that we require a vtable per interface in the weak identity. If the interface `IA` belongs to the primary identity as well as the weak identity, we'll need two vtables for `IA`: one to accommodate the `IUnknown` for each identity it appears in.

It shouldn't surprise you that the mechanics for implementing this in ATL turn out to be very similar to the mechanics that I used with alternate identities, and I'll illustrate this with the implementation of weak identity for the `Lot` class. The situation is slightly complicated by the fact that the `Lot` class has to implement several alternative identities *in addition to* implementing the weak identity.

In the following code, which comes from the `CLot` class definition, the highlighted areas correspond to my ATL extensions for weak identity. The rest of the code is standard ATL with my alternate identity extensions.

```
DEFINE_BIDVALIDATE(1)
DEFINE_LOTINITIALIZE(2)
DEFINE_AUCTIONINFO(3)
DEFINE_LOT(4)
DEFINE_AUCTIONINFOWEAK
DEFINE_FINISHINITWEAK

class ATL_NO_VTABLE CLot :
    public CComObjectRootSI<CComSingleThreadModel>,
    public CComCoClass<CLot, &CLSID_Lot>,
    public ISupportErrorInfo,
    public IDispatchImpl<ILot, &IID_ILot, &LIBID_WroxAuction>,
    public IDispatchImpl<IAuctionInfo, &IID_IAuctionInfo, &LIBID_WroxAuction>,
    public IDispatchImpl<
        ILotInitialize, &IID_ILotInitialize, &LIBID_WroxAuction>,
    public IDispatchImpl<IBidValidate, &IID_IBidValidate, &LIBID_WroxAuction>,
    public IDispatchImpl<ILotScript, &IID_ILotScript, &LIBID_WroxAuction>,
    public ISupportErrorInfoID1,
    public IDispatchImpl<IBidValidateID1, &IID_IBidValidate, &LIBID_WroxAuction>,
    public ISupportErrorInfoID2,
    public IDispatchImpl<
        ILotInitializeID2, &IID_ILotInitialize, &LIBID_WroxAuction>,
    public ISupportErrorInfoID3,
    public IDispatchImpl<IAuctionInfoID3, &IID_IAuctionInfo, &LIBID_WroxAuction>,
    public ISupportErrorInfoID4,
    public IDispatchImpl<ILotID4, &IID_ILot, &LIBID_WroxAuction>,
    public IFinishInitWeak,
    public IDispatchImpl<IAuctionInfoWeak, &IID_IAuctionInfo, &LIBID_WroxAuction>
{
public:
    CLot();
    ~CLot();
```

```
    void FinalRelease()
    {
        // Initiate breaking of split identity cycle
        m_spIBidsInfo.Release();
        m_spBidsIUnknown.Release();
    }

DECLARE_NOT_AGGREGATABLE_MI(CLot, CComObjectSIID4)
DECLARE_CLASSFACTORY_EX(CLotCO)

DECLARE_REGISTRY_RESOURCEID(IDR_LOT)
DECLARE_PROTECT_FINAL_CONSTRUCT()

BEGIN_COM_MAP(CLot)
    COM_INTERFACE_ENTRY2(IDispatch, ILotScript)
    COM_INTERFACE_ENTRY(ILot)
    COM_INTERFACE_ENTRY(IAuctionInfo)
    COM_INTERFACE_ENTRY(ILotInitialize)
    COM_INTERFACE_ENTRY(ILotScript)
    COM_INTERFACE_ENTRY(IBidValidate)
    COM_INTERFACE_ENTRY(ISupportErrorInfo)
END_COM_MAP()

BEGIN_COM_MAP2(CLot,1)
    COM_INTERFACE_ENTRY2(IDispatch, IBidValidateID1)
    COM_INTERFACE_ENTRY(IBidValidateID1)
    COM_INTERFACE_ENTRY(ISupportErrorInfoID1)
END_COM_MAP2(1)

BEGIN_COM_MAP2(CLot,2)
    COM_INTERFACE_ENTRY2(IDispatch, ILotInitializeID2)
    COM_INTERFACE_ENTRY(ILotInitializeID2)
    COM_INTERFACE_ENTRY(ISupportErrorInfoID2)
END_COM_MAP2(2)

BEGIN_COM_MAP2(CLot,3)
    COM_INTERFACE_ENTRY2(IDispatch, IAuctionInfoID3)
    COM_INTERFACE_ENTRY(IAuctionInfoID3)
    COM_INTERFACE_ENTRY(ISupportErrorInfoID3)
END_COM_MAP2(3)

BEGIN_COM_MAP2(CLot,4)
    COM_INTERFACE_ENTRY2(IDispatch, ILotID4)
    COM_INTERFACE_ENTRY(ILotID4)
    COM_INTERFACE_ENTRY(ISupportErrorInfoID4)
END_COM_MAP2(4)

BEGIN_IDENTITY_MAP(4)
    COM_IDENTITY_ENTRY(1)
    COM_IDENTITY_ENTRY(2)
    COM_IDENTITY_ENTRY(3)
    COM_IDENTITY_ENTRY(4)
END_IDENTITY_MAP

BEGIN_COM_MAP_WEAK(CLot)
    COM_INTERFACE_ENTRY(IAuctionInfoWeak)
    COM_INTERFACE_ENTRY(IFinishInitWeak)
END_COM_MAP_WEAK
```

If you look closely at the alternate identity code in the non-highlighted areas, you will realize that no changes are introduced as a result of having to support a weak identity as well. The structure of the remaining code strongly mirrors the equivalent alternate identity code.

Declaring the Interfaces

Each of the macros in the first highlighted area declares a weak identity for the corresponding interface. The two new interfaces are `IFinishInitWeak` and `IAuctionInfoWeak`.

Adding the Interfaces to the Inheritance List

The next highlighted area shows how the weak interfaces are included in the inheritance list. This is done in the most obvious manner, and is required to generate the appropriate vtables.

The FinalRelease() Method

Take a look at the `FinalRelease()` method in the next highlighted area. It contains not one, but two explicit calls to the `Release()` methods of smart pointers. Heresy! You're never supposed to do that! You're *supposed* to let the smart pointer's destructor do the cleanup when it goes out of scope. What's going on here?

The answer lies in the fact that an object with a weak identity has a two-stage destruction process. The object has to initiate destruction when its strong reference count goes to zero, but the destruction can only be completed if the weak reference has also gone to zero. In order for this to happen, any back pointers held by the composed object must also be released, and the only time that a composed object can be released safely is after the destruction process of the composing object has started. The releasing of the composed object eventually initiates the second stage of the composing object's destruction sequence.

This is the purpose of `FinalRelease()`. It is called when the destruction sequence of the outer object is initiated and goes about releasing all the interfaces on the contained object in turn. This generally causes the contained object to be destroyed, releasing the weak identity back pointer. This release causes the weak reference to go to zero, which allows the outer object to be destroyed. At that point, the outer object's destructor gets called.

Declaring the Class Object

The other macro in this highlighted area (`DECLARE_NOT_AGGREGATABLE_MI()`) uses a new variation on `CComObject<>` that implements `IUnknown` for the weak identity and the appropriate methods for alternate identities to work.

The Weak COM Map

Finally, the last highlighted area shows the COM map for the weak identity. It works in the same way as all the other COM maps that we have seen so far. In this example, the weak identity exposes `IAuctionInfoWeak` and `IFinishInit`, an interface that we will see shortly.

Exposing the Weak Identity

As was the case for alternate identities, there is no way for an object of your class to hand out a weak identity accidentally. The only way to hand out a weak identity is to be deliberate about it. In our case, this is done in a piece of code that we've already seen: the following snippet from `ILotInitialize`:

```
hr = spIBidsConstruct->CreateBids(
    reinterpret_cast<IUnknown*>(
        static_cast<IUnknownWeak*>(
            static_cast<IAuctionInfoWeak*>(this))),
    IID_IUnknown,
    reinterpret_cast<IUnknown**>(&m_spBidsIUnknown));
```

As you can see, the first parameter is passing in the weak identity. The `this` pointer of the `CLot` class is cast in two steps to the `IUnknownWeak` pointer. The `IUnknownWeak` pointer in turn is reinterpreted as `IUnknown`; this is a safe cast since it has exactly the same vtable structure as `IUnknown`.

Delayed Loading of Bids

You may be wondering why the `Lot` object keeps two smart pointers to the same `Bids` object – one to its `IUnknown` interface, and another to its `IBidsInfo` interface. For the answer, try to remember how lots are used in our use case. The reader initiates a find operation that results in a number of `Lot` objects being displayed in a grid. The bids associated with a lot are not actually made visible until the user double-clicks on an individual lot.

This sequence of operations actually reflects the underlying implementation. The data associated with `Bids` is not loaded until it is specifically requested. This seems to be a sensible design, since its cost structure is pay-as-you-go: the bids are not loaded unless the user actually wants to see them, so the cost of loading bids that the user isn't interested in is never incurred.

However, we've already seen that the `Lot` object creates the `Bids` object in its initialization sequence, so clearly the `Bids` object exists, albeit in an uninitialized state. At what point does the `Bids` object initialize itself? As we'll see later, this happens when you `QI()` for certain interfaces on it. More importantly, how does the `Lot` know if its `Bids` object is in a usable state? This is where the second smart pointer comes in.

Remember that the creation of the `Bids` object in the `Lot` initialization sequence only returned the `IUnknown` pointer on the `Bids` object. This was stored in `m_spBidsIUnknown`. The second smart pointer, `m_spIBidsInfo`, remains null until the `Bids` object has been initialized in one way or another.

As we'll see, the `Bids` object is responsible for initializing itself at the right time, and at this point the value of the `m_spIBidsInfo` pointer needs to change. The question is, who changes it? Clearly, the `Bids` object code that performs the initialization has to *initiate* the change, but that object cannot access a private member variable of the `Lot` object. What it needs is a sink interface on `Lot` that it can use to make a callback, and this is the function of the `IFinishInit` interface that shows up on the weak identity of `Lot`. It is a sink interface implemented by the `Lot` object that is used to assign to the `m_spIBidsInfo` member variable once the `Bids` object has been initialized. Code in the `Bids` object calls back on this interface at the appropriate time.

This sink interface is the same as any other sink interface, so do we need to implement registration of this event? Should we use connection points? In this object model, we have two objects whose implementations are very closely tied – the Bids object cannot even be created without a Lots object. No other object in this model needs to be informed that the Bids object has finished initializing – in fact, it is better if this initialization is completely transparent to every other object. That being the case, we don't really need to implement a generic registration mechanism for this event by means of connectable objects. Instead, we follow an implicit registration protocol with very simple semantics. The event can be fired *at any time* after the Bids object has been constructed with the back pointer. The event can fire at most once (the one time that the Bids object is initialized), at which point the event can be considered unregistered. The Bids object obtains a pointer to the sink interface by QI()'ing the weak identity that was used in its construction.

IFinishInit

Here is the declaration of IFinishInit:

```
interface IFinishInit : IUnknown
{
    [id(1), helpstring("Inform of Completed Initialization")]
    HRESULT Complete([in] REFIID a_riid,
                     [in, iid_is(a_riid)] IUnknown* a_piuk);
};
```

As you can see, the interface has been designed to be completely general. When initialization is complete, the source calls the Complete() method, passing in an interface of a late-bound type. This interface can be re-used in a completely generic setting, with or without a registration protocol.

The implementation of IFinishInit looks like this:

```
STDMETHOD(Complete)(REFIID a_riid, IUnknown* a_punk)
{
    ATLASSERT(InlineIsEqualGUID(a_riid, IID_IBidsInfo));
    ATLASSERT(m_spIBidsInfo == 0);
    m_spIBidsInfo = reinterpret_cast<IBidsInfo*>(a_punk);
    return S_OK;
}
```

As you can see, this is extremely simple. The code assigns the incoming interface parameter to its smart pointer member variable. The assertions make certain that

- ❑ The method is not being invoked with the wrong interface type
- ❑ The event has not been fired before

ILot

Let's now turn our attention to what looks like a fairly straightforward interface: ILot. It is declared as follows:

```
interface ILot : IDispatch
{
    [propget, id(1), helpstring("LotInfo")]
    HRESULT Info([out, retval] IAuctionInfo** a_ppai);
```

```
    [propget, id(2), helpstring("Bids")]
    HRESULT Bids([out, retval] IBids** a_ppbd);

    [propget, id(3), helpstring("IPlaceBid")]
    HRESULT IPlaceBid([out, retval] IPlaceBid** a_pppb);
};
```

Once again, the implementation of these properties is almost trivial. Here is the `propget` method for `Info`:

```
STDMETHOD(get_Info)(IAuctionInfo** a_ppai)
{
    if(a_ppai == NULL)
        return E_POINTER;
    *a_ppai = 0;

    return QueryInterface3(IID_IAuctionInfo, reinterpret_cast<void**>(a_ppai));
}
```

As you can see, it simply `QI()`'s for the returned interface on the appropriate alternative identity (ID 3 in this case) and returns the result. The `propget` method for `Bids` is just as simple:

```
STDMETHOD(get_Bids)(IBids** a_ppbd)
{
    if(a_ppbd == NULL)
        return E_POINTER;
    *a_ppbd = 0;

    HRESULT hr = m_spBidsIUnknown.QueryInterface(a_ppbd);
    ATLASSERT(SUCCEEDED(hr));
    return hr;
}
```

Since it is exposing an interface that is implemented as the primary `IDispatch` on a separate object (`Bids`), it simply `QI()`'s the `IUnknown` interface pointer it holds on the `Bids` object for the appropriate `IBids` interface.

The next piece of code is very interesting, because it shows a general technique that is occasionally necessary when dealing with alternate identities. In the previous case, we could simply `QI()` for `IBids` because it was the dispatch interface of the primary identity of the `Bids` object. The implementation of the `propget` method for `IPlaceBid` is complicated by the fact that it is the dispatch interface on an *alternate identity* of the `Bids` object (ID2). A simple `QI()` for `IPlaceBid` would return the correct interface pointer, but on the wrong identity.

```
STDMETHOD(get_IPlaceBid)(IPlaceBid** a_pppb)
{
    if(a_pppb == NULL)
        return E_POINTER;
    *a_pppb = 0;

    HRESULT hr;
    CComPtr<ICOMIdentity> spICOMIdentity;
    hr = m_spBidsIUnknown.QueryInterface(&spICOMIdentity);
    ATLASSERT(SUCCEEDED(hr));
```

```
        CComPtr<IUnknown> spIUnkAltID;
        spICOMIdentity->GetAlternateID(2, &spIUnkAltID);

        hr = spIUnkAltID.QueryInterface(a_pppb);
        ATLASSERT(SUCCEEDED(hr));
        return hr;
    }
```

The solution that you see uses an interface named `ICOMIdentity` that can be used to navigate to a specifically requested alternate identity. The call to the `GetAlternateID()` method on this interface returns the `IUnknown` pointer on the alternate identity. This `IUnknown` interface is then `QI()`'d for `IPlaceBid`. This gives the `IPlaceBid` interface on alternate identity 2, which is the interface that is returned.

IAuctionInfo

Now let us look at the `IAuctionInfo` interface:

```
interface IAuctionInfo : IDispatch
{
    [propget, id(1), helpstring("LotID"), restricted]
    HRESULT LotID([ref, out, retval] LONG* a_vlLotID);

    [propget, id(2), helpstring("Name String"), hidden]
    HRESULT NameString([ref, out, retval] BSTR* a_vstrName);

    [propget, id(3), helpstring("Description")]
    HRESULT Description([ref, out, retval] BSTR* a_pstrDescription);

    [propput, id(3), helpstring("Description"), hidden]
    HRESULT Description([in] BSTR a_vstrDescription);

    [propget, id(4), helpstring("Category")]
    HRESULT Category([ref, out, retval] LONG* a_vlCatID);

    [propget, id(5), helpstring("Starting Price")]
    HRESULT StartPrice([ref, out, retval] LONG* a_vl);

    [propget, id(6), helpstring("Bid Increment")]
    HRESULT BidIncrement([ref, out, retval] LONG* a_vl);

    [propget, id(7), helpstring("Lo Bid")]
    HRESULT LoBid([ref, out, retval] LONG* a_vl);

    [propget, id(8), helpstring("Hi Bid")]
    HRESULT HiBid([ref, out, retval] LONG* a_vl);

    [propget, id(9), helpstring("Auction Closes At")]
    HRESULT ClosesAt([ref, out, retval] DATE* a_vl);

    [propget, id(10), helpstring("Time of Last Bid")]
    HRESULT LastBidAt([ref, out, retval] DATE* a_vl);
};
```

The bulk of these property-accessing methods are implemented as members of the CLot class. For such properties, the implementation simply transfers a value from a member variable to the parameter or vice versa. I'll just show you a handful of these methods with parameters of different types. Remember that incoming, heap-allocated parameters are always getting copied onto the server heap even if that isn't immediately apparent.

```
STDMETHOD(get_LotID)(LONG* a_pl)
{
   if(a_pl == NULL)
      return E_POINTER;
   *a_pl = m_vlLotID;
   return S_OK;
}

STDMETHOD(get_Description)(BSTR* a_pstr)
{
   if(a_pstr == NULL)
      return E_POINTER;
   return m_vstrDescription.CopyTo(a_pstr);
}

STDMETHOD(put_Description)(BSTR a_vstr)
{
   m_vstrDescription = a_vstr;
   return S_OK;
}

STDMETHOD(get_ClosesAt)(DATE* a_pDat)
{
   if(a_pDat == NULL)
      return E_POINTER;
   cDateTime dt = CDateTime(m_vlClosesAt);
   *a_pDat = static_cast<DATE>(dt);
   return S_OK;
}
```

However, there are three properties that are a little unusual because they need to delegate to an interface on the Bids object: these are the properties LoBid, HiBid and LastBidAt. In fact, it ought to be intuitively obvious that these properties are associated with the Bids collection; here is the implementation of the propget method for LoBid:

```
STDMETHOD(get_LoBid)(LONG* a_pl)
{
   if(a_pl == NULL)
      return E_POINTER;

   if(m_spIBidsInfo == 0)
   {
      *a_pl = auctAIBSNoBid;
      return S_OK;
   }
   else
   {
      CComPtr<IBid> spIBid;
      HRESULT hr;
      hr = m_spIBidsInfo->get_LoBid(&spIBid);
```

```
        if(hr != S_OK)
        {
            *a_pl = auctAIBSNoBid;
            return S_OK;
        }
        return spIBid->get_Price(a_pl);
    }
}
```

We're finally using the m_spIBidsInfo smart pointer for something! This code checks to see if the Bids object has been initialized; if not, it simply returns the auctAIBSNoBid enum value to indicate that bid information is not available. If the smart pointer *has* been initialized, however, this code then retrieves the LoBid property of the interface. The value of this property is the IBid interface on the lowest bid, which can be used to retrieve the actual bid price. If the retrieval fails for any reason (usually because the collection is empty) the same auctAIBSNoBid value is returned.

The property-accessing methods for HiBid and LastBidAt have very similar implementations that delegate to the cached IBidsInfo interface.

IBidValidate

For a complete change, we'll look now at an interface that is actually completely straightforward to implement and involves no COM convolutions at all: IBidValidate:

```
interface IBidValidate : IDispatch
{
    [id(1), helpstring("Validate Bid information")]
    HRESULT IsValid1(
        [in] LONG a_vlPrice,
        [in] SHORT a_vsNumber,
        [in] DATE a_vdatTime,
        [out, retval] VARIANT_BOOL* a_pb);

    [id(2), helpstring("Validate Bid information")]
    HRESULT IsValid2 (
        [in] LONG a_vlPrice,
        [in] SHORT a_vsNumber,
        [in] LONG a_vlTime,
        [out, retval] VARIANT_BOOL * a_pb);
};
```

Here is the implementation:

```
STDMETHOD(IsValid1)(LONG a_vlPrice, SHORT a_vsNumber,
                                    DATE a_vdatTime, VARIANT_BOOL* a_pb)
{
    CDateTime dt(a_vdatTime);
    return IsValid2(a_vlPrice, a_vsNumber, static_cast<time_t>(dt), a_pb);
}
```

```
STDMETHOD(IsValid2)(LONG a_vlPrice, SHORT a_vsNumber,
                                    LONG a_vlTime, VARIANT_BOOL* a_pb)
{
    if(a_vlPrice > 0 && a_vsNumber > 0)
    {
        if(a_vlTime <= m_vlClosesAt)
        {
            *a_pb = VARIANT_TRUE;
            return S_OK;
        }
    }
    *a_pb = VARIANT_FALSE;
    return S_FALSE;
}
```

Notice that the first method is implemented by delegating to the second after converting a DATE value to a LONG using the CDateTime class. The second method then performs the basic validation by comparing the inputs against corresponding Lot member variables to determine legitimacy.

A production-quality validation function would return error codes that completely specified the nature of the error, rather than just a TRUE or FALSE value. Note also that the prefix S_ in S_FALSE indicates that it is an HRESULT success code.

ILotScript

The remaining interface on the Lot object that we haven't yet looked at is the default one, ILotScript. It's defined like this:

```
interface ILotScript : IDispatch
{
    [propget, id(1), helpstring("ILot")]
    HRESULT ILot([out, retval] ILot** a_pplt);

    [propget, id(2), helpstring("IBidValidate")]
    HRESULT IBidValidate([out, retval] IBidValidate** a_ppbv);

    [id(3), helpstring("Save Lot info to the named file")]
    HRESULT Copy2File(BSTR FileName);
};
```

Like the other interfaces whose names end in 'Script', its purpose is to serve as a navigational interface for scripting clients. To this end, it exposes ILot and IBidValidate using the "property get as QI()" idiom. You've already seen how such an implementation works for the IAuctionScript interface, so I will not go into the details again here.

The third method on this interface, Copy2File(), is a utility method for persisting the lot to a named file. It is not derived from the use case analysis, and is placed in this interface largely for convenience. In a production system it would probably be placed in a completely separate utility interface.

The Bids Class

I've been alluding to the Bids class throughout the latter half of the material on Lots, so it's about time we tackled it properly. Here's its definition in IDL:

```
coclass Bids
{
   [default] interface IBids;
   interface IPlaceBid;
   interface IBidsInfo;
   interface IBidsCustom;

   interface IPersistStream;
   interface IPersistStreamInit;
   interface IPersistPropertyBag;

   interface ISupportErrorInfo;
};
```

Object State

So far, we've been kicking off our discussions by examining the object states of the implementing class, and with no compelling reason to change, here are the member variables of the CBids class:

```
public:
   unsigned              m_bRequiresSave:1;   // IsDirty Bit

private:
   LONG                  m_vlLastBidAt;       // Time of Last Bid
   vector<CComPtr<IBid> > m_cbid;             // IBid* collection

   CComPtr <IUnknown>    m_spIUnknownParent;  // Back Pointer
   bool                  m_bInit;             // Is Initalized?

   bool                  m_bSorted;           // Is Sorted Collection UpToDate
   vector<CComPtr<IBid> > m_cbidOrdered;      // Sorted Collection
```

Lazy Initialization

One of the most interesting features of the Bids class is its initialization-on-demand implementation. The actual collection of Bid objects associated with the Bids class is not loaded until the Bids object is requested to do something that requires it to be initialized.

There are a large number of techniques for performing lazy initialization, but the one that I use is the one that I mentioned in Chapter 5. This technique delays initialization until an interface is requested that requires the object to have been initialized. The benefit of performing initialization in this manner is that it is possible to centralize the initialization code in the QueryInterface() implementation. The initialization is then performed only when QI() requests one of the interfaces that requires an initialized object. This guarantees that the initialization is performed before any method on such an interface is used.

I am using my own ATL extensions that support lazy initialization. Here is the class declaration for CBids:

```
DEFINE_BIDS(1)
DEFINE_PLACEBID(2)
DEFINE_BIDSINFO(3)

class ATL_NO_VTABLE CBids :
   public CComObjectRootEx<CComSingleThreadModel>,
   public CComCoClass<CBids, &CLSID_Bids>,
```

```
      public IPersistVariantImpl<CBids>,
      public IPersistFile,
      public IPersistStream,
      public IPersistStreamInit,
      public IPersistPropertyBag,
      public ISupportErrorInfo,
      public IBidsCustom,
      public ICOMIdentity,
      public IDispatchImpl<IBidsInfo, &IID_IBidsInfo, &LIBID_WroxAuction>,
      public IDispatchImpl<IBidsInfoID3, &IID_IBidsInfo, &LIBID_WroxAuction>,
      public IDispatchImpl<IPlaceBid, &IID_IPlaceBid, &LIBID_WroxAuction>,
      public IDispatchImpl<IPlaceBidID2, &IID_IPlaceBid, &LIBID_WroxAuction>,
      public IDispatchImpl<IBids, &IID_IBids, &LIBID_WroxAuction>,
      public IDispatchImpl<IBidsID1, &IID_IBids, &LIBID_WroxAuction>,
      public IDispatchImpl<
          IChildInitialize, &IID_IChildInitialize, &LIBID_WroxAuction>
{
public:
    CBids();
    ~CBids();

DECLARE_NOT_AGGREGATABLE_MI(CBids,CComObjectID3)
DECLARE_CLASSFACTORY_EX(CBidsCO)

DECLARE_REGISTRY_RESOURCEID(IDR_BIDS)
DECLARE_PROTECT_FINAL_CONSTRUCT()

BEGIN_COM_MAP(CBids)
    COM_INTERFACE_ENTRY(ICOMIdentity)
    COM_INTERFACE_ENTRY(IPersistStream)
    COM_INTERFACE_ENTRY(IPersistFile)
    COM_INTERFACE_ENTRY(IPersistStreamInit)
    COM_INTERFACE_ENTRY(IPersistPropertyBag)
    COM_INTERFACE_ENTRY(ISupportErrorInfo)
    COM_INTERFACE_ENTRY(IChildInitialize)
    COM_INTERFACE_ENTRY_DELAY_INIT(IDispatch, 0)
    COM_INTERFACE_ENTRY_DELAY_INIT(IBidsInfo, 0)
    COM_INTERFACE_ENTRY_DELAY_INIT(IPlaceBid, 0)
    COM_INTERFACE_ENTRY_DELAY_INIT(IBids, 0)
    COM_INTERFACE_ENTRY_DELAY_INIT(IBidsCustom, 0)
END_COM_MAP()

BEGIN_COM_MAP2(CBids,1)
    COM_INTERFACE_ENTRY_IID(IID_IUnknown, IBidsID1)
    COM_INTERFACE_ENTRY_DELAY_INIT(IDispatch, 1)
    COM_INTERFACE_ENTRY_DELAY_INIT(IBidsID1, 1)
END_COM_MAP2(1)

BEGIN_COM_MAP2(CBids,2)
    COM_INTERFACE_ENTRY_IID(IID_IUnknown, IPlaceBidID2)
    COM_INTERFACE_ENTRY_DELAY_INIT(IDispatch, 2)
    COM_INTERFACE_ENTRY_DELAY_INIT(IPlaceBidID2, 2)
END_COM_MAP2(2)

BEGIN_COM_MAP2(CBids,3)
    COM_INTERFACE_ENTRY_IID(IID_IUnknown, IBidsInfoID3)
    COM_INTERFACE_ENTRY_DELAY_INIT(IDispatch, 3)
    COM_INTERFACE_ENTRY_DELAY_INIT(IBidsInfoID3, 3)
END_COM_MAP2(3)
```

```
BEGIN_IDENTITY_MAP(3)
   COM_IDENTITY_ENTRY(1)
   COM_IDENTITY_ENTRY(2)
   COM_IDENTITY_ENTRY(3)
END_IDENTITY_MAP
```

The vast bulk of this code implements alternate identities on `CBids`, and is identical is essence to the alternate identity code that I've shown you before. What is new and different is that a few of the entries in each COM map have been modified to use my `COM_INTERFACE_ENTRY_DELAY_INIT()` macro, which identifies an interface entry that participates in lazy initialization. Whenever a `QI()` comes in for one of these entries, the initialization code is run.

In addition, each of the alternate `COM_MAPs` has an explicit entry for `IUnknown`, something you don't normally see in ATL. This is because the ATL `QI()` implementation uses the first entry in a COM map to satisfy a request for `IUnknown`, and unfortunately a `DELAY_INIT()` entry cannot be used for this purpose because it uses the ATL `QI()` thunking architecture.

Minor complications aside, that seems straightforward enough. However, this is only half the story — we still need to specify the initialization and `QI()` code, and that's next on my list of things to explain. Any class that uses a `DELAY_INIT()` map entry *must* implement a static function named `DIQueryInterface()` with the following signature:

```
typedef HRESULT (WINAPI _ATL_CREATORARGFUNC)
   (void* pv, REFIID riid, LPVOID* ppv, DWORD dw);
```

This function hooks into the `QI()` architecture and will get called at the appropriate time. In return, it must perform the initialization and complete the `QI()` operation. Here is the `CBids` implementation:

```
static HRESULT WINAPI DIQueryInterface(void* pv, REFIID iid,
                                       void** ppvObject, DWORD dw)
{
    if(ppvObject == NULL)
       return E_POINTER;
    *ppvObject = NULL;

    CBids* pBids = static_cast<CBids*>(pv);

    _ATL_DELAYINITQIDATA* pcd = reinterpret_cast<_ATL_DELAYINITQIDATA*>(dw);
    LONG vlID = pcd->m_vlID;

    HRESULT hr;
    hr = pBids->DoInit();
    if(FAILED(hr))
       return E_UNEXPECTED;

    if(InlineIsEqualGUID(iid, IID_IBidsCustom))
       *ppvObject = static_cast<IBidsCustom*>(pBids));
    else if(InlineIsEqualGUID(iid, IID_IBids) && (vlID == 0 || vlID == 1))
    {
       if(vlID == 0)
          *ppvObject = static_cast<IBids*>(pBids);
       else
          *ppvObject = static_cast<IBidsID1*>(pBids);
    }
```

```
      else if(InlineIsEqualGUID(iid, IID_IDispatch))
      {
         if(vlID == 0)
            *ppvObject = static_cast<IBids*>(pBids);
         else if(vlID == 1)
            *ppvObject = static_cast<IBidsID1*>(pBids);
         else if(vlID == 2)
            *ppvObject = static_cast<IPlaceBidID2*>(pBids);
         else if(vlID == 3)
            *ppvObject = static_cast<IBidsInfoID3*>(pBids);
         else
            return E_NOINTERFACE;
      }
      else if(InlineIsEqualGUID(iid, IID_IPlaceBid) && (vlID == 0 || vlID == 2))
      {
         if(vlID == 0)
            *ppvObject = static_cast<IPlaceBid*>(pBids);
         else
            *ppvObject = static_cast<IPlaceBidID2*>(pBids);
      }
      else if(InlineIsEqualGUID(iid, IID_IBidsInfo) && (vlID == 0 || vlID == 3))
      {
         if(vlID == 0)
            *ppvObject = static_cast<IBidsInfo*>(pBids);
         else
            *ppvObject = static_cast<IBidsInfoID3*>(pBids);
      }
      else
         return E_NOINTERFACE;

      if(*ppvObject)
         (reinterpret_cast<IUnknown*>(*ppvObject))->AddRef();

      return S_OK;
}
```

This method would have been much simpler if it didn't have to work seamlessly with alternate identities. Here is what it is doing. The first thing it does is cast the void* first parameter into a CBids pointer. This void* pointer is actually a this pointer, and the cast makes this explicit.

The next thing it does is to convert the fourth parameter, dw, into a pointer to an _ATL_DELAYINITQIDATA struct. This struct has the declaration:

```
struct _ATL_DELAYINITQIDATA
{
   LONG m_vlID;
   _ATL_CREATORARGFUNC* m_pFunc;
};
```

The important member here is the m_vlID value, which holds the ID of the alternate identity that is being used in the QI(). This ID is extracted into the local variable vlID.

Next, the method performs the actual initialization by calling the DoInit() method of the CBids class. We'll see what this does shortly.

Finally, the method completes the QI() by returning the requested interface, but there is an added complication here: the returned interface must match the identity that is performing the QI(). That means it cannot just call the 'standard' QI() after performing DoInit(), which is why the vlID value is being tested. This single QI() function is hooked into the QI() implementations of all the identities, and it has to return the correct interface for each identity.

Note especially what the QI() does on a request for IDispatch: depending on which identity is involved, a completely different IDispatch value is returned. Notice also that the method only handles interfaces that are DELAY_INIT(). QI()s for other interfaces never get into this code.

Next, let's take a look at the actual initialization method:

```
HRESULT DoInit()
{
   if(!m_bInit)
   {
      ATLASSERT(m_spIUnknownParent != 0);
      HRESULT hr;

      CComPtr<IAuctionInfo> spIAuctionInfo;
      hr = m_spIUnknownParent.QueryInterface(&spIAuctionInfo);
      ATLASSERT(SUCCEEDED(hr));

      CComPtr<IFinishInit> spIFinishInit;
      hr = m_spIUnknownParent.QueryInterface(&spIFinishInit);
      ATLASSERT(SUCCEEDED(hr));

      CComBSTR str;
      hr = spIAuctionInfo->get_NameString(&str);
      if(FAILED(hr))
         return hr;

      if(str)
      {
         hr = (static_cast<IPersistFile*>(this))->Load(str, 0);
         if(FAILED(hr))
            return hr;
      }
      else
      {
         m_bInit = true;
      }

      IBidsInfo* pIBidsInfo = static_cast<IBidsInfo*>(this);
      pIBidsInfo->AddRef();
      hr = spIFinishInit->Complete(IID_IBidsInfo, pIBidsInfo);
      pIBidsInfo->Release();
      if(FAILED(hr))
         return hr;
   }
   return S_OK;
}
```

As you can see, this method first checks to see if the initialization has already been performed. If so, it does nothing. If not, it goes into the initialization sequence. Essentially, the code retrieves the persisted state of the Bids object from the file that is in the NameString property of the IAuctionInfo interface. The name string is retrieved from the interface, and the IPersistFile interface on the object is used to load the contents of the file into the current object. This serves the purpose of initializing the object.

When initialization is complete, the IFinishInit::Complete() method is called on the sink interface. Notice that we don't actually QI() for the interface passed into the Complete() method. Instead, we use the C++ static_cast<>() operator to get the appropriate interface. However, we still need to call AddRef() and Release() on this interface to ensure compliance with the COM rules.

Persistence Implementation

Next, let me turn to the implementation of persistence for the Bids object. There are two noteworthy points here:

❑ ATL provides persistence support for simple objects that are composed of a fixed number of member variables of a VARIANT type. We'll see this support in the implementation of the next class. However, there is currently *no* ATL support for persisting collections, which is what we must do in this class.

❑ Persistence interfaces are frequently implemented by delegating to another persistence interface, and this code provides a good example of this technique. As you'll see, all the persistence interfaces are implemented by eventually delegating to IPersistStreamInit.

IPersist

The base persistence interface is IPersist. By itself it does next to nothing, simply providing a means of extracting the CLSID of the object that is being persisted. However, all the other standard persistence interfaces derive from it.

```
interface IPersist : IUnknown
{
    typedef [unique] IPersist* LPPERSIST;

    HRESULT GetClassID([out] CLSID* pClassID);
};
```

IPersistStream(Init)

The most widely used persistence interfaces are those that persist to an IStream interface. There are two related interfaces, IPersistStream:

```
interface IPersistStream : IPersist
{
    typedef [unique] IPersistStream* LPPERSISTSTREAM;

    HRESULT IsDirty();
    HRESULT Load([in, unique] IStream* pStm);
    HRESULT Save([in, unique] IStream* pStm, [in] BOOL fClearDirty);
    HRESULT GetSizeMax([out] ULARGE_INTEGER* pcbSize);
};
```

And `IPersistStreamInit`:

```
interface IPersistStreamInit : IPersist
{
    typedef IPersistStreamInit* LPPERSISTSTREAMINIT;

    HRESULT IsDirty();
    HRESULT Load([in] LPSTREAM pStm);
    HRESULT Save([in] LPSTREAM pStm, [in] BOOL fClearDirty);
    HRESULT GetSizeMax([out] ULARGE_INTEGER* pCbSize);
    HRESULT InitNew();
};
```

As you can see, the latter is the same as the former, but with one extra method at the end of its vtable. However, it is not actually derived from the former, so there is no IDL relationship between the two. An implementation of `IPersistStreamInit` serves automatically as an implementation of `IPersistStream` because of the similarity in their vtable structure and interface semantics. It is simply a matter of ensuring that `QI()` associates both IIDs with the same vptr.

We'll now go through the implementation of `IPersistStreamInit` for the `CBids` class. The simplest method is `IsDirty()`, which simply returns the status of the dirty bit `m_bRequiresSave`, translating it into an `HRESULT`:

```
STDMETHOD(IsDirty)()
{
    ATLTRACE2(atlTraceCOM, 0, _T("CBids::IsDirty\n"));
    return m_bRequiresSave ? S_OK : S_FALSE;
}
```

The implementation of `Load()` is more interesting: it reveals the format of the persisted data. First up is the time of last bid value, and after that comes the count of the number of elements in the collection. This is needed so that the correct number of `Bid` objects can be loaded.

```
STDMETHOD(Load)(LPSTREAM pStm)
{
    ATLTRACE2(atlTraceCOM, 0, _T("CBids::Load\n"));

    HRESULT hr;
    ULONG ulRead;
    hr = pStm->Read(
        reinterpret_cast<void*>(&m_vlLastBidAt),
        sizeof(m_vlLastBidAt),
        &ulRead);
    if(FAILED(hr))
        return hr;
    ATLASSERT(ulRead == sizeof(m_vlLastBidAt));

    ULONG ulElements;
    hr = pStm->Read(
        reinterpret_cast<void*>(&ulElements),
        sizeof(ulElements),
        &ulRead);
    if(FAILED(hr))
        return hr;
    ATLASSERT(ulRead == sizeof(ulElements));
    m_cbid.reserve(ulElements);
```

```
    int i;
    for(i = 0; i < ulElements; i++)
    {
        CComPtr<IBidScript> spIBidScript;
        hr = OleLoadFromStream(
            pStm,
            IID_IBidScript,
            reinterpret_cast<void**>(&spIBidScript));
        if(SUCCEEDED(hr))
        {
            Add(spIBidScript);
            continue;
        }
        return hr;
    }
    m_bRequiresSave = FALSE;
    m_bInit = true;
    return S_OK;
}
```

This code is fairly straightforward. The member variable m_vlLastBidAt and the local value ulElements are loaded from the stream using a call to IStream::Read(), a binary method that simply extracts a requested number of bytes from the stream without knowing the interpretation of those bytes. This method (and the corresponding Write() method) is what makes it difficult to implement a portable IPersistStream. A byte stream that can be interpreted as two long values on a specific OS with a specific compiler may be complete garbage when loaded on another. For an IPersistStream(Init) implementation to be portable it must define its own, NDR-style, architecture neutral format and do low-level formatting into this format before saving it into a stream.

The next section of code in the Load() method is also quite interesting. We need to load a sequence of Bid objects that has been serialized into the stream, and rebuild our Bid collection from this sequence.

The loading is performed by the OleLoadFromStream() function of the OLE API, which loads a COM object from the current position in the stream. Think of the implications here: the function has to create the object before loading it. How does it know what type of object to create? This is where the GetClassID() method of IPersist comes in. At the time the object is saved, its class ID is saved at the beginning of its serialized state. OleLoadFromStream() reads this ID, creates an object of the appropriate class, QI()s it for IPersistStream, and then uses *this* interface to finish the load. The only requirement is that the class *has* to implement IPersistStream (IPersistStreamInit doesn't work).

The code enters a loop where it loads ulElements Bid objects from the stream, requesting the IBidScript interface from each loaded object. This interface is then inserted into the Bids collection using the Add() method. When the loop is done, the load is complete. It resets the status variables m_bRequiresSave and m_bInit, and returns.

The counterpart of the Load() method is the Save() method. It stores the state of the Bids collection into the given stream. The data has to be saved in exactly the same order that it is loaded. The Load() and Save() methods must always be modified together so that they are in agreement about the persisted format.

```
STDMETHOD(Save)(LPSTREAM pStm, BOOL fClearDirty)
{
    ATLTRACE2(atlTraceCOM, 0, _T("CBids::Save\n"));
    vector<CComPtr<IBid> >::iterator ppIBid;

    HRESULT hr;
    ULONG ulWritten;
    hr = pStm->Write(
        reinterpret_cast<void*>(&m_vlLastBidAt),
        sizeof(m_vlLastBidAt),
        &ulWritten);
    if(FAILED(hr))
        return hr;
    ATLASSERT(ulWritten == sizeof(m_vlLastBidAt));

    ULONG ulElements = m_cbid.size();
    hr = pStm->Write(
        reinterpret_cast<void*>(&ulElements),
        sizeof(ulElements),
        &ulWritten);
    if(FAILED(hr))
        return hr;
    ATLASSERT(ulWritten == sizeof(ulElements));

    for(ppIBid = m_cbid.begin(); ppIBid < m_cbid.end(); ppIBid++)
    {
        CComPtr<IPersistStream> spIPersistStream;
        hr = (*ppIBid)->QueryInterface(
            IID_IPersistStream,
            reinterpret_cast<void**>(&spIPersistStream));
        if(SUCCEEDED(hr))
        {
            hr = OleSaveToStream(spIPersistStream, pStm);
            if(SUCCEEDED(hr))
                continue;
        }
        return hr;
    }
    if(fClearDirty)
    m_bRequiresSave = FALSE;
    return S_OK;
}
```

In this case, the data being saved is m_vlLastBidAt and ulElements, which is the current size (number of items) of the Bid object collection. This collection is stored in the STL collection class member variable, m_cbid.

The Save() method has a loop that corresponds to the loop in the Load() method. It serializes the individual Bid objects using the OleSaveToStream() function, the counterpart of the OleLoadFromStream() function we saw above. This function takes an IPersistStream interface and saves the corresponding object into the given stream. As we saw above, the serialized state must begin with the class ID, so that the Load() method can reverse the save. When the loop is done, status variables are reset, and the method exits.

The remaining methods of the interface (InitNew() and GetSizeMax()) are not implemented.

IPersistFile

Next, let's take a look at the implementation of `IPersistFile`. Here is the declaration of the interface:

```
interface IPersistFile : IPersist
{
    typedef [unique] IPersistFile* LPPERSISTFILE;

    HRESULT IsDirty();
    HRESULT Load([in] LPCOLESTR pszFileName, [in] DWORD dwMode);
    HRESULT Save([in, unique] LPCOLESTR pszFileName, [in] BOOL fRemember);
    HRESULT SaveCompleted([in, unique] LPCOLESTR pszFileName);
    HRESULT GetCurFile([out] LPOLESTR* ppszFileName);
};
```

I'll focus on the `CBids` implementations of the `Load()` and `Save()` methods. Here is the implementation of `Load()`:

```
STDMETHOD(Load)(LPCOLESTR a_pszFileName, DWORD a_vdwMode)
{
    HRESULT hr;
    CComPtr<IStorage> spIStorage;
    hr = StgOpenStorage(
        a_pszFileName,
        NULL,
        STGM_TRANSACTED | STGM_READ | STGM_SHARE_DENY_WRITE,
        NULL,
        0,
        &spIStorage);
    if(FAILED(hr))
        return hr;

    CComPtr<IStream> spIStream;
    hr = spIStorage->OpenStream(
        L"Lot",
        0,
        STGM_READWRITE | STGM_SHARE_EXCLUSIVE,
        0,
        &spIStream);
    if(FAILED(hr))
        return hr;

    CComPtr<IPersistStreamInit> spIPersistStreamInit;
    hr = QueryInterface(
        IID_IPersistStreamInit,
        reinterpret_cast<void**>(&spIPersistStreamInit));
    if(FAILED(hr))
        return hr;

    hr = spIPersistStreamInit->Load(spIStream);
    if(FAILED(hr))
        return hr;
    return S_OK;
}
```

The Load() function is pretty straightforward. It takes the incoming file name and opens the specified file as a storage object. It then opens a specific named stream (named "Lot" here) under that storage. This stream contains the persisted implementation of the object. The stream is then loaded by delegating to the IPersistStreamInit interface. As you can see, IPersistFile doesn't have to duplicate the work that IPersistStreamInit performed – it simply lets IPersistStreamInit do it. The purpose of the IPersistFile::Load() method is to perform the initialization for the IPersistStreamInit interface, requiring the extraction of the appropriate stream from the file it is given.

Unsurprisingly, the Save() method, the counterpart of Load(), is similar:

```
STDMETHOD(Save)(LPCOLESTR a_pszFileName, BOOL a_vbClearDirty)
{
    HRESULT hr;
    CComPtr<IStorage> spIStorage;
    hr = StgCreateDocfile (
        a_pszFileName,
        STGM_CREATE | STGM_TRANSACTED | STGM_READWRITE | STGM_SHARE_DENY_WRITE,
        0,
        &spIStorage);
    if(FAILED(hr))
        return hr;

    hr = spIStorage->SetClass(__uuidof(Lot));
    if(FAILED(hr))
        return hr;

    CComPtr<IStream> spIStream;
    hr = spIStorage->CreateStream(
        L"Lot",
        STGM_CREATE | STGM_READWRITE | STGM_SHARE_EXCLUSIVE,
        0,
        0,
        &spIStream);
    if(FAILED(hr))
        return hr;

    CComPtr<IPersistStreamInit> spIPersistStreamInit;
    hr = QueryInterface(
        IID_IPersistStreamInit,
        reinterpret_cast<void**>(&spIPersistStreamInit));
    if(FAILED(hr))
        return hr;

    hr = spIPersistStreamInit->Save(spIStream, a_vbClearDirty);
    if(FAILED(hr))
        return hr;

    hr = spIStream->Commit(STGC_DEFAULT);
    if(FAILED(hr))
        return hr;

    hr = spIStorage->Commit(STGC_DEFAULT);
    if(FAILED(hr))
        return hr;

    return S_OK;
}
```

This method overwrites the named file, creating a new storage in it. It also creates a new stream in this storage, gives it the right name ("Lot") and then hands this stream off to the IPersistStreamInit interface. As with the Load() method, the heavy lifting is done by the IPersistStreamInit interface.

IPersistVariant

Jonathan Pinnock defines this interface in his book *Professional DCOM Application Development*. He wanted a persistence interface that could be used from Visual Basic and scripting languages, so it only uses Automation-compliant types:

```
interface IPersistVariant : IDispatch
{
    [id(1), helpstring("GetClassID")]
    HRESULT GetClassID([out, retval] BSTR* pbstrCLSID);

    [id(2), helpstring("IsDirty")]
    HRESULT IsDirty([out, retval] VARIANT_BOOL* pbDirty);

    [id(3), helpstring("Save")]
    HRESULT Save([in] VARIANT_BOOL bClearDirty, [out, retval] VARIANT* pvar);

    [id(4), helpstring("Load")]
    HRESULT Load([in] VARIANT var);
};
```

What persistence medium does the interface work with? It can't work with an IStream interface, because scripting languages can't work with non-Automation interfaces. The persistence medium turns out to be a SAFEARRAY of bytes. The IPersistVariant interface persists the object state to and from a SAFEARRAY that is returned from the Save() method and passed into the Load() method.

Here is the implementation of IPersistVariant::Load(). It is based on Pinnock's implementation, but I had to make a small change to get it to work more generally:

```
STDMETHOD(Load)(VARIANT var)
{
    if(V_VT(&var) != (VT_UI1 | VT_ARRAY))
        return E_INVALIDARG;

    T* pT = static_cast<T*>(this);
    HRESULT hr = S_OK;
    SAFEARRAY* pArray = V_ARRAY(&var);

    long lBound;
    hr = SafeArrayGetLBound(pArray, 1, &lBound);
    if(FAILED(hr))
        return hr;

    long uBound;
    hr = SafeArrayGetUBound(pArray, 1, &uBound);
    if(FAILED(hr))
        return hr;

    ULONG size = uBound - lBound + 1;
```

```
        ULARGE_INTEGER cbSize = {0};
        cbSize.LowPart = size;
        cbSize.HighPart = 0;

        CComPtr<IStream> pStream;
        hr = CreateStreamOnHGlobal(NULL, TRUE, &pStream);
        if(FAILED(hr))
            return hr;

        hr = pStream->SetSize(cbSize);
        if(FAILED(hr))
            return hr;

        HGLOBAL hgData;
        hr = GetHGlobalFromStream(pStream, &hgData);
        if(FAILED(hr))
            return hr;

        BYTE* pStreamData = static_cast<BYTE*>(GlobalLock(hgData));

        BYTE* pData = NULL;
        hr = SafeArrayAccessData(pArray, reinterpret_cast<void**>(&pData));
        if(FAILED(hr))
        {
            return hr;
            GlobalUnlock(hgData);
        }

        memcpy(pStreamData, pData, size);

        SafeArrayUnaccessData(pArray);
        GlobalUnlock(hgData);

        hr = pT->Load(pStream);
        return hr;
    }
```

Once again, all the actual serialization is performed by the Load() method of IPersistStreamInit (the penultimate line of code). The rest of the code is performing initialization for IPersistStreamInit. It creates a stream of the appropriate size in memory (based on the size of the array) and then copies the data out of the SAFEARRAY and into the stream. Finally, it calls the stream Load() method.

Notice that the stream Load() method is delegating to the pT pointer. In the ATL architecture, the pT pointer points at the ATL class that you create and implement. Therefore, the method being accessed here is the Load(IStream*) method implemented in your main ATL class. This is the one line of code that is different from Pinnock's original.

Here is the corresponding Save() method:

```
    STDMETHOD(Save)(VARIANT_BOOL bClearDirty, VARIANT* pvar)
    {
        T* pT = static_cast<T*>(this);

        CComPtr<IStream> pStream;
        HRESULT hr = CreateStreamOnHGlobal(NULL, TRUE, &pStream);
```

```
        if(FAILED(hr))
            return hr;

        hr = pT->Save(pStream, bClearDirty == VARIANT_TRUE ? TRUE : FALSE);
        if(FAILED(hr))
            return hr;

        STATSTG stat = {0};
        pStream->Stat(&stat, STATFLAG_NONAME);
        ULONG cbSize = stat.cbSize.LowPart;
        if(!cbSize)
            return E_FAIL;

        HGLOBAL hgData = NULL;
        hr = GetHGlobalFromStream(pStream, &hgData);
        if(FAILED(hr))
            return hr;

        BYTE* pStreamData = static_cast<BYTE*>(GlobalLock(hgData));

        SAFEARRAY* pArray = SafeArrayCreateVector(VT_UI1, 0, cbSize);
        if(!pArray)
        {
            GlobalUnlock(hgData);
            return E_OUTOFMEMORY;
        }

        BYTE* pData = NULL;
        hr = SafeArrayAccessData(pArray, reinterpret_cast<void**>(&pData));
        if(FAILED(hr))
        {
            GlobalUnlock(hgData);
            return hr;
        }

        memcpy(pData, pStreamData, cbSize);

        SafeArrayUnaccessData(pArray);
        GlobalUnlock(hgData);

        V_VT(pvar) = VT_UI1 | VT_ARRAY;
        V_ARRAY(pvar) = pArray;

        return S_OK;
}
```

Predictably, this method performs the Load() actions in reverse. It creates a memory stream into which the IPersistStreamInit::Save() method can serialize the object state. After the serialization (performed by pT->Save()), it creates a SAFEARRAY of bytes of the appropriate size (based on the final size of the stream). The stream data is copied into the SAFEARRAY. This is then stuffed into a VARIANT, which is returned. Since the SAFEARRAY is an embedded out-only pointer, the memory for it has to be allocated by the server method. It is the caller's responsibility to free it.

IPersistPropertyBag

Why did I go to the trouble of modifying Pinnock's IPersistVariant? After all, I'm not directly exposing this object to a scripting client, so why bother giving it a scripting-compliant persistence interface? It turns out that IPersistVariant is extremely handy for implementing my final persistence interface, IPersistPropertyBag. Here is its declaration:

348

```
interface IPersistPropertyBag : IPersist
{
   typedef IPersistPropertyBag* LPPERSISTPROPERTYBAG;

   HRESULT InitNew(void);
   HRESULT Load([in] IPropertyBag* pPropBag, [in] IErrorLog* pErrorLog);
   HRESULT Save([in] IPropertyBag* pPropBag,
               [in] BOOL fClearDirty,
               [in] BOOL fSaveAllProperties);
};
```

One last time, here's the implementation of the `Load()` method:

```
STDMETHOD(Load)(LPPROPERTYBAG pPropBag, LPERRORLOG pErrorLog)
{
   ATLTRACE2(atlTraceCOM, 0, _T("CBids::IPersistPropertyBagImpl::Load\n"));

   CComVariant vvnt;
   pPropBag->Read(OLESTR("Bids"), &vvnt, pErrorLog);
   return (static_cast<IPersistVariant*>(this))->Load(vvnt);
}
```

Now the benefit of the `IPersistVariant` interface becomes clear! A property bag can only read and write `VARIANT` objects, and that leaves me two choices:

❑ Individually convert each piece of my state into a `VARIANT` and persist individually to a property bag

❑ Convert my entire object state into a `VARIANT` and persist this into the property bag in one shot

Because I can delegate to `IPersistVariant`, the second choice is ridiculously easy to implement, and this is what is done in `Load()`: it reads the `SAFEARRAY` of bytes out of the property bag. This is passed into `IPersistVariant`, which performs loading of the object state.

The `Save()` implementation is again similar:

```
STDMETHOD(Save)(LPPROPERTYBAG pPropBag,
                                    BOOL fClearDirty, BOOL fSaveAllProperties)
{
   ATLTRACE2(atlTraceCOM, 0, _T("CBids::IPersistPropertyBagImpl::Save\n"));

   CComVariant vvnt;
   HRESULT hr = (static_cast<IPersistVariant*>(this))->Save(fClearDirty, &vvnt);
   if(SUCCEEDED(hr))
       return pPropBag->Write(OLESTR("Bids"), &vvnt);
   else
       return hr;
}
```

The object state is persisted into a `SAFEARRAY VARIANT`. This is then passed into the `Write()` method of the property bag. Note that the `CComVariant` destructor will de-allocate the `SAFEARRAY` that was allocated in `IPersistVariant::Save()`, so there is no memory leak here. Once again, the Visual C++ compiler COM support classes simplify the code.

Using STL Collections

Let's turn our attention next to the various data structures and functions that are used actually to implement the collection of bids. The fundamental data structure we use is an STL `vector<>` organized as an STL heap.

Maintaining the Heap

We'll go through the methods one at a time. First, let me explain the member variables. The `CBids` class maintains two collections of `Bid` objects:

```
vector<CComPtr<IBid> >    m_cbid;          // IBid* collection

bool                      m_bSorted;       // Is Sorted Collection UpToDate
vector<CComPtr<IBid> >    m_cbidOrdered;   // Sorted Collection
```

`m_cbid` is an STL `vector<>` of items maintained as a heap. This makes it easy to insert items in a manner that maintains the heap property. The heap is initialized in the `CBids` constructor:

```
CBids::CBids()
{
    make_heap(m_cbid.begin(), m_cbid.end(), HeapLT<IBid>);
    m_bSorted = false;
    m_bInit = false;
}
```

The `make_heap()` operation converts the `m_cbid` vector into a heap, while the STL functor `HeapLT<IBid>` determines the ordering relationship used to maintain the heap. It is used as the third parameter to the heap maintenance functions `make_heap()`, `push_heap()` and `sort_heap()`.

`HeapLT<>` is an STL "strict weak ordering", which is a binary function that returns the result of a 'less than' operation applied to its two parameters. I define it as a template function with the following code:

```
template <class I>
bool HeapLT(I* a_pIL, I* a_pIR) throw(_com_error)
{
    CComPtr<IHeapNode> spL, spR;

    HRESULT hr;
    hr = a_pIL->QueryInterface(IID_IHeapNode, reinterpret_cast<void**>(&spL));
    ATLASSERT(SUCCEEDED(hr));
    hr = a_pIR->QueryInterface(IID_IHeapNode, reinterpret_cast<void**>(&spR));
    ATLASSERT(SUCCEEDED(hr));

    long lKeyL1, lKeyL2, lKeyL3;
    long lKeyR1, lKeyR2, lKeyR3;
    hr = spL->ThreeFields(&lKeyL1, &lKeyL2, &lKeyL3);
    ATLASSERT(SUCCEEDED(hr));
    hr = spR->ThreeFields(&lKeyR1, &lKeyR2, &lKeyR3);
    ATLASSERT(SUCCEEDED(hr));
```

```
    if(lKeyL1 != lKeyR1)
        return lKeyL1 > lKeyR1;

    if(lKeyL2 != lKeyR2)
        return lKeyL2 > lKeyR2;

    return (lKeyL3 > lKeyR3);
}
```

When instantiated with the type `IBid`, this function takes two `IBid` pointers and performs a 'less than' comparison between the two bid values. The first step of the comparison is to obtain the `IHeapNode` interface from each of these `Bid` objects; this interface is used to extract three fields of a sort key, which are then compared individually, beginning with the most significant. The result of this comparison is returned. If the 'value' of the first parameter was less than the 'value' of the second parameter, it returns `true`. The functor is used as the ordering relationship in this example, but notice that the `ThreeFields()` method of the `IHeapNode` interface actually *determines* the ordering. If this method were to be changed, a completely different ordering would ensue. Later on, you'll see how this method is implemented.

> *If we were implementing heaps of some object class* X *other than* Bid, *we would expose an* IHeapNode *interface on objects of this class, instantiate* HeapLT<> *with the appropriate interface, and obtain a working heap with close to no effort. The* IHeapNode *method for* X *would, of course, depend on state variables, keys and business rules that were relevant to* X.
>
> *In this sense, I have just defined a capabilities-based heap protocol that integrates mixin-based capabilities (*IHeapNode *implementation) with generics-based capabilities (*HeapLT<> *implementation). Any COM class that exports an* IHeapNode *interface can be maintained in a heap by using a variation on this code.*

The second vector, `m_cbidOrdered`, is actually a sorted version of the heap. There is a utility function `Order()` that ensures that the two vectors are in sync. Here is its definition:

```
void CBids::Order()
{
    if(!m_bSorted)
    {
        m_cbidOrdered.reserve(m_cbid.size());
        m_cbidOrdered = m_cbid;
        sort_heap(m_cbidOrdered.begin(), m_cbidOrdered.end(), HeapLT<IBid>);
        m_bSorted = true;
    }
}
```

This function repopulates `m_cbidOrdered` to contain the elements of `m_cbid` in sorted order. It tests the `m_bSorted` flag to check if the recalculation needs to be performed. The flag `m_bSorted` indicates whether `m_cbidOrdered` is currently up-to-date. Once again, the `HeapLT<IBid>` functor is used as the ordering relationship. The `m_cbidOrdered` vector is calculated on demand.

IBids

Moving on down the hierarchy, let us look at the code that maintains the collection of `Bid` objects. It is based on the STL `vector<>` collection class, and all of the hard work is done by the STL code – I simply glue it together. Here is the basic collection interface, `IBids`:

```
interface IBids : IDispatch
{
    [propget, id(DISPID_VALUE), helpstring("Item")]
    HRESULT Item([in] LONG a_vlIndex, [out, retval] IBidScript** a_ppbd);

    [propget, id(DISPID_NEWENUM), helpstring("_NewEnum"), restricted]
    HRESULT _NewEnum([out, retval] LPUNKNOWN* a_punk);

    [propget, id(1), helpstring("Count")]
    HRESULT Count([out, retval] LONG* a_pl);

    [id(2), helpstring("Add a new Bid to the collection"), restricted]
    HRESULT Add([in] IBidScript* a_punk);
};
```

First off, let's look at the `propget` method for the `Count` property:

```
STDMETHOD(get_Count)(LONG* a_pl)
{
    if(a_pl == NULL)
        return E_POINTER;

    *a_pl = m_cbid.size();
        return S_OK;
}
```

All this does is return the size of the member vector `m_cbid`, so we can move along quickly to the `propget` method for the `Item` property:

```
STDMETHOD(get_Item)(LONG a_vlIndex, IBidScript** a_ppbd)
{
    if(a_ppbd == NULL)
        return E_POINTER;

    Order();

    if(0 <= a_vlIndex && a_vlIndex < m_cbidOrdered.size())
        return m_cbidOrdered[a_vlIndex].QueryInterface(a_ppbd);

    return E_INVALIDARG;
}
```

This method simply returns the element at the requested index in the vector, calling the `Order()` function first to guarantee that the vector will be up-to-date. The next method is `Add()`:

```
STDMETHOD(Add)(IBidScript* a_pbid)
{
    HRESULT hr;

    CComPtr<IBid> spIBid;
    hr = a_pbid->QueryInterface(&spIBid);
    ATLASSERT(SUCCEEDED(hr));
    m_cbid.push_back(spIBid);
    push_heap(m_cbid.begin(), m_cbid.end(), HeapLT<IBid>);
    m_bSorted = false;
    return S_OK;
}
```

Astonishingly, this method adds a new item to the heap. As you can see, this involves two steps. First, the element is inserted into the vector using the `push_back()` method. Next, the function `push_heap()` is called on the vector. Like most of the heap operations, this takes the `HeapLT<>` functor as a parameter. Instead of immediately updating `m_cbidOrdered`, however, the `m_bSorted` flag is set to `false`, enabling lazy sorting when values from the vector are required.

IPlaceBid

You may have noticed that the `Add()` method in the `IBids` collection interface was a `restricted` method, and this is because a scripting user is not expected to use the `Add()` method directly. Instead, the specification object model exposes the `IPlaceBid` interface to enable insertion of bids. Here is its declaration:

```
interface IPlaceBid : IDispatch
{
    [id(1), helpstring("New Bid")]
    HRESULT InsertBid([in] IBidder* a_pmemMember,
                      [in] SHORT a_vsNumber,
                      [in] LONG a_vlPrice);
};
```

The implementation of the solitary `InsertBid()` method follows:

```
STDMETHOD(InsertBid)(IBidder* a_pmemMember, SHORT a_vsNumber, LONG a_vlPrice)
{
    HRESULT hr;

    CComPtr<IBidInitialize> spINewBid;
    hr = spINewBid.CoCreateInstance(CLSID_Bid);
    if(FAILED(hr))
        return hr;

    time_t lNow;
    time(&lNow);
    hr = spINewBid->Init(a_pmemMember, a_vlPrice, a_vsNumber, lNow);
    if(FAILED(hr))
        return hr;

    CComPtr<IBidScript> spIBidScript;
    hr = spINewBid.QueryInterface(&spIBidScript);
    if(FAILED(hr))
        return hr;

    hr = Add(spIBidScript);
    if(FAILED(hr))
        return hr;

    CComQIPtr<IAuctionInfo> spIAuctionInfo(m_spIUnknownParent);
    ATLASSERT(spIAuctionInfo);

    CComBSTR str;
    hr = spIAuctionInfo->get_NameString(&str);
    if(FAILED(hr))
        return hr;
    ATLASSERT(str);
```

```
    if(str)
    {
       hr = (static_cast<IPersistFile*>(this))->Save(str, TRUE);
       if(FAILED(hr))
          return hr;
    }
    m_vlLastBidAt = lNow;
    return S_OK;
}
```

This method creates a new instance of the `Bid` object and uses the `Init()` method on its `IBidInitialize` interface to initialize it. Just for a change, and to show you another way of doing things, I'm not using the `Bid` class factory and constructor interface. The newly-initialized `Bid` is then inserted into the vector by using the `Add()` method of the collection.

Finally, the method persists the new state of the `Bids` collection. No attempt is made to maintain transactional integrity of the persisted state (something that would be unacceptable in production) – that is, we're not checking to see if anyone else is using the same `Bids` collection at the same time prior to performing the persistence operation.

IBidsInfo

Let me now turn my attention to the `IBidsInfo` interface, to which several of the `IAuctionInfo` methods delegate. Here is its declaration:

```
interface IBidsInfo : IDispatch
{
    [propget, id(1), helpstring("Lo Bid")]
    HRESULT LoBid([ref, out, retval] IBid** a_ppbd);

    [propget, id(2), helpstring("Hi Bid")]
    HRESULT HiBid([ref, out, retval] IBid** a_ppbd);

    [propget, id(3), helpstring("Time of Last Bid")]
    HRESULT LastBidAt([ref, out, retval] DATE* a_pdat);
};
```

The `propget` method of the `LoBid` property is implemented as follows:

```
STDMETHOD(get_LoBid)(IBid** a_ppbd)
{
    if(a_ppbd == NULL)
       return E_POINTER;
    *a_ppbd = 0;

    Order();
    if(m_cbid.size() > 0)
    {
       m_cbidOrdered[0].CopyTo(a_ppbd);
       return S_OK;
    }
    else
       return S_FALSE;
}
```

As expected, this simply extracts the element of the sorted collection with the lowest index. Notice the use of the `CopyTo()` method to assign to the output parameter. This method performs the `AddRef()` that is required by the rules of COM. If the collection is empty, `S_FALSE` is returned instead.

The implementation of the `propget` method for `HighBid` is virtually identical, except that it extracts the element with the highest index. Here then is the implementation of the `propget` method of the `LastBidAt` property:

```
STDMETHOD(get_LastBidAt)(DATE* a_pDat)
{
   if(a_pDat == NULL)
      return E_POINTER;

   *a_pDat = static_cast<DATE>(CDateTime(m_vlLastBidAt));
   return S_OK;
}
```

This code simply returns the `m_vlLastBidAt` member after converting it to a `DATE` value.

IChildInitialize

We're almost there now. You'll recall that the constructor interface for the `Bids` class (`IBidsConstruct`) took a back pointer to the `Lot` object as its first parameter. That constructor interface (whose implementation mirrors that of the other constructor interfaces we've seen) eventually had to initialize the newly created `Bids` object with the back pointer, and this is accomplished with the only method of the `IChildInitialize` interface, declared as follows:

```
interface IChildInitialize : IDispatch
{
   [id(1), helpstring("Initialize Node with Parent Pointer")]
   HRESULT InitParent([in] IUnknown* a_piuk);
};
```

The implementation of this method is completely trivial: provided that no previous value has been assigned, the `m_spIUnknownParent` smart pointer is set to the value passed as an argument.

ICOMIdentity

Finally, before moving on to the `Bid` class, let me show you the `ICOMIdentity` interface. This is the interface that breaks identity encapsulation – in other words, it lets a client peek into alternate identities on the same object:

```
interface ICOMIdentity : IUnknown
{
   [id(1), helpstring("GetAlternateID")]
   HRESULT GetAlternateID([in] LONG a_vl,
                          [out, retval] IUnknown** a_ppuk);

   [id(2), helpstring("QIAltID")]
   HRESULT QIAltID([in] LONG a_vlid,
                   [in] REFIID a_riid,
                   [out, iid_is(a_riid), retval] IUnknown** a_ppuk);
};
```

The two methods, one of which returns `IUnknown` and the other any requested interface, are implemented as follows:

```
STDMETHOD(GetAlternateID)(LONG a_vl, IUnknown** a_ppuk)
{
    return _InternalQueryInterface(
        a_vl, IID_IUnknown, reinterpret_cast<void**>(a_ppuk));
}

STDMETHOD(QIAltID)(LONG a_vl, REFIID a_riid, IUnknown**a_ppuk)
{
    return _InternalQueryInterface(
        a_vl, a_riid, reinterpret_cast<void**>(a_ppuk));
}
```

As you can see, they are delegating to a method called `_InternalQueryInterface()`, which is another part of my ATL extensions for split interfaces. As usual, refer to Appendix B for more details.

The Bid Class

It must now be time to examine the `Bid` class, as implemented by `CBid`. As usual, I'll begin with a reminder of the coclass definition:

```
coclass Bid
{
    [default] interface IBidScript;
    interface IBid;
    interface IBidInitialize;

    interface ISupportErrorInfo;
};
```

Object State

The implementation of this class is relatively straightforward; its state is represented as follows:

```
public:
    unsigned            m_bRequiresSave:1;    // IsDirty bit

private:
    CComPtr<IBidder>    m_spmm;               // IBidder interface on Member object
    LONG                m_vlPrice;            // Price on Bid
    SHORT               m_vsNumber;           // Number of items in Bid
    LONG                m_vlTime;             // Time at which Bid is place
```

IBid

The most frequently used interface on the `Bid` object is the `IBid` interface. This is declared as:

```
interface IBid : IDispatch
{
    [propget, id(1), helpstring("Bidder")]
    HRESULT Bidder([out, retval] IBidder** a_ppmm);

    [propputref, id(1), helpstring("Bidder"), hidden]
    HRESULT Bidder([in] IBidder* a_pmem);
```

```
    [propget, id(2), helpstring("Price")]
    HRESULT Price([out, retval] LONG* a_pl);

    [propput, id(2), helpstring("Price"), hidden]
    HRESULT Price([in] LONG a_vl);

    [propget, id(3), helpstring("Number")]
    HRESULT Number([out, retval] SHORT* a_ps);

    [propput, id(3), helpstring("Number"), hidden]
    HRESULT Number([in] SHORT a_vs);

    [propget, id(4), helpstring("Time")]
    HRESULT Time([out, retval] LONG* a_pl);

    [propput, id(4), helpstring("Time"), hidden]
    HRESULT Time([in] LONG a_vl);
};
```

The first thing you'll notice is that this interface is different from the one I originally showed you in Chapter 5: it has a `hidden` 'put' method for each property, while the interface in Chapter 5 only had the 'get' methods. Although the use cases only require a get method, you'll discover why a put method is necessary in the sub-section on the *ATL Persistence Interfaces*.

The implementation of these methods is pretty straightforward: either they assign the parameter to a member variable, or vice versa. For this reason I'll just show you a couple of representative methods:

```
STDMETHOD(get_Bidder)(IBidder** a_ppmm)
{
    if(a_ppmm == NULL)
        return E_POINTER;
    *a_ppmm = 0;
    return m_spmm.CopyTo(a_ppmm);
}

STDMETHOD(putref_Bidder)(IBidder* a_pmem)
{
    m_spmm = a_pmem;
    return S_OK;
}

STDMETHOD(get_Price)(LONG* a_pl)
{
    if(a_pl == NULL)
        return E_POINTER;
    *a_pl = m_vlPrice;
    return S_OK;
}

STDMETHOD(put_Price)(LONG a_vl)
{
    m_vlPrice = a_vl;
    return S_OK;
}
```

The implementations of the `Price` property access methods are absolutely standard, but the ones for the `Bidder` property access methods are just a little more interesting.

To see what I mean, notice that the IDL for `Bidder` actually utilizes `propputref` rather than `propput`. Now, you may remember that `propputref` is used for properties that can be assigned a COM interface – in this case, `IBidder`. You may also remember that the ATL implementation of dual interfaces is driven by a type library, and this actually *requires* the `propputref` attribute in order to transmit the parameter through the dispatch side of the interface correctly.

The actual implementation of the `propputref` method, however, is simple: you just assign the parameter to the smart pointer member variable. The assignment operator automatically takes care of `AddRef()`'ing the interface. Similarly, the call to `CopyTo()` in the `get_Bidder()` method takes care of `AddRef()`'ing the outgoing interface.

ATL Persistence Interfaces

The implementation of the persistence interfaces in ATL is a table-driven system that serializes 'properties' of the class. The properties are listed in the property map, which in our example is defined by the following code:

```
BEGIN_PROP_MAP(CBid)
    PROP_ENTRY_EX("Bidder", 1, CLSID_NULL, IID_IBid)
    PROP_ENTRY_EX("Price", 2, CLSID_NULL, IID_IBid)
    PROP_ENTRY_EX("Number", 3, CLSID_NULL, IID_IBid)
    PROP_ENTRY_EX("Time", 4, CLSID_NULL, IID_IBid)
END_PROP_MAP()
```

This is a standard ATL table that will be used by the ATL serialization helpers to serialize the four properties of the `IBidder` dual interface. The properties are identified by the second parameter of the `PROP_ENTRY_EX()` macro, which specifies their DISPID within the `IBidder` interface.

> **The ATL persistence code winds up calling the Automation `put` and `get` methods in order to move data between the persisted format and the object, and this explains why we needed to have hidden `put` methods on `IBidder`.**
>
> **Although no client uses the `propput` methods, they are required by the ATL code to load data from the persisted format into the object.**
>
> **In general, you need to ensure that each property listed using the `PROP_ENTRY_EX()` macro is a *read-write* property of the corresponding (dual) Automation interface.**

Do you remember how the `Bids` object persisted the individual `Bid` objects by passing them into `OleLoadFromStream()` and `OleSaveToStream()`, which in turn delegated to the `IPersistStream` interface on the `Bid` object? Well, this issue comes up again when you look at the property map. It is easy to see what the ATL implementation has to do to persist the `Price`, `Number` and `Time` properties – they are all scalar values – but what is it supposed to do in order to persist an interface? Once again, delegation comes to the rescue. The ATL implementation delegates to the appropriate persistence interface on the `Member` object, which implements the `IBidder` interface. As you'll see, this is why we have to implement the persistence interfaces on `Member` as well.

The chain goes as follows: in order for the `Bids` object to persist itself, it needed to delegate to the persistence interfaces on the `Bid` object. For this to work, each property on the `IBidder` interface had to be read-write, and the corresponding persistence interfaces needed to be implemented on the `Member` object.

IPersistStream[Init]

Using the ATL `IPersistStreamInit` implementation is as easy as can be. After the property map has been created as described above, you simply add the following to the inheritance list for `CBid`:

```
public IPersistStreamInitImpl<CBid>
```

This brings the ATL implementation of the `IPersistStreamInit` into your code, as well as providing the vtable for `IPersistStreamInit`. Now we only need to provide an entry in the COM map to ensure that the interface is exported by `QI()`. This is the line:

```
COM_INTERFACE_ENTRY(IPersistStreamInit)
```

Recall that an `IPersistStreamInit` implementation is *also* an `IPersistStream` implementation, so we also have an `IPersistStream` implementation for free – with just one hitch. The `IPersistStreamInit` interface has no IDL relationship with `IPersistStream`, so we can't just use this macro:

```
COM_INTERFACE_ENTRY(IPersistStream)
```

Because `IPersistStream` is not actually in our inheritance list, the compiler will flag this as an error. We could try adding it, but this will not allow us to share the `IPersistStreamInit` implementation. Of course, there is a solution, and it turns out to be yet another macro:

```
COM_INTERFACE_ENTRY_IID(IID_IPersistStream, IPersistStreamInit)
```

This associates the IID `IID_IPersistStream` with the `IPersistStreamInit` C++ interface in the `QI()`, which then returns the `IPersistStreamInit` interface vtable when queried for the `IPersistStream` IID. This works just fine, since the latter's vtable is a subset of the former's.

IPersistPropertyBag

The implementation of `IPersistPropertyBag` turns out to be every bit as easy as that for `IPersistStreamInit`. We simply add this line to the inheritance list:

```
public IPersistPropertyBagImpl<CBid>
```

And this line to the COM map:

```
COM_INTERFACE_ENTRY(IPersistPropertyBag)
```

The ATL implementation of this interface also uses the property map that I described earlier.

IHeapNode

Next, let's take a look at the `IHeapNode` interface that was implemented by the `Bid` object in order to enable the `HeapLT<>` functor to sort the bid collection. Here is its declaration:

```
interface IHeapNode : IUnknown
{
    [id(1), helpstring("Single Key Field")]
    HRESULT Single([out, retval] LONG* a_plFld);

    [id(2), helpstring("Two Key Fields in Sort Order")]
    HRESULT TwoFields([out] LONG* a_plFld1,
                      [out] LONG* a_plFld2);

    [id(3), helpstring("Three Key Fields in Sort Order")]
    HRESULT ThreeFields([out] LONG* a_plFld1,
                        [out] LONG* a_plFld2,
                        [out] LONG* a_plFld3);
};
```

The methods of this interface return one, two or three sort keys, depending on the sorting algorithm in effect. The partial order of two different heap nodes is determined by comparing the keys one by one, in descending order of significance. The first key difference determines the partial order. If three fields were being used for sorting, `a_plFld1` on one object would be compared to `a_plFld1` on the other. The next field (`a_plFld2`) would only come into play if `a_plFld1` had the same value on both objects. Similarly, `a_plFld3` would be used only if `a_plFld2` could not determine the ordering. If all three fields were equal, the objects would be declared equal.

Here are the implementations of these methods:

```
STDMETHOD(Single)(LONG* a_plFld)
{
    if(a_plFld == NULL)
      return E_POINTER;

    *a_plFld = m_vlPrice;
    return S_OK;
}

STDMETHOD(TwoFields)(LONG* a_plFld1, LONG* a_plFld2)
{
    if(a_plFld1 == NULL || a_plFld2 == NULL)
      return E_POINTER;

    *a_plFld1 = m_vlPrice;
    *a_plFld2 = m_vsNumber;
    return S_OK;
}

STDMETHOD(ThreeFields)(LONG* a_plFld1, LONG* a_plFld2, LONG* a_plFld3)
{
    if(a_plFld1 == NULL || a_plFld2 == NULL || a_plFld3 == NULL)
      return E_POINTER;

    *a_plFld1 = m_vlPrice;
    *a_plFld2 = m_vsNumber;
    *a_plFld3 = - m_vlTime;
    return S_OK;
}
```

As you can see, `Single()` allows comparison on the `Price` field only, `TwoFields()` allows comparison on `Price` and `Number`, and `ThreeFields()` allows comparison on `Price`, `Number` and `Time`. In general, the parameters do not have to correspond individually to member variables as they do here. Any function of the object state can serve as a key that can be returned as any parameter. This allows a wide variety of business rules to be used in sorting a collection of `Bid` objects.

IBidInitialize and IBidScript

The `IBidInitialize` and `IBidScript` interfaces are implemented in a manner analogous to other such interfaces that I have already shown you:

```
interface IBidInitialize : IDispatch
{
    [id(1), helpstring("Initialize object with Bid information")]
    HRESULT Init([in] IBidder* a_pmem,
                 [in] LONG a_vlPrice,
                 [in] SHORT a_vsNumber,
                 [in] LONG a_vlTime);
};

interface IBidScript : IDispatch
{
    [propget, id(1), helpstring("IBid")]
    HRESULT IBid([out, retval] IBid** a_ppbd);

    [propget, id(2), helpstring("IBidInitialize"), hidden]
    HRESULT IBidInitialize([out, retval] IBidInitialize** a_ppbi);
};
```

The Member Class

To complete our tour of the application classes, here once again is the definition of the `Member` coclass:

```
coclass Member
{
    [default] interface IMemberScript;
    interface IBidder;
    interface IMemberInitialize;

    interface IPersistStream;
    interface IPersistStreamInit;
    interface IPersistPropertyBag;

    interface ISupportErrorInfo;
};
```

Object State

And for the final time, to aid your understanding of the various interface methods, here are the `CMember` class's member variables:

```
public:
    unsigned m_bRequiresSave:1;

private:
    LONG      m_vlMemberID;
```

```
    CComBSTR m_vstrFirstName;
    CComBSTR m_vstrLastName;
    CComBSTR m_vstrCity;
    CComBSTR m_vstrState;
```

IBidder

The primary interface of interest on the Member class is the IBidder interface:

```
interface IBidder : IDispatch
{
    [propget, id(1), helpstring("MemberID"), hidden]
    HRESULT MemberID([out, retval] LONG* a_pl);

    [propput, id(1), helpstring("MemberID"), hidden]
    HRESULT MemberID([in] LONG a_vl);

    [propget, id(2), helpstring("First Name")]
    HRESULT FirstName([out, retval] BSTR* a_pstr);

    [propput, id(2), helpstring("First Name"), hidden]
    HRESULT FirstName([in] BSTR a_vstr);

    [propget, id(3), helpstring("Last Name")]
    HRESULT LastName([out, retval] BSTR* a_pstr);

    [propput, id(3), helpstring("Last Name"), hidden]
    HRESULT LastName([in] BSTR a_vstr);

    [propget, id(4), helpstring("City")]
    HRESULT City([out, retval] BSTR* a_pstr);

    [propput, id(4), helpstring("City"), hidden]
    HRESULT City([in] BSTR a_vstr);

    [propget, id(5), helpstring("State")]
    HRESULT State([out, retval] BSTR* a_pstr);

    [propput, id(5), helpstring("State"), hidden]
    HRESULT State([in] BSTR a_vstr);
};
```

This is analogous to the IBid interface that we just saw on the Bid object – notice the presence of similarly-motivated hidden propput methods.

The implementation of these methods is very close in nature to other such methods that we have already seen. Data is moved between the method parameters and the corresponding member variables; memory allocation is performed as necessary, typically in the implementation of a smart C++ wrapper class.

Persisting an Alternate ID

The CMember class implements the IPersistStreamInit and IPersistPropertyBag methods. Recall that these were required for the implementation of the corresponding interfaces on the Bid object.

Unfortunately, we now have an additional problem that is related to alternate identities. This is the first time that we have had an alternate identity that needs to be persisted: we have to persist an identity in which `IBidder` is the primary dispatch interface. How do we ensure that a newly loaded object knows which identity was persisted? Clearly, we need to persist the actual identity along with the rest of the object.

The easiest way to do this, in a manner compliant with the rest of my ATL extensions, is to have separate implementations of the persistence interfaces for each identity. The identity-specific persistence interface will delegate to the primary persistence interface to perform the actual operation, but will also persist the identity number itself. Here is how this is done:

```
DEFINE_BIDDER(1)
DEFINE_MEMBERINITIALIZE(2)

class ATL_NO_VTABLE CMember :
    public CComObjectRootEx<CComSingleThreadModel>,
    public CComCoClass<CMember, &CLSID_Member>,
    public IPersistStreamInitImpl<CMember>,
    public IPersistPropertyBagImpl<CMember>,
    public ISupportErrorInfo,
    public IDispatchImpl<
        IMemberInitialize, &IID_IMemberInitialize, &LIBID_WroxAuction>,
    public IDispatchImpl<IBidder, &IID_IBidder, &LIBID_WroxAuction>,
    public IDispatchImpl<IMemberScript, &IID_IMemberScript, &LIBID_WroxAuction>,
    public IBidderCustom,
    public IPersistStreamInitID1,
    public IPersistPropertyBagID1,
    public IDispatchImpl<IBidderID1, &IID_IBidder, &LIBID_WroxAuction>,
    public IDispatchImpl<
        IMemberInitializeID2, &IID_IMemberInitialize, &LIBID_WroxAuction>
{
public:
    CMember()
    {
    }

    ~CMember()
    {
    }

DECLARE_NOT_AGGREGATABLE_MI(CMember,CComObjectIDPersist2)
DECLARE_CLASSFACTORY_EX(CMemberCO)

DECLARE_REGISTRY_RESOURCEID(IDR_MEMBER)
DECLARE_PROTECT_FINAL_CONSTRUCT()

BEGIN_COM_MAP(CMember)
    COM_INTERFACE_ENTRY2(IDispatch, IMemberScript)
    COM_INTERFACE_ENTRY(IMemberInitialize)
    COM_INTERFACE_ENTRY_IID(IID_IPersistStream, IPersistStreamInit)
    COM_INTERFACE_ENTRY(IPersistStreamInit)
    COM_INTERFACE_ENTRY(IPersistPropertyBag)
    COM_INTERFACE_ENTRY(IBidder)
    COM_INTERFACE_ENTRY(IBidderCustom)
    COM_INTERFACE_ENTRY(ISupportErrorInfo)
    COM_INTERFACE_ENTRY(IMemberScript)
END_COM_MAP()
```

```
BEGIN_COM_MAP2(CMember,1)
    COM_INTERFACE_ENTRY2(IDispatch, IBidderID1)
    COM_INTERFACE_ENTRY(IBidderID1)
    COM_INTERFACE_ENTRY_IID(IID_IPersistStream, IPersistStreamInitID1)
    COM_INTERFACE_ENTRY(IPersistStreamInitID1)
    COM_INTERFACE_ENTRY(IPersistPropertyBagID1)
END_COM_MAP2(1)

BEGIN_COM_MAP2(CMember,2)
    COM_INTERFACE_ENTRY2(IDispatch, IMemberInitializeID2)
    COM_INTERFACE_ENTRY(IMemberInitializeID2)
END_COM_MAP2(2)

IMPLEMENT_PERSISTABLE_ID
IMPLEMENT_PERSISTSTREAMINIT_ID(1)
IMPLEMENT_PERSISTPROPERTYBAG_ID(1)

BEGIN_IDENTITY_MAP(2)
    COM_IDENTITY_ENTRY(1)
    COM_IDENTITY_ENTRY(2)
END_IDENTITY_MAP
```

Much of this code is a 'standard' implementation of alternate identities, but I've added
`IPersistStreamInitID1` and `IPersistPropertyBagID1` to the inheritance list. The
appropriate entries are also made to the COM map for alternate ID 1, so that identity can be
persisted. The bulk of the actual work is being performed by `IMPLEMENT_PERSISTABLE_ID`,
`IMPLEMENT_PERSISTSTREAMINIT_ID(1)` and `IMPLEMENT_PERSISTPROPERTYBAG_ID(1)`,
which create the appropriate delegating implementations of `IPersistStreamInit` and
`IPersistPropertyBag`.

IMemberInitialize & IMemberScript

Finally, the `IMemberInitialize` and `IMemberScript` interfaces are declared and implemented
analogously to other interfaces of this kind:

```
interface IMemberInitialize : IDispatch
{
    [id(1), helpstring("Initialize object with Member information")]
    HRESULT Init([in] LONG a_vlMemberID,
                 [in] BSTR a_vstrFirst,
                 [in] BSTR a_vstrLast,
                 [in] BSTR a_vstrCity,
                 [in] BSTR a_vstrState);
};

interface IMemberScript : IDispatch
{
    [propget, id(1), helpstring("IBidder")]
    HRESULT IBidder([out, retval] IBidder** a_ppbr);

    [propget, id(2), helpstring("IMemberInitialize"), hidden]
    HRESULT IMemberInitialize([out, retval] IMemberInitialize** a_ppmi);
};
```

Implementing Enumerators

It can't have escaped your attention that, to this point, I haven't shown you any enumerator implementations, and it's time I put that right. Enumerators are exposed by the _NewEnum property of each collection interface, and their implementation as supported by ATL is extremely straightforward. As an example, I'll show you the implementation of the enumerator for the Bids collection.

Here is the declaration of the propget method for the _NewEnum property:

```
[propget, id(DISPID_NEWENUM), helpstring("_NewEnum"), restricted]
HRESULT _NewEnum([out, retval] LPUNKNOWN* a_punk);
```

What identifies this property as being an enumerator is the DISPID, which is DISPID_NEWENUM. You should also note that this is a restricted property.

> *Before the* restricted *keyword was introduced into IDL, a property name with a leading underscore signified a restricted property. Although it is no longer needed, the enumerator property is still frequently named* _NewEnum. *Old habits are hard to break, and fortunately there is no downside to this one.*

As I said earlier, an enumerator is an anonymous COM object that exports the IEnumVARIANT interface. ATL provides the template class CComEnum<> to support creation of enumerator interfaces. To illustrate the mechanism, let me show you the implementation of the propget method for the _NewEnum property outlined above:

```
STDMETHOD(get__NewEnum)(LPUNKNOWN* a_punk)
{
   if(a_punk == NULL)
      return E_POINTER;
   *a_punk = NULL;

   // Create Ordered Vector
   Order();

   // Create ATL Enumerator Object
   typedef CComObject<CComEnum<IEnumVARIANT,
                     &IID_IEnumVARIANT, VARIANT, _Copy<VARIANT> > > TEnumVar;
   TEnumVar* p = new TEnumVar;
   _ASSERTE(p);

   // Initialize Copy of Enumerator Array
   VARIANT* aVariant = new VARIANT[m_cbidOrdered.size()];
   vector<CComPtr<IBid> >::iterator ppIBid;
   VARIANT* pVariant = aVariant;

   // Iterate over collection, copying objects into array
   HRESULT hr = S_OK;
   for(ppIBid = m_cbidOrdered.begin();
                        ppIBid < m_cbidOrdered.end(); ppIBid++, pVariant++)
   {
      pVariant->vt = VT_DISPATCH;
      hr = ppIBid->CopyTo(reinterpret_cast<IBid**>(&(pVariant->pdispVal)));
      if(FAILED(hr))
         break;
   }
```

```
    // Give enumerator ownership of array
    if(SUCCEEDED(hr))
    {
        HRESULT hr = p->Init(&aVariant[0], &aVariant[m_cbidOrdered.size()],
                                            NULL, AtlFlagTakeOwnership);

        if(SUCCEEDED(hr))
            hr = p->QueryInterface(IID_IUnknown, reinterpret_cast<void**>(a_punk));
    }

    // Delete array on failure
    if(FAILED(hr))
    {
        delete p;
        delete [] aVariant;
    }
    return hr;
}
```

The code progresses through the following stages:

❑ The m_cbidOrderedVector is synched with m_cbid.

❑ A COM object of type TEnumVar is created. TEnumVar is a C++ class capable of creating an ATL enumerator that exposes the IEnumVARIANT interface. The template parameters to CComEnum<> specify the interface type, the interface IID, the type being enumerated over, and a class that knows how to copy the type. In this case, we use the ATL-supplied _Copy<VARIANT> class, and the remaining parameters are what you would expect.

❑ A new object of the TEnumVar class is created on the heap using the new operator. Why are we suddenly using new to create an ATL COM object? Don't be alarmed: the fact is that the COM creation mechanism doesn't really exist for anonymous classes (that's why they're anonymous), so this is the one case where you *can* use bare C++ with little downside. It's preferable to use the CComObjectXXXX::CreateInstance() mechanism, for the reasons that I mentioned earlier, but I'm going to ignore it in this case.

❑ This enumerator object knows how to implement IEnumVARIANT, but it needs an array of VARIANTs to iterate over. The code creates a suitably sized array of VARIANT objects.

❑ The for loop iterates over the elements of the collection, copying them into the VARIANT array. As usual, the C++ wrapper implementation of CopyTo() takes care of any necessary reference counting.

❑ When the array has been populated, it is used to initialize the new enumerator object. In this case, the method hands ownership of the array over to the enumerator. When the enumerator is done with it, it is expected to release the array. This also means that the method does not have to release any memory unless there is a failure. This condition is checked at the end of the method, and the code performs clean up of both the array and the output variable if necessary.

❑ The value that is returned via the output parameter is the IUnknown interface on the enumerator object. In order to use the IEnumVARIANT interface, the client has to QI() for it. This is an inefficiency in the COM enumerator protocol that can cause unnecessary performance degradation over a network, and it could have been avoided by giving the propget method for the _NewEnum property an iid_is() parameter that identified the actual interface to be returned.

User Defined Types & Pointers

So far, all the examples that we've seen have focused on relatively simple data types being passed as method parameters. However, we know that IDL allows much more complex types – in fact, just about any C-style data structure can be passed as a parameter. In practice, the interaction between embedded pointers and memory allocation turns some people off using complex structures, but things are not as complicated as they seem if you use some close-to-boilerplate code to help things along.

Avoiding the Cost of Interface Parameters

Here is some code from the MFC user interface to the auction services that we built in the previous chapter:

```
void CMainForm::BidsRefresh(IBidsPtr& a_spIBids)
{
   LONG iCount = a_spIBids->GetCount();

   m_ctlBids.Clear();
   m_ctlBids.SetRows(iCount + 1);
   m_ctlBids.SetFormatString(_T(
      "<Member           |<Location             |<Price |<Quantity "
      "|<Time                 "));

   LONG i;
   for(i = 0; i < iCount; i++)
   {
      IBidPtr spIBid = a_spIBids->GetItem(i);
      m_ctlBids.SetTextArray(
         faIndex(i + 1, 0, m_ctlBids),
         static_cast<LPCTSTR>(spIBid->GetBidder()->GetFirstName()
            + " " + spIBid->GetBidder()->GetLastName()));
      m_ctlBids.SetTextArray(
         faIndex(i + 1, 1, m_ctlBids),
         static_cast<LPCTSTR>(spIBid->GetBidder()->GetCity()
            + ", " + spIBid->GetBidder()->GetState()));

      CString str;
      str.Format("%d", spIBid->GetPrice());
      m_ctlBids.SetTextArray(
         faIndex(i + 1, 2, m_ctlBids),
         static_cast<LPCTSTR>(str));
      str.Format("%d", spIBid->GetNumber());
      m_ctlBids.SetTextArray(
         faIndex(i + 1, 3, m_ctlBids),
         static_cast<LPCTSTR>(str));

      COleDateTime datBid = TimeT2Ole(spIBid->GetTime());

      m_ctlBids.SetTextArray(
         faIndex(i + 1, 4, m_ctlBids),
         static_cast<LPCTSTR>(datBid.Format("%m/%d/%Y %h:%M:%S %p")));
   };
   m_ctlAddBid.EnableWindow(TRUE);
}
```

The `for` loop iterates over each item in the `Bids` collection. It uses the `IBid` interface to retrieve the various properties of each `Bid`. Remember, though, that one of these properties (`Bidder`) is itself an interface (`IBidder`), with its own properties.

Now think about the client code from the perspective of the remoting architecture that we have seen. Each call to a member of the interface results in an RMC if the server is in a different apartment to the client. Thus, each property lookup incurs the cross-apartment round trip cost. It's worse when the property belongs to the `IBidder` interface, since there are now *two* lookups. Looked at in this way, the information that is displayed for each bid requires twelve (potentially remote) method invocations.

Of course, we could optimize the code by using the enumerator interface to 'pre-fetch' an array of bids rather than getting them one at a time. We could also have reduced the number of calls to `GetBidder()` by caching the `IBidder` interface. In the best case, we could have reduced the number of (potentially cross-apartment) calls to nine.

Notice that this is not an artifact of the C++ client implementation, but a result of COM's transparent remoting architecture. We'd have exactly the same problem regardless of the client language.

How can we avoid all these method calls? Well, in truth the interfaces consist only of `propget` and `propput` methods, and we're really using these interfaces as object-oriented substitutes for structures (which we have to do on dual interfaces, since Automation cannot use IDL `struct`s). However, since this is a C++ client, and it *can* use `struct`s, why don't we introduce real structures to accomplish the same purpose?

Replacing Interfaces with C structs

Let's begin with a type that holds the information for a bidder. Here is the IDL:

```
struct tagBidder
{
    BSTR m_vstrFirstName;
    BSTR m_vstrLastName;
    BSTR m_vstrCity;
    BSTR m_vstrState;
};
typedef [public] struct tagBidder SBidder;
```

It looks just like a C structure declaration. Next we look at the declaration of the bid-holding structure:

```
struct tagBid
{
    [ref] SBidder* m_pbdrMember;
    LONG m_vlPrice;
    LONG m_vlTime;
    SHORT m_vsNumber;
};
typedef [public] struct tagBid SBid;
```

Notice that I've chosen to have the `SBid` structure aggregate the `SBidder` structure via a member pointer, rather than contain it directly. Again, this is pretty much straight C syntax, except for the `ref` attribute on the pointer. I'm following the guideline I proposed earlier of explicitly attributing the pointer instead of allowing the attribute to take on a default value depending on the interface that's using the `struct`. We know a `ref` qualification is safe, because `SBid` is aggregating the `SBidder` parameter (the semantics of `Bid` objects do not allow a null `Bidder`).

Defining an Enumerator Interface

If we wanted to rewrite the client example above to use these data types, what new interfaces would we need? Let's work backwards from the example. Clearly, I need some way of returning the SBid structure instead of the IBid interface described earlier. Instead of simply replacing the Item property, however, I'll implement an enumerator – that will give me extra efficiency and extra complexity, which makes it a more realistic example. Let me create such an enumerator, following the usual guidelines for enumerator interfaces. Here is the declaration for IEnumBid:

```
interface IEnumBid : IUnknown
{
    [helpstring("Try to fetch the next N elements")]
    HRESULT Next(
        [in] ULONG a_vulCount,
        [out, size_is(a_vulCount, 1), length_is(*a_pulFetched, 1)] SBid** a_abid,
        [out] ULONG* a_pulFetched);

    [helpstring("Skip over the next N elements")]
    HRESULT Skip([in] ULONG a_vulCount);

    [helpstring("Reset the enumeration to the beginning")]
    HRESULT Reset();

    [helpstring("Create a new enumerator with the same state")]
    HRESULT Clone([out] IEnumBid** a_ppEnum);
}
```

This interface is almost identical to the declaration of IEnumVARIANT, except for the type that is being enumerated (an SBid* rather than a VARIANT). Too bad IDL doesn't have templates!

The most interesting method declaration here is the declaration of Next(). Note that the second parameter is a two-dimensional, open (that is, varying and conformant), sized pointer array that contains a_vulCount pointers to SBid structures. I chose to have an array of pointers (rather than an array of structures) for two reasons. First, it is the normal C++ idiom for arrays of objects. Second, it better illustrates how memory allocation and marshaling are implemented.

Notice that the length_is() parameter, a_pulFetched, is out-only – the actual number of array elements returned from the method is determined by the server. The size of the array, or the maximum number of elements, is determined by the client via the in parameter a_vulCount.

The Collection Interface

Next, let us look at the declaration of the collection interface that will return the enumerator. This is the IBidsCustom interface:

```
interface IBidsCustom : IUnknown
{
    [helpstring("Item")]
    HRESULT Item([in] LONG a_vlIndex, [out, retval] SBid* a_ppbd);

    [propget, helpstring("NewBidEnum"), restricted]
    HRESULT NewBidEnum([in] REFIID a_riid,
                       [out, iid_is(a_riid), retval] LPUNKNOWN* a_ppuk);

    [propget, helpstring("Count")]
    HRESULT Count([out, retval] LONG* a_pl);
};
```

This is very similar to the IBids interface that you saw earlier. In fact, there are just three changes:

- ❑ The propget method of the Item property returns an SBid rather than an IBid pointer.
- ❑ The NewBidEnum() (corresponding to the _NewEnum) method takes an extra REFIID parameter, and uses the iid_is() idiom to return an enumerator interface. This gives us the flexibility to use a single interface to query for multiple enumerators (remember that our object implements an IEnumVARIANT enumerator in addition to the IEnumBid enumerator).
- ❑ I've dropped the Add() method.

Note that neither IEnumBid nor IBidsCustom can be a dual interface, since they both use a user-defined type.

Utility Interfaces

Let's think about what's required to implement IBidCustom. Clearly, we will need some way to break the encapsulation of the object in order to retrieve the structures, and I chose to do this through a couple of simple interfaces called IBidCustom and IBidderCustom. These are designed to extract SBid and SBidder values out of their respective objects:

```
interface IBidderCustom : IUnknown
{
    [propget, helpstring("Bidder")]
    HRESULT Bidder([out, ref, retval] SBidder* a_pbdr);
};

interface IBidCustom : IUnknown
{
    [propget, helpstring("Bid")]
    HRESULT Bid([out, ref, retval] SBid* a_pbid);
};
```

Implementing an Enumerator in ATL

Let us look now at the ATL code that implements these interfaces.

IBidderCustom

We'll begin with the simplest code of all, the implementation of IBidderCustom. Here is the implementation of the single propget method required:

```
STDMETHOD(get_Bidder)(SBidder* a_pbdr)
{
    if(a_pbdr == NULL)
        return E_POINTER;

    a_pbdr->m_vstrCity      = 0;
    a_pbdr->m_vstrFirstName = 0;
    a_pbdr->m_vstrLastName  = 0;
    a_pbdr->m_vstrState     = 0;

    HRESULT hr;

    hr = m_vstrFirstName.CopyTo(&a_pbdr->m_vstrFirstName);
    if(FAILED(hr))
        return hr;
```

```
        hr = m_vstrLastName.CopyTo(&a_pbdr->m_vstrLastName);
        if(FAILED(hr))
            return hr;

        hr = m_vstrCity.CopyTo(&a_pbdr->m_vstrCity);
        if(FAILED(hr))
            return hr;

        hr = m_vstrState.CopyTo(&a_pbdr->m_vstrState);
        if(FAILED(hr))
            return hr;

        return S_OK;
}
```

This method simply copies the member variables of the `CMember` class into the structure that is returned. Nevertheless, there are several noteworthy points:

❑ The test for a null pointer at the start of the function ensures that the pointer is a `ref` pointer, which will never be null.

❑ Because the embedded `BSTR` members of `SBidder` struct are out-only, they have to be allocated in the method implementation. This is done by the `CopyTo()` method of `CComBSTR`.

❑ The embedded `BSTR` pointers in the `SBidder` structure are initialized to zero on function entry. This is in compliance with the 'on error' requirement of interface memory allocation semantics. Of course, for this code to be compliant as written, the `CopyTo()` method of `CComBSTR` also has to comply with the convention. Since `CComBSTR` is a robust, production-quality template library, you can be reasonably sure that this is true. Being the paranoid type myself, I've actually checked the code, and it *is* compliant.

You will see soon how the 'on error' conventions drastically simplify the calling code, while allowing it to remain completely robust.

IBidCustom

The next piece of code to examine is the implementation of the `propget` method of the read-only `Bid` property of `IBidCustom`:

```
STDMETHOD(get_Bid)(SBid* a_pbid)
{
    if(a_pbid == NULL)
        return E_POINTER;
    a_pbid->m_pbdrMember = 0;

    CComPtr<IBidderCustom> spIBidderCustom;
    HRESULT hr = m_spmm->QueryInterface(
                    IID_IBidderCustom, reinterpret_cast<void**>(&spIBidderCustom));
    ATLASSERT(spIBidderCustom != 0);

    a_pbid->m_pbdrMember = reinterpret_cast<SBidder*>(
                                        CoTaskMemAlloc(sizeof(SBidder)));
```

```
    hr = spIBidderCustom->get_Bidder(a_pbid->m_pbdrMember);
    if(FAILED(hr))
    {
        CoTaskMemFree(a_pbid->m_pbdrMember);
        a_pbid->m_pbdrMember = 0;
        return hr;
    }

    a_pbid->m_vlTime    = m_vlTime;
    a_pbid->m_vlPrice   = m_vlPrice;
    a_pbid->m_vsNumber  = m_vsNumber;

    return S_OK;
}
```

This is very similar to the get_Bidder() function we just saw, but again there are a few points worthy of note:

❑   Even though the call to the get_Bidder() function is being made to a C++ object compiled in the same executable, I chose to use a COM-style QueryInterface() and method invocation rather than performing a dynamic_cast<> that cross-casts to the other interface method. Although the dynamic cast is probably a little more efficient, I find it conceptually cleaner, as well as more portable, to stick to one interface discovery paradigm within a single module.

❑   The parameter SBid is an out-only parameter. That makes the SBidder pointer member m_pbdrMember an embedded out-only ref pointer. According to the memory allocation conventions, the server has to allocate the memory for this pointer. The code calls the COM task allocator to do so.

❑   Since we do have an embedded out-only pointer, we need to ensure that it is zero on entry to simplify compliance with the 'on error' memory allocation convention.

❑   Notice how get_Bidder()'s compliance with the 'on error' memory convention simplifies the error return for get_Bid(). The only clean up required is for local memory allocation.

❑   Finally, notice that I set the m_pbdrMember member variable of the SBid parameter to zero on failure. This has to be done to be in compliance with the on-error allocation conventions.

IBidsCustom

Next, let's look at the implementation of the IBidsCustom interface. It turns out that we don't have to implement the Count() method on this interface, as we can simply share the implementations already created for the IBids interface. This is one of the nice features of the ATL technique for implementing COM interfaces via multiple inheritance. Whenever the same method is duplicated in more than one interface, its implementation can be re-used (assuming the semantics remain the same).

The Item() Method

Here's the implementation of the Item() method. Remember that get_Item() is supposed to return the item at a given index:

```
STDMETHOD(Item)(LONG a_vlIndex, SBid* a_pbid)
{
    if(a_pbid == NULL)
        return E_POINTER;
    a_pbid->m_pbdrMember= 0;
```

```
      Order();

      if(0 <= a_vlIndex && a_vlIndex < m_cbidOrdered.size())
      {
         CComPtr<IBidCustom> spIBidCustom;
         HRESULT hr = m_cbidOrdered[a_vlIndex]->QueryInterface(
                        IID_IBidCustom, reinterpret_cast<void**>(&spIBidCustom));
         if(SUCCEEDED(hr))
         {
            hr = spIBidCustom->get_Bid(a_pbid);
            ATLASSERT(a_pbid->m_pbdrMember != 0);
         }
         return hr;
      }
      return E_INVALIDARG;
   }
```

This code is fairly straightforward and lets the get_Bid() function do all the work.

- ❑ We use the same technique of doing a QueryInterface() on a C++ object, rather than a dynamic_cast<>.

- ❑ Since we are once again in a situation where we have an embedded out-only ref pointer, the method needs to allocate memory for the pointer. Instead of doing so directly, it hands off to the get_Bid<> method whose IDL type indicates that it is required to allocate memory for the embedded pointer. Just to be on the safe side, we insert an assertion to check that the call allocated the memory as it should have.

- ❑ Once again, we need do nothing special in the case of failure, since it is assumed that get_Bid() will behave correctly if problems arise. We just pass the error back out.

The NewBidEnum Property

Finally, let us look at the implementation of get_NewBidEnum(). The purpose of this propget method is to return an enumeration interface – either IEnumVARIANT or IEnumBid. The caller gets to select the interface that it wants to request.

This is a long and interesting function, so I've broken it into sections that begin with an identifying comment for ease of description:

```
   STDMETHOD(get_NewBidEnum)(REFIID a_riid, LPUNKNOWN* a_ppuk)
   {
      // Section 1
      if(a_ppuk == NULL)
         return E_POINTER;
         *a_ppuk = NULL;

      // Section 2
      if(InlineIsEqualGUID(a_riid, IID_IEnumVARIANT))
      {
         CComPtr<IUnknown> spIUnk;
         HRESULT hr = get__NewEnum(&spIUnk);
         ATLASSERT(SUCCEEDED(hr));
         hr = spIUnk->QueryInterface(IID_IEnumVARIANT,
                                      reinterpret_cast<void**>(a_ppuk));
         ATLASSERT(SUCCEEDED(hr));
         return hr;
      }
```

```
   if(!InlineIsEqualGUID(a_riid, IID_IEnumBid))
      return E_NOINTERFACE;

// Section 3
Order();

typedef CComObject<CComEnum<IEnumBid,
                            &IID_IEnumBid, SBid*, _Copy<SBid*> > > TEnumVar;
TEnumVar* p = new TEnumVar;
ATLASSERT(p);

SBid** apBid = new SBid*[m_cbidOrdered.size()];
vector<CComPtr<IBid> >::iterator ppIBid;
SBid** ppBid = apBid;

HRESULT hr = S_OK;
for(ppIBid = m_cbidOrdered.begin();
                          ppIBid < m_cbidOrdered.end(); ppIBid++, ppBid++)
{

   // Section 4
   CComPtr<IBidCustom> spIBidCustom;
   hr = (*ppIBid)->QueryInterface(IID_IBidCustom,
                                  reinterpret_cast<void**>(&spIBidCustom));
   if(FAILED(hr))
      break;

   SBid* pBid = reinterpret_cast<SBid*>(CoTaskMemAlloc(sizeof(SBid)));
   if(pBid == 0)
   {
      hr = E_OUTOFMEMORY;
      break;
   }

   pBid->m_pbdrMember= 0;
   hr = spIBidCustom->get_Bid(pBid);
   *ppBid = pBid;
   if(FAILED(hr))
      break;
}

if(SUCCEEDED(hr))
{
   HRESULT hr = p->Init(&apBid[0], &apBid[m_cbidOrdered.size()],
                                          NULL, AtlFlagTakeOwnership);
   if(SUCCEEDED(hr))
      hr = p->QueryInterface(IID_IEnumBid, reinterpret_cast<void**>(a_ppuk));
}

// Section 5
if(FAILED(hr))
{
   delete p;
   ppBid = apBid;
```

```
         for(ppIBid = m_cbidOrdered.begin();
                             ppIBid < m_cbidOrdered.end(); ppIBid++, ppBid++)
      {
         if(*ppBid)
         {
            FreeBidEmbeds(*ppBid);
            CoTaskMemFree(*ppBid);
         }
         else
            break;
      }
      delete [] apBid;
   }
   return hr;
}
```

Section 1

Section 1 of the code consists of the standard method entry protocol, with which you ought to be familiar by now!

Section 2

The first part of section 2 checks the incoming IID to see if it is IEnumVARIANT. If it is, the existing get_NewEnum() method is called. Since this is actually a method of the same C++ class, it's OK to call it directly without doing a QI().

The most interesting point is what happens next. Instead of returning the value retrieved from the method call, the code does a QI() for IEnumVARIANT and returns that interface after casting it to IUnknown. Why cast back to IUnknown? Why is the return value different from that of get_NewEnum()?

The answer is that get_NewEnum() returns the actual IUnknown interface on the enumerator, which the client then queries for IEnumVARIANT. In the case of get_NewEnumBid(), the client (and more importantly, the MIDL-generated marshaling code) assumes the actual IEnumVARIANT interface is returned. It would be wrong to return the IUnknown pointer, because the marshaling code will fail when you try to invoke non-IUnknown methods on the returned interface. The cast to IUnknown is required only to satisfy the type system of the C++ compiler.

Note, by the way, that I'm ASSERT()'ing the success codes rather than testing them. This is because we can be confident to a high degree of certainty that the calls will succeed, since the implementation is defined within this class.

The last piece of section 2 returns if the incoming IID is not IEnumBid. Thus, this method will only work if the requested interface is IEnumBid or IEnumVARIANT.

Section 3

Section 3 sets up the ATL enumerator machinery and the STL iterators over the bid collection data member. Remember that the bid collection is actually an STL vector of type CComPtr<IBid> (a smart pointer wrapper around IBid), from which we need to extract the IBidCustom interface that is actually used to retrieve the SBid structure. This is done in Section 4.

Section 4

It's especially important to notice how I've followed the memory allocation conventions here. The `get_Bid()` function expects a pointer whose IDL signature is `[out, ref]`. The memory for the top-level pointer must be allocated before it is called, and the embedded `ref` pointer should be set to zero (this is not strictly necessary, but our code asserts if it isn't true). As we've seen, the `get_Bid()` function is responsible for allocating the embedded `ref` pointer.

Who should allocate the memory for the top-level `SBid` pointer? Let's think for a second about how this pointer is used. The pointer is created to go into an STL collection that is used internally by the anonymous ATL enumerator class. This enumerator class has methods that implement the `IEnumBid` interface, which will return one or more `SBid` pointers on demand. The marshaling code will then need to clean up the objects pointed at by these pointers. All of this magic is accomplished by the `_Copy<>` templatized class that is a template parameter to the `CComEnum` declaration, and we will look at this class in the next section. For now, all you need to know is that the memory for each `SBid` structure is allocated using `CoTaskMemAlloc()`, and will eventually be freed when the enumerator object is destroyed.

At the end of section 4 is the actual initialization of the enumerator object.

Section 5

Section 5 contains code for the usual rigorous clean up of allocated memory on failure. Remember that the clean up must not only free memory that has already been allocated, it must also leave all parameters in the appropriate 'on error' state.

Notice that there is a helper function called `FreeBidEmbeds()` being used to do the actual clean up of the `SBid` structure, and in the next section we'll take a look at this and other helper functions that perform valuable tasks.

Deep Copy Helpers

We need two kinds of helper functions: one kind to do deep copies of variables that have embedded pointers, and another kind to free the embedded pointers in such variables. Let's begin, though, by looking at some simpler utility functions.

Utility Functions

The utility functions `SysFree()` and `CoFree()` are wrappers around `SysFreeString()` and `CoTaskMemFree()`. They reset the pointer to the released memory to zero:

```
inline void SysFree(BSTR& a_vstr)
{
    ::SysFreeString(a_vstr);
    a_vstr = 0;
}

inline void CoFree(void** a_p)
{
    CoTaskMemFree(*a_p);
    *a_p = 0;
}
```

```
inline HRESULT SysCopyTo(BSTR& a_vstrL, BSTR& a_vstrR)
{
    BSTR vstr;
    vstr = ::SysAllocString(a_vstrR);
    if(vstr == 0)
    {
        a_vstrL = 0;
        return E_OUTOFMEMORY;
    }
    else
    {
        a_vstrL = vstr;
        return S_OK;
    }
}
```

SysCopyTo() is a wrapper around SysAllocString() that leaves the LHS pointer zeroed out on failure. It also returns an HRESULT on failure instead of a size. As we'll see, this makes it a lot easier to use from our helper functions.

Freeing Embedded Pointers

We've seen that IDL semantics expect the server code to be responsible for releasing embedded pointers, while the marshaler releases the top-level pointers. This means that we must create helper functions that free embedded memory but *not* top-level memory. Here are the helper functions for SBidder and SBid:

```
void FreeBidderEmbeds(SBidder* a_pbdr)
{
    ::SysFree(a_pbdr->m_vstrCity);
    ::SysFree(a_pbdr->m_vstrState);
    ::SysFree(a_pbdr->m_vstrFirstName);
    ::SysFree(a_pbdr->m_vstrLastName);
}

void FreeBidEmbeds(SBid* a_pbid)
{
    FreeBidderEmbeds(a_pbid->m_pbdrMember);
    CoFree(reinterpret_cast<void**>(&a_pbid->m_pbdrMember));
}
```

The first function frees the memory embedded in SBidder, and the second frees the memory embedded in SBid. Notice that they're calling the SysFree() and CoFree() utility functions, which means that they will leave all embedded pointers 'nulled-out', in addition to freeing them. This feature makes these helpers usable when cleaning up after an error.

Deep Copying

Similar issues need to be addressed when creating deep copy helpers. The helpers need to allocate memory for embedded pointers, while assuming that the top-level pointers are pre-allocated. They also need to clean up on failure. Here are the deep copy methods:

```
HRESULT CopyBidderEmbeds(SBidder* a_pbdrL, SBidder* a_pbdrR)
{
    HRESULT hr;
    hr = SysCopyTo(a_pbdrL->m_vstrCity, a_pbdrR->m_vstrCity);
    hr = SysCopyTo(a_pbdrL->m_vstrState, a_pbdrR->m_vstrState);
    hr = SysCopyTo(a_pbdrL->m_vstrFirstName, a_pbdrR->m_vstrFirstName);
    hr = SysCopyTo(a_pbdrL->m_vstrLastName, a_pbdrR->m_vstrLastName);
```

```
    if(FAILED(hr))
        FreeBidderEmbeds(a_pbdrL);

    return hr;
}

HRESULT CopyBidEmbeds(SBid* a_pbidL, SBid* a_pbidR)
{
    a_pbidL->m_vlPrice   = a_pbidR->m_vlPrice;
    a_pbidL->m_vlTime    = a_pbidR->m_vlTime;
    a_pbidL->m_vsNumber  = a_pbidR->m_vsNumber;

    a_pbidL->m_pbdrMember = reinterpret_cast<SBidder*>(
                                        CoTaskMemAlloc(sizeof(SBidder)));
    if(!a_pbidL->m_pbdrMember)
        return E_OUTOFMEMORY;

    HRESULT hr = CopyBidderEmbeds(a_pbidL->m_pbdrMember, a_pbidR->m_pbdrMember);
    if(FAILED(hr))
        CoFree(reinterpret_cast<void **>(a_pbidL->m_pbdrMember));

    return hr;
}
```

These methods do what they are supposed to. Notice particularly how the control flow is kept simple in the case of errors; all the functions are designed to keep the memory in a consistent state in this case. Note also how the copying methods depend on the freeing methods to clean up, demonstrating why these helper methods need to be created in pairs.

The _Copy<> Template Specialization

Finally, let's look at the specialization of the _Copy<> template class that is required by the ATL CComEnum<> class. We need to specialize this class for the SBid structure, since it requires deep copy semantics (although you *can* get away with shallow copy semantics, if you only use the enumerator in certain restricted ways). Here is the template specialization:

```
template<>
class ATL::_Copy<SBid*>
{
public:
    static HRESULT copy(SBid** p1, SBid** p2)
    {
        HRESULT hr = S_OK;
        (*p1) = reinterpret_cast<SBid*>(CoTaskMemAlloc(sizeof(SBid)));
        if(*p1 == NULL)
            hr = E_OUTOFMEMORY;
        else
            hr = CopyBidEmbeds(*p1, *p2);
        return hr;
    }
    static void init(SBid** p)
    {
        *p = NULL;
    }
    static void destroy(SBid** p)
    {
        FreeBidEmbeds(*p); CoTaskMemFree(*p);
    }
};
```

This class has three methods: the first to do a deep copy, the second for initialization and the third for releasing memory. A couple of points are noteworthy:

- ❑ The functions are easy to write because we already had our helpers written.
- ❑ The `copy()` function actually allocates memory for the top-level bid structure. This is the right thing to do, since the bid copies will be used in a context where they are `out`-only embedded pointers (in the `Next()` method).

The Auction Client

You may just remember that the whole point of this exercise was to see if we could gain performance improvements by replacing the Automation interface with a nested structure. The theory was that the latter option should have much better marshaling characteristics. We must therefore build a client that uses several different enumeration methods in order to test the actual performance characteristics.

In the source code archive for this book that you'll find on the Wrox web site, you'll find a pair of projects called `InitPerf` and `PerfMeas`, with instructions as to how you should go about installing them. The code in this section comes from the `PerfMeas` (performance measuring) example.

Different Ways to Enumerate

The code is actually very simple: we just populate an auction lot with a large number of bids. We then step through the lot one bid at a time, assigning the bid values to a stack variable. We then measure the elapsed time for the entire operation.

Enumerating with IEnumVARIANT::Next()

```
long CAuctionClient::MeasureVariantRefresh()
{
    IBidsCustomPtr spIBids = m_spILot->GetBids();
    int iCount = a_spIBids->GetCount();

    _variant_t* aVariant = new _variant_t[iCount];

    CStopClock sc;

    IEnumVARIANTPtr spIEnumVARIANT;
    HRESULT hr = spIBids->get_NewBidEnum(
        const_cast<GUID*>(&__uuidof(IEnumVARIANT)),
        reinterpret_cast<IUnknown**>(&spIEnumVARIANT));
    _ASSERTE(SUCCEEDED(hr));

    ULONG ulFetch;
    hr = spIEnumVARIANT->Next(iCount, aVariant, &ulFetch);
    _ASSERTE(SUCCEEDED(hr));

    int i;
```

```
    for(i = 0; i < iCount; i++)
    {
        IBidPtr spIBid(aVariant[i]);
        _bstr_t vstr1(spIBid->GetBidder()->GetFirstName());
        _bstr_t vstr2(spIBid->GetBidder()->GetLastName());
        _bstr_t vstr3(spIBid->GetBidder()->GetCity());
        _bstr_t vstr4(spIBid->GetBidder()->GetState());
        int i1(spIBid->GetPrice());
        short s1(spIBid->GetNumber());
        long t1(spIBid->GetTime());
    };

    sc.Stop();

    delete [] aVariant;

    return sc.TimeMS();
}
```

Retrieving a Named Interface

The first part of the code gets the `IEnumVARIANT` interface of our bids enumerator. Note that we do not use the `get__NewEnum()` method to do this. Instead, we use the new `get_NewEnumBid()` method and pass in the IID of the `IEnumVARIANT` interface. Once this interface has been fetched, we proceed as we did before, using the smart pointer wrappers to the `IBid` and `IBidder` interfaces.

Memory Allocation

You might now be thinking, "Just a minute! Where did the memory for all these parameters get allocated? Why didn't I have to free it?" The Automation properties are all `out` properties, so memory has to be freed by the client. Let's begin by considering the `Next()` method.

The IDL for this method takes a sized pointer at the top-level to hold the returned array. The top-level storage has to be allocated on the client, and that means storage for the *entire* array – in this case, `iCount` elements. Since the storage is allocated and freed on the client, we don't need to use the task memory allocator – plain old `new` and `delete` work just fine. This array is allocated in the variable `aVariant`. I chose an element type of `_variant_t` (storage compatible with `VARIANT`) so that cleanup (of the returned `IDispatch` interface) is done automatically by the class destructor.

How about cleanup of the `BSTR`s returned by the individual Automation properties? The answer, you might recall from the previous chapter, is in the smart pointer wrappers.

Time Measurement

Finally, note the `CStopClock` variable, `sc`. This is a C++ class (even I use pure C++ classes from time to time!) that was created to get access to the fine granularity system timer. The `TimeMS()` method returns the elapsed time between the `stop()` and `start()` methods in milliseconds.

Enumerating with IEnumBid::Next()

Here is the equivalent code using `IEnumBid` instead of `IEnumVARIANT`:

```
long CAuctionClient::MeasureBidRefresh()
{
    IBidsCustomPtr spIBids = m_spILot->GetBids();
    int iCount = spIBids->GetCount();

    SBid** apBid = new SBid*[iCount];
```

```
      CStopClock sc;

      IEnumBidPtr spIEnumBid;
      HRESULT hr = spIBids->get_NewBidEnum(const_cast<GUID*>(&__uuidof(IEnumBid)),
                                  reinterpret_cast<IUnknown**>(&spIEnumBid));
      _ASSERTE(SUCCEEDED(hr));

      ULONG ulFetch;
      hr = spIEnumBid->Next(iCount, apBid, &ulFetch);
      _ASSERTE(SUCCEEDED(hr));
      int i;

      for(i = 0; i < iCount; i++)
      {
          SBid * pBid = apBid[i];
          _bstr_t vstr1(pBid->m_pbdrMember->m_vstrFirstName);
          _bstr_t vstr2(pBid->m_pbdrMember->m_vstrLastName);
          _bstr_t vstr3(pBid->m_pbdrMember->m_vstrCity);
          _bstr_t vstr4(pBid->m_pbdrMember->m_vstrState);
          int i1(pBid->m_vlPrice);
          short s1(pBid->m_vsNumber);
          long t1(pBid->m_vlTime);
          FreeBid(apBid[i]);
      };
      sc.Stop();

      delete [] apBid;

      return sc.TimeMS();
  }
```

Once again, the most important aspect of this code is the memory allocation behavior. The allocation of the top-level structure passed into the Next() method is similar to the case we've just been dealing with, except that the element type is now an SBid pointer. The memory for the pointers embedded in the array ([out, ref, unique]) is allocated by the server, and so the client needs to free it. This is accomplished by the FreeBid() routine, which is a wrapper around FreeBidEmbeds() that frees the SBid structure as well.

Enumerating with IBidsCustom::Item()

Finally, here is the code that enumerates using the Item() method of the IBidsCustom collection interface:

```
long CAuctionClient::MeasureItemBidRefresh()
{
    IBidsCustomPtr spIBids = m_spILot->GetBids();
    int iCount = spIBids->GetCount();

    CStopClock sc;
```

```
    for(int i = 0; i < iCount; i++)
    {
        SBid bid = spIBids->Item(i);
        _bstr_t vstr1(bid.m_pbdrMember->m_vstrFirstName);
        _bstr_t vstr2(bid.m_pbdrMember->m_vstrLastName);
        _bstr_t vstr3(bid.m_pbdrMember->m_vstrCity);
        _bstr_t vstr4(bid.m_pbdrMember->m_vstrState);
        int i1(bid.m_vlPrice);
        short s1(bid.m_vsNumber);
        long t1(bid.m_vlTime);
        FreeBidder(bid.m_pbdrMember);
    };

    sc.Stop();

    return sc.TimeMS();
}
```

This code does not use an enumeration interface at all. Instead, it iterates through the collection using the `Item()` method. Recall that this method takes a single `[out, ref, retval]` pointer parameter, but since it is a top-level parameter, allocation is done on the client. Since it is a single *element*, allocation can be done on the heap. The actual call is of course wrapped by the `#import`-generated code, which looks like this:

```
inline SBid IBidsCustom::Item(long a_vlIndex)
{
    SBid _result;
    HRESULT _hr = raw_Item(a_vlIndex, &_result);
    if(FAILED(_hr))
        _com_issue_errorex(_hr, this, __uuidof(this));

    return _result;
}
```

As you can see, an `SBid` structure (not a pointer) is being allocated on the stack, and its address passed into the method call. There is a slight inefficiency introduced here by the conversion from `ref` pointer to return value, because the entire structure is being copied out.

That takes care of the top-level pointer, but the embedded pointer is still allocated on the server, and must be freed. This is done via the `FreeBidder()` function, a wrapper around `FreeBidderEmbeds()`.

Performance Characteristics

So, what did the performance measurements look like? Here are the measurements I got in milliseconds:

Out-of-process Server	100 elements	1000 elements	10000 elements
`IEnumVARIANT::Next()`	731	7841	166329
`IEnumBid::Next()`	20	120	1602
`IBidsCustom::Item()`	40	390	3926

In-process Server	1000 elements	10000 elements
`IEnumVARIANT::Next()`	240	3045
`IEnumBid::Next()`	90	1842
`IBidsCustom::Item()`	80	852

Notice the pronounced improvement in performance of using `struct`s rather than method calls in the out-of-process case. There is even a significant performance difference in the in-process case.

Detecting Leaked Memory

As you have probably figured out by now, memory allocation in interface method calls can become quite complicated due to the interplay between pointer types and directional parameters. Now that you've read the rest of this chapter, however, you should have a systematic understanding of the memory allocation framework, and be able to debug hairy memory allocation situations.

However, as all old C programmers know, dynamic memory allocation is a persistent source of bugs and performance problems. The situation in C++ is considerably better because of the lifetime management framework provided by the language, and as a result C++ has a greatly reduced incidence of heap allocation problems. The use of Wizards and C++ smart pointer wrappers should make life simpler for the ATL COM programmer as well. However, heap allocation problems will continue to persist.

One of the best tools to ensure software quality is the **instrumented heap**. Typically, this is a special heap that runs from debug builds, keeping extra bookkeeping information on each heap operation. At the end of execution, it reports on any memory leaks that occurred during that run. Visual C++ 6.0 comes with such an instrumented heap built in.

Unfortunately, the COM task memory allocator *cannot* be replaced with a different heap implementation, so instead the designers left in a hook by means of which heap allocations can be monitored. The user can register an implementation of the `IMallocSpy` interface with the COM task memory allocator. Immediately before and after each heap operation, the allocator calls into the implementation of this interface, which can perform fairly sophisticated instrumentation of heap operations.

In the `MemChekr` project, I have provided a reasonably sophisticated implementation of the `IMallocSpy` interface. My object keeps track of each allocation, and the corresponding release. On demand, it dumps a list of the memory blocks that are left unreleased (the leaked memory) onto the debug window. If the report is clean, there are no memory leaks.

The allocator spy is accessed through a C API consisting of `MallocSpyRegister()`, `MallocSpyRevoke()` and `MallocSpyDump()`.

Here is some code that demonstrates its use:

```cpp
int main(int argc, char* argv[])
{
   CoInitialize(NULL);
   MallocSpyRegister();
   {
      // Rest of program
   }
   MallocSpyRevoke();
   CoUninitialize();

   MallocSpyDump();

   return 0;
}
```

The interesting point here is that `MallocSpyDump()` must be called *after* `CoUninitialize()`. If this is not the case, the spy will report memory that is used by the COM runtime as leaks!

Let's take a quick look at the implementation of this spy. First of all, some globals that you'll find in the source file `MallocSpy.cpp`: a critical section object controlling access to the spy, an ATL object pointer to the spy object, and a Boolean flag indicating spy registration:

```cpp
CComCriticalSection g_vcsMS;
CComObject<CMallocSpy>* g_pMS = 0;
bool g_vbReg = false;
```

Here is the code that initializes these globals:

```cpp
bool WINAPI MSInit()
{
   g_vcsMS.Init();
   HRESULT hr = CComObject<CMallocSpy>::CreateInstance(&g_pMS);
   ATLASSERT(SUCCEEDED(hr));
   if(SUCCEEDED(hr))
   {
      g_pMS->InternalAddRef();
      return true;
   }
   else
      return false;
}
```

Notice that we're using a C++ rather than a COM creation mechanism to create the object; this is to avoid COM memory allocation operations associated with this creation. Also, we do not want this object to get de-allocated by accident, so we artificially bump up its reference count.

Next, look at the code for `MallocSpyRegister()`:

```cpp
STDAPI MallocSpyRegister()
{
   HRESULT hr;
   g_vcsMS.Lock();
   if(!g_vbReg)
   {
      CComPtr<IMallocSpy> spIMallocSpy;
```

```
        hr = g_pMS->QueryInterface(&spIMallocSpy);
        if(SUCCEEDED(hr))
        {
            hr = CoRegisterMallocSpy(spIMallocSpy);
            if(SUCCEEDED(hr))
                g_vbReg = true;
        }
    }
    else
        hr = CO_E_OBJISREG;

    g_vcsMS.Unlock();
    return hr;
}
```

This code uses the `CoRegisterMallocSpy()` API to register our spy interface with the task memory allocator. For thread safety, we guard the code with a critical section variable.

The `MallocSpyRevoke()` function performs the corresponding unregistration:

```
STDAPI MallocSpyRevoke()
{
    HRESULT hr;
    g_vcsMS.Lock();
    if(g_vbReg)
    {
        hr = CoRevokeMallocSpy();
        g_vbReg = false;
    }
    else
        hr = CO_E_OBJNOTREG;

    g_vcsMS.Unlock();
    return hr;
}
```

Finally, the `MallocSpyDump()` function calls the `Dump()` method of the `IDiagnostic` interface on the object:

```
STDAPI MallocSpyDump()
{
    g_vcsMS.Lock();
    (static_cast<IDiagnostic*>(g_pMS))->Dump();
    g_vcsMS.Unlock();
    return S_OK;
}
```

The actual object implementation simply keeps an STL vector of the memory blocks that have been allocated so far. Each 'allocate' operation adds to this list, and each 'release' operation removes an item from it. At each dump, the remaining elements in the vector are output.

Every block that gets allocated is prefixed with a header that contains bookkeeping information on the block. This header info forms part of the dump report.

To give you a flavor of the implementation, here is the code for the `PreAlloc()` and `PostAlloc()` interface methods, which get called before and after the actual `CoTaskMemAlloc()`:

```
ULONG CMallocSpy::PreAlloc(ULONG cbRequest)
{
    m_vulRequest = cbRequest;
    return m_vulRequest + HeaderSize + FooterSize);
}

VOID* CMallocSpy::PostAlloc(VOID* pHeader)
{
    Add(USERS_OFFSET(pHeader));
    HEAD_SIGNATURE(pHeader) = HeadSign;
    BUFFER_LENGTH(pHeader) = m_vulRequest;

    static ULONG ulID = 0;
    BUFFER_ID(pHeader) = ++ulID;

    memset(USERS_OFFSET(pHeader), AllocSign, m_vulRequest);
    TAIL_SIGNATURE(pHeader) = TailSign;

#ifdef FINDLEAKS
    ATLTRACE(L"-- IMallocSpy Alloc - 0x%08x, ID=%08lu, %lu bytes\n",
        USERS_OFFSET(pHeader), ulID, m_vulRequest);
#endif

    return USERS_OFFSET(pHeader);
}
```

`PreAlloc()` stores the size of the request and then changes the request size to include room for the header and footer.

`PostAlloc()` receives the actual buffer returned from the allocation, adds it to its collection, initializes the header information, places a signature around the block that can be checked for memory corruption, and finally returns the user an adjusted pointer to the user area of the block. This strategy lets us place arbitrary amounts of information in the header and footer.

Building a DHTML Control

To conclude this chapter (and the book), I'll give you a very rapid overview of the implementation of the DHTML control that we used for the DHTML-based client in Chapter 6. You've doubtless already tested the client and seen how it works, and it turns out that ATL 3.0 has support for building controls of exactly this kind.

> *As ever, the source code for this example is included in the archive that's available for download, and this particular project is called* `htAddBid`.

The Architecture of a DHTML Control

A DHTML control is yet another way of building controls that display a user interface; it is a composite control that has other controls embedded within it. What makes DHTML controls different from other composite controls, however, is that the form is laid out using HTML as the page description language, rather than some custom form layout language. What makes this seem especially bizarre is that a DHTML control may itself be embedded in a web page, or even in some other DHTML control.

How is this accomplished? It's actually simpler than you might think. A DHTML control is an ActiveX control that has an embedded web browser control. The web browser control is used to display the DHTML resource that defines the form. The form is just a DHTML page like any other, which can include text, graphics, form controls and script.

From the form, scripting languages gain access to the outer DHTML control via a designated Automation-capable interface on that control. This means that the outer control must expose *two* incoming Automation-capable interfaces: one for its own container (which I shall call IA1 in the ensuing explanations) and another for the script in the DHTML page (called IA2). In addition, the outer control can expose one or more *outgoing* interfaces via the connection point mechanism, and we'll call the default source interface ISA.

The Inner Script Interface

You may remember that the control in Chapter 6 exported an outgoing interface called DWebBridgeEvents (which translates to ISA here) and a regular incoming interface called IAddBid (which is therefore IA1). The third interface – IA2 – is called IAddBidUI in the ATL project, and it's declared as follows:

```
interface IAddBidUI : IDispatch
{
    [propget, id(1), helpstring("property Quantity")]
    HRESULT Quantity([out, retval] short* a_ps);

    [propput, id(1), helpstring("property Quantity")]
    HRESULT Quantity([in] short a_vs);

    [propget, id(2), helpstring("property Price")]
    HRESULT Price([out, retval] long* a_pl);

    [propput, id(2), helpstring("property Price")]
    HRESULT Price([in] long a_vl);

    [id(3), helpstring("FireAddBid")]
    HRESULT FireAddBid(BidState a_ve, VARIANT a_vvntEvent);
};
```

The Control Class

If you now take a look at the ATL project, the complete declaration of the DHTML control's coclass looks like this, in keeping with the explanations I've just provided:

```
importlib("mshtmlwb.dll");

...

coclass AddBid
{
    [default] interface IAddBid;
    [default, source] dispinterface DWebBridgeEvents;
    interface IAddBidUI;
};
```

The DHTML Form

To get a feel for how these interfaces ought to be implemented, let's now examine the HTML form and its associated script. As you've seen, the form simply has two edit controls named txtPrice and txtQuantity, into which the user can type bid parameters. When the user is done, they press either the Add or the Cancel button.

The Add button should validate the inputs, store them somewhere where they will be available to the main form (in which this control is embedded), and then fire the appropriate method on its event interface. The Cancel button simply lets the main form know that it has been pressed, again by firing the appropriate method on the event interface.

I said at the beginning of this discussion that scripting languages gain access to the outer DHTML control via a designated interface on that control, and it turns out that this designation is made by a call to CAxWindow::SetExternalDispatch() in the OnCreate() method of your DHTML control; you can see this in action in the project file AddBid.h:

```
hr = wnd.SetExternalDispatch(static_cast<IAddBidUI*>(this));
```

Hence, the script only has access to the IAddBidUI interface on the DHTML control, and so it must use this interface to initiate event firing. Here is the code involved:

```
Sub window_onload()
    txtPrice.value    = window.external.Price
    txtQuantity.value = window.external.Quantity
End Sub

Sub cmdAdd_onclick()
    If BidValidate() Then
        window.external.Price = txtPrice.value
        window.external.Quantity = txtQuantity.value
        window.external.FireAddBid 1, window.event
    End If
End Sub

Sub cmdCancel_onclick()
    window.external.FireAddBid 0, window.event
End Sub
```

In this code, the window.external variable is actually the IAddBidUI interface of the DHTML control, and so the window_onload() function initializes our form's edit controls to the Price and Quantity properties of the IAddBidUI interface on the control.

cmdAdd_onclick(), which is the event handler for the Add button in the form, sets the same properties using the edit controls as the source. It then calls the IAddBidUI::FireAddBid() method.

cmdCancel_onclick(), which is the event hander for the Cancel button on the form, simply calls IAddBidUI::FireAddBid() with a different first parameter.

Implementing the Interfaces

Let us now look at the C++ code that enables the script to operate in the way we want it to. The implementations of the `Price` and `Quantity` properties are trivial; here are the property access methods for `Price` (this implementation is used for both `IAddBid` and `IAddBidUI`, since the properties have the same semantics and types in both interfaces):

```
STDMETHOD(get_Price)(/*[out, retval]*/ long * a_pl)
{
   *a_pl = m_vlPrice;
   return S_OK;
}

STDMETHOD(put_Price)(/*[in]*/ long a_vl)
{
   m_vlPrice = a_vl;
   return S_OK;
}
```

The `Enabled` property is more interesting: the `get` method is trivial, but recall that the `put` method has to be able to make the control disappear. Here is its implementation:

```
STDMETHOD(put_Enabled)(/*[in]*/ BOOL a_vb)
{
   m_vbEnabled = !!a_vb;
   if(!m_vbEnabled)
   {
      m_vlHeight = m_rcPos.bottom - m_rcPos.top;
      m_vlWidth = m_rcPos.right - m_rcPos.left;
      RECT vrcPos = {m_rcPos.left, m_rcPos.top, m_rcPos.left, m_rcPos.top};
      return m_spInPlaceSite->OnPosRectChange(&vrcPos);
   }
   else
   {
      RECT vrcPos = {m_rcPos.left, m_rcPos.top, m_rcPos.left + m_vlWidth,
         m_rcPos.top + m_vlHeight};
      return m_spInPlaceSite->OnPosRectChange(&vrcPos);
   }
}
```

This method makes use of the `m_spInPlaceSite` smart interface pointer to the `IInPlaceSite` interface on the container. This interface can be used to resize the control to make it appear and disappear (size zero) on demand.

Finally, let's look at `FireAddBid()`. This is a very simple function that allocates a BSTR (because the type signature of the string variable is `out`-only) and calls the event firing code. Depending on the first parameter, the string is either "addbid" or "cancel"; this is as I described it when we briefly discussed the operation of this client at the end of Chapter 6.

```
STDMETHODIMP FireAddBid(BidState a_veBS, VARIANT a_vvntEvent)
{
   BSTR vstr;
   switch(a_veBS)
   {
   case bsAddBid:
      vstr = SysAllocString(OLESTR("addbid"));
```

```
        Fire_onscriptletevent(vstr, a_vvntEvent);
        break;
    case bsCancel:
        vstr = SysAllocString(OLESTR("cancel"));
        Fire_onscriptletevent(vstr, a_vvntEvent);
        break;
    default:
        return E_INVALIDARG;
    }
    return S_OK;
}
```

That concludes our whistle-stop tour of this implementation, and I hope that I've covered enough to give you a feel for how the interfaces of the DHTML control fit together. Should you so choose, you ought to be able to delve further into the source code of the sample project with a good idea of what's going on.

Summary

I've covered an enormous amount of ground in this chapter, and careful (re) reading of it should pay you handsome dividends when you're designing and building your COM object models. Way back when, I began with a description of IDL bindings to C++ ATL. During the course of this first section, we looked at:

- The data type bindings of IDL to C++/ATL, especially the bindings for BSTRs and VARIANTs
- The bindings for UUIDs, and IDL enums, structs and unions
- The raw C/C++ bindings for IDL interfaces, as well as smart pointer classes
- The overall structure of the ATL classes
- A simple server implementation in ATL, including method implementation details such as preparing out parameters, creating custom HRESULTs, transforming HRESULTs, and providing support for dual interfaces, COM error objects and the connectable object protocol

Next, I described the design of the implementation model for the auction server; the realization of the specification object model that we put together in Chapter 5. In this section, we discussed:

- The variety and purpose of persistence interfaces
- The role of construction interfaces on class objects, and the structure of construction methods
- The need to define anonymous class objects to implement construction interfaces
- The place of singleton classes, and how they are implemented by the class factory mechanism
- How to implement multiple scriptable interfaces on a single object by using the alternate identity technique
- How to enforce encapsulation of the specification model by using the alternate identity technique
- The interaction between alternate identities and persistence interfaces
- How to break reference cycles using the weak (or split) identity technique
- How enumerator objects fit into the object model
- What a box-spoon diagram for a full-fledged COM object model looks like

The ensuing section – a long one – dealt with building this object model using ATL and a few of my own extensions. The implementation saw a number of real-world problems being solved, including:

- Structuring a data schema for storing an object model in a relational database
- Using OLE DB consumer classes to gain access to the object model
- Implementing an `IPersistRowset` interface that uses OLE DB interfaces and the OLE DB consumer classes to load a collection of objects from a relational database
- The details of implementing alternate identities, including code for declaring the alternate interfaces, declaring the class object, having multiple COM maps for multiple alternate identities, and exposing alternate identities
- Implementing collection interfaces using STL collections
- Implementing custom constructor interfaces on top of ATL class objects
- Constructing a part/whole relationship, and breaking a reference cycle using a weak identity
- Implementing weak identities
- Implementing delayed loading of an object – that is, lazy initialization
- Implementing a custom event registration protocol
- Implementing persistence, including the use of delegation to implement one persistence interface with another
- Implementing `IPersistStreamInit` on a collection of COM objects
- Implementing `IPersistFile`, `IPersistVariant` and `IPersistPropertyBag` in sequence, each implementation using the previously implemented interface
- Using STL heaps to maintain sorted collections with complex partial orders
- Implementing identity navigation for objects that implement alternate or weak identities
- Using the ATL persistence interface implementation for `IPersistStreamInit` and `IPersistPropertyBag`
- Persisting the alternate identity on an object
- Implementing COM enumerators using ATL support

The penultimate section dealt with the use of user-defined types (UDTs) with embedded pointers in interface methods. It gave motivation for the use of such types by replacing object references with UDTs in an attempt to improve performance. By the end of this example, you should have seen:

- The performance benefits of using UDTs instead of object references
- How to use UDTs in interface design
- Designing enumerators and collections of UDTs
- The memory allocation rules for UDTs in interface method calls
- How to implement enumerators over complex UDTs in ATL
- The specialization of template helper functions to support such enumerators
- The helper functions that are needed for deep copy and memory release when dealing with UDTs
- The dramatic performance improvements that result from replacing object references with UDTs
- How to detect leaked memory by using the `IMallocSpy` interface to implement the COM task allocator

Finally, the chapter and the book closed with implementation details on the DHTML control that was designed and used in Chapter 6.

MIDL Compilation

You may have noticed that I have not focused too much on the details of MIDL compilation, and this might seem strange in a book called *COM IDL and Interface Design*. However, the reasons for my decision are simple: once you understand the peculiarities of the MIDL compilation process that are due to its varied legacy (as explained in Chapter 2), you've recognized about 95% of the interesting features of MIDL compilation as it pertains to COM.

If you read the MIDL documentation that comes with the Platform SDK, it is easy to get very confused. Part of the problem is that most of the documentation is describing the semantics of RPC IDL, and it isn't always easy to find the COM IDL sections. Fortunately, COM IDL is much simpler and has fewer options than RPC IDL, which is what makes the compilation of COM IDL relatively easy to understand.

In this Appendix, I shall clearly indicate the compiler switches and IDL keywords that apply only to RPC so you don't get confused when you come across them.

Compiler Options

The MIDL compiler processes IDL and corresponding ACF (RPC only) files to generate the RPC files, COM proxy-stub files, and a type library.

The following tables contain the various compiler options to MIDL. For the most part, these are extracted from the explanations in the 'MIDL /?' help information.

Mode

MIDL can run in various modes. Several of these modes (those that select the specific language being compiled) only apply to straight RPC (rather than COM), and are therefore not of particular interest. These switches allow the use of MS RPC instead of DCE RPC.

Flag	RPC only	Description
/ms_ext	Y	Microsoft extensions to the IDL language (allow by default).
/c_ext	Y	Allow Microsoft C extensions in the IDL file (default).
/osf	Y	OSF mode – disables /ms_ext and /c_ext options. Strict compliance with DCE RPC.
/app_config	Y	Selected ACF attributes can be placed in the IDL file instead of the ACF file.
/mktyplib203		MkTypLib Version 2.03 compatibility mode. This flag forces MIDL to operate in strict compatibility with the last version of MkTypLib. The syntax of the IDL file must conform strictly to the ODL syntax that was recognized by MkTypLib. This should only be necessary for legacy ODL code.

Input

The following flags permit finer control over the inputs into the MIDL compiler.

Flag	RPC only	Description
/acf filename	Y	Specify the attribute configuration file.
/I directory-list		Specify one or more directories for include path.
/no_def_idir		Ignore the current and the 'include' directories.

Output File Generation

The following flags permit finer control over the output files of the MIDL compiler.

Flag	RPC only	Description
/client none	Y	Do not generate client files. Applies only to RPC interfaces.
/client stub	Y	Generate client stub file. Applies only to RPC interfaces.
/out directory		Specify destination directory for output files.
/server none	Y	Generate no server files. Applies only to RPC interfaces.
/server stub	Y	Generate server stub file. Applies only to RPC interfaces.
/syntax_check		Check syntax only; do not generate output files.
/Zs		Check syntax only; do not generate output files.
/oldtlb		Beginning with NT 4.0, there is a new, richer format for type libraries. The format is generated/read using functionality in OLEAut32.dll. By default, MIDL checks for the presence of the newer version of the DLL and uses it if it's present. If /oldtlb is used, the old type library format will be generated, even if the newer DLL is present.
/newtlb		See the description under /oldtlb. If /newtlb is specified and the newer version of OLEAut32.dll is not present, an error is generated.

Output File Names

The following options control the naming of output files. This allows you to specify names other than those selected by MIDL as defaults.

Flag	RPC only	Description
/cstub filename	Y	Specify client stub filename. RPC only.
/dlldata filename		Specify 'dlldata' filename.
/h filename		Specify header filename.
/header filename		Specify header filename.
/iid filename		Specify interface UUID filename.
/proxy filename		Specify proxy filename.
/sstub filename	Y	Specify server stub filename. RPC only.
/tlb filename		Specify type library filename.

Compiler and Preprocessor Options

The following options allow you to fine-tune the behavior of the C preprocessor used by MIDL. *Beware* the use of such options. Under ordinary circumstances, you should never need to fiddle with 'cpp' options for your IDL files. Their only real utility lies in supporting legacy code.

Flag	RPC only	Description
/cpp_cmd cmd_line		Specify name of the C preprocessor.
/cpp_opt options		Specify additional C preprocessor options.
/D name[=def]		Define a name (with an optional value) in the C preprocessor.
/no_cpp		Turn off the C preprocessing option.
/nocpp		Turn off the C preprocessing option.
/U name		Remove any previous definition ('undefine').

Environment

The following options allow you to customize MIDL compilation for different environments. These include different operating systems, different compilers and different locales. The switches also include options for customizing the names of functions.

Flag	RPC only	Description
/char signed		C compiler default char type is signed.
/char unsigned		C compiler default char type is unsigned (default).
/char ascii7		char values limited to 0-127.
/dos		Target environment is MS-DOS client (obsolete).
/env dos		Target environment is MS-DOS client (obsolete).
/env mac		Target environment is Apple Macintosh (obsolete).
/env powermac		Target environment is Apple PowerMac.
/env win16		Target environment is 16-bit Windows (obsolete).
/env win32		Target environment is 32-bit Microsoft Windows.
/lcid		Locale ID for international locales.
/mac		Target environment is Apple Macintosh (obsolete).
/ms_union		Use MIDL 1.0 non-DCE wire layout for non-encapsulated unions.
/ms_conf_struct		Use MIDL 3.x and earlier non-DCE wire layout for complex structures.
/oldnames		Do not mangle version numbers into names.
/powermac		Target environment is Apple PowerMac.
/rpcss	Y	Automatically activate rpc_sm_enable_allocate.

Table Continued on Following Page

Flag	RPC only	Description
/use_epv	Y	Generate server side application calls via entry-point vector.
/no_default_epv	Y	Do not generate a default entry-point vector.
/prefix client str		Add 'str' prefix to client-side entry points.
/prefix server str		Add 'str' prefix to server-side manager routines.
/prefix switch str		Add 'str' prefix to switch routine prototypes.
/prefix all str		Add 'str' prefix to all routines.
/win16		Target environment is 16-bit Windows (obsolete).
/win32		Target environment is 32-bit Microsoft Windows.

Runtime Error Checking by Stubs

The proxy-stub marshaling code that is generated by MIDL can have varying levels of error checking capability. The following switches control the level of checking performed by the code.

Flag	RPC only	Description
/error none		Turn off all error checking options.
/error allocation		Check for out of memory errors.
/error bounds_check		Check size vs. transmission length specification.
/error enum		Ensure enum values in allowable range.
/error ref		Ensure ref pointers are non-null.
/error stub_data		Perform an additional check for server-side stub data validity.
/robust		Generate additional information to validate parameters.

Optimization

The following switches control various optimization features in the generated proxy-stub code, including the degree of packing to be used for structures, the style of proxy-stub code that is generated, and the presence of debug options.

Flag	RPC only	Description
/align {1|2|4|8}		Designate packing level of structures. The number specifies the byte alignment boundary.
/pack {1|2|4|8}		Designate packing level of structures.
/Zp {1|2|4|8}		Designate packing level of structures.
/no_format_opt		By default, MIDL eliminates the string representation of duplicate type and procedure descriptors to reduce the size of the proxy-stub DLL. This flag disables the optimization.
/Oi		Generate fully interpreted stubs; old style /Oicf is usually better.
/Oic		Generate fully interpreted stubs for standard interfaces and stub-less proxies for object interfaces as of NT version 3.51. Using /Oicf instead is usually better.
/Oicf		Generate fully interpreted stubs with extensions and stub-less proxies for object interfaces as of NT version 4.0.
/Oif		Same as /Oicf.
/Os		Generate inline stubs.
/hookole		Generate "HookOle" debug information for local object interfaces. This is used in conjunction with the HookOle diagnostic library.

Miscellaneous

Flag	RPC only	Description
@response_file		Accept input from a response file – that is, a file that contains the rest of the command line switches.
/?		Display a list of MIDL compiler switches.

Table Continued on Following Page

Flag	RPC only	Description
/confirm		Display options without compiling MIDL source.
/help		Display a list of MIDL compiler switches.
/nologo		Suppress display of banner lines.
/o filename		Redirect output from screen to a file.
/W{0|1|2|3|4}		Specify warning level 0-4 (default = 1).
/WX		Report warnings at specified /W level as errors.
/no_warn		Suppress compiler warning messages.

Keywords

Here is a matrix of IDL keywords and the declarations that they can decoratete.

General

Keyword	library	interface	dispinterface	coclass	module	module member	method	property	arguments	coclass member	typedef	struct member
aggregatable				Y								
appobject				Y								
bindable								Y				
control	Y			Y								
default										Y		
defaultbind								Y				
defaultcollelem								Y				
defaultvalue									Y			

Table Continued on Following Page

Keyword	library	interface	dispinterface	coclass	module	module member	method	property	arguments	coclass member	typedef	struct member
defaultvtbl										Y		
displaybind									Y			
dllname					Y							
dual		Y										
entry						Y						
helpcontext	Y	Y	Y	Y	Y		Y	Y			Y	
helpfile	Y											
helpstring	Y	Y	Y	Y	Y		Y	Y			Y	
helpstringdll	Y											
hidden	Y	Y	Y	Y			Y	Y				
id							Y	Y				
immediatebind								Y				
lcid	Y								Y			
licensed				Y								
nonbrowsable									Y			
noncreatable				Y								
nonextensible		Y	Y									
oleautomation		Y										
optional									Y			
propget								Y				
propput								Y				

Table Continued on Following Page

Keyword	library	interface	dispinterface	coclass	module	module member	module member	method	property	arguments	coclass member	typedef	struct member
propputref									Y				
public												Y	
readonly									Y	Y			
replaceable		Y											
requestedit									Y				
restricted	Y					Y		Y	Y		Y		
retval										Y			
source											Y		
string								Y	Y	Y		Y	Y
uidefault									Y	Y			
usesgetlasterror						Y							
uuid	Y	Y		Y	Y								
vararg									Y				
call_as									Y	Y			
first_is										Y			Y
ignore										Y			Y
iid_is										Y			Y
In										Y			
last_is										Y			Y
length_is										Y			Y
local		Y						Y	Y				
max_is										Y			Y

Table Continued on Following Page

Keyword	library	interface	dispinterface	coclass	module	module member	module member	method	property	arguments	coclass member	typedef	struct member
object		Y											
out										Y			
pointer_default	Y												
ptr										Y		Y	Y
ref										Y		Y	Y
size_is										Y			Y
switch													Y
switch_is										Y			Y
switch_type										Y			Y
transmit_as													Y
unique										Y		Y	Y
v1_enum													Y
wire_marshall													Y

Currently Unimplemented/RPC Specific

idempotent   broadcast   maybe   message

RPC Specific

context_handle   handle   ms_union   pipe
callback   endpoint   version

This Appendix takes a more detailed look at my ATL extensions for alternate and split identities. These extensions are dependent on the internal workings of the ATL architecture, but if you restrict your usage of the extensions to the attribute-style programming macros, you should be able to insulate yourself from any changes to that architecture. I will make every effort to keep these extensions up-to-date; the latest versions are available from the Wrox web site, which can be found at http://www.wrox.com.

Alternate Identities

The problems that need to be solved to implement alternate identities are the following:

❑ Each identity needs its own implementation of QI(), but should share the AddRef() and Release() implementation with all the other identities.

❑ Each interface in the alternate identity should share the QI() implementation of that identity. The implementations of the custom (non-inherited) methods of the interface are shared by all identities.

As mentioned in the Chapter 7 text, the simplest way to deal with this situation is to have a separate IUnknown interface (vtable) for each identity. In addition, each interface that participates in an alternate identity should have an independent vtable for each identity that it participates in. Like all other interfaces implemented by an ATL class, these interfaces will have to appear in the inheritance list for the class.

The other issue to be tackled in setting up this architecture is to ensure that the appropriate implementations of the various IUnknown methods get plugged into the vtable in the right places. This involves appropriate naming of the interface methods, as well as creating alternatives to the CComObjectXXXX<> classes that are used to make the ATL COM classes concrete. In the case of singleton class factories, it also becomes necessary to override the ATL class factory class.

All of this is encapsulated from the programmer through the use of appropriate attribute-defining macros. The ATL extensions are present in the files `atlex.h`, `atlmi.h`, `atlsi.h`, `auctsrvrmi.h` and `atlmipv.h` (the last is not really an ATL extension; rather it's an extension that works with Jonathan Pinnock's `IPersistVariant` interface), which can be downloaded from the Wrox web site.

Alternate IUnknown and IDispatch

The alternate `IUnknown` methods are declared by the following macro:

```
#define DEFINE_UNKNOWN_ID(n) \
    MIDL_INTERFACE("00000000-0000-0000-C000-000000000046") \
    IUnknownID##n \
    { \
    public: \
        BEGIN_INTERFACE \
        virtual HRESULT STDMETHODCALLTYPE QueryInterface##n( \
            /* [in] */ REFIID riid, \
            /* [iid_is][out] */ void __RPC_FAR* __RPC_FAR* ppvObject) = 0; \
        virtual ULONG STDMETHODCALLTYPE AddRef(void) = 0; \
        virtual ULONG STDMETHODCALLTYPE Release(void) = 0; \
        END_INTERFACE \
    };
```

This is based on the standard definition of `IUnknown`, but it creates an interface whose name is `IUnknownID`n, where n is the macro parameter. The macro can thus be used as:

```
DEFINE_UNKNOWN_ID(5)
```

This would declare `IUnknownID5`, the `IUnknown` interface for alternate identity 5.

Notice that the `QI()` method is the only one whose name gets modified – it is now named `QueryInterface`n`()`, where n is once again the macro parameter. Thus, the `QI()` on identity 5 would be named `QueryInterface5()`. `AddRef()` and `Release()` are still named `AddRef()` and `Release()`, because the alternate identities share these implementations.

Analogous to `IUnknown`, we need `IDispatch` for each identity, because many of the interfaces that we define are dual interfaces. This is declared using another macro:

```
#define DEFINE_DISPATCH_ID(n) \
    DEFINE_UNKNOWN_ID(n) \
    MIDL_INTERFACE("00020400-0000-0000-C000-000000000046") \
    IDispatchID##n : public IUnknownID##n \
    { \
    public: \
        virtual HRESULT STDMETHODCALLTYPE GetTypeInfoCount( \
            /* [out] */ UINT __RPC_FAR* pctinfo) = 0; \
        virtual HRESULT STDMETHODCALLTYPE GetTypeInfo( \
            /* [in] */ UINT iTinfo, \
            /* [in] */ LCID lcid, \
            /* [out] */ ITypeInfo __RPC_FAR* __RPC_FAR* ppTInfo) = 0; \
```

```
        virtual HRESULT STDMETHODCALLTYPE GetIDsOfNames( \
            /* [in] */ REFIID riid, \
            /* [size_is][in] */ LPOLESTR __RPC_FAR* rgszNames, \
            /* [in] */ UINT cNames, \
            /* [in] */ LCID lcid, \
            /* [size_is][out] */ DISPID __RPC_FAR* rgDispId) = 0; \
        virtual /* [local] */ HRESULT STDMETHODCALLTYPE Invoke( \
            /* [in] */ DISPID dispIdMember, \
            /* [in] */ REFIID riid, \
            /* [in] */ LCID lcid, \
            /* [in] */ WORD wFlags, \
            /* [out][in] */ DISPPARAMS __RPC_FAR* pDispParams, \
            /* [out] */ VARIANT __RPC_FAR* pVarResult, \
            /* [out] */ EXCEPINFO __RPC_FAR* pExcepInfo, \
            /* [out] */ UINT __RPC_FAR* puArgErr) = 0; \
    };
```

With this definition in place, calling the macro like this:

```
    DEFINE_DISPATCH_ID(5)
```

declares an interface called `IDispatchID5` that is derived from `IUnknownID5`. All the `IDispatch` method names remain unchanged.

Note that the IIDs declared using `MIDL_INTERFACE()` in these two definitions are the *actual* `IUnknown` and `IDispatch` IIDs. This is as it should be, since the interfaces being declared are still `IUnknown` and `IDispatch`.

Interface Declarations

This next step is the only one where the programmer currently needs to write some simple code of their own, rather than just using my macros. I am, however, writing a Wizard to automate this step (check out the Wrox web site), so you shouldn't have to do this for too long!

For each interface that is going to participate in an alternate identity, you need to create a macro similar to the one above for `IDispatch`: you need a way to create a name for the interface, and a mechanism to inherit from the `IUnknown` of the appropriate identity. For instance, here is the declaration of the macro for the `IPlaceBid` interface:

```
    #define DEFINE_PLACEBID(n) \
    · MIDL_INTERFACE("A5C2C850-3825-11d2-A5FC-000086056448") \
    IPlaceBidID##n : public IDispatchID##n \
    { \
    public: \
        virtual /* [helpstring][id] */ HRESULT STDMETHODCALLTYPE InsertBid( \
            /* [in] */ IBidder __RPC_FAR* a_pmemMember, \
            /* [in] */ SHORT a_vsNumber, \
            /* [in] */ LONG a_vlPrice) = 0; \
    };
```

This is very similar to the equivalent macro for IDispatch, and in the same way this line:

```
DEFINE_PLACEBID(5)
```

declares an interface called IPlaceBidID5 that is derived from IDispatchID5. If IPlaceBid were not dual, this line in the macro:

```
IPlaceBidID##n : public IDispatchID##n \
```

would have to be replaced by this line to indicate inheritance from IUnknown:

```
IPlaceBidID##n : public IUnknownID##n \
```

Note that the IID in the MIDL_INTERFACE() macro must be identical to the IPlaceBid IID.

Inheritance List

Recall that the interface that is added to the inheritance list of the ATL class is the one that is generated from the appropriate DEFINE_XXXX() macro. Thus, if IPlaceBid had to participate in alternate identity 5 of the COM class, the following line would need to be added to the inheritance list:

```
public IPlaceBidID5
```

Alternate COM Maps

My COM map macros are designed to do the same thing as the ATL COM map, which acts as a table that is used by a table driven implementation of QI(). As a matter of fact, I actually re-use the ATL QI() architecture – I just supply it with a different table. The COM map for each alternate identity exposes *only* those interfaces that should be exposed by that identity. In addition, it allows the programmer to have a different primary IDispatch interface.

Here are the declarations for my COM map macros:

```
#define BEGIN_COM_MAP2(x,n) public: \
    HRESULT _InternalQueryInterface##n(REFIID iid, void** ppvObject) \
    { \
        return InternalQueryInterface(this, _GetEntries##n(), iid, ppvObject); \
    } \
    const static _ATL_INTMAP_ENTRY* WINAPI _GetEntries##n() { \
    static const _ATL_INTMAP_ENTRY _entries##n[] = { DEBUG_QI_ENTRY(x)

#ifdef _ATL_DEBUG
#define END_COM_MAP2(n) {NULL, 0, 0}}; return &_entries##n[1];} \
    STDMETHOD(QueryInterface##n)(REFIID, void**) = 0;
#else
#define END_COM_MAP2(n) {NULL, 0, 0}}; return _entries##n;} \
    STDMETHOD(QueryInterface##n)(REFIID, void**) = 0;
#endif // _ATL_DEBUG
```

If you compare this with the declaration of the ATL COM map macros, you will see that the only change is that the table and QI() implementation names are different – the QI() has the identity number appended to it. However, exactly the same helper function is called as is called by the normal ATL implementation of QI(): InternalQueryInterface().

Identity Map

The identity map macros are used to set up a QI() that is sensitive to the identity being queried for. Its declaration is:

```
#define BEGIN_IDENTITY_MAP(n) \
    HRESULT _InternalQueryInterface(LONG l, REFIID iid, void** ppvObject) \
    { \
        const _ATL_IDMAP_ENTRY* pEntry; \
        for(pEntry = _GetIDMapEntries(); pEntry->m_pEntry; pEntry++) \
        { \
            if(l == pEntry->m_vlID) \
                return InternalQueryInterface(this, pEntry->m_pEntry, \
                    iid, ppvObject); \
        } \
        ATLASSERT(FALSE); \
        return QueryInterface(iid, ppvObject); \
    } \
    const static _ATL_IDMAP_ENTRY* WINAPI _GetIDMapEntries() { \
    static const _ATL_IDMAP_ENTRY _idmapentries[] = {

#define END_IDENTITY_MAP {0, 0}}; return _idmapentries;}
```

Without getting into too many details, the _InternalQueryInterface() function is an overloaded function that dispatches to the QI() implementation of the ID that has been requested. It iterates through the table of known IDs in order to do so.

Concrete Classes

If you're familiar with the implementation of ATL, you'll know that the actual implementation of QueryInterface() is provided by the CComObjectXXXX<> template classes that derive from your ATL class via a template parameter.

My ATL extensions provide implementations of classes that derive from CComObjectXXXX<>, but give support for alternate identities. By way of an example, this declaration:

```
DEFINE_OBJECT_CLASS_ID_3(CComObject)
```

is declaring a class that derives from CComObject<> and supports three alternate identities. The macro declaration is shown overleaf:

```
#define DEFINE_OBJECT_CLASS_ID_3(T) \
template <class B> \
class T##ID3 : \
    public T <B> \
{ \
public: \
    T##ID3 () \
    { \
    } \
    T##ID3 (void *p) \
        : T <B> (p) {} \
    STDMETHOD(QueryInterface1)(REFIID iid, void** ppvObject) \
        {return _InternalQueryInterface(1, iid, ppvObject);} \
    STDMETHOD(QueryInterface2)(REFIID iid, void** ppvObject) \
        {return _InternalQueryInterface(2, iid, ppvObject);} \
    STDMETHOD(QueryInterface3)(REFIID iid, void** ppvObject) \
        {return _InternalQueryInterface(3, iid, ppvObject);} \
};
```

As you can see, this (not very elegant) macro is declaring a template class that is derived from
CComObject<B>, where B is your ATL class. It is also providing the implementation of
QueryInterface() for each of three alternate identities.

A separate macro is also necessary to ensure that the appropriate concrete class is used; this is the
macro declared as:

```
#define DECLARE_NOT_AGGREGATABLE_MI(x, c) public:\
    typedef CComCreator2<CComCreator<c<x> >,
        CComFailCreator<CLASS_E_NOAGGREGATION> > _CreatorClass; \
    LONG m_vlID;
```

and which is used in the class declaration.

Persistence

How should persistence for alternate identities work? Clearly, the persistence interfaces must keep
track of the identity that was persisted, implying the need for an extra variable that is loaded and
stored whenever the object is persisted. The details of this technique can be viewed in the header
files, particularly atlmi.h.

Weak/Split Identity

The weak identity infrastructure is very similar to that for alternate identities. The one major point of
departure is that the weak IUnknown must implement its own version of AddRef() and Release()
in addition to its own version of QI().

Since the AddRef() and Release() implementations come from CComObjectRoot<>, this class
needs to be replaced by one that can work with weak identities. I will not show you the entire
implementation, but comparing the code for the strong Release() and the weak Release()
should illustrate the essentials of how weak identities work.

Here's the declaration of the strong `Release()`. It calls `InternalRelease()`, a function that decrements the strong reference count `m_dwRef` in a way appropriate to the threading model:

```
STDMETHOD_(ULONG, Release)()
{
   ULONG l = InternalRelease();
   if(l == 0)
   {
      WeakAddRef();
      BeginDestroy();
      WeakRelease();
   }
   return l;
}
```

If the strong reference count goes to zero, it begins the destruction sequence for the object. It brackets a call to `BeginDestroy()` (the function that releases any object that holds a weak reference) within calls to `WeakAddRef()` and `WeakRelease()`. If the weak reference count goes to zero as a result of `BeginDestroy()`, the `WeakRelease()` will complete the destruction of the object as follows:

```
STDMETHOD_(ULONG, WeakRelease)()
{
   ULONG l = InternalWeakRelease();
   if(l == 0 && m_dwRef == 0)
      delete this;
   return l;
}
```

Note the call to `InternalWeakRelease()`, which is the function for decrementing the weak reference count. Only if both the weak *and* the strong reference counts are zero will the object be destroyed.

Index

Index

I

Professional NT Services

Author: Kevin Miller
ISBN: 1861001304
Price: $59.99 C$83.95 £55.49

Professional NT Services teaches developers how to design and implement good NT services using all the features and tools supplied for the purpose by Microsoft Visual C++. The author develops a set of generic classes to facilitate service development, and introduces the concept of *usage patterns* — a way of categorizing the roles that services can fulfil in the overall architecture of a system. The book also gives developers a firm grounding in the security and configuration issues that must be taken into account when developing a service.

To date, the treatment of NT services has been sketchy and widely scattered. This book is aimed at bringing the range of relevant material together in an organized way. Its target readership is C/C++ Windows programmers with experience of programming under Win32 and basic knowledge of multithreaded and COM programming. At an architectural level, the book's development of usage patterns will be invaluable to client-server developers who want to include services as part of a multi-tiered system.

ATL COM Programmer's Reference

Authors: Richard Grimes
ISBN: 1861002491
Price: $22.99 C$44.95 £27.49

The Active Template Library is the method for making lightweight COM components for C++ programmers. First available as a download for use with Visual C++ 4.2, the ATL is now an integral part of Microsoft's premier development tool. This book covers ATL 3.0, which is found in all versions of the Visual C++ 6.0 product. ATL already comes with a growing family of wizards to make your development easier and is based on well-established C++ language disciplines.

Who is this book for?
This book is for anyone needing an easy reference point for the fundamental techniques and guidelines for programming in ATL. You should be a competent C++ programmer, familiar with basic Template theory and usage. You should also be competent in Windows programming and using Visual C++.

Professional ATL COM Programming

Authors: Dr. Richard Grimes
ISBN: 1861001401
Price: $59.99 C$89.95 £45.99

For experienced Visual C++ programmers with experience of COM and ATL (Active Template Library) The coverage throughout, is for the latest ATL version 3.0 and as such is essential reading for getting the most out of your COM servers.

Author, Richard Grimes - famous for his definitive text on DCOM, has applied all his specialist knowledge of ATL usage in the field to give you *the* book on ATL architecture and usage. If you've ever looked at Wizard-generated ATL code and wondered what's behind it. If you've ever wondered how it works, why it's implemented in that way and the options for customising and extending it – then the answer is in these pages. You will learn all about the plumbing behind ATL via example code that will be useful in your own projects. You should read this if you wish to: debug, get the right factory, thread, marshal, use Windows classes, use connection points, sink events, build composite controls and understand the COM object wizard.

Professional COM Applications with ATL

Authors: Sing Li and Panos Econompoulos
ISBN: 1861001703
Price: $49.99 C$69.95 £45.99

This book examines how and why you should use COM, ActiveX controls and DNA Business Objects, and how these components are linked together to form robust, flexible and scalable applications.

A key part of the book is the extended case study in which we produce a distributed events calendar that fits Microsoft's Distributed interNet Applications (DNA) model. This three-tier application uses flexible browser-based controls for the client user interface, business objects on both client and server to process the required information efficiently and Universal Data Access to perform the queries and updates. It depends on the support for component-based development now available for Windows NT server.

The additions and changes to this book make it both significant and relevant to readers of the first edition, Professional ActiveX/COM Control Programming.

Beginning ATL COM Programming

Authors: Various
ISBN: 1861000111
Price: $39.95 C$55.95 £36.99

This book is for fairly experienced C++ developers who want to get to grips with COM programming using the Active Template Library. The Beginning in the title of this book refers to COM and ATL. It does not refer to Programming.

We don't expect you to know anything about COM. The book explains the essentials of COM, how to use it, and how to get the most out of it. If you already know something about COM, that's a bonus. You'll still learn a lot about the way that ATL works, and you'll be one step ahead of the COM neophytes.

Neither do we expect you to know anything about ATL. ATL is the focus of the book. If you've never touched ATL, or if you've been using it for a short while, but still have many unanswered questions, this is the book for you.

Clouds to Code

Authors: Jesse Liberty
ISBN: 1861000952
Price: $40.00 C$56.00 £36.99

"In Clouds to Code, I document the design and implementation of a real project, from start to finish, hiding nothing. Books on theory are all well and good, but there is nothing like living through the process. You'll watch as we struggle to understand the requirements, as we conceive a design, implement that design in C++, then ready it for testing and rollout. You'll see the complete iterative development process as it happens. This is not an example or a thought experiment, it's a real life case study written in real time.

Along the way you'll learn about object- oriented analysis and design with UML, as well as C++, design patterns, computer telephony, and COM. You'll also learn about professional software development and what it takes to ship a product on time and on budget. This is programming in the trenches."

Professional DCOM Application Development

Authors: Jon Pinnock
ISBN: 1861001312
Price: $44.99 C$69.95 £45.99

As befits a book that has as its ultimate goal end-user satisfaction, Professional DCOM Application Development is firmly rooted in practical examples. To my mind, there is no better way to understand a technology than to program your way around it (and there are a lot of technologies covered here). Sure, I'm happy to provide you with the theory, with words and pictures (and don't worry, I do), but that's no substitute for rolling up your sleeves and getting stuck in to the code. Generally speaking, all the examples are self-contained within each chapter, so if you want to skip a chapter because it isn't your immediate concern, you can do. (But do come back to it later!) So let's get programming – let's make lots of end-users happy, and make the world a more beautiful place. OK, I made the last bit up.

Professional DCOM Programming

Authors: Richard Grimes
ISBN: 186100060X
Price: $49.95 C$69.95 £46.99

DCOM is an enabling technology, but it is also perceived as being difficult to use. During training courses I've given, people have expressed this concern, often suggesting that they could use Winsock or RPC solutions. My response was to demonstrate how DCOM can actually simplify your code by providing a solid infrastructure that could take months to develop with those old technologies. I aim to show you the same thing. If you're already comfortable with COM, you're probably interested in extending your knowledge beyond the confines of a single machine. I'll show you how to configure your existing components for remote use and, more importantly, how you can create new components that exploit core DCOM functionality.